Critique and Affirmation in Erich Fromm

Critique and Affirmation in Erich Fromm explores the relations between Erich Fromm's theory and practice in politics and the psychoanalytic clinic – their points of continuity and contradiction.

Drawing on a systematic reading of Fromm's published output, as well as extensive research in the Fromm archives, Matheus Romanetto extracts the fragments of ontology, logic, and ethics implicit in his writings, leading to a re-evaluation of Fromm's place in 20th century intellectual history. Interpolated with the theoretical argument are three historical chapters thematizing Fromm's practice in political life, religious life, and the psychoanalytic clinic, setting the grounds for a new political sociology of radical humanism and critical theory.

Critique and Affirmation in Erich Fromm will be of great interest to psychoanalysts and to scholars of psychoanalytic studies, sociology, contemporary philosophy, political theory, and critical theory.

Matheus Romanetto is a Brazilian sociologist. His work brings together aspects of social theory, psychoanalysis, and philosophy in the investigation of intellectual, political, and religious movements, exploring their social psychology and structure.

Critique and Affirmation in Erich Fromm

Humanistic Politics
and the Psychoanalytic Clinic

Matheus Romanetto

LONDON AND NEW YORK

Designed cover image: CC BY 4.0 Wien Museum, Foto: Birgit und Peter Kainz, Wien Museum

First published 2025
by Routledge
4 Park Square, Milton Park, Abingdon, Oxon OX14 4RN

and by Routledge
605 Third Avenue, New York, NY 10158

Routledge is an imprint of the Taylor & Francis Group, an informa business

© 2025 Matheus Romanetto

The right of Matheus Romanetto to be identified as author of this work has been asserted in accordance with sections 77 and 78 of the Copyright, Designs and Patents Act 1988.

All rights reserved. No part of this book may be reprinted or reproduced or utilised in any form or by any electronic, mechanical, or other means, now known or hereafter invented, including photocopying and recording, or in any information storage or retrieval system, without permission in writing from the publishers.

Trademark notice: Product or corporate names may be trademarks or registered trademarks, and are used only for identification and explanation without intent to infringe.

British Library Cataloguing in Publication Data
A catalogue record for this book is available from the British Library

Library of Congress Cataloging-in-Publication Data
A catalog record has been requested for this book

ISBN: 9781032708454 (hbk)
ISBN: 9781032708447 (pbk)
ISBN: 9781032708560 (ebk)

DOI: 10.4324/9781032708560

Typeset in Times New Roman
by Taylor & Francis Books

To Herminio Cezar, in memoriam

Contents

List of figures   9
Acknowledgments   13

Introduction: Problems, Methods, Solutions   1

PART I
Metapsychology and Society   7

I   Phenomenology and Dynamics of Erich Fromm's Works   9

PART II
Life and Politics   47

II   Anthropology and Sociology   49

III   To Go to the Roots: Fromm and Marcuse After the *Dissent* Debate   84

PART III
Ontology and the Clinic   123

IV   Aspects of Ontology (1937–1964)   125

V   To Touch Reality: Language and Experience in Erich Fromm's Clinics   153

PART IV
Critique and Praxis   183

VI   Aspects of Logic and Ethics (1964–1980)   185

VII To Fill the Hearts of Men with a New Spirit: Politics in Erich
  Fromm's Thought and Action   223
VIII
Conclusion: Toward a Political Sociology   270

  Index   280

Figures

IV.1 Psychic structure and existential needs in Fromm's theory.   131

Acknowledgments

The theoretical chapters in this book were funded by CAPES and supervised by Ricardo Musse at the University of São Paulo. The historical chapters were funded by the Erich Fromm Stiftung and supervised by Rainer Funk at the Erich Fromm Institut Tübingen. I am grateful to them and several other scholars whose assistance and criticism helped shape my ideas.

Neil McLaughlin introduced me to Erich Fromm, and helped form my approach to historical sociology. Kieran Durkin kept my political and theoretical senses in tune. Daniel Burston assisted intensely in researching and editing Chapter III, as well as with various subjects in religious and intellectual history. Catherine Silver helped me understand what Frommian clinics feel like. She was crucial in turning Chapter V into what it is now. Ralph Dumain discussed critical theory and Marxism with me for many years; his honesty and criticism inspired Chapter VII. Lynn Chancer shared important insights on gender and social psychology, and gave me a chance to discuss my ideas with a lively group of students. David Norman Smith encouraged me to seek an integration of empirical rigor, theoretical insight, and clear expression. Ansgar Schwarzer awoke my speculative imagination. Erick Vidal strengthened my theoretical self-awareness. Inara Marin's, Christian Dunker's, and Josué Pereira da Silva's comments helped consolidate my results.

Martha Bergler kindly assisted me throughout my research at the Fromm archives. Jonathan Keir and Alisa Jones gave me intellectual, moral, and institutional support at crucial points. Several meetings organized by the Erich Fromm Gesellschaft, the Erich Fromm Study Center at the IPU Berlin, and CEBRAP's Bancada do Inconsciente were important for developing my theses. Júlia Galvez, Felipe Steinacker de Paula, Julius Leonhardt, Gustavo Dean-Gomes, Erick Vidal, Ansgar Schwarzer, Catherine Silver, David Smith, Neil McLaughlin, and Rainer Funk all helped me with comments and editing in the final stages of the manuscript preparation.

***

Quotations from Erich Fromm's correspondence and from previously unpublished excerpts, drafts and writings by Erich Fromm are published here with the kind permission of the Literary Estate of Erich Fromm. Use by third parties is only possible upon written request (fromm-estate@fromm-online.com).

I thank Harold Marcuse and Peter-Erwin Jansen for using the materials, quotations from the Marcuse-Archiv Frankfurt.

Introduction
Problems, Methods, Solutions

Erich Fromm was a German psychoanalyst and sociologist. Born in Frankfurt in 1900 to an Orthodox Jewish family, he pursued his religious education until the mid-1920s. A few years later, already a non-theist, he started collaborating with the Frankfurt Institute for Social Research in developing a critical theory of society. Fromm was compelled to leave Germany during the rise of Nazism, and found housing alternately in the United States, Mexico, and Switzerland. He worked as a university professor, a clinician, and a training psychoanalyst. His writings brought together depth psychology, historical materialism, and sociology under a paradigm called "radical humanism". As one of his main theoretical outcomes, Fromm developed a "social characterology" – a typology and dynamics of human passions, as they are formed and organized by experiences common to certain social classes and groups. He passed away in 1980, victim of a heart attack (cf. Funk, 1999; Hardeck, 2005).

Throughout the 1930s, Fromm helped shape an analytic social psychology, based mainly on Freud, Marx, Bachofen, and formal sociology. Later in that decade, he broke with the Frankfurt Institute, and went to develop a different form of critical theory, based on a normative humanism. Fromm undertook an extensive revision of Freud; his relation to Marx yes was specified as a Marxist humanism, and he multiplied his sources in the social sciences, especially in anthropology. Fromm's later critical theory is deeply rooted in Jewish prophetic literature. It displays a unique porosity to opposing philosophical, scientific, and religious systems, while still being guided by the same concern that oriented his earlier output: the attempt at coupling a theory of social change with a theory of subjective change.

Fromm's core political convictions were formed very early on, as an outcome of his ethical education in Judaism – but his activism developed mainly after he left the Institute for Social Research. From the 1950s onwards, Fromm worked as a public intellectual and political organizer. He promoted democratic socialism, and took stance in a number of international issues as a representative of pacifism (cf. Friedman, 2013). Fromm's later critical theory corresponds to his experience within these political movements. It is grounded on a different social basis and practice than the writings of his former Frankfurt colleagues. This is reflected in their logical structure: whereas Horkheimer, Adorno, and for some time Marcuse, work with negation as a basic form, Fromm proposes a unity of negation and affirmation as the basis for critique (compare Wiggershaus, 1986).

This contrast is the starting point for our research. Unlike other critical theories, Fromm's articulates an explicit political program: its *logical* form includes affirmation. His politics are derived from certain experiential values, whose realization would be the task of socialism. The core of Fromm's normative stance is given as an *ethics,* objective and universalistic in character: a better society is one which allows a better life for its members. Since Fromm gives up the theological grounding of his earlier religious precepts, these ethics are formulated as immanent to human experience and practice. They presuppose an *ontological* assessment of human beings and their social relations: only if we know how subjects and society change can we judge the viability of a normative program. Unlike his ethics, however, Fromm's ontology remains mostly implied to his psychoanalytic notions. Conversely, the forms of political organization and mobilization he favored are to a large extent sublimated in his logic. We are given a crystal clear determination of normative criteria for political action, but their practical and psychological presuppositions are only partly spelled out.

The purpose of this book is to clarify the above relations. We will address two interrelated problems. The first is a *theoretical* one: is it possible to ground a universal normative theory immanently? This requires examining the relation between Fromm's ethics and his ontological assumptions. The second problem is a *sociological* one: how do theoretical stances translate into practice, and what are their practical origins? In Fromm's writings, these questions affect the relation between ethics and logic. In his activities, they correspond to experiences developed in different realms – most importantly religion, politics, and the psychoanalytic clinic. Of these, the last two shall be our main concerns. We will investigate a number of historical sources evidencing the pragma of Fromm's political and clinical action, searching for its points of continuity and contradiction with his thought. Solving these problems amounts to developing a critical balance of Fromm's theoretical and political positions.

Since we are interested in the relations between Fromm's critical theory and his practice, *periodization* follows accordingly. Our historical inquiries cover material between 1947 and 1980, which are Fromm's most active years in politics, and his most characteristic in the clinic. By that time, Fromm had already formulated some of his most significant concepts and theses; most importantly, he had also started to update them into his revised theory. For that reason, we will be especially interested in Fromm's writings from 1937 onwards, when the theoretical groundwork for his later social psychology is first laid out. From then on, Fromm's works are updated in a series of relevant points – most importantly his biological and anthropological assumptions. They display nonetheless a basic continuity in purpose and style, which authorizes considering them in their unity, emphasizing new developments only to the extent of necessity.

Two important consequences follow from this periodization. The first concerns Fromm's relation to *psychoanalysis* and *sociology*. His writings between 1926 and 1936 were still formulated in Freudian terms; and between roughly 1922 and 1932, we may as well count a critical appreciation of Max and Alfred Weber, Georg Simmel, and several currents of Marxism among Fromm's main intellectual tasks. These are fundamental steps in his theoretical development – to a large degree consistent with his post-1937 theory, and presupposed to it. Writings and documents from this time are taken into account throughout this book, but mostly subsumed to their relation with Fromm's later critical theory, which is our main subject matter.

The second consequence concerns Fromm's relation to *religion*. Fromm's adult activism brought him together, in action and thought, with a number of religious traditions and personalities – most importantly in Judaism, Catholicism, Protestantism, and Buddhism. By that time, he had long broken with his youthful Judaism and Zionism. Fromm's ethics in many ways developed out of his earlier religious precepts – however, they were not anymore practiced within the same institutional and conceptual frames. One of the peculiarities of the humanistic movements Fromm championed is precisely that they fostered alliances between competing religious organizations, transposing the corresponding social relations onto new political forms. We will be interested in understanding the significance of Fromm's ideas within these plural political formations, but will mostly refrain from discussing their *sources* in his youthful education, as well as their social *origins* within several religious and philosophical institutions. The historical development of humanistic norms, as well as their primary assimilation by Fromm, will be taken as presuppositions – as they were in fact for the political and religious movements which actualized them in the mid-20th century.

***

The above qualifications are related to the *method* adopted in this book, which is a sociological, not a biographical one. While theoretical chapters are thoroughly devoted to Fromm's ideas, historical chapters strive to extrapolate their broader political and clinical implications. They examine the social relations around Fromm, not with the aim of characterizing the man and his life, but in search of significant regularities, pointing toward the structural implications to these relations. This approach allows us to rehearse the categories for a critical political sociology.

The *sources* consulted for this investigation are located at the Erich Fromm Institut Tübingen, and at the Marcuse Archives in the Goethe-Universität Frankfurt – both in Germany. They include letters, drafts, typescripts, unpublished writings, audio recordings, video interviews, marginalia to books, and other study materials. Their significance is very different in each case. Theoretical extrapolations are often unsafe without comparison to Fromm's writings: he was a rigorous editor of his own texts, privileging consistency and clarity over speculation. Many unfinished arguments can only be tallied in comparison with the writings he authorized for publication. However, these same lines of reasoning prove crucial for an appreciation of Fromm's practical activities. Here, contradiction and hesitation are as significant as conviction. The same caution which guaranteed Fromm's crisp theoretical prose sometimes resulted in suppressing his most incisive positions, both on psychoanalytic and political matters.

To the best of my capacity, I have striven to control the authenticity and significance of unpublished sources through a systematic comparison with Fromm's published writings, allowing them to speak in their mutual criticism. These documents allow a surprising wealth of conclusions regarding Fromm's stances on concrete political and clinical issues, and in many cases a specification of his theory. They also determine the limitations of this book. The relations examined here concern mostly theoreticians, clinicians, politicians, and religious leaderships. Clinically relevant documents don't convey the analysand's point of view, and I ventured little into institutional history. Politically relevant documents don't allow equal insight into the whole structure of the movements and organizations at stake, but especially into the relations between their representatives. To the extent that relations between intellectuals and leaders shape broader political formations, they illuminate their historical effectiveness and social nature. Nonetheless, the social bases of humanistic alliances are very diverse, internationally spread, and mostly inaccessible to my sources. We must therefore consider this investigation, not as a completed political sociology, but as a way into it – a study in political superstructure.

Fromm's published writings are quoted following Rainer Funk's systematic notation for the German *Gesamtausgabe*. His and Marcuse's unpublished documents are quoted following their identifying codes in the respective archives. All sources, published or otherwise, were read in their original language and translated here when necessary. Whenever a bibliographic reference is in German, Spanish, or French, but quoted in English, the reader may assume the translation is mine. For reasons of space, I refrain from detailed discussion with the secondary literature. The books and papers I found essential in the development of my point of view – either out of agreement or disagreement – are listed at the end of each chapter. Taking these qualifications into account, the argument is divided as follows:

Part I: *Chapter I* characterizes Fromm's psychoanalysis and social psychology by comparing it to other major intellectual currents of his times: Freudianism, critical theory, systems theory, cultural anthropology, and structuralism. It examines the development of Fromm's early writings toward his break with the Freudian paradigm, connecting them to our main subjects of inquiry: his later ontology, ethics, and logic.

From this point onwards, each part is divided in two chapters: a theoretical one, and a historical one, whereby the practical implications of the previous discussion are developed.

Part II: *Chapter II* presents Fromm's anthropological and sociological premises, comparing them with their antecedents in Freud and Marx. *Chapter III* investigates their political consequences by studying Fromm's relation with Herbert Marcuse, the New Left, and other movements from the 1960s and 1970s – some of which assimilated Freud's and Marx's legacies differently.

Part III: *Chapter IV* deducts a series of ontological categories from Fromm's psychoanalytic and social psychological concepts. Their origins and application in clinical practice are discussed in *Chapter V*, which reconstructs Fromm's take on psychoanalytic treatment and technique.

Part IV: *Chapter VI* addresses Fromm's normative theory and its ambiguities. It differentiates several strains within his ethics, each of which stands in a particular relation to the ontological categories developed before. The logical structure of Fromm's critical theory is correspondingly led back to its experiential models in politics and in psychoanalysis. *Chapter VII* completes this line of reasoning with a characterization of Fromm's political thought and action, and an analysis of the social psychology typical for the humanistic associations around him.

The categories developed in Chapter VII are recovered in the *Conclusion*, summarizing the connections and contradictions between Fromm's model of political action and his theoretical positions.

Bibliography

Burston, Daniel. Erich Fromm: a brief biography. Michael Maccoby, Mauricio Cortina (eds.). *A prophetic analyst*. London: Jason Aronson Inc., 1996.
Friedman, Lawrence. *The lives of Erich Fromm*. New York: Columbia University Press, 2013.
Funk, Rainer. *Liebe zum Leben*. Stuttgart: DTV, [1999]/2011.
Hardeck, Jürgen. *Erich Fromm*. Darmstadt: Wissenschaftliche Buchgesellschaft, 2005.
Hardeck, Jürgen. Fact and fiction about Erich Fromm's life and work. Rainer Funk, Neil McLaughlin (eds.). *Towards a human science*. Gießen: Psychosozial-Verlag, 2015.
Roazen, Paul. Erich Fromm's courage. Michael Maccoby, Mauricio Cortina (eds.). *A prophetic analyst*. London: Jason Aronson Inc., 1996.
Schaff, Adam. Mexikanische Erinnerungen. Lutz von Werder (ed.). *Der unbekannte Fromm*. Frankfurt: Haag und Herchen, 1987.
Wiggershaus, Rolf. *The Frankfurt school*. Cambridge: The MIT Press, [1986]/1995.

Part I

Metapsychology and Society

This part explores the origins and characteristics of Erich Fromm's metapsychology and way of theorizing, in preparation for our later inquiries into his logic, ontology, and ethics.

Chapter 1

1 Phenomenology and Dynamics of Erich Fromm's Works

Erich Fromm's thought formulates a particular mode of experience – a way of grasping psychic and social life. It expresses the results of previous experience, and sets forth the categories allowing its further development. However, these categories are among the least clarified aspects of his writings. Whereas Fromm's concepts are brilliantly developed in clear prose, the categories underlying them often occupy an intermediary position between what is said and what is left unsaid, offering themselves to our knowledge in minor formulations, particularities of expression, details, metaphors – in everything that is closer to images than to concepts.

The purpose of this chapter is to prepare the remaining theoretical sections of this book, in which we will explore Fromm's logical, ontological, and ethical categories. Most of them only fully crystallized after Fromm laid the grounds for his own psychoanalysis and philosophical anthropology, from around 1937 onwards. Up to that point, Fromm had already developed some of his most important concepts and methodological tenets – but they were still couched in Freudian metapsychology. This chapter examines the reasons for Fromm's transition out of the Freudian paradigm, situating him in relation to some of the major intellectual currents of his time: Freudianism, critical theory, systems theory, cultural anthropology, and structuralism.

1 Style and Idea

The most important text documenting Fromm's transition out of libido theory is known nowadays as "Man's impulse structure and its relation to culture". It is dated precisely 1937, but was only published in 1992(e). It is one of the clearest presentations of the new foundations adopted by Fromm. What is most impressive, however, is the very fact that this document remained unpublished for such a long time. In the history of Fromm's publications, this represents a rather typical event. The archives reveal a pervasive tendency for suppressing the more abstract presuppositions to his way of thinking. He cuts off speculative trains of thought, formal definitions, diagramatic representations – and where these are allowed, they often result inadequate (cf. Fromm, 1962a; 1964a; d-1973a-eng-type-06:4; d-RoHD). We might as well speak of a resistance to formalization.

The reasons for these omissions are of various kinds – editorial, stylistic, theoretical, and political. However, incurring so often in the suppression of the same kind of abstraction, they result in a meaningful pattern. Toward the end of his life, Fromm would claim to have "no gift for abstract thought" (1974b:105) – a sentence we can value for its sincerity, but may also suspect conceals something. In Freud, and even in Ronald Laing, whom Fromm strongly admired, he censored the tendency for "constructing too much", both in theoretical speculation and in the clinical reconstruction of facts. He was averse to the tendency of wild conjecture to leave experience behind and produce an "obsessive" insistence in false ideas (Fromm, 1979a:16). At the same time, Fromm praised in Laing the fact that "he sees and he describes what he sees and has tremendous faith, patience and toughness to see" (d-1991d-002-eng-draft-04:165). This preference for leading abstraction back into "intuition" is at the very core of Fromm's (1960a:40) mode of experience.

Let us not be misunderstood. Fromm was not a proponent of irrationalism. He was an admirer of philosophy, from Spinoza to Hegel, advocating for the "vigour of theoretical thought" (1966n:4). In Carl Jung, he censored the tendency towards obscurantism, and in Otto Rank, what he saw as a fascistic impetus in his voluntarism (cf. 1939a; 1963e). He thought the development of reason was a vital issue, and included scientific research as an indispensable requirement for a progressive politics (cf. 1947a; 1960b). The retreat of formalization in his writings is thus not the result of a misgiving with theoretical language. It is rather related to Fromm's openness to religious traditions emphasizing the insufficiency of thought against experience – especially the mystical and active tendencies in Judaism, Buddhism, and Christianity.

What kept Fromm in dialogue with these and other sources was an *ethical* affinity with their precepts. Fromm's first encounter with religion was a thoroughly practical one, as he grew embedded in the Jewish tradition (cf. Akrap, 2011). As a young doctoral student, he tried to reconcile his then sociological approach with an ethical evaluation of the right way of living: the essence of Jewish law was, for him, the "active healing of the world" (1989b:177). He abandoned his belief in God later in the 1920s, but religious precepts remained an important source for his political activity – especially from the late 1950s on, when Fromm helped shape an international humanistic movement. He tried to foster an alliance between representatives of distinct doctrinal positions based on a common ethical program. "Humanists in the most divergent doctrinal and conceptual camps find more in common among themselves, therefore, than they find differences", Fromm thought (1966i:49). There would be a "new alternative of a frame of reference that would be common to the theistic and the non-theistic person" (1992l:56).

This ecumenical strategy coincides, in Fromm, with the subordination of thought to practice of life: "shared concern and experience are more important than shared concepts" (1968a:141). Fromm valued scientific and speculative behavior as a necessary aspect in human development – but only one among others. Being the work of a thinker, his writings know the valuation of science as an ultimate end – but they also recognize the evanescence of thought in face of action and experience: "the only way in which the world can be grasped ultimately lies, not in thought, but in the act, in the experience of oneness" (1956a:61).

To the extent that formalization fixates thought, displacing emphasis away from the vital process and towards ideas, Fromm avoids it. Contrariwise, to the extent that he is concerned with theorizing, his ideas are clearly delineated. He often shows greater concern for presenting his results than for evidencing the reasoning behind them. Hence the remarkable character of his writings. They are rich in quality, saturated with concreteness, and organize their contents in clear concepts – but the categorial articulation between these concepts is not manifest. Fromm's concepts bear more experience than they are able to express. They say more, in what is said, than what is merely said.

2 Two Methods Meet

Fromm's works confront us with an immense thematic variety. We find writings on religion, foreign policy, sexuality, social movements, and a number of other subjects. What gives them unity is an experience of the human psyche, of its modes of development and conditions of existence. As an ethical thinker, Fromm asks himself who we *could be*. As the proponent of an "analytic social psychology" (1932a) or "sociopsychoanalysis" (1976a:112), he asks how we become who we in fact *are*. Fromm's critical theory is born as he joins these perspectives together.

Fromm's thought is the fruit of an alliance between sociological concerns and clinical work. Graduated as a doctor in sociology in 1922, and as a psychoanalyst in the second half of the 1920s, Fromm sought to integrate both disciplines into a common thought structure. The psychoanalytic clinic remained his most constant empirical source, although he also employed sociological, psychiatric, historical, and ethnographic methods on occasion (cf. Fromm and Maccoby, 1970b). However, clinical problems are among the subjects Fromm discusses the least in print. A formal psychopathology is almost completely absent from his writings. Rather, they center on developing a "pathology of normalcy" (1955a:6). Fromm saw that as a necessary extension of the psychoanalytic field, since "Freud's discoveries were applied mainly to the cure of neurosis, more than to the understanding and diagnosis of the normal personality, or as we should better say, the medium type personality" (1967i:xi).

To understand the origins of this framing, we must go back to Fromm's years in psychoanalytic training. In the late 1920s, psychoanalysis was beginning to develop a new nosology. Psychoanalytic characterology was passing from its previous position in Freudian literature – as a complement to the study of resistance and tentative ego psychology – into greater clinical and theoretical centrality. There were many causes for that. Freud's (1923) second topology induced a large segment of the analytic field to investigate the formation of the ego – to which psychoanalytic characterology in its classical formulation would have pertained. Karl Abraham's (1921; 1924; 1925) last works brought the study of character to an unprecedented systematization, illuminating the relation between specific character traits and the stages of psychosexual development. Melanie Klein's (1921) works show how the study of character was also important for the pedagogical application of psychoanalysis, which was flourishing together with child analysis in the 1920s. Finally, the increasing demand for therapy exposed psychoanalysts to a new contingent of analysands. They didn't count among those cases of chronic neurosis whose treatment analysis was originally intended for (cf. Freud, 1904). Clinics were now filled with people who suffered in other ways. This prompted the treatment of what came to be called "character neurosis" (cf. Alexander, 1930) – a concept initially found in Adler (1912–22), but now stripped off its straight connection with "inferiority feelings".

In Ferenczi (1927, 1928), the treatment of unpleasant character traits is a necessary step towards a complete psychoanalysis. Balint's work (1932) developed in part this same tendency. In Reich (1925; 1933), character analysis leads certain forms of resistance back to particular resolutions of the Oedipal conflict. In Alexander (1927, 1930), "character neurosis" is put in systematic relation to other nosological categories, but we also find an attempt at accommodating the results of ego and id analysis in an integrated approach to the "whole personality". Despite the plurality of their premises and results, these works have a common effect. They destabilize the central concepts upon which they are based: character, character trait, neurosis, ego. Fromm's approach begins to be formed as the clinical meaning of these terms is being redefined.

Fromm's penchant for analytic characterology represents an outgrowth of his youthful religious interests. Now already a non-theist, he finds in this research field an Archimedean point between his moral and scientic passions, allowing him to give his ethical aspirations a new form of expression – previously in religious language, now in a psychological one. A notion like Karl Abraham's (1925) "genital character" prefigures the possibility of a normative psychology. In Ferenczi (1928), we find more than once an aversion to everything that, not being a "symptom", remains nonetheless disturbing for others. Freud (1912–13) had previously described the transference neuroses as associal – but Alexander (1930) came to understand the "associality" of character neurosis in terms of its kinship with criminality. Indeed, character analysis was concomitant with the development of a psychoanalytic criminology (cf. Reik 1925; 1932). By the late 1920s, ego psychology had become a realm of negotiation between the clinic and social norms – ego and superego problems went hand in hand.

Fromm's early output participates in all the major tendencies of the psychoanalysis of his times. His first psychoanalytic publication is a small report on the genesis of an anal character trait, intended as a contribution for analytic pedagogy (cf. 1926a). There soon follow essays on penal justice (cf. 1930b; 1930d; 1931a). Fromm (1932a) shares with Reich the interest in studying the motivations recurring in certain human types. He shares with Alexander an extended understanding of psychoanalytic treatment – "symptom analysis" is for him only a partial aspect in the "analysis of the whole character" (1991a:67). With Ferenczi, he shares a conception of the goals and means of analytic cure (cf. Fromm, 1935a). By the end of a short development, contrary to much of previous psychoanalysis, Fromm's concept of "character" comes to be displaced out of classic ego psychology. It is redefined as typologically structural and topologically unconscious (cf. Fromm, 1930a). From 1930 until the end of his life, the project of a characterology under these premises remains the vital nucleus of Fromm's theory (cf. 1932b; 1947a; 1976a).

While Fromm's ethical impulse is the seed of his intellectual endeavor, we cannot understand his study of character without taking into account its *political* interest (cf. Frie, 2019). As he abandons Zionism, and next Jewish theism as a whole, Fromm consolidates his socialist creed. Hence the importance of Marx, which he claimed all his life as one of his main sources, together with Freud, Bachofen, and other religious writers (cf. Fromm, 1962a; 1974b). Even more important than this intellectual heritage was the impact of Marxism as a political movement. The sensibility for political problems attracts Fromm's social psychology towards mass movements and ideologies – toward everything which, now in statistical terms, would pertain to "normality", not to "pathological" idiosyncrasies. Fromm was especially interested in investigating, not ideology in general, but those ideal formations (and the corresponding character structures) which are vastly diffused in social life, entering the political arena as main competitors for the "hearts" of political agents (Fromm, 1955a:343).

Fromm (1929a) recognized, with Marx and Engels (1845–7), the contingency of character formation on the "conditions" and "practice of life" confronted by each subject. This allowed him to ground his view of psychic development in a broader understanding of the social process. Among Freudians, society was often represented by the institutions socializing subjects into certain norms: education, morality, logical and aesthetic customs (cf. Rank and Sachs, 1913). Fromm (1930a; 1949c) acknowledged the relevance of cultural norms, but only as secondary elements, fixating and organizing the affective tendencies originated in praxis. Customs and ideologies themselves needed to be explained as emerging from a certain practice of life. They were, together with character, concomitant results of a society's mode of production, both expressing a certain emotional matrix and sedimenting it into rules. The relevance of unconscious processes for social life was still acknowledged – but their ultimate origin was displaced onto the specific process of production and reproduction of life found in each society.

Fromm's collaboration with the Institute of Social Research in Frankfurt was initiated under these premises. Some of his first contributions discuss the place a social psychology could have in understanding social movements, particularly those of political and religious significance (cf. Fromm, 1931b). But nothing expresses Fromm's interests as clearly as the first big study he coordinates with the Institute, which was published posthumously as *The Working Class in Weimar Germany* (1980a). He intended to interpret, from the responses given to an open questionnaire, which were the unconscious tendencies characteristic for workers in the Weimar republic, and their corresponding political affinities. The Weimar study was Fromm's only piece of work to live through the transformation of his theoretical paradigm: he was busy with its redaction to the end of the 1930s (cf. Smith, 2020). Significantly, Fromm would later employ the same method, refined and adapted to his post-Freudian theory, in a research study on the prevailing character types in a Mexican village through the late 1950s and the 1960s (cf. Fromm and Maccoby, 1970b), suggesting similar pieces of research in a number of other political contexts (cf. 1964a).

Even though Fromm's later Mexican study combined the open questionnaire with clinical interviews and other techniques as a control, the continuity of the sociopsychoanalytic *method* through his works corresponds to the continuity of a political *research interest*, which is itself not situated in the dimensions of the clinical interview with therapeutic purposes (compare Brunner, 1994). Trying to reconcile statistical and theoretical generalization, Fromm's theory reached a type and degree of abstraction which was not anymore identical to the one we find in classical psychoanalytic casuistry. The figure of "character" one obtains in interpreting the latent meaning of answers to a questionnaire is of a more general kind. It cannot easily be decomposed in more singular aspects than those appearing "in common" for members of the same group or class. Fromm himself would say: "it is extremely difficult to achieve the dynamic understanding of character if one does not dispose of the psychoanalytic interview" (1967i:xi).

Fromm's articulation between these two experiential spheres – clinic and politics – is distinct from its Freudian predecessors in its rejection of phylogenetic speculation. By the 1920s, the analysis of "mass psychology" had already taken a few steps away from the strict analogy between neurotic, infantile, and "primitive" cultural phenomena, as it was practiced earlier by Freud (1907) or Rank (1919). Reik (1920) came to formulate repression as an effect of historical commonalities in a group's life; Freud (1921) sketched the possibility of decomposing the structure of mass formations into typical psychic mechanisms. Still, the earlier paradigm remained dominant, even in the works of these same authors (cf. Freud, 1929–30; Reik, 1923). On his side, Fromm (1930a) discarded the possibility of building direct analogies between collective phenomena and individual psychic formations. This allowed him to develop a more sophisticated understanding of socialization. In doing so, however, he severed the connection allowing classical psychoanalysis to formulate the *process* leading to the formation of shared ideas, attitudes, and acts.

This peculiarity is evident in the scarcity of explicit references to dynamic categories in Fromm's writings. In Freud (1901; 1911a), notions such as condensation and displacement, projection and introjection, allowed the translation between deformed conscious forms and their primary contents – at first unconscious, later discovered by way of construction, interpretation, or remembrance. Freudian analysis could thus guarantee an uninterrupted transit between the phenomenology and the dynamics of clinical facts as they evolved (cf. Freud, 1938). This corresponded also to the experience that the morphology of psychic formations changes only tentatively: the same material returns in many different forms, and the process of its translation is a process transcurring *in time*, and which needs time (cf. Ferenczi, 1919). Each appropriation of Freudian analysis communicated the tenacity of clinical facts in its particular form of theorization and literary style. Freud himself (1911b) expressed the clinical experience of duration through theoretical figuration: he formulated sequences of nodal points in the processes under consideration, casting them as the most important reliefs shaping the course of clinical cases, of symptom formation etc. Reik (1927), the most musical of the early analysts, came to an intensive experience of duration, emphasizing the metamorphosis of historical and psychic formations. Tausk (1919) achieved an experience of deep retard, as in the relationship between metronome and melody, meticulously severing symptom formation in its stages.

It is not different with Fromm – but, in his writings, the temporality of social phenomena dominates that of psychic formations. His central concepts, such as that of "social character", refer to the psychic consequences of the "common experience for the group as such" (1939b:179). They are adapted to processes developing over the course of entire generations, not over the individual lifetime: "in many centuries, the process of change is so slow that the two lines, namely that of social and economic development on the one hand and character development on the other, can adjust to each other" (Fromm, 1992f:81). The priority of social over psychic categories has for Fromm the retroactive effect of suspending the specifically clinical intuition of time. The orientation of research to problems in historical scale and the refusal of the analogical method – after all, another expression of the refusal of formalism – both obfuscate the clinical origins of his ideas. Fromm's parsimony in expressing dynamic processes results in a transition without apparent mediations between the primary form of psychic formations and their conscious deformation and unfolding. Being a psychoanalyst, Fromm forgets nothing of this difference. But his mode of expression does not convey, in form, what it acknowledges in content. The translucent, concrete impression his style conveys corresponds to this way of theorizing, which moves freely between conscious formations and unconscious content, but omits the key allowing to translate ones into the others.

3 Time, Force, and Experience

Taken together, the above two aspects in Fromm's writing – the omission of formal articulations, and the inhibition in expressing temporality – result in a peculiar difficulty in delineating *processes*, or treating categories as parts of a becoming. But Fromm's psychoanalysis starts with the very idea that everything pertaining to life has this character of becoming: "man is not a thing; he is a living being caught up in a continual process of development" (1983d:140). Lost with formalization is the capacity to effect, *in* Fromm's concepts, what he says *about* them. This is evidenced by the scarcity of notions such as "fixation" and "regression" in his writings – which is as impressive as the fact that, despite everything, they are still there. These terms are fundamentally connected to the temporal dimension of psychic formations, but also to their topological inscription. Fromm's writings are as quiet in this respect as in the case of dynamic categories. His post-Freudian theory gives up the idea of strongly differentiated psychic *topoi*, favoring a purely functional understanding: the modalities of unconsciousness must be explained in terms of their inner necessity for the total psychic process (cf. Fromm, 1962a). The effect is once again the same. At first sight, we have the impression of an immediate passage between the phenomenon and its explanation.

This is the source for the accusation of a relapse into ego psychology, which was held by some of Fromm's opponents (cf. Fenichel, 1944; Adorno, 1952). These contentions are not justified – Fromm's psychoanalysis was never reduced to a psychology of conscious and preconscious facts. However, they point to a real contradiction in his writings, which would better be formulated in other terms. The more Fromm gives up developing his concepts as a process, the greater his capacity to differentiate between psychic strata. Conversely, the more the aspect of processuality is effected in his notions, the more phenomenology and dynamics are confused (compare Burston, 1991 on biophilia and necrophilia). After all, the topological stratification of psychic processes corresponds also in part to the stages in their formation. In loosening this mode of consideration, Fromm is forced to give expression always to the extremes of psychic development, abstracting from the path between them. The path must then be resumed in its results – that is, in what appears in the end as phenomenon.

Other peculiarities of Fromm's way of theorizing take part in this problem as well. One of them is his option, in many cases, for formulating his concepts as ideal types (cf. Fromm, 1947a). Pure types have a hard time expressing processes if they must refer to the totality of a certain object, and not to constitutive relations and partial determinations between objects, as Weber (1904) once wanted. We must also take into account Fromm's conduct towards Freud's works. An ongoing revision of Freud's output characterizes Fromm's whole development from 1937 on, culminating in his last book, *Greatness and limitations of Freud's thought* (1979a). Fromm considered his own work as presupposing Freud's. His concept of scientific revision was not one of theoretical revolution, but one that strives to "preserve the essence of the original teaching by liberating it from time-conditioned, restricting theoretical assumptions" (Fromm, 1970c:26). Even though he was treated as a "neo-Freudian", having first emphasized his divergences with Freudian "orthodoxy" in America, Fromm gave ever greater expression to his indebtedness to Freud as he got older: "I never abandoned Freudianism" (Jay_Martin_1971-05-14-to). He eventually reached a parsimonious posture, expressing openly the points in which he thought the original body of thought should be changed, but largely dispensing with the reaffirmation of the aspects he thought remained valid. In fact, the blindspots in Fromm's writings correspond precisely to the points in which he valued Freud with less reserves.

Fromm's greatest limitations, as well as the richness of his works, both derive from his intuition of the modes of becoming of psychic facts – of *psychodynamics* as such. He praised in Freud having shown that "man's unconscious motivations can be recognized by inference (interpretation) from his dreams, symptoms, unintentional small acts" (1990e:14) – which is but an enumeration of the concrete ways through which Freudianism led the transit between consciousness and the unconscious. Contrary to many others, Fromm left this aspect of the Freudian corpus untouched. However, his clinical intuition ended up differing fundamentally from Freud's over time. The same categories came to subsume a different experience of the psyche. Thus, where Fromm speaks of "psychic forces", he ultimately does not mean the same as Freud. The concept anticipates a different way of relating clinical phenomena – of conceptualizing and explaining them. Not only Fromm's economy and topology, but also his psychodynamics were modified. Unlike the other two, however, his dynamics were still formulated in Freudian terms – and so couldn't speak in their own voice. This is the reason Fromm's formulations couldn't fully spell out the *way* in which what is hidden betrays itself in the phenomenon. It is thus out of the question to imagine that Fromm's "revision" would have led him away from a psychology of the unconscious. The problem was not that he stuck too little to Freudian theory – but it may have been that he stuck too much to it. The missing "formal" element in his writings is in fact the basic condition for every experience of the psyche as a psychodynamic one.

Force, energy, compromise, conflict – some of the basic terms under which Freud apprehended the mind – are substantive categories according to their theoretical content, but act as "forms" or basic conditionants of experience as soon as we enter clinical practice. They capture the intuited mode of effectiveness of psychic processes – the way in which their component elements act upon each other over time. Even more than the economic and the topological points of view, the dynamic appreciation of psychic formations delineates what would be their sufficient explanation. It allows us to express efficient psychic relations – not as relations in general, undifferentiated, but as relations of a specific *type*. Early psychodynamic categories relied on the physics and psychophysics of Freud's time (cf. Freud, 1920; Bateson and Ruesch, 1951). Fromm (1955a; 1962a), who nodded modestly towards 20th century physics, came to criticize the *economic* point of view in Freudian analysis as informed by a mechanicist, bourgeois materialism. However, he didn't explicitly unfold the question: would a psychodynamics be possible on other grounds than the ones supplied by classic mechanics and thermodynamics? Had he formulated this question, Fromm would have been in a position to clarify the peculiarity of his own intuition of psychic processes. He might have reached a new body of psychodynamic categories.

This absent body makes itself felt all through Fromm's works – including his epistemology. Fromm generalizes the notion of "force" as a category pertaining to all forms of explanation. Science would always follow the "principle of trying to arrive at the *forces behind observable phenomena*" (1955e:362). To be sure, the idea of force is employed here more as metaphor than as concept – but this does not spare it from having consequences for thought. If the experience of magic has much to do with sharing subjective categories with the inanimate world, social scientific experience often develops in the opposite direction – introjecting back into the sphere of the spirit categories originated in the relation to other objects. In the Freudian paradigm, the notion of force had been incorporated and made to configure the "dynamic" apprehension of psychic processes. In Fromm, it is expelled back as the scheme for scientific explanation in general – including Marx, who would have seen "society" as "an intricate structure with various contradictory yet ascertainable forces" (1962a:25). This is a symptom of the unspoken kernel of Fromm's intuition. What is left unresolved in the clinic is generalized onto every other experience.

***

We considered before the extent to which Fromm's political interest affects his formulation of psychic phenomena. Taking the opposite route, inquiring if clinical work determines his dealings with social problems, we find a peculiar inversion. In Freudianism, the understanding of society centered mainly around *formal* analogies between collective phenomena and unconscious formations. In Fromm, to the contrary, the path of analytic treatment becomes the *substantive* model for social change. Nothing expresses his clinical experience of human becoming as clearly as his conception of the struggle for emancipation. "The cure of social pathology must follow the same principle" of the cure of individual pathology, he thinks, "since it is the pathology of so many human beings, and not of an entity beyond or apart from individuals" (Fromm, 1955a:273). A critical theory would also be a "therapeutically oriented" one (1962a:151).

Let us give words their right meaning. Fromm rejected very early on the idea that there could be a therapeutic "of society" as such:

> The quasi-neurotic behavior of the masses, which is an adequate reaction to actual, real, albeit also damaging and inappropriate conditions of life, will not let itself be "cured" by means of analysis, but only through the *modification and elimination of those very conditions of life*. One can understand a series of political phenomena better with the help of psychoanalysis, but it would be a disastrous illusion to believe that psychoanalysis can replace politics.
>
> (Fromm, 1931b:36)

Fromm made clear his rejection of any notion of supraindividual subjectivity, of a "soul of the mass" (1929a:3). In that, he remained consistent with Freud (1921) himself, who expressed only very carefully the possibility of a "pathology of cultural communities" (cf. 1929–30). Freud began precisely with the caveat that a therapy of entire societies wouldn't be possible, and that the criterion for normality and pathology would be lost once one did not contrast the individual with his own community, but communities between themselves. Fromm preserved the first premise, but discarded the second one. His socialism wouldn't allow him to hand in the problem. Political issues should have political solutions – but in reference to clear criteria for a better society. Fromm tried to delineate these criteria starting from the analysis of the "conflict between human needs and our social structure" (1955a:275). Hence, what the generalization of the notion of "therapy" denotes is not the social form implied to clinical practice – the analytic dyad, the relationship between analyst and analysand. It is rather the insight that the contents and stages characteristic for the therapeutic process are met again in social emancipation, once subjects act politically: "*conflict* with the requirements of human nature and resulting suffering, *awareness* of what is shut out, and *change* of the realistic situation and of values and norms" (Fromm, 1955a:273). The dynamic of suffering and liberation is consubstantial in the clinical and political spheres.

Fromm's thought aspires to unify these two poles of emancipatory activity – not in a single act, but in a single *experiential nucleus*. The search after this nucleus is the life-long consequence of Fromm's break with religious creed, as well as the source for his continued relationship with religious groups and personalities. Fromm's departure from Judaism and his entrance in psychoanalytic training mark the beginning of his adult intellectual path. Correspondingly, his first contribution to applied psychoanalysis is an interpretation of the unconscious meaning of the Jewish sabbath (cf. Fromm, 1927a). A few years later, his first empirical investigation based on the synthesis between Marxism and Freudianism is also centered on a religious phenomenon: Christian dogma and its development in early Christianity (cf. Fromm, 1930a). Whereas these early writings still treat theistic cosmology and ritual as collective elaborations of unconscious phantasy, Fromm's later work seeks to retrieve the ethical values underlying doctrinal irrationality: "knowledge (reason, truth, *logos*), brotherly love, reduction of suffering, independence, and responsibility" (1950a:18); the "full affirmation of life and all that is alive as against the worship of the mechanical and dead" (1921:56).

Fromm's theoretical path may thus be understood as the series of metamorphoses suffered by his ethical impulse, once it is severed from its early religious forms and transposed onto political and scientific practice (cf. Funk, 1988). In his own words: "I gave up all theistic belief, but retained an attitude which I would describe as religious, if one does not imply by this belief in God" (Jay_Martin_1971–05–14-to). Fromm's articulation between the psychoanalytic clinic and politics is the successor to his earlier Jewish ethical standpoint, which tries to revert the problem of who we "should" be into the problem of who we effectively "are" and "can be". What is then lost in translation is not so much the knowledge of Fromm's practical goals, but that of its intellectual conditions of possibility. Implicit to Fromm's psychological and sociological formulations, we find a covert intuition of the process of human passions, of their nature and development in time, which then feeds back into his overt *"normative humanism"* (1955a:12). The formal aspect we found missing corresponds to a specific *conception of psychic determination* – that is, of the form of effectiveness psychic processes have one over the other, and the mode of explanation supposed sufficient in their theoretical reproduction.

4 Process, System, and Language

There is a point around which Fromm's conception of psychic determination can be delineated: his notion of *system*. Introduced rather timidly in his vocabulary already at an early stage, the term is treated as equivalent to two others – "structure" and "totality" (Fromm, 1947a:234). Between 1966 and 1974, its recurrence is greatly increased. As Fromm tells Vladimir Dobrenkov in 1969: "I have recently found quite useful to think in terms of what in sociology and economy is now often called 'system analysis'" (Dobrenkov_Vladimir_1969-03-10-to). The texts published in this period stress his approach to the human being and society as "system" (1968a:4) – psychic and social change can only be effected through a total rearticulation of the elements therein contained: "a systemic change is possible only if a whole set of circumstances is changed in such a way that it applies to the system as a whole, and brings forth other latent systems which until then have remained dormant" (Fromm and Maccoby, 1970b:22).

This subtle change in emphasis calls our attention due to the difficulty in tracing its origins back to Fromm's major intellectual sources. Only one document seems to bring some light into the discussion: his correspondence with Heinz von Foerster, of which we have registers between 1971 and 1973. It was Ivan Illich who first recommended von Foerster's works to him (cf. Foerster_H_Von_1971–10–01-to). Fromm's initial intention in reading them must have been part of his studies for *The anatomy of human destructiveness* (Fromm, 1973a). He also consulted Ludwig von Bertalanffy, whose *General systems theory* Fromm annotated a few times, together with other comments of his on aggression (cf. e-Q7; e-N93). Von Foerster seems to have impressed Fromm more strongly for his "humanism", which prompted the two to stay in touch for some time. In one of Fromm's letters, we discover that he was particularly interested in von Foerster's distinction between "verbs and nouns" (Foerster_H_Von_1971–10–01-to). His study notes allow us to track this distinction back to a paper on "Molecular ethology" (von Foerster, 1970), where the biophysicist discusses the notion of "process" (cf. e-N15–16) – precisely the one in which the greatest lacks in Fromm's formulations are reunited for us. He may have felt a similar disquietude to ours towards the end of his life.

Fromm's research in neurophysiology and systems biology, which was part of his investigation on aggression, is one chapter in a larger revision he took of his concept of *life*. This had long been an important notion for him. Already in his Freudian phase, "conditions of life" and "practice of life" are the pivotal social determinations of psychic facts; even his interpretation of Freud emphasizes the category of "self-preservation" (cf. Fromm, 1932a). However, it is only towards the 1960s that this concept starts being more accurately defined (cf. Fromm, 1962a). This theoretical movement was also prompted by practical problems. "Life" is the meeting point between many of Fromm's political convictions. It is relevant for his participation in the movements against nuclear war and the Vietnam war; it creates room for dialogue between progressive religious factions and Marxist humanists (cf. Fromm, 1965a). Much of Fromm's output from the 1960s on is centered around the diagnosis of an increasing "indifference to life" from the 1st World War on (cf. 1990s). His political activities correspondingly revolved around preventing the extinction of the species – be it as a result of nuclear bombing, be it as an outcome of ecological disaster.

This process of revision led to a more accurate presentation of the "sociobiological" presuppositions to Fromm's (1990d:4) social psychology – the organic and social determinations conditioning every psychic fact. Whereas Fromm's posthumous writings clarify much in this respect, it remains harder to track his correlate interest in the formulation of vital processes through language, which developed in the late 1970s. An emphasis on the process of verbal expression is practically without precedents in Fromm's previous printed work, which discussed language in terms of "social patterns of thought" (1962a:121) and dream symbolism (cf. 1951a), but not of speech and writing. This changes with *To have or to be?* and subsequent writings (cf. 1976a; 1977b; 1978b; 1979a). Fromm saw the primacy of nouns over verbs in contemporary English as significant of a tendency towards reification, and reached a new understanding of the place of science and language in the social process. Once we arrive at this stage in his works, the emphasis on the notion of "system" seems to have recoiled already. However, it leaves a permanent trace in his keen capacity for expressing vital developments as a becoming – as well as his change of perspective regarding language. Form of expression and theoretical content are better reconciled than ever – albeit without fully overcoming the problems we discussed before.

Fromm's late conception of language allows us to clarify his previous intellectual path retrospectively. Still nowadays, it is commonplace to frame him as a "culturalist", implying his relationship to other psychoanalyses and anthropologies – Karen Horney, Clara Thompson, Margaret Mead, Abraham Kardiner etc. – in which the greater weight in determining psychic processes would fall over "culture". Doing so means confusing Fromm's personal relations with his theoretical position. It is true that, especially in the 1930s, he was close to the circle of researchers we now know as the "culture and personality" school. Franz Alexander once invited Fromm to a panel discussing this relationship because his would be the most adequate method up to that point (cf. Alexander_Franz_1937–01–08-by). In 1948, Fromm taught in collaboration with Ralph Linton, and his relationship to Margaret Mead continued for years, albeit with long periods of silence (cf. Mead_Margaret_1968–04–20-to). A series of handbooks and papers from the times portray him as a culturalist, both among friends and foes (cf. Thompson, 1950; Marcuse, 1955). Fromm himself took decades to make his differences with his peers clearer on print (cf. 1970c, 1973a). When he expressed himself in this respect earlier, he didn't deny their intellectual kinship altogether, treating disagreements as matters of "emphasis" instead (cf. 1955e). Again in this case, an important part of his arguments was only published posthumously (cf. Fromm, 1990d).

Despite these difficulties, two major differences distinguish Fromm's work from others associated to "culturalism". First, his Marxism poses a connection between social class and subjectivation without equivalents elsewhere. Second, Fromm took psychodynamics, not behavior, as the basis for understanding human action. He assimilated categories framed in behavioristic terms, such as "cultural pattern", only on a secondary level – as modes of "static adaptation", determinations of consciousness, more superficial and ephemeral than those pertaining to "dynamic adaptation" or "character" (cf. 1941a). In acting according to such "patterns", he thought, we merely "behave the way society expects us to behave" – we "conform" (1972a:61–2) to the degree demanded by self-preservation. The primary social determinants in character formation fell for him elsewhere, on the side of socio-economic conditions and the affects they excite. He thought culture has a retroactive power over psychic formations, but already presupposes subjectivity as it emerges from the immediate life process (cf. 1962a). Taking him as a "culturalist" hence betrays his theoretical purpose in two fundamental aspects. It inverts the logical priority he assumed between social process and cultural structure, and implies a lack of difference between his depth psychology, and the many blends of psychoanalysis and behaviorism emerging in the 1930s.

At the same time, it is true that North American cultural anthropology remained Fromm's major model in the exploration of conscious processes. Still his later theory of aggression in the 1970s reports back to Margaret Mead's and Ruth Benedict's results (cf. Fromm, 1972c). Even though Fromm recognized their behaviorism and cultural relativism as problematic, he didn't develop a systematic criticism of the implications their concept of "culture" would have for depth psychology. In Fromm's works, the idea that certain "behaviors" and "opinions" are acquired by conditioning or suggestion is merely superimposed onto the sphere of unconscious dynamics. It implies their suspension into a different kind of determinacy, based on "learning and conditioning" (1990d:4). Instead of the old distinction between primary and secondary process (cf. Freud, 1911a), we now have (unconscious) determinations of character on the one side, and (conscious) determinations of behavior on the other. The tendency in this counterposition is to severe the conceptual connection between language and the drives, which was integral to the Freudian way of thinking. This could only have been reversed if the very notion of behavior would be framed semiotically (cf. Bateson, 1972) – a measure Fromm's sources in the 1930s still didn't take.

A linguistics such as Whorf's (1956), not very sympathetic towards Freudianism, operates in abstraction of the positive relationship between language and the affective process. It privileges the connection between language and perception, inferring differences in the way we organize sensoria from *syntactic* properties – a different concept of subjectivity than the one arrived at by Freudians, which base their theory on a "talking cure", whence *speech* becomes central. Despite all these differences, Whorf, Mead, Benedict, as well as Schachtel's (1947) "categories of consciousness", remained Fromm's main references in this respect. Because of that, language appeared in his works only in its negative efficacy, as a component of the "social filters" (1960a:55) limiting conscious thought and experience. In the late 1970s, he started exploring the complementary relation: the extent to which social experience limits linguistic and logical development (cf. 1978b). A positive articulation between language and affection remained undiscussed.

It is in this state that Fromm's thought runs to its encounter with systems theories. It may as well have been an accidental encounter. Fromm read von

Foerster and von Bertalanffy first of all as biologists, not as systems theorists. But he discovered with them a mode of abstraction that puts the blindspots in his own formulations at the center of discussion. Then-developing cybernetics and systems theories were characterized by their formalism and homological thinking: "this is a logical-mathematical field, whose task is the formulation and derivation of those general principles that are applicable to 'systems' in general", following from "terms which occur in all sciences dealing with 'systems' and imply their logical homology" (von Bertalanffy, 1968:253). The concern with the description of evolutionary processes led to a revision of semantics, and introduced variation in time as part of what models had to consider (cf. von Bertalanffy, 1950). Fromm remained distant from this way of reasoning; but his experimentation with the corresponding vocabulary reveals a secret affinity, whose effects we can feel in his subsequent writings – even though he never fully displaced his theoretical presuppositions onto cybernetics.

What is then the character of this encounter, which fertilizes and produces intellectual fruits, but remains a subterranean and passing relation? – Its ambiguity derives from the political valency of cybernetics, which presented itself as a plainly instrumental form of thought. From Wiener (1948) to Margaret Mead's (1969) last writings, the application of cybernetics to human facts is followed by the anticipation of a well-succeeded social engineering. It promises the rise in industrial productiveness through automation, social integration without frictions – and an increasing conceptual undifferentiation between human beings and machines. Fromm is appalled by that. His prospects on "cybernation" are far from optimistic: he sees the potential for liberation from work through the machine, but believes the prevailing tendency in capitalism would be for an alienation of human beings' autonomy into calculus (cf. Fromm, 1968a). So much for the worse if this calculating tendency, as expressed for example in von Neumann's and Morgenstern's (1944) game theory, would reemerge among the strategists of the cold war – some of Fromm's biggest political rivals (cf. Fromm and Maccoby, 1962b).

There was therefore not only a "formal" resistance with the mode of thinking characteristic for cybernetics and correlated fields, but also an antagonism between their prevailing political tendency and Fromm's socialist humanism. All through the 1960s, Fromm had been criticizing what he saw as an idolatric aspect in the fascination with space travel. The project for his book *The crisis of psychoanalysis* (1970a) originally included a chapter on the "psychological and spiritual meaning of the Moonflight" (d-1970a-001-eng-draft-01:1). He thought he was testimonying the rise of a "cult of technology", a "cybernetic religion" (1976a:138). All of these practical developments involved the engineering of "systems".

With that in mind, Fromm must have felt incorporating systems theories integrally would violate his ethics. It is maybe no accident that his contact with systemic reasoning was initiated through sources in biology, where technocratic and instrumental interpretations were often weaker than among physicists, psychologists, and social scientists. If Wiener started from the model of the machine, von Bertalanffy would write that:

> Last century's mechanistic world picture was closely related to the domination of the machine, the theoretical view of living beings as machines and the mechanization of man himself. Concepts, however, which are coined by modern scientific developments, have their most obvious exemplification in life itself. Thus, there is a hope that the new world concept of science is an expression of the development toward a new stage in human culture.
>
> (1968:253)

This difference in attitude may have contributed for Fromm's receptiveness to organism-oriented systems theories – but he still didn't incorporate, either their logical formalism, or the mathematics of communication. What was then left for him? Precisely the *conception of determination* characteristic for systemic outlines, which is based on self-referentiality, circularity, and generalized covariance.

Fromm's only work intending an explicit incorporation of systems-theoretical concepts was presented in 1969 at the National Academy of Medicine in Mexico, in a "Symposium on the concept of death". The abstract tells us that "the difference between linear cause and effect and systemic thinking in terms or process is emphasized" (d-1992k-001-eng-type-01:1). This text discusses "the disintegration of societies": "a system can be changed only if, instead of changing only one single factor, real changes are made within the whole system so that a new integration of all its parts can take place" (Fromm, 1992k:43). In the Mexican symposium, Fromm discussed "disintegration" in reference to political violence in the US. But the same formulation recurs when he discusses the transformation of character in the therapeutic process:

> the character structure is a system, and like every other system it has a great power of cohesion because each part is geared to every other part, and a change in one part necessitates a change in every other part.
>
> (Fromm and Maccoby, 1970b:22)

Fromm is thus not attracted by cybernetic theorizing in general, but only by its attempt at expressing evolutionary processes as a function of the reciprocal relations between elements in the "system". A rather abstract, "formal" property – but one which offers him for the first time a chance at expressing his own understanding of causation. We should not frame Fromm as a "systems theorist" – an exaggeration leading to absurdity. What matters is to understand the peculiar dialectic in his thought: a critical theorist according to his social theory and political purpose, Fromm is closer to systemic reasoning according to his implied ontology. Unable to give full expression to the intricacy of this structure, he underestimated his own originality, and saw his own thought reflected in that of his masters. He believed "Freud's theory is a critical theory, as Marx's was" (1979a:24) – but also that both were at the same time systems thinkers:

> Freud saw the person as a system, as a form, as structure, or, to allude to Hegel, as *a totality*. He did not piece apart the person, but understood him or her as a system. Although the system theory was significant only since the 1920s, Freud – without calling it this – had already developed a system theory, in which every factor in the human system is actually connected and works with every other factor, so that change in one factor never goes without also affecting the whole and each part of the system. (The same is also true, by the way, of Marx's system. Because system thinking is very difficult for most so-called adherents to follow, both systems were by and large not understood by them.)
> (1992h:129)

***

Had Fromm remained so close to North American cultural anthropology as is usually held, he might have participated way more heavily in the development of cybernetics. Think of Margaret Mead: a participant in the Macy Conferences, her thought took the informational turn of the 1940s to its last consequences. Nothing of the sort happens with Fromm. He remained a strict opponent of the economic and scientific currents to which automation was related. For that reason, contending that his discovery of systems theory represents a late encounter with aspects of his own thought poses a historical problem. For this to be true, Fromm's works would have to imply forms of thinking which only blossomed at a later stage in the development of the sciences – and mostly outside his usual circle of scientific and philosophical references.

While this may sound implausible at first, it has its probability once we take into account that some of Fromm's acquaintances in the 1930s were already developing theoretical insights which would later be regrouped in cybernetic terms. For example: Karen Horney's (1936) and Harry Sullivan's (1953) works prefigure a systemic formulation of psychic economy. However, both of them passed away at a time when the infusion of information theory into the humanities was in a precocious stage. Fromm developed the seeds of his form of theorizing at a moment when the systemic experience of the world had not yet originated a general set of concepts, and then distanced himself from the thinkers which further formulated them. His later works still bear the mark of this precocious interruption.

We can understand the effect this had over Fromm's thought if we compare it to an experience contemporary to his – that of structuralism in France, which developed a much closer connection to the natural sciences and mathematics. Fromm's main contacts with natural scientists seem to have revolved around political issues, not theoretical ones. With Linus Pauling, he collaborates in fighting against nuclear war (Pauling_Linus_1961-01-15-by); with Albert Einstein, he elaborates a plea for peace between Jews and Arabs in Palestine (cf. Fromm, 1990t); Werner Heisenberg signs him an inscription in *Der Teil und das Ganze*, thanking him for "the book and some other teachings" (cf. e-N354). Fromm's main interest falls, not so much on the methods of contemporary natural science, but on the general epistemological consequences one could extrapolate from probabilistics, as well as the experimental and speculative boldness of physicists and chemists (cf. 1962a). In a work like Lévi-Strauss' (1958), to the contrary, the very mode of abstraction and method characteristic for information science and related areas is transposed onto anthropology, providing a general scheme for apprehending phenomena of communication. In psychoanalysis, a similar movement leads Lacan (1953–4) to a rearticulation between the symbolic and the imaginary registers. The "subject" itself finds its inner workings undermined and redescribed with the tools learned from physics, from logic, from mathematics. There is no equivalent movement in Fromm. His thought lends itself only tentatively to approximations with structuralism, since it considers human variety and history as actualizations of path-dependent possibilities – but we cannot say his method was a thoroughly probabilistic one (cf. Fromm, 1964a).

The specificity of Fromm's position lies in his desire to retain the effects of systemic explanation without fully making the passage from psychic energetics to the paradigm of communication. His way of grasping phenomena is similar to structural analysis in its aspiration to understand totality as a product of multilateral relationality. However, he does not accept the idea that the relative consideration of phenomena has analytic primacy over their consideration in themselves, as would be typical for some forms of structuralism. Halfway between Freud's "psychic determinism" and Bateson's "ecology of mind", Fromm is compelled to formulate in substantive terms what structural analysis would treat relatively. His very concept of "object relation" (Fromm, 1992e:19) remains unilateral, being introverted into one of the two (or more) *relata*. Thinking language primarily as an *expressive* phenomenon, only secondarily as a phenomenon of *communication*, Fromm is deprived of the elements making possible Lacanianism in France, the pragmatics of communication in the US, and other developments based on the interface between "information" and "meaning". As an inhabitant of this theoretical interstice, his thought may appear as formally incoherent. On the other hand, precisely because of its position between opposing intellectual tendencies, it finds greater freedom to pursue things in their substantive contradictions, opening the pathway for a singular way of experiencing the psychic world.

5 Quality and Quantity

We are now sufficiently informed to understand Fromm's break with classic Freudianism around 1937. The long delayed reflection on the influx of language over affection corresponds, in Fromm, to a primacy of "experience" as such – in the sense of its plain psychic reality, of the effectiveness of one's relatedness to others. This is the basis for his fondness for mystical discourse in the religious sphere (cf. 1966a), as well as for therapies valuing coming to grips with affective life (cf. Ferenczi and Rank, 1924). Thence springs the concrete, deeply felt trace in his writings. An affinity with the quality of affective phenomena is the very basis of Fromm's psychoanalysis. It must be deemed the stronger force motivating his clash with Freudian materialism.

In reading Fromm's output previous to 1937, we find several signs of the process leading him to abandon libido theory. In 1932, he takes a first step by detaching object relations from sexual stimulation, and calling for a "critique of the central role given to the erogenous zones" (1932b:137). A few years later, he asserts that drives must be "generate[d] and regenerate[d]" by a "specific practice of life" (1936a:80). The activation of drives is not anymore seen as a spontaneous bodily process, and the very notion of "adaptation" – previously related to the ego drives – is turned inward, to mean unconscious affection in relatedness to others. By that time, Fromm (1935a) had already expressed his misgivings with the authoritarian traces in the orthodox attitude towards the patient – a break in clinical conduct. It would not be long until this reverted into a break in theory as well. He then affirms an irreducible difference between "attitudes", grounded in affects excited in the life process, and sexual drives (cf. 1992e).

Fromm presents clinical work as the main reason for this change. Still in 1971, he tells Martin Jay his turn against Freudian "metapsychology" was empirically motivated (Jay_Martin_1971–05–14-to). He came to believe his therapeutic success was limited when he intervened in Freudian terms. We have no reason to doubt this affirmation, but must qualify it by noting that Fromm's criticism does not concern Freud's whole metapsychology. The main target is his energetics. This alone is good evidence that, around 1937, Fromm's systemic intuition of clinical phenomena is already developing. Liberated from Freudian economic dualism, he is now able to apprehend the mutual conditionality of psychic processes, as they fold over one another. This is the theoretical achievement underlying his last essay for the journal of the Institute for Social Research, "*On the feeling of powerlessness*". "Character structure" is there finally understood as a "reaction to the outside world", and a variety of drives, compulsions, and phantasies are portrayed as "compensations" against a repressed *feeling* (1937a:109).

The form of analysis Fromm develops in this essay can be seen as an attempt at resolving a difficulty inherent in Freudianism. Freud's and Breuer's (1893) cathartic method still worked with the idea that affective reactions were the primary contents underlying hysterical symptoms. Psychic *qualia* were seen as responding to particular situations, and turned pathogenic once their discharge was impeded. The transition into the psychoanalytic method was followed by a change in this respect. Affects were gradually subsumed to a unified libidinal economy, and increasingly identified with their quantitative determination (cf. Freud, 1894). This allowed to account for the history of displacements in patient's desires, as it unveils itself in association, as well as for non-hysteriform symptoms, where affection is often less pronounced (cf. Freud, 1896). However, even if desires and memories were still theorized as awakened by outside stimuli (cf. Freud, 1900–30), the causative role of objects was weakened. Arousal and frustration of drives came to be seen as modulating their intensity and proneness to fixation, but their activity was increasingly treated as spontaneous (cf. Freud, 1905–24). This brought about a primacy of drives over feelings, which were lastly expelled out of the dynamic unconscious. Repressed were, after all, only representations of drives (cf. Freud, 1915b).

We find the first sign of this change in Freud's theory of anxiety. All through its many reformulations, neurotic anxiety is still understood as presupposing the clash between repression and the repressed; realistic anxiety and guilt owe their specificity to the danger they react to (their object or originating instance), not to the system they are inscribed in (cf. Freud, 1900–30; 1916–7; 1926). From this point on, the dominating trend in Freudianism is to understand the qualitative peculiarity of affects and feelings as a secondary manifestation of the dynamics between forces which – considered economically – appear as amounts of a substance of identical quality (cf. Freud, 1914b; 1919; Ferenczi, 1912). Even in countercathexis, libido represses libido, and the difference between libido and interest becomes secondary (cf. Freud, 1915c). The derivation of more nuanced affective qualities can then only happen by overdetermination between independent unconscious processes (cf. Reik, 1929). Quality must otherwise be presupposed, either negatively – as with reaction formations, such as disgust, shame and social feelings (cf. Freud, 1921) – or affirmatively – as being implied by the kinds of energy at stake in a certain process (cf. Reik, 1917).

Indeed, object libido, narcissistic libido, interest, and the energy of the death drive are not purely quantitative categories. They contain a rudimentary qualification of different kinds of pleasure, from which psychic *qualia* can in part be derived. However, they still imply the emergence of consciously felt qualities as a result of displaced, dammed, discharged *quanta*. This organizes the whole intuition of the clinical process. If the same forces move between different forms of expression, then libido theory suggests that the substrat for this variety be imagined as the displacement of energy between representations – here, their decathexis; there, their irruption in conversive innervation, and so on. This implies an essential undifferentiality underneath phenomenal differences. Hence the contradictory result: if affective qualities are seen as reactions to real events, they remain unanalyzable. If they are made available to analysis, their plurality has to be deduced from qualitatively homogeneous processes.

Classic Freudianism lives within this contradiction – a consequence of its way of relating the dynamic and the economic points of view. Any change of balance in this respect opens the path for revision or rupture – and the corresponding theoretical problems start breaking down in opposing tendencies precisely around the 1920s. Symptoms of that abound in many forms. Freudian literature vacillates between the derivation of secondary affects and feelings (shame, guilt, the uncanny), and the assumption of certain primary reactions (original anxiety, normal jealousy, envy), themselves left without a clear dynamic origin (cf. Freud, 1921; 1922; 1926). In Freud (1923), the implied equivalence between "unconscious guilt feelings" and masochistic "need for punishment" collapses the two sides of the antagonism (drives and feelings) into one, but at the cost of giving up the strictly *pcs-cs* topology of affection. On the clinical side, updating trauma theory is turned urgent with the advent of war neuroses, in which emotional reactions to real events are again a symptomatic source (cf. Simmel, 1918; Reik, 1929). A reevaluation of the therapeutic function of affects leads Rank (1929) to his will therapy, and Ferenczi (1929) to a neocathartic method.

On the opposite extreme, the dominant form of Freudian characterology may be seen as a field of compromise. It staggers the problem by introducing the intermediary notion of *emotional attitudes*, conceived as rigid, partly conscious "modes of reaction", to which unconscious drive dynamics are presupposed (cf. Alexander, 1922). Character traits, once conceived as attitudes, function as a middle-term, partaking of both drive-like and affect-like qualities. Affection by specific objects can then be retained together with the primacy of quantitative over qualitative factors. This allows a postponement of the central difficulties at stake for some time, but not their overcoming. Years later, a number of major revisions are reached precisely through the theory of affects. Jones achieves a theory of jealousy in which the homosexual etiology assumed by Freud is subordinated to a deeper cause: unresolved guilt and a "lack in the capacity to love" (1930:166). Alexander strives for a "combination of the metapsychological with the qualitative analysis of mental processes", in which the "opposed polar strivings" of contradictory drives would be themselves causative of conflict (1933:90,111). Out of Karl Abraham's and Ferenczi's late works, the grounds are set for object-relations theories, beginning with Klein (1928). The time is then ripe for others to perform more radical changes. One need only remember Reich, once a brilliant character analyst, whose departure from Freud happens once he resolutely subordinates dynamics to the economic point of view: "whereas the psychoanalytic organization developed the qualitative angle, i.e., the ideas, their interconnection, and so on, I picked up the energy angle" (1967:120). Fromm's development is symmetrical and opposite. He gives primacy to *qualia* and does away with speculative economics. Because of that, libido theory is the first aspect of classic Freudianism he rejects.

Once the Freudian knot between economy and dynamics is severed, it must lead into a conceptual revolution. In Freud (1905–24), the "plasticity" of sexuality had been the plasticity of its modes of satisfaction: his model for quality was *sensation*, not the affects. While psychic economy is thought of in terms of the pleasure-unpleasure series, the content of desires remains in a status of relative clinical indifference. It matters only in its relation to social norms, since the moral and practical viability of their satisfaction determines their participation in suffering. A drive's aim and object are ultimately secondary to its source and pressure, and the conflict emerges only between drive and repression. To this corresponds also a formal aspect in Freud's understanding of the unconscious. Departing from the treatment of hysteria, Freudianism grew to take *compromise formations* as its model for derivatives of the unconscious. This notion was first introduced to account for obsessional and paranoid symptoms, but its meaning was generalized as soon as the theory of repression was extended beyond strict symptomatology, and the return of the repressed was not restricted to remembrance (cf. Freud, 1899). Psychic mechanisms then ceased to be seen as "ways of repression" (cf. Freud, 1896), and were taken as presupposing it. Since other mechanisms already presume the conflict between drives and repression, they always imply the concept of compromise – a partial satisfaction of both opposing tendencies (cf. Freud, 1914a). Only later was the question of their relative independence raised again, with reference to a generalized notion of "defense" (cf. Freud, 1926). By contrast, Frommian analysis privileges *affects* as models for psychic *qualia,* and favors the concept of "compensation" over that of defense. Developing for years in the study of the "normal" bourgeois character, Fromm's approach works with a generalized notion of *reaction formation* as its model, taking repressed processes to be basically "compulsive" in nature (cf. 1931b). Hence its greater affinity with the analysis of obsessional phenomena, and the corresponding interest Fromm displays for problems in sadomasochism and narcissism all through the 1930s.

Elsewhere, Freudian analysis worked with the complementary opposition between psychic tendencies, as it recurs in particular drives and their modification (displacement upwards, aim inversion – cf. Freud, 1905; 1909a; 1915a; Ferenczi, 1911). Only in the analysis of obsessional phenomena occurs also the idea that repression is sustained by way of attraction and repulsion between incompatible *qualia.* They are indifferently ambivalent in the unconscious, but turn into contradiction by the secondary process (cf. Freud, 1894; 1909b). This *polar* understanding of psychic forces is essential to Frommian psychoanalysis. He thinks different psychic tendencies can be activated by one another, eventually for the purpose of sustaining their own unconsciousness. Primary affective reactions (to objects) are then seen as kept in repression by a foliage of conscious formations, which unfold as secondary reactions of the psyche (to itself). They are responses against the affective nucleus of one's own experience, implying a *reflexive* character to psychic processes. These "compensatory" reactions may be phenomena of any kind – feelings, ideas, drives, acts – as long as they function for reproducing unconsciousness. With that, the dynamics of their underlying "mechanism" does not anymore equate their *formal* deduction out of primary material. Rather, the interest falls on the *substantive* connection between different psychic tendencies. By their very nature, they imply or negate each other in the process of reproducing psychic existence. Contrary to Freud (1910; 1915c), ambivalence is recognized as capable also of unconscious contradiction. This generalized conditionality of psychic tendencies by one another, already in their unconscious state, is what specifies Fromm's concept of character as a *structural* one.

Fromm's social psychology starts with the premise that the predominance of some forms of satisfaction over others is not indifferent for human activity. Loving and hating don't count as simple alternatives for pleasure, but as forces implying different psychic constitutions. The primary conflict is not anymore that between drives and repression, but that between distinct aims in the unconscious – that is, between contradictory passional qualities. Hence Fromm's late incursion in systems theoretical vocabulary. He was attracted by the way it allowed him to develop the idea of a multilateral negativity of the drives, towards the formation of a singular "totality". On the other hand, we see why he remained so distant, both from cybernetic formalism, and from Freudian energetics. Abstracting from the particular content of phenomena would betray the most fundamental tenet of his clinical intuition. Fromm's aspiration is not to deduce generally valid isomorphisms between psychic processes, which would derive a generalized psychodynamics, but rather to grasp the psychodynamics specific to each kind of psychic material. Contrary to Abraham (1924), regularities in the employment of psychic mechanisms are not anymore ascribed to developmental stages, but to unconscious contents themselves. Fromm's is a materialism of the immanence of form in matter. His works move in the contradiction between a thought pregnant with interest for differentiated quality, and a formally undifferentiated mode of expression.

6 Logic

The refusal to treat distinct forms of satisfaction indifferently is a theoretical continuation of Fromm's ethical impulse. Among classic philosophical formulations of ethics, he was most at home with eudaimonics (cf. 1947a). This raises the problem of understanding Fromm's grounding of normativity in comparison to other critical theories – among which we will take Adorno's (1951) as a pivot for contrast, since for him an investigation of the problem of "good life" had to take an emphatically negative form. Both in Fromm's case and in Adorno's, the normative and the logical aspects of theory are mutually dependent. This stems from a problem inherited by all the members of the Frankfurt Institute: the integration of categories originated in absolute idealism into the structure of historical materialism.

At first sight, this aspect seems to point at a strong discrepancy. Other than a few notes and excerpts from the *Logic* and the *Philosophy of religion*, nothing in the archives indicates that Fromm would have systematically engaged with Hegel (cf. e-N280–81; e-N828; e-A-011–12). In his correspondence with Raya Dunayevksaya, he remains unresponsive to technical issues in the interpretation of idealism (Dunayevskaya_Raya_1964–02–14-to). In his published works, the treatment of alienation is the most direct Hegelian (1807) inflection, and even then interpolated with Marx's (1844) reinterpretation (cf. Fromm, 1962a). Isolated aspects of Hegelianism abound in less specific form. He thought "Hegel's great contribution to the understanding of man and history" was the notion that "one cannot understand any living phenomenon [...] unless one sees it as a process" (d-1961h-eng-draft-03:6), and derived his understanding of historical "alternatives" from the notion of "real possibilities (in the Hegelian sense)" (Adams_James_Luther_1963–11–08-to). His concept of normality and pathology was partly inspired by an interpretation of the Hegelian notion of necessity – "what Hegel meant in his own system by 'real' was 'real inasmuch as it is necessary'" (1991f:85). Finally, he came to develop a particular understanding of the "resolution of polarities", whose "most important influence" would have been "Marx and Hegel" (Adams_James_Luther_1970–02–21-to) – to which we should also add Bachofen, since it was heavily based on a metaphysics of sexual polarity inspired by the theory of matriarchy (cf. Fromm, 1934a; 1949b).

A "dialectics of polarities" is the closest we find in Fromm to an overt dialectic:

> Now, there is always the problem of how polarity is met, and I think there are only three possibilities. First, the two poles unite, and in this union they become one, at least for the moment. [...] Or, second, the two poles cannot unite. [...] What we find in modern industrial culture is the third possibility – the two poles tend to neutralize each other.
>
> (1965f:216)

The meaning of idealist notions is thus profoundly changed: the concept of a "dialectical logic" is turned interchangeable with that of a "paradoxical logic" (1956a:60), to which Fromm subsumed also Freudian dynamics. These "paradoxical" relations do not always follow the triadic movement characteristic for Hegel's logic. They are sometimes interrupted in aporia – "I experience myself, at the same time, and the same subject, I, as completely unique, and as completely not unique" (Fromm, 1992g:88). In other cases, they fall back into undifferentiated unity – "man can perceive reality only in contradictions, and can never perceive in *thought* the ultimate reality-unity, the One itself" (Fromm, 1956a:60). Finally, they sometimes move toward sublation. Then Fromm speaks of the "negation of negation" as a "new [...] positive" (1991e:25).

This logical eclecticism has its roots partly in the incorporation of Buddhistic motives into Fromm's (1960a) thought, but it is also conditioned by his clinical experience. We saw that he extended the classes of relation apprehended in the clinic onto other spheres, taking them as general categorial forms. Thus, also when it comes to "dialectics", Fromm speaks in terms of "opposing forces" (1990f:27). A general logic of polarities is the displaced expression he gives to psychic polar relations, as intuited during therapeutic practice. The meaning of "affirmation", "negation", "sublation" is not anymore derived from predicative relations, as in Aquinas (1255), or from the determinations met in the pure space of speculative logic, as in Hegel (1812–16), but from a particular experiential domain, in which logical forms adhere to more specific processes. Fromm is after all interested in the "the true experience of two contradictory facts, two contradictory statements, and the capacity or the willingness to live on these contradictions" (1992g:90) – ultimately in their "perception" or "awareness" (1956a:59–60; 1960a:52).

This sublation of conceptual thinking into immediate experience remains foreign to Adorno (1966–7). However, both him and Fromm share the tendency for a particularization of logical terms in reference to specific experiential spheres. Abstract and determined negation, position, sublation, do not anymore function as the skeleton of a systematic ontology, but let themselves be saturated with concrete political, aesthetic, or psychological values. Marx's (1844) early works already participate in this tendency – and it is ultimately to be found in Hegel (1817–30a) himself, who aspired to modify his trans-categorial notions according to the singular determinations met within each category. However, Hegel's thought still comprised an "ontology" in the strict sense of the term. The common tissue reuniting the various modalities of affirmation, negation, and return was still the identity between thought processes and real processes, as presumed by idealism (cf. Hegel, 1807). The materialistic turn originating Marxism problematizes this equivalence. The particularization of Hegelian vocabulary may thus be understood as one of the effects of the dissolution of its systematic aspiration. 20th century critical theories still respond to this process, and it is in reference to it that we can clarify Fromm's and others' logical positions.

Adorno's (1966–7) negative dialectics mistrust sublation. They anticipate the infinity of the thought process in the infinity of things themselves, and propose a logic of non-identity as a way of avoiding that the conceptual movement be exhausted in false reconciliation. This had indeed been a partial tendency in Hegel – but only one among others. Certain passages could only be resolved speculatively by compressing the particular and the general meaning of the corresponding categories into the same movement. This happens in the derivation of life species in the *Phenomenology* (1807), in the introduction of good infinity in the *Logic* (1812–32), culminating in the subsumption of individuals to their status as persons in the *Encyclopedia* (1817–30b), and of civil society to the state in the *Philosophy of Right* (1821). Marx (1843) saw in this an empirical problem, and Adorno (1966–7) a logical-political one – there would be an ideological subsumption of singularity to universality. Fromm himself would have agreed: "Hegel exchanged his youthful revolutionary sympathies for the glorification of the State in his later years" (1967b:25). Hegel's handling of right does sometimes imply a suspension of particular contradictions into generality – but even then not with a total erasure of political conflict (cf. 1837). The more we regress into more abstract categories, the more that assessment displays its inaccuracies. The specific forms of negation embodied in certain categories are retained within the corresponding entities; the movement towards higher forms does not imply their real dissolution (cf. 1812–32).

Contrariwise, if sublation and reconciliation are made one, the notion of "positive" has to recoil from its character as a mediated derivative (that which is set) and fall back into immediate identity. It then remains to negation to represent all difference – but a difference now lingering in the margins of identity, expelled from it. This grows to be Adorno's (1951) main experiential *topos*: the movement of difference as a fleeting glimpse behind an overwhelming homogeneity. Adhering to aesthetic, political, and bodily experience alike, this formulation often redounds in antinomical thinking (cf. Adorno, 1961). "Moments of truth" lose their true character as *moments*, disintegrating into isolated singularities. The "negative", formally ascribed as immanent to things, is only really acknowledged outside actual existence – as a remnant, a weakling. It functions ultimately not as *negating,* but as *negated*. The primacy of the object then falls back into a primacy of phantasy – a remembrance, through the object, of the subject's unfulfilled desires.

Fromm (1947a) is also mistrustful of the wish for definitive reconciliation. However, he retains a greater differentiation between sublation of conflict and reconciliation. His is not a logic of non-identity, but one of differentiated unity – of complexification and development of contradictions. Sublation works intensively, not extensively. Radical humanism then "comprehends the process of the unfolding of oppositions and aims at a new synthesis which negates *and* affirms" (Fromm, 1970k:7–8) – so much so that Fromm subscribes to a negative psychology: "psychology can show us what man is *not*. It cannot tell us what man, each one of us, *is*" (1957a:195). This sends us back to the articulation between clinic and politics. The dynamics of suffering and liberation provide Fromm with the model for his notions of "affirmation", "negation", and "synthesis". Instead of acting as trans-categorial articulations, as in Hegel (1812–16), they express a particular understanding of the relation between unconscious process and political action.

In Fromm, contrary to Adorno, immediate "affirmation" is more clearly distinguished from the "positive", which is already mediated by its negation. His critical theory is thus not opposed to others by its "affirmative", least of all its "positive" character. It is rather the fruit of a different understanding of the *relation* between affirmation, negation, and position. This amounts lastly not to a different logic, as to a contrasting experiential paradigm. Hegel's idealism allowed his political and religious preferences to infiltrate philosophy in the guise of the Idea – but logic was still left free to express the particularities of opposition, counterposition, and contradiction as they present themselves in each case. In Adorno and Fromm, materialism prescribes a dissociation between ideas and the Idea. But this constrains logic, now freed from its identity with the particular movement of things, to reintegrate political and religious desire into the thought process. Logical functions thus express a specific experience of difference – of its *situation* in a particular setting. Adorno tends to fixate norms around an experience of the negative as negated. Fromm tends to give primacy to the moment of return and overcoming, of successful operation of potentiality into existence. His logic freezes the moment in which difference, freed from its previous constraints, announces a new beginning – and hence appears anew as affirmation. Hence his belief that

> the culmination of all of Hegel's thinking is the concept of the potentialities inherent in a thing, of the dialectical process in which they manifest themselves, and the idea that this process is one of active movement of these potentialities.
>
> (1961b:25)

The opposition between these thought forms is dissolved as soon as we recognize them for what they are – fixated gestures, different moments in a single movement. Their real contradiction lies in their distinct social bases. All critical theories may agree that society "already develops in itself the elements which contradict it" (Fromm, 1955b:348), but they may disagree on which social formations fulfill this role. Hence the relevance of the religious model for Fromm's thought and action. His understanding of logic is a sublimation of what he deemed a trustable basis for political activity. It is modeled after radical religious movements, which fought against institutional dogma and carried out reforms in the history of various confessions (cf. Fromm, 1992s). Therein Fromm's conception of socialism as "secular messianism" (1961b:58): revolutionary movements would share a common psychological basis in politics and religion, despite the differences in the languages they employ:

> Europe, since the end of the Middle Ages, has not found a form yet to express the substance of this "religious" experience in thought concepts adequate to

modern scientific thought. I believe that in the philosophy of Spinoza to Hegel and Marx we find a new form of expressing the old substance in philosophical language.

(Bottomore_Tom_B_1962-05-31-to)

This affinity between Marxist humanism and the religious sphere remained foreign to other critical theories, which start from different social models for political relatedness. This as well is reflected in their logical structures. Adorno (1966–7) retains, from Judaism, the taboo of images, whereas Fromm (1950a) sees in the very concept of "God" an anticipation of the experience of a multilateral human development. Where Adorno emphasizes the rigor of the concept, Fromm sees the passage into a practice seeking a yet-undeveloped experience. This allows for a partial convergence between Fromm's approach and Adorno's notion of non-identity, but the procedure is all the more divergent. In Adorno, experience is for the concept; in Fromm, the concept is for experience. Thus also the political formations their works foster are fundamentally different.

These oppositions culminate in a different reception of the idealist inheritance in Marxism. Fromm's greatest affinity with Hegel lies not on the formal aspect of thought, but on its content and problematic: absolute knowledge would also lead to a return to immediacy (cf. Hegel, 1807). In Hegel (1821; 1837), freedom had been the telos of both individual human beings and social development. However, it was derived either from will – in its most abstract stage, "will that wills itself" – or from thought, which is "one with its object" (free from difference) in the concept. Through its relationship to will, liberation redounded for Hegel (1817–30b) in formal, legal freedom – with a primacy of ego relations over real individuation. Fromm's Marxism is a critique of this Hegelian tenet. Instead of a formal concept of freedom, based on conscious determination of action and subsumption of difference to generality, Fromm (1941a) strives for a concept of real freedom, based on unconscious indeterminacy and its productiveness of singular difference. His critical theory and his socialism are a pursuit of this insight, after all also found in Hegel: "freedom lies neither in indeterminacy nor in determinacy, but is both" (1821:57).

Bibliography

Primary Sources

Fromm's correspondence

Adams_James_Luther_1963–1911–08-to: Fromm to James Luther Adams, November 8th, 1963
Adams_James_Luther_1970–1902–21-to: Fromm to Adams, February 21st, 1970

Alexander_Franz_1937–1901–08-by: Franz Alexander to Fromm, January 8th, 1937
Bottomore_Tom_B_1962–1905–31-to: Fromm to Tom Bottomore, May 31st, 1962
Dobrenkov_Vladimir_1969–1903–10-to: Fromm to V. Dobrenkov, March 10th, 1969
Dunayevskaya_Raya_1964–1902–14-to: Fromm to Raya Dunayevskaya, February 14th, 1964
Foerster_H_Von_1971–1910–01-to: Fromm to Heinz von Foerster, October 1st, 1971
Jay_Martin_1971–1905–14-to: Fromm to Martin Jay, May 14th, 1971
Mead_Margaret_1968–1904–20-to: Fromm to Margaret Mead, April 20th, 1968
Pauling_Linus_1961–1901–15-by: Linus Pauling to Fromm, January 15th, 1961

Drafts, typescripts, and study materials by Fromm

d-1961h-eng-draft-03: draft for "*Russia, Germany, China: remarks on foreign policy*"
d-1970a-001-eng-draft-01: a prospective listing of chapters for *The crisis of psychoanalysis*.
d-1973a-eng-type-06: typescripts for *The anatomy of human destructiveness*.
d-1991d-002-eng-draft-04: transcription of the recordings published as *The art of listening*.
d-1992k-001-eng-type-01: typescripts for "*The Disintegration of Societies*".
d-RoHD: drafts for *The revolution of hope*. Still without an official identifying code.
e-A-011–12: excerpts from Hegel's *Wissenschaft der Logik and Religionsphilosophie*.
e-N15–16: study notes on Heinz von Foerster's "*Molecular ethology*".
e-Q7: study notes on Ludwing van Bertalanffy's "*Comments on aggression*".
e-N282: marginalia to Fromm's copy of Hegel's *Enzyklopädie*.
e-N280–1: marginalia to Fromm's copy of Hegel's *Wissenschaft der Logik*.
e-N93: marginalia to Fromm's copy of von Bertalanffy's *General systems theory*.
e-N354: marginalia to Fromm's copy of Heisenberg's *Der Teil und das Ganze*.

Published sources

Abraham, Karl. Ergänzungen zur Lehre vom Analcharakter. *Psychoanalytische Studien zur Charakterbildung*. Frankfurt: Fischer Verlag, [1921]/1969.
Abraham, Karl. Beiträge der Oralerotik zur Charakterbildung. *Psychoanalytische Studien zur Charakterbildung*. Frankfurt: Fischer Verlag, [1924]/1969.
Abraham, Karl. Zur Charakterbildung auf der "genitalen" Entwicklungsstufe. *Psychoanalytische Studien zur Charakterbildung*. Frankfurt: Fischer Verlag, [1925]/1969.
Adler, Alfred. *Über den nervösen Charakter*. Munich: Verlag von J. F. Bergmann, 1912–1922.
Adorno, Theodor. *Minima Moralia*. Frankfurt: Surkhamp, [1951]/1969.
Adorno, Theodor. *Die revidierte Psychoanalyse. Gesammelte Schriften 8*. Frankfurt: Surkhamp Verlag, [1952]/2020.
Adorno, Theodor. Vers une musique informelle. *Quasi una fantasia*. Frankfurt: Surkhamp, [1961]/1963.
Adorno, Theodor. *Negative Dialektik*. Frankfurt: Surkhamp, [1966–1967]/1970.
Alexander, Franz. The castration complex in the formation of character. *The scope of psychoanalysis*. New York: Basic Books Inc., [1922]/1961.

Alexander, Franz. *Psychoanalyse der Gesamtpersönlichkeit.* Vienna: Internationaler Psychoanalytischer Verlag, 1927.
Alexander, Franz. The neurotic character. *The scope of psychoanalysis.* New York: Basic Books Inc., [1930]/1961.
Alexander, Franz. The relation of structural and instinctual conflicts. *The scope of psychoanalysis.* New York: Basic Books Inc., [1930]/1961.
Aquinas, Thomas of. *On being and essence.* Wetteren: Universa, [1255]/1991.
Balint, Michael. Character analysis and new beginning. *Primary love and psycho-analytic technique.* London: Tavistock Publications, [1932]/1965.
Bateson, Gregory. *Steps to an ecology of mind.* Chicago: Chicago Univ. Press, [1972]/2000.
Bateson, Gregory; Ruesch, Jurgen. *Communication.* New York: W. W. Norton and Company, Inc., [1951]/1968.
Bertalanffy, Ludwig von. An outline of general systems theory. *British Journal for the Philosophy of Science*:1 (2):134–165.
Bertalanffy, Ludwig von. *General systems theory.* New York: George Braziller, 1968.
Fenichel, Otto. Psychoanalytic remarks on Erich Fromm's book "Escape from Freedom". *Psychoanalytic Review*:31:133–152.
Ferenczi, Sándor. Über passagère Symptombildungen während der Analyse. *Bausteine II.* Bern: Verlag Hans Huber, [1911]/1927.
Ferenczi, Sándor. Ein Fall von "dejà vu". *Bausteine II.* Bern: Verlag Hans Huber, [1912]/1927.
Ferenczi, Sándor. Technische Schwierigkeiten einer Hysterieanalyse. *Bausteine III.* Bern: Verlag Hans Huber, [1919]/1939.
Ferenczi, Sándor. Das Problem der Beendigung der Analysen. *Bausteine III.* Bern: Verlag Hans Huber, [1927]/1939.
Ferenczi, Sándor. Die psychoanalytische Therapie des Charakters. *Bausteine III.* Bern: Verlag Hans Huber, [1928]/1939.
Ferenczi, Sándor. Relaxationsprinzip und Neokatharsis. *Bausteine III.* Bern: Verlag Hans Huber, [1929]/1939.
Ferenczi, Sándor; Rank, Otto. *Entwicklungsziele der Psychoanalyse.* Vienna: Internationaler Psychoanalytischer Verlag, 1924.
Foerster, Heinz von. Molecular ethology. *Molecular mechanisms in memory and learning.* New York: Plenum Press, 1970.
Freud, Sigmund. Die Abwehr-Neuropsychosen. *Gesammelte Werke I.* London: Imago Publishing, [1894]/1952.
Freud, Sigmund. Weitere Bemerkungen über die Abwehr-Neuropsychosen. *Gesammelte Werke I.* London: Imago Publishing, [1896]/1952.
Freud, Sigmund. Zum psychischen Mechanismus der Vergesslichkeit. *Gesammelte Werke I.* London: Imago Publishing, [1899]/1952.
Freud, Sigmund. Die Traumdeutung. *Gesammelte Werke II-III.* Frankfurt: S. Fischer Verlag, [1900–1930]/1961.
Freud, Sigmund. Über den Traum. *Gesammelte Werke II-III.* Frankfurt: S. Fischer Verlag, [1901]/1961.
Freud, Sigmund. Die Freudsche psychoanalytische Methode. *Gesammelte Werke V.* Frankfurt: S. Fischer Verlag, [1904]/1968.
Freud, Sigmund. Drei Abhandlungen zur Sexualtheorie. *Gesammelte Werke V.* Frankfurt: S. Fischer Verlag, [1905–1924]/1968.

Freud, Sigmund. Bruchstück einer Hysterieanalyse. *Gesammelte Werke V.* Frankfurt: S. Fischer Verlag, [1905]/1968.
Freud, Sigmund. Zwangshandlungen und Religionsübungen. *Gesammelte Werke VII.* Frankfurt: S. Fischer Verlag, [1907]/1966.
Freud, Sigmund. Allgemeines über den hysterischen Anfall. *Gesammelte Werke VII.* Frankfurt: S. Fischer Verlag, [1909a]/1966.
Freud, Sigmund. Bemerkungen über einen Fall von Zwangsneurose. *Gesammelte Werke VII.* Frankfurt: S. Fischer Verlag, [1909b]/1966.
Freud, Sigmund. Über den Gegensinn der Urworte. *Gesammelte Werke VIII.* London: Imago Publishing, [1910]/1955.
Freud, Sigmund. Formulierungen über zwei Prinzipien des psychischen Geschehens. *Gesammelte Werke VIII.* London: Imago Publishing, [1911a]/1955.
Freud, Sigmund. Psychoanalytische Bemerkungen über einen autobiographisch beschriebenen Fall von Paranoia (Dementia Paranoides). *Gesammelte Werke VIII.* London: Imago Publishing, [1911b]/1955.
Freud, Sigmund. Totem und Tabu. *Gesammelte Werke IX.* London: Imago Publishing, [1912–1913]/1940.
Freud, Sigmund. Zur Geschichte der psychoanalytischen Bewegung. *Gesammelte Werke X.* London: Imago Publishing, [1914a]/1949.
Freud, Sigmund. Über Fausse Reconnaissance ("Déjà Raconté") während der psychoanalytischen Arbeit. *Gesammelte Werke X.* London: Imago Publishing, [1914b]/1949.
Freud, Sigmund. Triebe und Triebschicksale. *Gesammelte Werke X.* London: Imago Publishing, [1915a]/1949.
Freud, Sigmund. Die Verdrängung. *Gesammelte Werke X.* London: Imago Publishing, [1915b]/1949.
Freud, Sigmund. Das Unbewußte. *Gesammelte Werke X.* London: Imago Publishing, [1915c]/1949.
Freud, Sigmund. Vorlesungen zur Einführung in der Psychoanalyse. *Gesammelte Werke XI.* Frankfurt: S. Fischer Verlag, [1916–1917]/1969.
Freud, Sigmund. Das Unheimliche. *Gesammelte Werke XII.* Frankfurt: S. Fischer Verlag, [1919]/1966.
Freud, Sigmund. Jenseits des Lutsprinzips. *Gesammelte Werke XIII.* Frankfurt: S. Fischer Verlag, [1920]/1967.
Freud, Sigmund. Massenpsychologie und Ich-Analyse. *Gesammelte Werke XIII.* Frankfurt: S. Fischer Verlag, [1921]/1967.
Freud, Sigmund. Über einige neurotische Mechanismen bei Eifersucht, Paranoia und Homosexualität. *Gesammelte Werke XIII.* Frankfurt: S. Fischer Verlag, [1922]/1967.
Freud, Sigmund. Das Ich und das Es. *Gesammelte Werke XIII.* Frankfurt: S. Fischer Verlag, [1923]/1967.
Freud, Sigmund. Hemmung, Symptom und Angst. *Gesammelte Werke XIV.* London: Imago Publishing, [1926]/1955.
Freud, Sigmund. Das Unbehagen in der Kultur. *Gesammelte Werke XIV.* London: Imago Publishing, [1929–1930]/1955.
Freud, Sigmund. Some elementary lessons in psycho-analysis. *Gesammelte Werke XVII.* London: Imago Publishing, [1938]/1955.

Freud, Sigmund; Breuer, Joseph. Über den psychischen Mechanismus hysterischer Phänomene (Vorläufige Mitteilung). Sigmund Freud. *Gesammelte Werke I*. London: Imago Publishing, [1893]/1952.

Fromm, Erich. Dauernde Nachwirkung eines Erziehungsfehlers. *Zeitschrift für psychoanalytische Pädagogik*:1:327f, 1926a.

Fromm, Erich. Der Sabbath. *Imago*:13:223–234, 1927a.

Fromm, Erich. Psychoanalyse und Soziologie. *Gesamtausgabe, Band I*. Stuttgart: Deutsche Verlags-Anstalt, [1929a]/1999.

Fromm, Erich. The dogma of Christ. *The dogma of Christ*. New York: Holt, Rinehart and Winston, [1930a]/1992.

Fromm, Erich. Der Staat als Erzieher: Zur Psychologie der Strafjustiz. *Gesamtausgabe, Band I*. Stuttgart: Deutsche Verlags-Anstalt, [1930b]/1999.

Fromm, Erich. Ödipus in Innsbruck: Zum Halssman-Prozess. *Gesamtausgabe, Band I*. Stuttgart: Deutsche Verlags-Anstalt, [1930d]/1999.

Fromm, Erich. Zur Psychologie des Verbrechers und der strafenden Gesellschaft. *Gesamtausgabe, Band I*. Stuttgart: Deutsche Verlags-Anstalt, [1931a]/1999.

Fromm, Erich. Politik und Psychoanalyse. *Gesamtausgabe, Band I*. Stuttgart: Deutsche Verlags-Anstalt, [1931b]/1999.

Fromm, Erich. The method and function of an analytic social psychology. *The crisis of psychoanalysis*. New York: Holt, Reinehart and Winston, [1932a]/1970.

Fromm, Erich. Psychoanalytic characterology and its relevance for social psychology. *The crisis of psychoanalysis*. New York: Holt, Reinehart and Winston, [1932b]/1970.

Fromm, Erich. The theory of mother right and its relevance for social psychology. *The crisis of psychoanalysis*. New York: Holt, Reinehart and Winston, [1934a]/1970.

Fromm, Erich. Die gesellschaftliche Bedingtheit der psychoanalytischen Therapie. *Gesamtausgabe, Band I*. Stuttgart: Deutsche Verlags-Anstalt, [1935a]/1999.

Fromm, Erich. Sozialpsychogischer Teil. Max Horkheimer (ed.). *Studien über Autorität und Familie*. Frankfurt: Dietrich zu Klampen Verlag, [1936a]/1987.

Fromm, Erich. Zum Gefühl der Ohnmacht. *Gesamtausgabe, Band I*. Stuttgart: Deutsche Verlags-Anstalt, [1937a]/1999.

Fromm, Erich. The Social Philosophy of "Will Therapy". *Psychiatry*:2:229–237, 1939a.

Fromm, Erich. Selfishness and self-love. *Love, sexuality, and matriarchy*. New York: Fromm International Edition, [1939b]/1997.

Fromm, Erich. *Escape from freedom*. New York: Henry Holt & Company, [1941a]/1994.

Fromm, Erich. *Man for himself*. New York: Henry Holt & Company, [1947a]/1990.

Fromm, Erich. The Oedipus complex and the Oedipus myth. Ruth Nanda Anshen (ed.). *The family*. New York: Harper and Bros, 1949b.

Fromm, Erich. Psychoanalytic characterology and its application to the understanding of culture. *Fromm Forum*: 12:5–10, [1949c]/2008.

Fromm, Erich. *Psychoanalysis and religion*. New York: Bantam Books, [1950a]/1967.

Fromm, Erich. *The forgotten language*. New York: Holt, Rinehart and Winston, [1951a]/1960.

Fromm, Erich. *The sane society*. New York: Henry Holt & Company, [1955a]/1990.

Fromm, Erich. The human implications of instinctivist "radicalism": a reply to Herbert Marcuse. *Dissent*: 2:342–349, 1955b.

Fromm, Erich. Psychoanalysis. J.R. Newman (Ed.): *What Is Science?* New York: Simon and Schuster, 1955e.

Fromm, Erich. *The art of loving*. London: Thorsons Editions, [1956a]/1995.

Fromm, Erich. On the limitations and dangers of psychology. *The dogma of Christ*. New York: Holt, Rinehart and Winston, [1957a]/1992.
Fromm, Erich. Let man prevail: a socialist manifesto and program. *On disobedience*. New York: Harper Perennial, [1960b]/2010.
Fromm, Erich. *Marx's concept of man*. New York: Bloomsbury, [1961b]/2013.
Fromm, Erich. *Beyond the chains of illusion*. New York: Continuum, [1962a]/2001.
Fromm, Erich. Psychoanalysis and Zen Buddhism. *Psychoanalysis and Zen Buddhism*. London: Unwin Paperbacks, [1960a]/1987.
Fromm, Erich. C.G. Jung: Prophet of the Unconscious. A Discussion of "Memories, Dreams, Reflexions" by C.G. Jung. *Scientific American*:209:283–290, 1963e.
Fromm, Erich. *The heart of man: its genius for good and evil*. New York: Harper and Row, 1964a.
Fromm, Erich (ed.). *Socialist humanism*. New York: Doubleday, 1965a.
Fromm, Erich. Interview with Richard Heffner. *McCaws*: 29:132f, 213–219, 1965f.
Fromm, Erich. *You shall be as gods*. New York: Fawcett Premier, [1966a]/1983.
Fromm, Erich. A global philosophy of man. *On disobedience and other essays*. London: Routledge & Kegan Paul, [1966i]/1984.
Fromm, Erich. La investigacion cientifica en el Psicoanálisis. *Revista de Psicoanálisis, Psiquiatría y Psicología*:3:3–6, 1966n.
Fromm, Erich. Prophets and priests. *On disobedience*. New York: Harper Perennial, [1967b]/2010.
Fromm, Erich. Prefacio. A. Hinojosa and A.C. Pascal. *Analísis Psicologico de estudiante universitario*. México: La Prensa Medica Méxicana, 1967i.
Fromm, Erich. *The revolution of hope*. New York: Bantam Books, 1968a.
Fromm, Erich. The crisis of psychoanalysis. *The crisis of psychoanalysis*. New York: Holt, Rinehart and Winston, [1970c]/1970.
Fromm, Erich. Introduction. *Ivan Illich. Celebration of Awareness*. New York: Doubleday and Co., 1970k.
Fromm, Erich. Dreams are the universal language of man. *For the love of life*. New York: The Free Press, [1972a]/1986.
Fromm, Erich. The Erich Fromm Theory of Aggression. *The New York Times Magazine*: (02/27/1972):14f,71,76,80f,84,86, 1972c.
Fromm, Erich. In the name of life: a portrait through dialogue. *For the love of life*. New York: The Free Press, [1974b]/1986.
Fromm, Erich. *To have or to be?* New York: Bantam Books, [1976a]/1981.
Fromm, Erich. Interview with Alfred A. Häsler: Das Undenkbare denken und das Mögliche tun. *Ex Libris*:22 (5):13–19, 1977b.
Fromm, Erich. Das Undenkbare, das Unsagbare, das Unaussprechliche. *Psychologie heute*: 5:23–31, 1978b.
Fromm, Erich. *Greatness and limitations of Freud's thought*. New York: Harper and Row, Publishers, [1979a]/1980.
Fromm, Erich. *Arbeiter und Angestellt am Vorabend des Dritten Reiches*. Giessen: Psychosozial-Verlag, [1980a]/2019.
Fromm, Erich. Who is man? *For the love of life*. New York: The Free Press, [1983d]/1986.
Fromm, Erich. *Das jüdische Gesetz*. Gießen: Psychosocial-Verlag, [1989b]/2020.
Fromm, Erich. On my psychoanalytic approach. *The revision of psychoanalysis*. Boulder: Westview Press, [1990d]/1992.

Fromm, Erich. The necessity for the revision of psychoanalysis. *The revision of psychoanalysis*. Boulder: Westview Press, [1990e]/1992.
Fromm, Erich. The dialectic revision of psychoanalysis. *The revision of psychoanalysis*. Boulder: Westview Press, [1990f]/1992.
Fromm, Erich. Martyrs and Heroes. *Fromm Forum*:13:25–30, [1990s]/2009.
Fromm, Erich. For a Cooperation Between Jews and Arabs. *New York Times* (04/18/1948). 1990t.
Fromm, Erich. *The art of listening*. London: Constable, [1991a]/1994.
Fromm, Erich. Modern man's pathology of normalcy. *The pathology of normalcy*. New York: American Mental Health Foundation, [1991e]/2010.
Fromm, Erich. The concept of mental health. *The pathology of normalcy*. New York: American Mental Health Foundation, [1991f]/2010.
Fromm, Erich. Man's impulse structure and its relation to culture. *Beyond Freud*. New York: American Mental Health Foundation, [1992e]/2010.
Fromm, Erich. Dealing with the unconscious in psychotherapeutic practice. *Beyond Freud*. New York: American Mental Health Foundation, [1992g]/2010.
Fromm, Erich. The relevance of psychoanalysis for the future. *Beyond Freud*. New York: American Mental Health Foundation, [1992h]/2010.
Fromm, Erich. The search for a humanistic alternative. *On being human*. New York: Continuum, [1992l]/2005.
Fromm, Erich. The disintegration of societies. *On being human*. New York: Continuum, [1992k]/2005.
Fromm, Erich. Meister Eckhart and Karl Marx on having and being. *On being human*. New York: Continuum, [1992s]/2005.
Fromm, Erich; Maccoby, Michael. A Debate on the Question of Civil Defence, *Commentary*: 33:11–23, 1962b.
Fromm, Erich; Maccoby, Michael. *Social character in a Mexican village*. New York: Routledge, [1970b]/1996.
Hegel, Georg. *Phänomenologie des Geistes*. Frankfurt: Surkhamp, [1807]/1986.
Hegel, Georg. *Wissenschaft der Logik I*. Frankfurt: Surkhamp, [1812–1832]/1986.
Hegel, Georg. *Wissenschaft der Logik II*. Frankfurt: Surkhamp, [1812–1816]/1986.
Hegel, Georg. *Grundlinien der Philosophie des Rechts*. Frankfurt: Surkhamp, [1821]/1986.
Hegel, Georg. *Enzyklopädie der philosophischen Wissenschaften im Grundrisse, I*. Frankfurt: Surkhamp, [1817–1830a]/1986.
Hegel, Georg. *Enzyklopädie der philosophischen Wissenschaften im Grundrisse, III*. Frankfurt: Surkhamp, [1817–1830b]/1986.
Hegel, Georg. *Vorlesungen über die Philosophie der Geschichte*. Frankfurt: Surkhamp, [1837]/1986.
Horney, Karen. The problem of the negative therapeutic reaction. *The psychoanalytic quarterly*: 5:29–44, 1936.
Jones, Ernest. Die Eifersucht. *Psychoanalytische Bewegung*: II(2):154–166, 1930.
Klein, Melanie. The development of a child. *The writings of Melanie Klein, vol. I*. New York: The Free Press, [1921]/1975.
Klein, Melanie. Early stages of the Oedipus complex. *The writings of Melanie Klein, vol. I*. New York: The Free Press, [1928]/1975.
Lévi-Strauss, Claude. *Anthropologie structurale*. Paris: Plon, [1958]/1996.
Lacan, Jacques. *Le Séminaire, Livre 1*. Paris: Editions du Seuil, [1953–1954]/1975.

Marcuse, Herbert. The social implications of Freudian "revisionism". *Dissent*: 2 (3):221–240, 1955.

Marx, Karl. Zur Kritik der Hegelschen Rechtsphilosophie. *MEGA I.2*. Berlin: Akademie Verlag, [1843]/2009.

Marx, Karl. Ökonomische-philosophische Manuskripte. *MEGA I.2*. Berlin: Akademie Verlag, [1844]/2009.

Marx, Karl; Engels, Friedrich. Die deutsche Ideologie. *MEGA I.5*. Amsterdam: Akademie Verlag, [1845–1847]/2017.

Mead, Margaret. Crossing Boundaries in Social Science Communication. *Social Science Information*:8:7–15, 1969.

Neumann, John von; Morgenstern, Oskar. *Theory of games and economic behavior*. Princeton: Princeton University Press, [1944]/1953.

Rank, Otto. *Psychoanalytische Beiträge zur Mythenforschung*. Vienna: Internationaler Psychoanalytischer Verlag, 1919.

Rank, Otto. *Technik der Psychoanalyse* II. Vienna: Internationaler Psychoanalytischer Verlag, 1929.

Rank, Otto; Sachs, Hanns. *Die Bedeutung der Psychoanalyse für die Geisteswissenschaften*. Wiesbaden: Verlag von J. F. Bergmann, 1913.

Reich, Wilhelm. *Der triebhafte Charakter*. Vienna: Internationaler Psychoanalytischer Verlag, 1925.

Reich, Wilhelm. *Charakteranalyse*. Vienna: Im Selbstverlag des Verfassers, 1933.

Reich, Wilhelm. *Reich speaks of Freud*. New York: Noonday Press, 1967.

Reik, Theodor. Beitrag zur psychoanalytische Affektlehre. *Internationale Zeitschrift für ärztliche Psychoanalyse*: IV(3):148–153, 1917.

Reik, Theodor. Über kollektives Vergessen. *Internationale Zeitschrift für Psychoanalyse*: VI(3):203–215, 1920.

Reik, Theodor. *Der eigene und der fremde Gott*. Vienna: Internationaler Psychoanalytischer Verlag, 1923.

Reik, Theodor. *Geständniszwang und Strafbedürfnis*. Vienna: Internationaler Psychoanalytischer Verlag, 1925.

Reik, Theodor. *Dogma und Zwangsidee*. Vienna: Internationaler Psychoanalytischer Verlag, 1927.

Reik, Theodor. *Der Schrecken und andere psychoanalytische Studien*. Vienna: Internationaler Psychoanalytischer Verlag, 1929.

Reik, Theodor. *Der unbekannte Mörder*. Vienna: Internationaler Psychoanalytischer Verlag, 1932.

Schachtel, Ernest. On memory and childhood amnesia. *Metamorphosis*. New York: Basic Books, [1947]/1959.

Simmel, Ernst. *Kriegsneurosen und "psychisches Trauma"*. Munich: Verlag von Otto Nemnich, 1918.

Sullivan, Harry Stack. *The interpersonal theory of psychiatry*. New York: W. W. Norton & Company, 1953.

Tausk, Viktor. Über die Entstehung des "Beeinflussungsapparates" in der Schizophrenie. *Internationale Zeitschrift für ärztliche Psychoanalyse*: V(1):1–33, 1919.

Thompson, Clara. *Psychoanalysis*. New York: Hermitage House, Inc., [1950]/1951.

Weber, Max. Die Objektivität sozialwissenschaftlicher und sozialpolitischer Erkenntnis. *Gesammelte Aufsätze zur Wissenschaftslehre*. Tübingen: Verlag von J. C. B. Mohr, [1904]/1922.

Whorf, Benjamin. *Language, thought, and reality.* New York: John Wiley & Sons, [1956]/1959.
Wiener, Norbert. *Cybernetics.* Cambridge: The MIT Press, [1948]/1961.

Secondary literature

Abromeit, John. *Max Horkheimer and the foundations of the Frankfurt School.* Cambridge: Cambridge University Press, 2011.
Akrap, Domagoj. *Erich Fromm.* Münster: LIT-Verlag, 2011.
Bakhtin, Mikhail. *O freudismo.* São Paulo: Perspectiva, [1926]/2001.
Bastide, Roger. *Sociologia e psicanálise.* São Paulo: EdUSP, 1974.
Blomert, Reihhard. Das vergessene Sanatorium. N. Giovannini, J. Bauer, H. Mumm (eds.). *Jüdisches Leben in Heidelberg.* Heidelberg: Wunderhorn, 1992.
Brunner, José. Looking into the hearts of workers, or: how Erich Fromm turned critical theory into empirical research. *Political psychology*: 15 (4):631–654, 1994.
Burston, Daniel. *The legacy of Erich Fromm.* Cambridge: Harvard University Press, 1991.
Durkin, Kieran. Erich Fromm and Theodor W. Adorno reconsidered: a case study in intellectual history. *New German Critique*: 41(1[136]):103–126, 2019.
Falzeder, Ernst. *Psychoanalytic filiations.* London: Karnac Books, 2015.
Frie, Roger. Psychoanalysis, persecution and the Holocaust: Erich Fromm's life and work during the 1930s. *Fromm Forum*: 23:70–79, 2019.
Funk, Rainer. The Jewish roots of Erich Fromm's humanistic thinking. *Symposium: Erich Fromm. Life and Work*, 1988.
Funk, Rainer. *Liebe zum Leben.* Stuttgart: DTV, [1999]/2011.
Gay, Peter. *Freud.* London: J. M. Dent & Sons, [1988]/1995.
Jay, Martin. *The dialectical imagination.* Berkeley: The University of California Press, [1973]/1996.
Roazen, Paul. *Encountering Freud.* London: Transaction Publishers, 1990.
Rouanet, Sérgio. *Teoria crítica e psicanálise.* Rio de Janeiro: Tempo Brasileiro, 2001.
Smith, David. Antiauthoritarian Marxism: Erich Fromm, Hilde Weiss, and the politics of radical humanism. Kieran Durkin, Joan Braune (eds.). *Erich Fromm's critical theory.* New York: Bloomsbury, 2020.
Szekacs-Weisz, Judit; Keve, Tom (eds.). *Ferenczi and his world.* London: Karnac, 2012.

Part II

Life and Politics

This part explores Fromm's *anthropology*, his *sociology*, and their political implications. Chapter II provides a systematic development of Fromm's concepts in these domains, showing that they contain the basic determinants for his normative assessments and their logical structure. Chapter III studies the way the corresponding theoretical choices played out in the political arena by examining Fromm's relation to Herbert Marcuse, the New Left, and other social movements in the 1960s and 1970s.

Chapter 2

II Anthropology and Sociology

This chapter presents a systematic development of Fromm's anthropological and sociological concepts. They unfold a dialectic of necessity and freedom, beginning with its most immediate forms in the concept of life, and evolving into a complex balance of mediations in human psychology and society. These are the presuppositions to Fromm's psychoanalysis and political theory, which will later become our main field of inquiry. With some important exceptions, we here refrain from extensive criticism. On occasion, we shall have the opportunity to notice a recurring pattern in Fromm's concepts – the introversion of reciprocal relations into reflexive or unilateral determinations. This pattern will prove relevant in our later examination of his ethics.

To the extent of necessity, Fromm's concepts are here translated into their logical functions, and compared with analogous notions in Marx and Freud. This is done with the purpose of clarifying an important aspect of his intellectual heritage, and preparing our understanding of his critical theory.

1 The Concept of Life

a Organic and Psychic Life

Fromm assumed there was a "fundamental difference between life and non-life, between 'organisms' and 'things'" (1973a:526). Things are "fixed and *describable*" (1976a:75), whereas life is an endless process of setting itself forth, realizing what is given potentially in the organism. It is "not subject to strict control or prediction" (1964a:57), since it "never remains the same" (1968a:16). Freud (1912–3; 1920a; 1938a) saw ontogenesis as repeating phylogenesis, and later each drive as an attempt at repeating its originating conditions. Only later did he limit repetition compulsion to the scope of the death drive. Fromm's understanding is coherent with this late reformulation: "nothing in life is repeated" (1991a:56). Thus conceived, "life is characterized by growth in a structured, functional manner" (1964a:41). It is "a process of changing and unfolding; a process also of constant interaction between the [organism's] constitutional structure and the environment into which it has been born" (1967e:198). The concept of life is thus given as a *process of structured growth in relation with the environment.*

Growth is "constant birth", "constant change" (1962a:175): life poses what is given within itself, and changes in doing so. Hegelian (1812–32) vocabulary would maybe recognize this as one of the figures of the negative – something which differentiates itself, specifies itself further, breaking with its circumscription to previous determinacies. In Fromm, life's pressure for singularization is an imperative: the forces developing the organism are also its "necessities of growth" (1973a:225). For that reason, in Frommian vocabulary, the aspect of "growth" corresponds to the affirmative moment within the concept of life.

Effected as pure growth, life would appear in its "flowering quality" (1992s:167): as infinite profusion of difference, absolute diversification – with that, amorphous. Absolute determination would correspond to absolute indetermination: the specimen would be nothing more than an aggregate of contradictory attributes. Growth finds its negative, its *limitation*, in its being "structured": for "any structure requires constraint" (1973a:225). Life contains a series of such constitutionally given, "autonomous restrictions" (1976a:68). It "does not grow wild and unstructured; every living being has its own form and structure implanted in its chromosomes. It can grow more fully, more perfectly, but it cannot grow into what it was not born to become" (1967e:197).

As a self-limiting development, life "forms itself" (1970h:144) and takes form. It is neither absolutely determinable, nor absolutely undetermined: its evolution in time is an increasing organization of determinations. This is true for the singular specimen – and life does not exist in general, since it can "be experienced only in its individual manifestations" (1964a:57). It is also true for the set of organisms in their interaction – life process as natural history. In this determinacy, "being alive is to grow, to develop", but also "to respond" (1966a:142). In its inner determination, the organism appears as capable of setting itself forth. In its relation to others, it appears as "incomplete", "precarious" (1968a:147; 1973a:286). Marx (1844) saw nature as the human species' inorganic body, and life as manifest only in its relation with effective sensuous objects. In Fromm, correspondingly, growth only occurs if life finds appropriate objects in the fight to "preserve its existence" (1964a:45). Without responsiveness to objects, life is not fulfilled.

Pure growth would amount to an amorphous profusion of the organism's possibilities; pure structure would degenerate into reified "order" (1976a:156). The relation to the objective world allows both aspects – affirmative and negative – to develop into moments of a *process*. In Hegel (1807), life is substantial in its subsistence to the death of singular beings. In Fromm, as life's possibilities relate to their limits, the living being becomes itself *living substance* (1947a:67) – a being subsisting its own metamorphoses. Now "there is simultaneously permanence and change in any living being" (1966a:17): life seeks "to preserve and affirm its own existence" (1947a:19). To *preserve*: for the organism tries to retain the structure resulting from its previous development, without which no further change would be possible. To *affirm*: for life, the weariless weaver of its own elements, wills actualizing more of its inner potencies. Freud (1920) thought Eros tends to unite living beings into ever greater unities. Fromm would have agreed: "life always tends to unite and integrate" (1967e:197); but its synthetic force was introverted: productiveness is first of all inner productiveness, only mediately production of others. At each moment, the living being "is not yet what he can be and what he may yet become" (1983d:140).

"Living structures can only be if they become; they can exist only if they change" (1976a:13). Change proceeds from the organism's inner possibilities, and its relations to the objects it can appropriate. Correspondingly, the living being is determined by its "biological constitution" (1973a:291), and also by the "favorable and unfavorable conditions which incline" his development (1962a:175). In its relation to itself, the moment of "growth" appears as a *necessity*: if it wants to live, the organism *must* develop. In its relation to others, growth is the representative of *freedom*. The moment of "structure", on its turn, is for the living being a condition of possibility for *freedom*. Without it, it wouldn't dispose of its own forces. In its relation to others, however, structuralization acts as a moment of *necessity*: the already formed structure must be preserved, and this imperative sets the specimen negatively against its others. Each moment expresses a different aspect depending on how it is considered. However, since Fromm seldom discusses the living being in isolation, but only in the process of relating to others, their constitutive significance predominates over their determinative significance. Growth is taken mostly in its spontaneous character, and structure in its character of necessity.

These moments are reunited as a series of inherent tendencies in the specimen (cf. 1941a:267). The structural moment corresponds to the "self-replenishing function of all living substance" (1947a:67). The moment of growth is found in life's tendency "to be expressed, to be lived" (1941a:182). Brought together, both aspects result in "innate strivings for health and happiness" (1951a:140): the "supreme biological law" is that "every living being" wills "its most perfect functioning and the fullest realization of its potentialities" (1974b:112; 1989a:4). Each organism wants to become "more full of life" (1983b:37). In its becoming, its seeks the conditions to continue becoming.

Freud (1920a) thought organisms seek their own disintegration. For Fromm, there is no such thing. Life's tendency toward health and multilateral development is first given objectively, in the body. In sentient life forms, it is specified in the "activity inhering in the nerve cells" (1976a:88), and acquires a subjective expression: the "brain [...] has the capacity to recognize which kinds of goals are conducive to man's health and growth, physically as well as psychically" (1973a:285) – an organic adjudication whose ethical implications we will explore later. For this reason, life is not restricted to its organic substance: there is also a "psychological equivalent of the identical biological tendency" (1941a:286). Life's affirmative tendency is furthered into a "process of birth on the mental plane" (1947a:91), appearing as an impulse to *vital self-expression* – "a true luxury not serving any biological purpose", "except the general aim of increased life energy, in well-being, aliveness" (1974a:102; 1989a:88–9). The negative tendency is expressed in the impulse to *survival* (with Maccoby, 1970b:15).

The clash between necessity and freedom acquires a subjective form: we have "shifted our inner gears from the biologically necessary act to the realm of freedom; from 'animal' to 'human' existence" (1989a:88). This change is effected in "the creation of man in history" (1968a:89). Should historical development result in appropriate conditions of life, survival and self-expression result in a "polarity" between "two forms of human existence", "two forms of living" (1968a:72–3). Should this not be the case, both tendencies are dissociated. The task of survival takes the lead, subordinating growth to structural preservation: "the individual and society are primarily concerned with the task of survival", and "only when survival is secured can they proceed to the satisfaction of other imperative human needs" (1955a:80).

b Organic and Psychic Death

Life conditions may be bad conditions. The absolute limit in this relation is death itself – the undoing of life's structure, its "return to the past, the inorganic state of matter" (1955a:25). Death – "the most crucial phenomenon of existence" (1967e:203) – grounds two human *existential dichotomies* (1947a:41): the fact that we die, and the fact that this finitude amounts to a precocious interruption of the life process. Their acknowledgment (or lack of it) will shape an otherwise unavoidable suffering. The process of structured growth is finite according to its real possibilities, but infinite according to its own determination:

> while every human being is the bearer of all human potentialities, the short span of his life does not permit their full realization under even the most favorable circumstances. Only if the life span of the individual were identical with that of mankind could he participate in the human development which occurs in the historical process.
>
> (1947a:42)

Every specific manifestation of life is fated to unilateral development: "by necessity we can only realize a limited part of all the potentialities within us" (1950a:94). Absolute growth, which would result for the specimen in lack of structure, is fulfilled at the level of species development, which may encapsulate the "infinite versions of life" (1950a:94) within a corresponding multitude of bodies. Accordingly, the mission of developing human endowments is "the mission of humanity", not only of the individual: "the task of life" is "the development toward totality through individuality" (1962a:29). The more so since this is only possible through the relation between organisms: the human being "enhances the other's sense of aliveness by enhancing his own" (1956a:19).

Organic death terminates in the fall of the organism – psychic death, in its *stagnation*: "cessation of growth, ossification, repetition" (1962a:175; 1968a:16). For Marx (1844), each species was characterized by its own form of activity. For Fromm, "to be alive" means "to use one's powers" (1947a:248), to *exercise* them freely. If the organism cannot act, psychic growth cannot happen, and the "wish" to live is "paralyzed" (1989a:1). It is possible to be "alive biologically", but "dead emotionally and mentally" (1941a:254) – to "becomes a thing" (1966a:142), for "only mechanical things can be repeated" (1991a:56). Hence the significance of "growth" in its negative function, as vital imperative. Self-preservation is a necessary condition for free expression – but if there is no freedom whatsoever, life loses the responsiveness it needs for self-preservation. Reduced to survival, life is not able to survive.

2 The Human Being

a Evolution

Fromm believes animals live in immediate *harmony* with nature – a "preindividual", "preconscious" state of "oneness" (1941a:23; 1960a:92). Sentient species have a "simple consciousness" (1960:47), akin to Marx and Engel's (1845–7) animal sensuous consciousness. The process of evolution develops for each species a series of objective *physiological needs*, whose subjective expression are the *instincts*: "answers to [...] *physiological* needs" (1973a:26), "perceived subjectively as desire" (1947a:183). Their satisfaction is the minimum condition for "remaining alive" (1973a:255). When they pass from impulses into acts, instincts appear as action patterns (cf. 1955a:22), which can be "modified" and "controlled" – but never extinguished – through "learning" (1973a:244; 1974a:70). They are centrally: "sexual desires, aggression, fright, hunger, and thirst" (1968a:77). Fromm provides a more accurate description for only some of these.

Animal sexual instinct is desire for physical distension and bodily proximity, aiming at "reproduction" (1973a:215). It is still "nonerotic" (1990f:68).

Animal aggression is inhibitory of sexuality, except when it is self-assertive (cf. 1973a:216). It has two main forms, one of which is shared with humans. Carnivorous species display interspecific, *predatory aggression*: they "attack to obtain their food" (1983c:43). The aggressive tension is dissolved once this purpose is fulfilled. Human beings are omnivorous, sharing with other animals – with some modifications – *reactive* or *defensive* aggression "against threats to vital interests" (1973a:210). Defensive aggression is mostly, but not always interspecific. It is activated only in the presence of outer dangers, and aims at preserving the organism's integrity, the safety of children, the possibility of mating, access to food, and to the extent of necessity for each species, also space (cf. 1973a:119,139,221). Human beings add a series of "emotional" threats to these "material" ones (1941a:179).

Fromm believed evolution led to an increasing liberation from instinctual patterns. "The lower an animal is in the scale of [evolutionary] development, the more are its adaptation to nature and all its activities controlled by instinctive and reflex action mechanisms" (1941a:31). Conversely, "the higher an animal has risen in the stages of evolution, the less is the weight of stereotyped behavior patterns" (1973a:251). Also in this sense, the process of life amounted for him to a progressive conquest of freedom: "There was no single step or moment that marked the completion of that development. It was a long process in which quantitative factors underwent a very gradual transformation into qualitative ones" (1983b:17).

b Conditions of Existence

In the most advanced species, Fromm found a "surplus energy" (1947a:186), an *abundance* manifest in play and in animal love (cf. 1973a:279). The older he grew, the more he emphasized the similarities between ours and other species, taking into account other animal social structures, the animal's need for self-expression, its individuality (cf. 1973a). However, he always maintained that human life is peculiar: "elements of the human condition already exist among the prehuman primates, but [...] qualitative differences led to a qualitative 'jump'" (Foerster_H_Von_1972–04–29-to). For him, the animal has no "conscience of a moral nature", and hence "cannot be evil" (1955a:22; 1964a:148). It has no "self-awareness" or "reason", even though it has pragmatic "intelligence" – which means it "has no concept of the truth, even though it may have an idea of what is useful" (1955a:22). Like Marx (1844), Fromm thought "the capacity for material production is specific for man" (1947a:84). Like Freud (1924), he thought other species are predominantly autoplastic – the animal modifies itself while adapting to the environment –, whereas humans also display alloplastic behavior – our adaptation being "passive and at the same time active" (1992e:42).

For Fromm, the human species is "still in the process of birth" (1973a:251). Evolutionary hominization unfolds into psychic humanization through history. The species' biological past is embodied in its present anatomical and neurophysiological structure: they are a conditioning factor to all further psychic experience. Because the body cannot subsist without outer objects, the environment fulfills the same function. Taken together, body and environment compose the *human conditions of existence* or *human situation* – its "biologically given existential situation" (1973a:26).

Human conditions of existence behave negatively. "Environmental factors further or hinder the development of certain traits and set the limits within which man acts" (1973a:296); biological factors determine its set of anatomic and neurological possibilities. Before, we considered the life process as an articulation between three moments – growth, structure, and an other. Now this relation is specified. Structure is represented by the body and the neurological characteristics of the species; its "other" is generalized into the social conditions within which the organism develops. They build a "system of factors": "biological" and "economic" conditions finally result in a "mental" output (1973a:250,292). The first belongs to Fromm's anthropology, whereas the others will be treated in the scope of his sociology.

***

For Fromm, human speciation happened when two factors were combined: "instinctive determination had reached a minimum and the development of the brain a maximum" (1976a:123). This he calls the human *existential dichotomy* (1990f:24). Like Freud (1926), Fromm believes this increases the dependency of the newborn on her caretakers (cf. 1955a:23). Its most important consequence is an indetermination of action: "man has to act and make decisions" (with Maccoby, 1970b:12). However, a minimal instinctual determination is not the same as its lack. We must update our previous discussion, tracking what changes instincts undergo among humans.

Freud (1913) opposed the ego drives – sleep, thirst, hunger, excretion, aggression – to sensuous sexual drives, counterposing the preservation of the specimen to the preservation of the species. Each mobilized different kinds of psychic energy. Fromm includes "sexual" needs, as well as "physical exercise" and "protection", among the instincts concerned with "self-preservation" (1941a:15; 1947a:183; 1983d:142). For him, all these organic impulses have a cyclic, rhythmic arousal, imposed by the body's "self-regulating mechanisms" (1947a:187; 1955a:91). They have a "self-propelling dynamism; [...] become more and more intense, and end in a rather sudden climax in which satisfaction is achieved and nothing more is wanted" (1951b:129). Later in his life, Fromm added the possibility that they might be aroused by "passivating stimuli" (1973a:271). Sensuous pleasure and self-preservation are united, and the concept of energy suffers a corresponding change. For Fromm, "there is no reason to separate various kinds of energy or to speak of desexualized energy as it is suggested by the ego psychologists" (1977g:3).

In Freud (1911), energy is subject to *discharge*. In Marx (1844), it is subject to *externation* and *objectivation* of life. In Fromm, it is subject to *expression*

(1941a:139). Like Marx (1867–90), Fromm thought human needs are modified historically as they acquire new objects. The body is hungry, thirsty, tired – but the specific food, drink, repose it obtains are "socially conditioned" (1992e:45). The pleasure these instincts seek remains nonetheless identical: it is *satisfaction*, or *"relief from painful tension"* (1947a:183). Fromm considered only as a form of pleasure what Freud (1911) took as the concept of pleasure in general.

i Sexual instinct and eroticism

Human sexual instinct only behaves rhythmically up to a certain point (cf. 1956a:28). Sex belongs to the *organism* to the extent that it is grounded in the body; when it is "loveless sex" (1976a:104), and object choice is limited by the availability of bodies (cf. 1994f:151). Thus abstracted, "sexual desires per se are not characterized by great stability" (1979a:29): they move between objects according to convenience – without this preventing them from being an "expression of life", "of mutual giving and sharing of pleasure" (1973a:314). "Sexual experience can be simply sensuously pleasant without the depth of love but also without a marked degree of greed" (1968a:80).

Sex belongs to *social life* to the extent that the expectancy of pleasure is *stimulated, mobilized* by historical human passions (cf. 1956a:42; 1992h:135). In Fromm's opinion, "there are many motivations for the sexual urge that in themselves are not sexual" (1951b:127). He thought "sexual desire may easily be combined and stimulated by any strong emotion", as well as by "non-sexual passions": "every character trait [...] is expressed" in "sexual behavior" (1956a:43; 1973a:97,315) – noting only years later that "there are also many passions that cannot mobilize sexuality" (1992h:135). Among the passions calling sex in their service, Fromm found love, narcissism, sadism, masochism, destructiveness; one's sense of adventure, the desire for richness; the wish to escape fear, boredom, aloneness (cf. 1948b:143; 1956a:28; 1964a:64,133; 1968a:80; 1973a:97; 1979a:25–6). Even though the sexual instinct "serves life *biologically*", it doesn't necessarily do it when considered "*psychologically*" (1964a:46).

Fromm still subscribes to Freud's (1905–24) notions of infantile sexuality and universal psychic bisexuality, albeit timidly (cf. 1956a:26; 1973a:219; 1991a:133). Sexuality loses its character as source for secondary psychic phenomena, being understood as one of the spheres of expression of human character:

> The fact that sexual behavior is determined by character is not in contradiction to the fact that the sexual instinct itself is rooted in the chemistry of our body. This instinct is the root of all forms of sexual behavior, but it is the particular way of satisfying it, not the instinct itself, which is determined by the character structure, by the particular kind of person's relatedness to the world.
>
> (1948b:139)

For Freud (1908), sexual behavior was the model for behavior in other spheres. For Fromm, "sexual behavior is determined by character" (1948b:139). Even "sensuality" – a "basically erotic attitude" in one's "readiness" to arousal (1939b:189) – is a composite character trait. This did not prevent Fromm (1943b) from deriving character traits he took as "masculine" and "feminine" from the anatomic differences between sexes, and their supposed "functions" in coitus – "penetrating" and "receiving" (1956a:27). In this second formulation, sexuality was taken as a sphere of experience, among the many contributing for the generation of character traits – the same traits which later rebound into sexual desire (compare Wilde, 2004).

Freud (1915a; 1920b; 1931) had previously subsumed the sexual difference between "masculinity" and "femininity" to activity and passivity, eventually extending this opposition into homosexual object choice. Characterological femininity was understood in connection with castration, masochism, and the degree of repression imposed on each gender. Fromm reduced the problem of object choice to the assertion that any organism may be excited by any other (cf. 1991a:24; 1994f:150–1). He saw masculinity and femininity as a polarity inhering in living substance, sexuated or not. This led him to an understanding of "bisexuality" in a "psychological sense". What he understood as masculine and feminine was not free from the social prescriptions of his time: "the masculine character can be defined as having the qualities of penetration, guidance, activity, discipline and adventurousness; the feminine character by the qualities of productive receptiveness, protection, realism, endurance, motherliness". He ultimately still assumed "masculine" and "feminine" conduct falls together with particular bodies: "in each individual both characteristics are blended, but with the preponderance of those appertaining to 'his' or 'her' sex" (1956a:26,29).

Fromm subscribed to a deeply gendered metaphysics of nature (compare Chancer, 2020). He took the attraction between masculine and feminine as a "*primary* phenomenon underlying sexual desire" (1990f:30), "a fundamental attraction in all living substance" (1968h:55). "Sexual polarisation" (1956a:26) was for him not only coextensive with life – it would pertain also to the opposition of "earth and rain, of river and ocean, of night and day, of darkness and light, of matter and spirit" (1956a:27). We would find "the male and the female aspect in the world, in the universe, in each of us" (1951b:123). In the living being, this polarization would impel to a "need for fusion" (1964a:46) between both sides – sexual union being only one of its manifestations (cf. 1956a:28). This would be the "biological" basis of *eroticism*, as opposed to "physiological" *sexuality* (1956a:26; 1990f:68). Eroticism would not lead to "satisfaction", but to *sexual joy* – the enduring pleasure in combining physical and loving intimacy (cf. 1956a:69; 1976a:104). It stood in opposition to "falling in love", which was for Fromm a "short-lived" experience of "sudden intimacy" (1956a:41–2) – the opposite of Freud's

(1921) "being in love", which extended relations by inhibiting libido in its aim.

***

In Freud (1922), sexual development was always coupled with a corresponding psychosexual movement. Fromm dissociated the two moments. For him only eroticism proper was in a deeper sense a *psycho-biological* (1956a:28) relation – a middle-term between strictly physiological and psychic determinations. Each side implied a restriction of the concept. The psychic moment tied eroticism to "tenderness" (1956a:43); the biological aspect tied it to heterosexual love: "woman is a manifestation of life for man just as man is a manifestation of life for woman" (1967b:36).

These restrictions should be understood as a compromise between Fromm's stances in the spheres of gender and of sexuality. *He was in favor of gender equality, but opposed the equality of sexual practices.* Fromm (1933a; 1934a; 1951b; 1978b; 1979a) remained all his life a critic of patriarchalism and the inequality between culturally-ascribed "sexual roles". He believed women should be freed from patriarchal coercion, which he saw as ultimately debilitating for all genders. Once the women's liberation movement was on the rise, he championed it as one of the most significant political movement of the times, but remained deeply ambivalent regarding its political tactics (cf. 1977c). His understanding of gender liberation was at odds with the prevailing political currents. He saw social equality between genders, not as producing a new determination (or indetermination) of masculinity and femininity, but as the social realization of naturally-given differences:

> I ascribe the biggest significance to the women's movement in the struggle for a new society, because I am now – as always – deeply convinced that the woman embodies certain ideas and experiences of humanity in greater measure than man, and can teach people. However (here is a big "however") for the women's movement to be one, it must be a movement which does not align with men, and its aim cannot be to go as far as men [in domination].
>
> (1980f:3)

Culturally prevailing inequalities should give way to a society in which the natural differences between man and woman flourish unimpeded: "the male-female polarity [...] is only possible if male and female are equals, though different" (1970d:40).

In accepting a strongly gendered metaphysics, Fromm thought he was safeguarding the equality between genders, not precluding it. This concept could reach interesting consequences when taken together with psychic "bisexuality". The room was left open for acknowledging variations in gendered expression as equal in status: "the polarity between masculine and feminine principles exists also *within* each man and each woman [...] Man –

and woman – finds union within himself only in the union of his [inner] female and his male polarity" (1956a:26). It also allowed for a modification in the gendered division of labor – "maternity" was taken as a "feminine" attribute, but a father "can be a mothering figure" (1964a:103). More often, however, Fromm's position amounted only to a defense of heterosexual genital love against other forms of sexuality.

Fromm didn't take homosexuality as a "pathology" – it "is not a clinical entity" (1994f:150). At the same time, he could not treat it as equal to heterosexuality: it remained a "symptom", even if non-specific, of varied etiology, and not very grave (cf. 1994f:158–60). At first Fromm thought "the union of male and female genitals" would provide "the most satisfactory type of sexual gratification" (1994f:151); later he conceded that "differences between homo- and heterosexuality are somewhat blurred" (1990f:68). Considered in its physiological aspect, homosexuality appeared as equal to any other form of gratification: "there are as many different types of homosexual behavior as of heterosexual, and the interpersonal relations of homosexuals present the same problems as are found in heterosexual situations (1994f:159). However, he could not admit a "psychobiological" equality. Homosexuality would amount to a "failure to attain this polarised union" with an other – even if it would also be precluded for the "heterosexual who cannot love" (1956a:26).

Freud (1922) had taken narcissistic object choice as one of the possible sources for homosexuality. Fromm echoed this motif in the idea that "there is always a trace of desire for sameness and identification in homosexual love" (1936a:10). He denied homosexuals the capacity for true eroticism, which he thought was only possible when "one can love 'the stranger'" (1948b:142). He could not understand that there may be deep psychic otherness among any two bodies. To the end of his life, he would still say: "I don't think homosexuality is a sickness, but nevertheless I think it is a restriction in the growth of a person" (1991a:114). Fromm's treatment of perversions was similar: "all physical instinctual appetites, including sex, are harmless even in their deviations and perversions and are no threat to the welfare of the human race in comparison with the damage done by those irrational passions" of historical origin (1948b:141).

Freud (1905–24; 1920a; 1927b; 1938b) had explained fetishes as displacements away from the woman's missing penis, followed by an ego split, in reaction to castration anguish – or otherwise as derivative from peculiar fixations in childhood sexual experience. He treated sadism and masochism first as partial drives in psychosexual development, later as derivative from the death drive. Fromm (1973a; 1990g) recognized the susceptibility of perversions to be defined in reference to social taboos. He didn't include homosexuality, and had little to say about fetishism. His few casual remarks on "coprophilia" or "necrophagia" are without a clear psychogenesis (cf. 1990g:89). He provided a way clearer picture of sadism and masochism – but their sexual expression was understood only as a particular form of their broader activity within character (cf. 1990g:93). He thought "the intensity of characterological sadism may be somewhat reduced because of its direct satisfaction in the sexual act" (1990g:94) – but its origin, like that of all historical passions, lay outside sexuality proper.

Fromm thought perversions result from "the blending between life and death" (1964a:46). They would amount to ways of perverting "a life-serving impulse into a life-strangling one" (1973a:314). Sadism and masochism, for example, would preclude genuine "affection" by turning people into "things": "the sadistic perversion, by its very nature, excludes love, intimacy, and respect" (1990g:96–7). Sadistic and masochistic sex would give sex a compulsive, non-free quality (cf. 1990g:89), whereas "full relaxation" and "concentration" in erotic love would allow a deeper "*quality* of sexual experience", both "bodily and mental" (1990f:35,67–8; 1991a:178). He rejected them, not on the ground that they deviated from procreation, but in seeing them as ways of paralyzing "structured growth". He thought satisfying perversions would hamper the inner productiveness of life.

ii Aggressive instinct

From the late 1960s onwards, Fromm updated his theory with a revised *neurophysiological* concept. His concept of human instinctual aggression was modified accordingly, deviating in part from the general determination of organic drives. He didn't think the need for aggression was cyclical as the need for hunger or sleep. Rather, it was taken as a "possibility" (1983c:44) inhering in our constitution, needing appropriate circumstances to be activated:

> a *readiness* for aggression is present in human psychology, but a readiness which doesn't [...] act spontaneously and growing out of itself, as sexuality, but which must first be activated by certain stimuli; if these stimuli are not apparent, aggressiveness does not emerge, since it is always impeded by the simultaneous active tendency to [its] restriction, which, from the neurophysiological point of view, has its own cerebral center.
>
> (1973a:140)

Fromm differentiates between *pseudoaggression*, which is not intended to hurt; *malignant* aggression – historically developed passions such as sadism and destructiveness –; and *benign* aggression, which is defensive and serves self-preservation (cf. 1973a:20,213,246). Only the latter is given as "instinct", even though either may be mixed or even prompt the others (cf. 1968e). Phenomenologically, human benign aggression responds to "anxiety" or "fear" (1964a:25; 1991f:95), being an alternative to flight from danger. In Freud (1915a; 1916–17; 1938a), this would have corresponded to aggression in response to "realist anxiety", following from frustration or the expectation of displeasure. In Fromm, it is reported to objective criteria: the animal fights to protect its "vital interests". The sphere of vital interests to be protected by the human being is larger, beginning with the fact that the "fear" may be "real or imagined, conscious or unconscious" (1964a:25), and even induced by "suggestion" (1983c:51). Besides the bodily interests we pointed before, the human being reacts also to threats to health, freedom, dignity, and property (cf. 1964a:25; 1973a:221). Each of these leads to a special form of reactive violence – their prevalence varying in different historical circumstances. While the basic impulse is still in the interest of self-preservation, it is in each case related to socially-generated irrationality.

Property is only felt as a vital interest "in those societies where private property exists and is highly valued" (1973a:221). There, "greed" is confused with "interest" (1973a:246), and leads to *instrumental* aggression – "the greedy person who does not have the necessary means must attack if he wants to satisfy his desires" (1973a:236). Conversely, inaccessibility to the desired good will lead to *frustration*, and a corresponding attempt "to attain the frustrated aim through the use of violence" (1964a:26). This violence will be specified further if an element of *envy* or *jealousy* is present – for each is "a special kind of frustration" (1964a:27).

Freedom is, for Fromm, a "condition for the full growth of a person, for his mental health and well-being; its absence cripples man and is unhealthy". *Revolutionary* aggression finds its biological basis in its defense (1973a:225–6). Its opposite is *conformist* aggression, practiced out of obedience for an authority: "the impulse not to obey or not to conform constitutes for many an inner threat, against which they defend themselves by performing the required aggressive act" (1973a:234).

Health is our entry point into specifically human psychology. In Fromm's concept of life the moment of growth functions as affirmative in relation to others, but as negative in itself: it is an impulse to active self-expression, but a *necessary* one, whose unfulfillment is not without consequence. The living being must exercise its capacities, lest they perish. When specified in human psychology, life's attributes are further differentiated. The structural moment is expressed as need for *physical survival*. The moment of growth appears as free *self-expression* in its affirmativeness – but it recurs as a need for *mental survival* or *sanity* according to its imperative character (cf. 1977g:3). The human being fights against death for the preservation of her body, but she fights against *insanity* for the preservation of her psychic structure: "all passions and strivings of man are attempts at finding an answer to his existence, or, as we can also say, they are an attempt to avoid insanity" (1955a:29). Where the Freudian (1900–30) psyche evades unpleasure, the Frommian psyche evades psychosis. Mental survival is the middle-term between freedom and necessity in the psychic sphere: the same psychic acts satisfying one's spontaneity appear as preserving one's sanity when considered functionally.

"For man everything necessary for the maintenance of his psychic equilibrium is of the same vital interest as that which serves his physical equilibrium" (1973a:223). For this reason, threats to mental health may also initiate benign aggression. "Any attack on compensatory ideas, figures or institutions" – on "values", "symbols" and "idols" with which the individual "identifies" – "constitutes a serious threat" (1970h:141; 1983c:51; 1990f:77). The more so, the more one's conduct and self-experience is dependent on them. *Resistance* in the clinic corresponds to this tendency: attempts at breaking repression also threat one's current psychic existence. If the threatened ideas are narcissistically invested, a *narcissistic aggression* adds to resistance, avenging the wounded self-image (1973a:223).

Even though Fromm considered narcissism one of the historical, irrational passions, he thought narcissistic aggression aligned with the benign, life-serving forms of aggression. Freud (1916–7) saw narcissism as the libidinal complement to egoism. Fromm agreed, but displaced his point of view away from the specimen, into the species. He thought narcissism fulfilled a biological purpose in centering subjective experience in oneself, thus contributing to "do what is necessary for survival" (1964a:72). Both narcissistic and resisting aggression represented for him a triumph of psychic self-preservation at the expense of psychic growth: "the biological interest of the survival of the race requires a certain amount of narcissism among its members; the ethico-religious goal of the individual, on the contrary, is the maximal reduction of narcissism toward the zero point" (1979a:45).

c Human Nature

The nucleus of Fromm's anthropology is his view of human nature: a characterization of the species in terms of its "psychic organization" (1962a:27). From human nature must be distinguished its "conditions of existence", but also "existence" itself (cf. 1979a:62; 1990f:26). *Existence* is the "*process* in the course of which a person" (1973a:250) becomes who she is. As a living being, the human is "living process" (1983d:140), setting forth her qualities in her becoming. *Human nature* is the content of this becoming, whose general form we first knew in the determination of "structured growth". It is specified in its "qualities, laws, and alternatives" (1968a:4). In Hegel (1812–16), essentialities are moments, whereas essence is absolute negativity. In Fromm, as a set of *essential qualities* or essentialities, human nature bears the elements which are articulated in the process of growth, both individual and generic. As governed by *laws*, it interacts with its others in determinable ways. As *essence,* it is "essence of human existence" (1992f:81). It determines the direction of the vital movement, the multiplicity of *alternatives* left open for the human being – in a word, the way in which the human being *changes* over time.

i Essential qualities

The human being's essential qualities are those resulting from her organically given faculties: sociality; the capacity to produce with a goal; the capacities to symbolize, to negate, to have fun, to promise, to build tools and to hope (cf. Fromm, 1964a:116; 1968a:59–60; 1973a:247). Even though they are characteristic of the species, neither of these attributes qualifies the human according to its own mode of development. A simple listing of essentialities "suffers from the fact that it is purely descriptive and enumerative, is unsystematic, and makes no attempt to analyze" the "common conditions" (1973a:249) for their emergence. We must consider them in their relation to such conditions – the specimen's inner constitution and its environment.

Given with the human organism are three *spheres of activity*, whose free exercise satisfies life's imperative of expression – the *sensory, affective,* and *intellectual* spheres (1941a:28,109,139; 1947a:84,117). Sometimes a *sexual* sphere is also included (1941a:289). These "realms of human experience" should be differentiated form the social *spheres of life* which are formed through social differentiation: economy, politics, religion etc. (1976a:84). Spheres of activity appear as *essential faculties* in their immediate determination, as *powers* in their relation to human energy, as *capacities* in their relation to human will (cf. 1992s:156). They are given first as isolated from each other, prior to any social relation. Their development and inner *differentiation* only happens when they are related to each other. The work of *individuation* – of increasing *organization of life* (cf. 1950a:93–4) – will be that of *integrating* them (1941a:28,35) through their "factual expression" (1939b:195). In their practical social exercise, these faculties pass from the state of potency into that of *existence* (1941a:257). Each individual develops a particular mode of communication between them, such that they become mutually conditioned.

The articulation between essential capacities will later build the form of the act as a response to the problem of psychic survival. Here, human faculties are still taken in isolation – but they are already active, in need of development. Fromm identifies the *potency* of a faculty – "the capacity to direct" the "will toward a goal and sustain" the "effort until the goal is achieved" (1964a:31) with the *necessity* of expressing it and developing it: "*the power to act creates a need to use this power*". Contrariwise, "failure to use and to spend what he has is the cause of sickness and unhappiness" (1947a:219): if "man is not able to *act*, if he is impotent, he suffers" (1964a:31). The pressure Freudian (1915a) libido exerted for discharge is generalized: also human powers are *forces* in need of "expression" (1941a:139; 1947a:234).

Notice the similarities and differences: in Marx (1844), the human being is endowed with active, objective vital forces, which act as *drives* impelling toward fulfillment of their possibilities. At the same time, as a bodily being, she is lacking, and develops *passions* toward objects in response to her suffering. In their relation to sensuous objects, passions affirm one's being; in the absence of lack, drives lead to free activity in production. Passions contain the moments of vital affirmation and necessity, whereas drives contain the moments of negation and freedom. In Fromm, historical passions do not emerge from bodily lack, but from the development of the vital forces behind them. This changes their function. The "drive" of vital forces is now seen as the necessity of their practice, a psychic lack; passions are its specification, acting as affirmations of life only given appropriate conditions: "affirmation is related to the essence of the 'object', not merely toward partial qualities" (1939b:186,195). In Freud (1915a) drives are the most immediate psychic mobiles, but they already presuppose an articulation of all human powers. In the *ucs* representation of an object and aim, they involve sensation; in the *pcs* cathexis of word representations, they involve the intellect, and their pressure is manifest in an emotional quality. In Fromm, passions behave the same way (excluding their rootedness in bodily pressure), but all three human powers are already active beforehand. Freud (1938a) sees psychic development as progressive differentiation of the primary "id-ego". Fromm sees individuation as the process of bringing the isolated human faculties into relation.

ii Laws

The exercise of the human capacities appears as a set of "responses" (with Maccoby, 1970b:71) to the objective world. Fromm believes these responses are determinable, though historically variable: "if one assumes a certain *substance* as constituting the essence of man, one is forced into a nonevolutionary, unhistorical position" (1964a:115). In the beginning, Fromm sees human nature as bearing certain "inherent mechanisms and laws" which are "immutable", "fundamental – but at the same time, as "not fixed" (1941a:13; 1947a:22; 1950a:72,80). The contradiction is only apparent. For Fromm, laws don't express immediate imperatives. They are of the form of *relations* between human (organic, psychic) imperatives and their objects. "Which reaction occurs, depends on many factors: on economic and political ones, and on the spiritual climate in which people live" (1955a:19) – but the range or possible responses is finite, and determinable in relation to their conditions. Thus considered, "laws" amount to a knowledge of "the needs man has as man" (1962a:30), and what happens when they are frustrated.

Over time, this notion loses its strength: "the possibility of generalization and the formulation of laws is limited" (1979a:14). There is little in Fromm's works to fill the concept with a positive content. In practice, the "laws of human nature" function as conceptual representatives of the negativity of life. They don't determine what human beings are, but rather the threshold of *inhumanity*, of what is intolerable for us. Life is characterized by inner limitations. Correspondingly, "laws" determine the human being as not "infinitely malleable" (1968a:4) in her relation to others: there are "certain basic elements which are part of human nature and will react in the very same way as our body reacts if their laws are violated": "to be completely inhumane" leaves the individual "close to insanity" (1963c:172–3; 1973a:330).

iii Essence

"Laws" gave us the formal determination in the "interaction between the nature of man and the nature of the external conditions in which he lives" (1962a:81). We achieved only a negative concept of human nature, as limited by the ways it *cannot* go – human situation – and the ways it *shouldn't* go: "*the aim of man's life* [...] is to be understood as *the unfolding of his powers in accordance with the laws of his nature*" (1947a:20). We still miss a positive understanding. This is what the concept of essence expresses.

We must begin by differentiating between concrete and abstract human nature. In the first sense, "humanity [...] is not an abstraction, but a reality" (1963f:1) resulting from evolution and historical development. In the second sense, we deal with a concept formed, not in "metaphysical speculations" (1973a:27), but through empirical observation and self-experience. "Human nature in general we can never see" (1962a:29), but only infer as a "*nucleus*" of commonalities between the "various manifestations of man as they appear in various cultures" (1991g:102): "*how different can we be and yet be human?*" (1968a:61). Since this differentiation is a historical process, and history is not over, any knowledge remains provisional: "it is possible that" a definitive assertion "will never be possible to make" (1968:61). Still, a relative determinability is still given: the concept circumscribes the set of human "*possibilities*" (1968a:61) – the "fundamental question" (1955a:29) whose attempt at resolution initiates the process of individuation.

Biologically, the species emerges from the combination between minimal instinctual determination and maximal growth of neural connections. Psychologically, these characteristics result in a new property: "the biological dichotomy [...] results in psychic dichotomies" (1990f:27) which require resolution. The human brain is the basis for *imagination* and *reason* – and the relation between reason and imagination originates *self-awareness* (1955a:23). Self-awareness implies a "new quality" (1973a:253) of human thought. Animals are "aware of objects; they know that this is one thing, and that is another" (1983b:17) – but they don't know that they know. The human, contrariwise, is "life aware of itself" (1960a:37) – the only form of life which knows that it is alive, and knows that it knows (cf. 1973a:253). Psychic life is folded into being for itself, and experiences its own estrangement from the world. Life aware of itself is split life, differentiated from its objects in its own experience: already the first human being "knew that he exists and that he was something different, something apart from nature, apart from other people, too. He experienced himself. He was aware that he thought and felt" (1983b:17).

In Marx (1844), the human being is sensuous life, but it is also "generic being" – capable of thought, existing for itself, confronted with the objects of its passions, and knowingly dependent on then. The counterposition between sensibility and reason dominates the concept: each specimen is related to generic life first through their common action upon sensuous needs – self-preservation –, later through language, as instinct is brought into consciousness (cf. Marx and Engels, 1845–7). In Fromm, to the contrary, a new sphere of "conflict and suffering" (1966a:98) is originated by reflexivity in self-awareness. The human being "is *in* nature, and yet he *transcends* nature" (1960a:29). Thought "can reach beyond the satisfaction of his physical needs" (1983d:140) – but it cannot suppress them. He is "free in his thoughts", but "cannot rid himself of his mind" or "his body" (1964a:117; 1973a:253). Capable of reflection, the human being remains nonetheless under the yoke of finitude and lack; she *recognizes herself as finite* – and thus suffers not only from lack, but from knowing herself as lacking. We will see later that this knowledge is first of affective nature – it corresponds immediately to the *effect* of thought over affection, mediately to conscious reasoning.

In Freud (1927a), primitives are haunted by the magnitude of nature; in Fromm, the human being is haunted by itself. "Gifted with self-awareness and reason, man [...] is aware of his powerlessness, of his ignorance; he is aware of his end: death" (1973a:253). He knows the "dangers" of the world and his "smallness" against them; he knows his "lostness and weakness", and thus feels *helpless* (cf. 1966b; 1992h:139; 1992m:75; 1992q:100). Helplessness resumes the human experience of being split from the world. Consciousness is opposed to the objects of its needs, but also in part to these needs – to its inner nature, if we may. The human being is "split between awareness and being determined as an animal" (1991a:124): passions and intellect do not immediately correspond. This subjective split is felt as *separation*: the human being "is aware of itself as a being separate from nature and others" (1973a:253), as well as from herself. She is thus susceptible to *shame* (cf. 1960a:30). As a desiring being, she goes to the world in her helplessness. As a being who is aware, she is estranged from her desire and its object.

For Freud (1925) the differentiation of the reality-ego from the pleasure-ego happened as the child was frustrated and learned to differentiate inner and outer phenomena. Fromm agrees, but provides no clear description of the corresponding process. The subjective split appears immediately as a result of the "development of one's intellect" (1960a:91). We can only infer that this inner partition of the subject – her *existential split* (1973a:156) – is followed by the corresponding split between subject and object. As she desires, the human being relates to others, even if she remains separate from them; as split from her desire, she is her own other, and risks falling in *isolation* (1962a:127): "man is alone and he is related at the same time" (1947a:43). This is the third of the existential dichotomies (plural) Fromm recognized as unavoidable human sufferings. The first two – death and the unfulfillment of potentialities – could be deduced from pure organic conditions. This third one presumes the extension of the life process into psychic life, as it follows from the existential dichotomy (singular) between instincts and brain power.

The split between subject and object and the inner subjective split were resumed in the feelings of helplessness and separation (compare Burston, 1991, and Philipson, 2017). Taken together, they result in *objective alienation* (cf. 1960d:212) – a qualification I suggest introducing to differentiate this anthropological concept from "subjective alienation", which denotes a historically variable "mode of experience" (1955a:120; compare Funk, 1978). Hegel (1807) saw the self-alienation of the spirit as an imperative of its own movement, presupposing its domestication in family life; Marx (1844) saw it as a necessary outcome of the division of labor. Fromm reverts historical into anthropological necessity. In Marx (1844), alienation was the outcome of the work process: exteriorization of the life forces in the product of labor resulted in estrangement from the object, from one's essence, and from others. In Fromm, likewise, the human being ends up "alienated from himself, from his fellow men, and from nature" (1956a:67). However, objective alienation, being grounded on the organic constitution of the human being, is invariable and "insoluble" (1990f:24). It is a *"necessary"* step in individuation: "only when I can distinguish between the world outside and myself, that is, only if the world outside becomes an *object*, can I grasp it and make it my own world, become one with it again" (1962a:57). Only afterwards do social determinations such as the function of repression come into play, fostering *subjective alienation* as a "socially conditioned" "psychological fact", modifiable in "form and intensity" (1955c:102; 1962a:59,129):

> During the emergence from primitive unconsciousness to self-consciousness, the world is experienced as an alienated one on the basis of the split between subject and object, of separation between the universal man and the social man, between unconsciousness and consciousness.
>
> (1960a:97)

Just as life's generative capacity was introverted into organic self-productiveness, here alienation is displaced into the individual life process, being socialized only afterwards. For Fromm, objective alienation is the source of a "state of constant disequilibrium" (1973a:254). Splitting desire from its object, the human being is threatened with absolute isolation: *madness*. Being in need of relation, the individual is also a barrier to her own relations, and experiences the risk of absolute lack of touch with other – psychic death. For this reason, the human being "needs to find new ties with his fellow beings":

"his own sanity depends on that. Without strong affective ties with the world, he would suffer from utter isolation and lostness" (1973a:262). Hence the determination of psychic survival as avoidance of psychosis.

What was originally an objective "dichotomy", later a subjective "split", now develops into an *existential contradiction* (1973a:254). Abandoned to itself, human maturation does not secure "structured growth" as demanded by life. In Freud (1937), maturation was complicated by an impulse to physical self-annihilation. In Fromm, maturation risks mental self-annihilation: unity with objects is dissolved without an immediate replacement. For that reason, they are not only the objects of organic needs, but establish a new need – that, through contact with them, the individual reestablish psychic "equilibrium" (1947a:50). Objects are now the supports for the movement of life: they must move the human powers – sensibility, affection, intellect –, removing them from their original isolation. Without that, the existential "split" remains still in its suffering.

The content of this movement – the attempt at *reestablishing unity with oneself through unity with others* – is what Fromm calls human *essence*. In formal terms, essence is "that in virtue of which a thing is what it is" (1992m:66). Correspondingly, in talking about human essence, we talk about "that by virtue of which man is man" (1964a:117): his nature as particular in reference to other beings, universal in reference to his formal diversity, or simply "man in general" (1992m:66). In Marx and Engels (1845–7), essence grew into an equivalence with the set of social relations. In Fromm, it is the specimen's inner "contradiction" (1964a:120), *demanding* social relations. Thus conceived, human nature is not in the element of freedom, but in the necessity engendered with its inner fracture and torment. Human freedom is then mediated by this necessity – one possible outcome of the movement of the human powers as they attempt to find unity.

Objective alienation was determined as unity of existential dichotomy and split. Essence is contradiction, the attempt at overcoming it: "the various forms of human existence are not the essence, but they are the answers to the conflict which, in itself, is the essence" (1964a:117). We answer, "not with a thought, but with our whole existence" (1992g:109), with our "mode of being", "feeling and acting" (1962a:174; 1964a:117) – with a particular way of bringing the human faculties into relation. From the point of view of structure, each existence is indifferent – "every answer to these contradictions can really satisfy the conditions of helping man overcome the sense of separation" (1992q:100). From the point of view of growth, however, they are not the same. Not every form of living satisfies life's expressive tendencies equally well. This leads Fromm to reintroduce a more determined meaning in his concept of essence. Now, "good consists of transforming our existence into an ever increasing approximation to our essence; evil into an ever increasing estrangement between existence and essence" (1964a:149). The essence ceases to be a "question", and becomes the best possible "answer" one would give to it: freedom emerging from necessity. This opposition will be reflected within Fromm's ethics.

Two classes or *alternatives* of resolution are given as "inclinations" and "real possibilities": "man is inclined to regress *and* to move forward" (1964a:123,149). For Fromm, psychic *progression* has a single general form, whereas *regression* is stratified in "different forms" and "several levels" (1960a:32). Each implies a different way of producing "unity". Regressive forms of life are attempts at a "return [...] to nature" (1962a:157) – a suspension of the effects of reason and self-awareness over psychic life by going back to "pre-individuation", to "the state of unity which existed before awareness had emerged" (1960a:30; 1964a:118). For Fromm, this solution is "bound to failure" (1962a:175): intellectual maturation cannot be abolished. Here, life is preserved at the cost of its affirmation: "only in death or in insanity can the return be accomplished – not in life and sanity" (1960a:32). The progressive form of life is characterized by the desire to be "*fully* born" (1960a:30) – the "full development of" the "human powers" (1962a:175). The vital moment coincides with the plain humanization of the individual; physical and mental survival cooperate with expression. Regressive alternatives correspond to "compensations" for the anxiety aroused by the risk of insanity, whereas the progressive alternative represents its "overcoming" (1992g:98).

3 Society

"The essence of each individual is identical with the existence of the species" (1973a:27). The totality of singular life courses (or "existences") gives us the explicit, developed figure of what the human essence contains as an incognito – an inner drive engendering each of those courses. As the life process originates new social forms throughout history, conditions of existence change, originating new subjective arrangements: "at any new level man has reached new contradictions appear which force him to go on with the task of finding new solutions" (1964a:120):

> Man's existential, and hence unavoidable disequilibrium can be relatively stable when he has found, with the support of his culture, a more or less adequate way of coping with his existential problems. But this relative stability does not imply that the dichotomy has disappeared; it is merely dormant and becomes manifest as soon as the conditions for this relative stability change.
>
> (1973a:254)

Fromm's anthropology oscillates between the promise of definitive resolution and the inevitability of the existential contradiction. In the first conception, "this process continues until" the human being "has reached the final goal of becoming fully human and being in complete union with the world" (1964a:120). "The interest of society and of the individual need not be antagonistic forever" (1944a:384) – harmonious human diversification must be possible. In the second conception, we are reminded that no given society ever achieved this goal – and while it may be approximated, it may never fully succeed. Since all known forms of society restrict human development and freedom, none of them refrained from activating regressive tendencies. "We are never free from" the "two conflicting tendencies" (1955a:27), and thus the process of production of human unity is infinite: what was conquered may be lost, the next step may be succeeded by regression. "Each individual and each group of individuals can at any given point regress to the most irrational and destructive orientations and also progress toward the enlightened and progressive orientation" (1964a:123). The main historical task of the human being would be to create conditions of life dispensing the need for regressive alternatives to life, fostering the development of human powers. We would thus be taken to *"ever-higher forms of unity with nature"* (1955a:25), but never definitive ones.

Freud (1912a; 1915b; 1920a) also thought collective regressions were possible. He conditioned individual regression to the avenues left open for pleasure by cultural repression; later, with the introduction of the repetition compulsion, a return to previous experience was made coextensive with drives. In Fromm regression and progression are not immediate forms of drive activity. They are in reference to humanization and social development, not to biographical experience and phylogenetic inheritance. Passions are their subject only mediately: they refer in the first place to human essential capacities and their modes of articulation in history.

a Phylogenesis and Evolution

Freud (1912b; 1912–3; 1921; 1927a; 1929–30) thought civilization was born out of guilt. Human prehistorical groups would be living under the yoke of powerful patriarchs, who monopolized sex with the females at the expense of their sons' satisfaction. The resentful brothers would have gathered and murdered the father. A brief period would follow under the rule of women, until patriarchy would emerge victorious again in retrospective obedience of the dead father. In their repentance, the brothers would institutionalize a fraternity of male equals. Inhibited in its aim and blended with self-preservation, homosexual libido would have originated social feelings. Aggression would have gone taboo, being vented only in punishing infractions of the fraternal agreement. Religion, morality, society, would all have emerged as reaction formations, the fruit of collective renunciation, based on fear of authority – and the toil of work, upon which society depends for its survival, at the expense of sexual gratification. The phylogenetic history of mankind would be repeated in abbreviated form in ontogenetic development, guaranteeing an ever increasing predisposition of each new generation to accept more severe renunciation.

Marx might have agreed that work is toil – but not for anthropological reasons, and not for every possible society. Earlier in life, he even considered work as part of the essential determinations of human nature (cf. 1844). Nothing in it should contradict the worker, if not for alienation based on the division of labor (cf. 1844), or the conditions imposed by a given mode of production – in capitalism, the subsumption of the work process to valorization of value (cf. 1867–90). No more natural would be the inequality between men and women, which Marx took first as an effect of human self-estrangement (cf. 1844), later as an outcome of the sexual division of labor and the development of capital (cf. 1845–7 with Engels; 1867–90). His later anthropological notebooks indicate he would not be willing to take patriarchy as a social given, like Freud. Most importantly, he would not have defined society in moral terms. In Marx (1857–58), society is the effective interdependence of producers in the social process – in the capitalist mode of production, particularly their interdependence as commodity exchangers under a developing division of labor. Instead of the abrupt establishment of law, history develops in continuity with natural history, as human activity engenders new conditions of life for the species. Law and morality participate in the social process, but already presuppose it – instead of originating it, as was the case for Freud.

Freud (1921) thought he was writing a scientific myth – Marx would have taken it as the myth of bourgeois society. Where Freud was concerned with pre-historical *hominization*, the young Marx was concerned with *humanization* in history. Fromm drew from both sources. His anthropology is neither phylogenetic nor natural-historical, but *sociobiological* (1990d:4). Freudian (1915; 1920a; 1929–30) phylogenesis encompassed the whole history of life, compressing previous stimuli into current drives, organic repression, and predispositions to renounce. For most of his writings, Fromm opposed this form of reasoning: prehistory would be present only in the "phylogenetically programmed" (1973a:97) organic drives – not as psychic inheritance. Memory would still be indelible, but only as individual memory (cf. 1951a). Toward the end of his life, he updated the Freudian paradigm with his new model of the brain. Instead of organic repression and inherited experience, we would find a "constitutional-genetic basis" (1973a:510) allowing a "neurophysiological regression" (1973a:327) – at which point we could "use our unconscious as a key to the understanding of pre-history" (1973a:257). With exception of these late speculations, Fromm thought always in evolutionary and historical terms. For Marx (1844), the human senses and fruition would develop as each new generation assimilated the material and intellectual sediment left by its ancestors. For Fromm, likewise:

> Evolutionary thinking is historical thinking. We call historical thinking "evolutionary" when we deal with bodily changes that have occurred in

the history of the development of animals. And we speak of historical change's when we refer to those that are no longer based on changes in the organism. [...] The "historical" changes (i.e., the evolution of man) are not changes in man's anatomical or physiological structure but, rather, are mental changes, which are adapted to the social system into which he is born.

(1990d:5)

For Marx (1844), generic being was endowed with the capacity for free, conscious vital activity. Fromm saw this capacity for teleological work as resulting from our species endowments – imagination, reason, self-awareness. They at the same time pose a problem and offer a solution. In his partial emergence from nature, the human being is filled with doubt: he doesn't immediately know how to act – "and this doubt would eventually paralyze his ability to act – that is, to live" (1941a:20). Imagination allows to "remember the past, to visualize the future"; reason allows to "denote objects and acts by symbols" and to "plan" (1947a:39; 1990d:5); self-awareness allows subjecting these faculties to will. They fulfill the biological function of making survival possible. At the same time, they develop in history. Reason is the fruit of a "long evolutionary process" (1955a:64); self-awareness "varies" in "degree" (1941a:19). In this development, they find new ways to fulfill their possibilities in freedom. For Marx and Engels (1845–7), human beings make each other, but don't make themselves. For Fromm, correspondingly, there is "both the furthering and the inhibiting impact of society on man" (1955a:77).

b Cooperation and Relatedness

Both Marx (1867–90) and Fromm agreed: "*man is a social animal*" (1990d:6); "sociability is an essential attribute" of his (1968g:18). The younger Marx (1844) had already argued against opposing society abstractly to the individual: the individual *is* the social being. Fromm took it as his mission to demonstrate the natural foundation of this assertion. For Fromm, self-preservation is also collective: "the survival of society is a biological necessity for the survival of man" (1990d:8). However, the human being must survive not only physically, but also mentally. As we treated the human specimen in isolation, these terms appeared as a simple opposition. When we consider him in his concreteness – as participating in *social* life – they engender a new relation:

> His physical constitution is such that he has to live in groups and therefore must be able to cooperate with others, at least for the purposes of work and defense. The condition for such cooperation is that he must be

sane. And in order to remain sane – that is, to survive mentally (and, in an indirect sense, physically) – man must be related to others.

(1990d:6)

In Freud (1927a; 1929–30) culture defends human beings against nature; it imposes renunciation of libidinal gratification for the sake of survival, and later offers cultural goods as substitute compensations for the previous sacrifice. In Fromm, mental and physical self-preservation are immediately presupposed to each other. To have a mind, sane or not, one must be alive. But to remain alive, one must be sane – and sanity is fundamentally: relation to others. Conversely, the main motivation for repression is the *fear of ostracism* – of going mad with isolation (1962a:69,127).

Physical survival is socially resumed in practical cooperation, whereas mental survival is resumed in affective relatedness. Marx (1867–90) took cooperation, in the strict sense of the term, as a form of organization of labor. He and Engels (1845–7) had earlier seen every social relation as cooperation between many individuals, regardless of its ends and conditions. For Freud (1916–7), the weight fell over the affective bonds between individuals, whether tender or hostile: relations would be formed as others would appear as objects of one's lacks. Fromm held an intermediary position. He didn't think relations to others were primarily tied to the "mutual satisfaction of needs" (1977g:2) – not of physical needs, by any means. Relations were for him primarily affective, subsequently sensory and intellectual – *interpersonal, intersubjective* relations (1949c; 1968g:19), filled with emotion and meaning. In Marx (1844; 1857–8), social activity is not always immediate communitarian activity. Neither does it presuppose affective ties to others – exchange of commodities is relation without "relatedness", in indifference to the peculiarities of others. Similarly for Fromm:

> To the extent that man is an animal in need of food and, for that purpose, of adapting to the material or social structure in which he lives, he can be seen as a "thing" or an "ego". Man, as I relate to him, instead of selling or buying from him, is a process, a self. In other words, man appears as a thing or as a process, depending on the nature of his relation to others.
>
> (d-RoHD:I:1:12)

Relatedness is thus a specifically psychological concept, just like for Freud (1916–7) affective ties needn't report to an immediately available object. It derives first from the biological dichotomy. Considered organically, it is a *condition* of human existence (cf. 1947a). Reduction of instinctual determination results in indetermination of action: one's orientation in the world must be built again – beginning with affects, which represent objects within the structure of action. Here, society supports the individual: relatedness develops in the process of practical cooperation, since there is no living individual without a living society. On the other hand, the increase in brain power leads to self-awareness, hence to anxiety, helplessness, powerlessness – all of which motivate the attempt at relating emotionally to others. Here, "it is not because society exists that each of us exists: society exists because otherness belongs to each of us individually. Man is, in his own nature, a being for others" (1968g:19). Psychologically considered, relatedness becomes an *existential need*, without whose satisfaction psychic structure falls into psychosis:

> Subjectively, the awareness of having been torn away from his natural basis and of being an isolated and unrelated fragment in a chaotic world, would lead to insanity (the insane person is one who has lost his place in a structured world, one which he shares with others and in which he can orient himself.)
> (1977g:2)

Thus far, relatedness contains the moment of necessity in life. It contains vital freedom in the lack human powers have for their objects, without which they cannot be practiced. From this point of view, human beings are "primarily related" (cf. 1968h) to the extent that others are *for them*.

c Mode of Production and Alienation

Since they need to cooperate and relate, human beings partake in the reproduction of their lives. The particular form of their joint activity is their *mode of production*:

> Societies have lives of their own; they are based on the existence of certain productive forces, geographical and climatic conditions, techniques of production, ideas and values, and a certain type of human character that develops under these conditions. They are organized in such a way that they tend to continue existing in the particular form to which they have adapted themselves.
> (1961a:3)

A "mode of production" engenders a "mode of life" (1947a:241): it

> must not be considered simply as being the reproduction of the physical existence of individuals. Rather, it is a definite form of activity of these individuals, a definite form of expressing their life, a *mode of life* on their part.
> (1961b:9)

As "economic development" succeeds – proportional to "objective factors, such as the natural productive forces, technique, geographical factors"

(1941a:295) – forms of life and human relations are modified accordingly: "the mode of production [...] comes first, as it were, and determines the other spheres of his [man's] activity" (1961b:10). Thereby included are also differences in power. Each mode of production engenders a corresponding social stratification: the social product is unevenly distributed among classes, allowing the domination of one class over others (cf. 1961a).

For Fromm (1961b:13), as for Marx (1859), a mode of production is characterized by the relation between the historically available *productive forces* and the *relations of production* in which they are effected. In Marx, these relations and the division of labor supporting them are variously called "social structure" (with Engels, 1845–7) or "economic structure" (1867–90:746). Fromm (1966a) used the same names, but implied at times that a society's "political structure" was equally fundamental – in opposition to Marx (1859), for whom it would be part of the superstructure based on economic relations. More importantly, Fromm tended to emphasize "productive forces" unilaterally. From them, he thought, derives the division in classes; from them also the distinct practices of life each class develops: "the method of production" and the "productive forces underlying it" in turn "determines the social relations existing in a given society" (1955a:80; 1961b:10). The complementary moment – relations of production, presupposing a certain distribution of the productive forces – is mostly left out of consideration, or equated with "class relations" in the remaining spheres of life. Here, as before in the concept of life, relations are introverted into one of their elements. The same tendency recurs in Fromm's early formulation of social character. In Freud (1921), libidinal structure was the name for the set of relations between subjects in a mass. In Fromm (1932b), it became equivalent to "character structure" – that is, the set of relations within the subject, taken in isolation.

The concept of society is correspondingly less developed in Fromm than in Marx: the social consequences of exchange relations are deduced from the general concept of the "market" (cf. 1955a), as a complement to the more important *practice of life* characteristic for each class, according to their position in the social structure (cf. 1941a:16,102). Circulation is not without effect for human relations in general – "we experience and treat ourselves as commodities" (1947a:248) – but production remains the central factor for subjective life. In Marx (1852), feelings, illusions and ways of thinking emerge from social conditions of existence and the corresponding social relations. In Fromm, one's immediate relation to survival – to work – has the upper hand over social relations. In characterological terms: modes of assimilation of goods have an implied primacy over modes of socialization.

Because work is the central determinant of subjectivity, the category expressing the most general mode of subjectivation within capitalism is, for Fromm, subjective *alienation*. In Marx (1844), the exteriorization of labor is felt as mortification. Its subjective counterpart – estrangement – is such that productive activity, the work object, and human generic being all appear as external, hostile, independent powers. Alienation at first engenders private property, and may later be abolished by sublating it. In Fromm, alienation is to be translated into its psychological mechanism:

> If we want to really understand what alienation is, we cannot conceive this term only abstract-philosophically, but also see what happens empirically and psychologically in the alienated man: in which ways he feels weak and powerless, which anxieties he endures, and what safety he finds in worshiping forces which become the stronger, the more impotent man feels.
>
> (1966j:6)

From this approach derives a concept of alienation as *mode of experience*, in which the human being "does not experience himself as the center of his own world, as the creator of his own acts – but his acts and their consequences have become his masters, whom he obeys or whom he may even worship" (1955a:120). Alienation is manifest in a series of relations: not only work, but also the relation to others, to oneself, to thought, to language, to consumption (cf. 1955a). Specified by transference and projection, subjective alienation takes the form of *idolatry* (cf. 1990f):

> life forces have been transformed into things and institutions; and these things and institutions have become idols. They are experienced not as the result of man's own efforts but as something apart from him, which he worships and to which he submits.
>
> (1955c:98)

In Marx and Engels (1845–7; 1848), social relations were indeed objectified into "social powers", standing seemingly above people – but history was the history of class struggle. In Fromm (1966a:17), it is "the history of idol worship" – that is, of human submission to our own objectified potencies.

Alienated experience is one in which human beings project their "*living substance*" (1955a:124) onto the outside – precisely that substance which presses for freedom, for something more than mere subsistence. Alienation of one's vital forces demands, therefore, the reduction of activity to the scope of self-preservation. It is the process in which human possibilities are abstracted and subordinated to a foreign determination – the conservation of society itself, at the expense of the individuals from which it is constituted. There is then "a conflict between the interests of most societies in the continuity of their own system as opposed to the interest of man in the optimal unfolding of his potentialities" (1990e:21).

d Potency and Existence

In Freud (1900–30; 1904–05), desire is awakened by the object, but preexists in its bodily rootedness. In Fromm, the encounter with the object happens before desires are formed. Human powers are marked by a lack: they have "the dynamic quality of having to strive for an object they can relate to and unite with" (1968h:49). This is so before any topological differentiation between psychic functions develops: their separation is original, and the division of labor only *reinforces and reproduces* the disconnection between the parts (cf. 1959b).

A *potentiality* is a specification of human powers in their relation to objects – a "future existence" which is "prepared in the present" (1947a:217). It manifests in case appropriate conditions for its development are given (cf. 1942b). These conditions are historical in nature: they are the economic, moral, and political requisites for the individual to dispose of herself in freedom – not in subordination to outer demands or urgency (cf. 1947a:171–2; 1964a). A class's *conditions of life* provide the objects with which potentialities are exercised, the scope of their freedom, the mode of their operation. A collective *mode of life* is the process of this operation in the interaction between human beings. The middle-term between both categories is one's *practice of life*: the "total process of man" (1956a:72) – the active, actual exercise of capacities, resulting in their biographical and historical development (cf. Fromm, 1961a).

The degree of development achieved by subjective capacities is conditioned by the concrete conditions in which they are practiced. But there is also an inner determination to the process. Sensory, affective, and intellectual powers move of their own will, even when the appropriate object and means are lacking:

> Each of these potentialities has a dynamism of its own. Once they have developed in the process of evolution they tend to be expressed. This tendency can be suppressed and frustrated, but such suppression results in new reactions, particularly in the formation of destructive and symbiotic impulses.
>
> (Fromm, 1941:285–6)

Hence the introduction of a difference between *primary and secondary potentialities* (1955a:28). They are now not anymore as abstract possibilities, but express a *telos* of their own – an expressive "drive", in the Marxian sense of the term. Those potentialities are "primary" to which the process of individuation tends "if the proper conditions are present" (1947a:218) – that is, when material, moral, and political conditions are affirmative of one's life. In acting toward an appropriate object, the subject *confirms* herself in relatedness (cf. 1968h:50). Opposed to these potentialities are those Fromm calls "secondary", which develop "with necessity" within "pathogenic conditions", in which the individual finds her life negated, "blocked" (1941a:179–80; 1947a:218; 1962a:177). To the first class belong all passions and modes of activity which confirm and further individuality: creative work, love, reason. To the second class belong destructiveness, hatred, irrationality (cf. 1947a).

Both classes of potentialities are "real possibilities" (1973a:296) in human life. Considered as pure potencies, they delineate all possible modes of feeling, thinking, and acting – but still as ineffective, prior to expression; capable of determination, but still undetermined. In this state, they are free – or rather, demanding of freedom. Once they seek their object, they enter historical relations, and must participate in the satisfaction of psychic needs:

> Man's inherent dichotomy is the basis for his passionate strivings. Which of these is activated and becomes dominant in the character system of a society or an individual depends largely on the social structures, which, by their specific practice of life, teachings, rewards, and sanctions, have a selective function with regard to the various potential drives.
>
> (1990f:27).

Within history, potentialities lose their character of immediate, *possible* freedom. They must conquer it as mediated, *effective* freedom – as the fruit of real relations to objects affirming them. The same endowments we first considered as participants in the process of self-preservation now pertain also to life's expressive moment.

The category resuming all the previous development is human *existence:* "the manifest reality" of the "potentiality" (1947a:207). Being an "anthropologico-philosophical" category (1947a:45), existence is irreducible to economic imperatives, containing also the moments of psychic potentiality and relatedness. It expresses the unity of self-preservation and expression, necessity and freedom: "*existence and the unfolding of the specific powers of an organism are one and the same*". "Preserving existence" and "realizing" one's "inherent potentialities" (1947a:19–20,133) coincide *in practice*, whereby existence turns into *actual life-process* (1962a:103). Now "the process of becoming" and "the process of being" are reunited: "using any kind of human power" and "relating" coincide in the act (cf. 1973a:250; 1992g:97). The individual is *potent* to the extent that he is "able to realize his potentialities on the basis of freedom and integrity of his self" (1941a:161). Conversely, "the sense of being condemned to ineffectiveness – i.e. to complete vital impotence (of which sexual impotence is only a small part) – is one of the most painful and almost intolerable experiences" (1973a:266): it blocks life's movement in its aspiration to freedom.

Bibliography

Primary sources

Fromm's correspondence

Foerster_H_Von_1972-1904-29-to: Fromm to Heinz von Foerster, April 29th, 1972.

Drafts, typescripts and study materials by Fromm

d-RoHD: drafts for The revolution of hope. Still without an official identifying code.

Published sources

Freud, Sigmund. Die Traumdeutung. *Gesammelte Werke II-III*. Frankfurt: S. Fischer Verlag, [1900–1930]/1961.
Freud, Sigmund. Drei Abhandlungen zur Sexualtheorie. *Gesammelte Werke V*. Frankfurt: S. Fischer Verlag, [1905–1924]/1968.
Freud, Sigmund. Die "kulturelle" Sexualmoral und die moderne Nervosität. *Gesammelte Werke VII*. Frankfurt: S. Fischer Verlag, [1908]/1966.
Freud, Sigmund. Formulierungen über zwei Prinzipien des psychischen Geschehens. *Gesammelte Werke VIII*. London: Imago Publishing, [1911]/1955.
Freud, Sigmund. Über neurotische Erkrangungstypen. *Gesammelte Werke VIII*. London: Imago Publishing, [1912a]/1955.
Freud, Sigmund. Beiträge zur Psychologie des Liebeslebens II. *Gesammelte Werke VIII*. London: Imago Publishing, [1912b]/1955.
Freud, Sigmund. Totem und Tabu. *Gesammelte Werke IX*. London: Imago Publishing, [1912–1913]/1940.
Freud, Sigmund. Das Interesse an der Psychoanalyse. *Gesammelte Werke VIII*. London: Imago Publishing, [1913]/1955.
Freud, Sigmund. Triebe und Triebschicksale. *Gesammelte Werke X*. London: Imago Publishing, [1915a]/1949.
Freud, Sigmund. Zeitgemäßes über Krieg und Tod. *Gesammelte Werke X*. London: Imago Publishing, [1915b]/1949.
Freud, Sigmund. Vorlesungen zur Einführung in der Psychoanalyse. *Gesammelte Werke XI*. Frankfurt: S. Fischer Verlag, [1916–1917]/1969.
Freud, Sigmund. Jenseits des Lutsprinzips. *Gesammelte Werke XIII*. Frankfurt: S. Fischer Verlag, [1920a]/1967.
Freud, Sigmund. Über die Psychogenese eines Falles von weiblicher Homosexualität. *Gesammelte Werke XIII*. Frankfurt: S. Fischer Verlag, [1920b]/1967.
Freud, Sigmund. Massenpsychologie und Ich-Analyse. *Gesammelte Werke XIII*. Frankfurt: S. Fischer Verlag, [1921]/1967.
Freud, Sigmund. Über einige neurotische Mechanismen bei Eifersucht, Paranoia und Homosexualität. *Gesammelte Werke XIII*. Frankfurt: S. Fischer Verlag, [1922]/1967.
Freud, Sigmund. Das Ich und das Es. *Gesammelte Werke XIII*. Frankfurt: S. Fischer Verlag, [1923]/1967.

Freud, Sigmund. Der Realitätsverlust bei Neurose und Psychose. *Gesammelte Werke XIII*. Frankfurt: S. Fischer Verlag, [1924]/1967.
Freud, Sigmund. Die Verneinung. *Gesammelte Werke XIV*. London: Imago Publishing, [1925]/1955.
Freud, Sigmund. Hemmung, Symptom und Angst. *Gesammelte Werke XIV*. London: Imago Publishing, [1926]/1955.
Freud, Sigmund. Die Zukunft einer Illusion. *Gesammelte Werke XIV*. London: Imago Publishing, [1927a]/1955.
Freud, Sigmund. Fetischismus. *Gesammelte Werke XIV*. London: Imago Publishing, [1927b]/1955.
Freud, Sigmund. Das Unbehagen in der Kultur. *Gesammelte Werke XIV*. London: Imago Publishing, [1929–1930]/1955.
Freud, Sigmund. Über die weibliche Sexualität. *Gesammelte Werke XIV*. London: Imago Publishing, [1931]/1955.
Freud, Sigmund. Die endliche und die unendliche Analyse. *Gesammelte Werke XVI*. London: Imago Publishing, [1937]/1961.
Freud, Sigmund. Abriss der Psychoanalyse. *Gesammelte Werke XVII*. London: Imago Publishing, [1938a]/1955.
Freud, Sigmund. Die Ichspaltung im Abwerhvorgang. *Gesammelte Werke XVII*. London: Imago Publishing, [1938b]/1955.
Fromm, Erich. Psychoanalytic characterology and its relevance for social psychology. *The crisis of psychoanalysis*. New York: Holt, Reinehart and Winston, [1932b]/1970.
Fromm, Erich. Robert Briffaults Werk über das Mutterrecht. *Gesamtausgabe, Band I*. Stuttgart: Deutsche Verlags-Anstalt, [1933a]/1999.
Fromm, Erich. The theory of mother right and its relevance for social psychology. *The crisis of psychoanalysis*. New York: Holt, Reinehart and Winston, [1934a]/1970.
Fromm, Erich. Sozialpsychogischer Teil. Max Horkheimer (ed.). *Studien über Autorität und Familie*. Frankfurt: Dietrich zu Klampen Verlag, [1936a]/1987.
Fromm, Erich. Selfishness and self-love. *Love, sexuality, and matriarchy*. New York: Fromm International Edition, [1939b]/1997.
Fromm, Erich. *Escape from freedom*. New York: Henry Holt & Company, [1941a]/1994.
Fromm, Erich. Faith as a character trait. *Psychiatry: V*:307–319, 1942b.
Fromm, Erich. Sex and character. *The dogma of Christ*. New York: Holt, Rinehart and Winston, [1943b]/1992.
Fromm, Erich. Individual and social origins of neurosis. *American Sociological Review*:9:380–384, 1944a.
Fromm, Erich. *Man for himself*. New York: Henry Holt & Company, [1947a]/1990.
Fromm, Erich. Sexuality and character. *Love, sexuality, and matriarchy*. New York: Fromm International Edition, [1948b]/1997.
Fromm, Erich. Psychoanalytic characterology and its application to the understanding of culture. *Fromm Forum*:12:5–10, [1949c]/2008.
Fromm, Erich. *Psychoanalysis and religion*. New York: Bantam Books, [1950a]/1967.
Fromm, Erich. *The forgotten language*. New York: Holt, Rinehart and Winston, [1951a]/1960.
Fromm, Erich. Man – Woman. *Love, sexuality, and matriarchy*. New York: Fromm International Edition, [1951b]/1997.

Fromm, Erich. *The sane society.* New York: Henry Holt & Company, [1955a]/1990.
Fromm, Erich. The present human condition. *The dogma of Christ.* New York: Holt, Rinehart and Winston, [1955c]/1963.
Fromm, Erich. *The art of loving.* London: Thorsons Editions, [1956a]/1995.
Fromm, Erich. Values, psychology, and human existence. A. H. Maslow (ed.). *New knowledge in human values.* New York: Harper and Row, 1959b.
Fromm, Erich. Psychoanalysis and Zen Buddhism. *Psychoanalysis and Zen Buddhism.* London: Unwin Paperbacks, [1960a]/1987.
Fromm, Erich. The prophetic concept of peace. *The dogma of Christ.* New York: Holt, Reinhart and Winston, [1960d]/1992.
Fromm, Erich. *May man prevail?.* New York: Doubleday & Company, Inc, [1961a]/1961.
Fromm, Erich. *Marx's concept of man.* New York: Bloomsbury, [1961b]/2013.
Fromm, Erich. *Beyond the chains of illusion.* New York: Continuum, [1962a]/2001.
Fromm, Erich. Medicine and the ethical problem of modern man. *The dogma of Christ.* New York: Holt, Reinhart and Winston, [1963c]/1992.
Fromm, Erich. Humanismo y Psicoanálisis. *La Prensa Medica Mexicana*:28:120–126, 1963f.
Fromm, Erich. *The heart of man: its genius for good and evil.* New York: Harper and Row, 1964a.
Fromm, Erich. *You shall be as gods.* New York: Fawcett Premier, [1966a]/1983.
Fromm, Erich. Die Grundpositionen der Psychoanalyse. *Fortschritte der Psychoanalyse, Band II.* Göttingen: Verlag für Psychologie Hogrefe, 1966b.
Fromm, Erich. Marxismus, Psychoanalyse und "wirkliche Wirklichkeit". *Tagebuch*:21(9):5f, 1966j.
Fromm, Erich. Prophets and priests. *On disobedience.* New York: Harper Perennial, [1967b]/2010.
Fromm, Erich. Do we still love life?*Love, sexuality, and matriarchy.* New York: Fromm International Edition, [1967e]/1997.
Fromm, Erich. *The revolution of hope.* New York: Bantam Books, 1968a.
Fromm, Erich. On the sources of human destructiveness. L. Ng (ed.). *Alternatives to violence: a stimulus to dialogue.* New York: Time Inc., 1968e.
Fromm, Erich. Introduction. Erich Fromm and Ramón Xirau (eds.). *The Nature of Man.* New York: Macmillan, 1968g.
Fromm, Erich. Marx's contribution to the knowledge of man. *The crisis of psychoanalysis.* New York: Holt, Reinehart and Winston, [1968h]/1970.
Fromm, Erich. On the theory and strategy of peace. *On disobedience and other essays.* London: Routledge & Kegan Paul, [1970h]/1984.
Fromm, Erich. *The anatomy of human destructiveness.* New York. Henry Holt & Company, [1973a]/1992.
Fromm, Erich. Psychology for nonpsychologists. *For the love of life.* New York: The Free Press, [1974a]/1986.
Fromm, Erich. In the name of life: a portrait through dialogue. *For the love of life.* New York: The Free Press, [1974b]/1986.
Fromm, Erich. *To have or to be?*New York: Bantam Books, [1976a]/1981.
Fromm, Erich. Interview with Adelbert Reif. *Arbeiter-Zeitung*:16:1,8,10, 1977c.
Fromm, Erich. My own concept of man. *Fromm Forum*:17:5–10, [1977g]/2013.
Fromm, Erich. Das Undenkbare, das Unsagbare, das Unaussprechliche. *Psychologie heute*: 5:23–31, 1978b.

Fromm, Erich. *Greatness and limitations of Freud's thought*. New York: Harper and Row, Publishers, [1979a]/1980.
Fromm, Erich. Interview with Veio Zanolini. *Südschweiz* (02/19/1980):3, 1980f.
Fromm, Erich. Affluence and ennui in our society. *For the love of life*. New York: The Free Press, [1983b]/1986.
Fromm, Erich. On the origins of aggression. *For the love of life*. New York: The Free Press, [1983c]/1986.
Fromm, Erich. Who is man? *For the love of life*. New York: The Free Press, [1983d]/1986.
Fromm, Erich. *The art of being*. New York: Continuum, [1989a]/1998.
Fromm, Erich. On my psychoanalytic approach. *The revision of psychoanalysis*. Boulder: Westview Press, [1990d]/1992.
Fromm, Erich. The necessity for the revision of psychoanalysis. *The revision of psychoanalysis*. Boulder: Westview Press, [1990e]/1992.
Fromm, Erich. The dialectic revision of psychoanalysis. *The revision of psychoanalysis*. Boulder: Westview Press, [1990f]/1992.
Fromm, Erich. Sexuality and sexual perversions. *The revision of psychoanalysis*. Boulder: Westview Press, [1990g]/1992.
Fromm, Erich. *The art of listening*. London: Constable, [1991a]/1994.
Fromm, Erich. The concept of mental health. *The pathology of normalcy*. New York: American Mental Health Foundation, [1991f]/2010.
Fromm, Erich. The humanistic science of man. *The pathology of normalcy*. New York: American Mental Health Foundation, [1991g]/2010.
Fromm, Erich. Man's impulse structure and its relation to culture. *Beyond Freud*. New York: American Mental Health Foundation, [1992e]/2010.
Fromm, Erich. Psychic needs and society. *Beyond Freud*. New York: American Mental Health Foundation, [1992f]/2010.
Fromm, Erich. Dealing with the unconscious in psychotherapeutic practice. *Beyond Freud*. New York: American Mental Health Foundation, [1992g]/2010.
Fromm, Erich. The relevance of psychoanalysis for the future. *Beyond Freud*. New York: American Mental Health Foundation, [1992h]/2010.
Fromm, Erich. A new humanism as a condition for the One World. *On being human*. New York: Continuum. [1992m]/2005.
Fromm, Erich. Some beliefs of man, in man, for man. *On being human*. New York: Continuum. [1992q]/2005.
Fromm, Erich. Meister Eckhart and Karl Marx on having and being. *On being human*. New York: Continuum, [1992s]/2005.
Fromm, Erich. Changing concepts of homosexuality. *Love, matriarchy, sexuality*. New York: Fromm International Publishing Corporation, [1994f]/1997.
Fromm, Erich; Maccoby, Michael. *Social character in a Mexican village*. New York: Routledge, [1970b]/1996.
Hegel, Georg. *Phänomenologie des Geistes*. Frankfurt: Surkhamp, [1807]/1986.
Hegel, Georg. *Wissenschaft der Logik I*. Frankfurt: Surkhamp, [1812–1832]/1986.
Hegel, Georg. *Wissenschaft der Logik II*. Frankfurt: Surkhamp, [1812–1816]/1986.
Marx, Karl. Ökonomische-philosophische Manuskripte. *MEGA I.2*. Berlin: Akademie Verlag, [1844]/2009.
Marx, Karl. Der 18. Brumaire des Louis Bonaparte. *MEGA I.11*. Berlin: Dietz Verlag, [1852]/1985.

Marx, Karl. Ökonomische Manuskripte 1857–8. *MEGA II.1*. Berlin: Akademie Verlag, [1857–1858]/2006.
Marx, Karl. Zur Kritik der politischen Ökonomie. *MEGA II.2*. Berlin: Dietz Verlag, [1859]/1980.
Marx, Karl. Das Kapital, Erster Band. *MEGA II.10*. Berlin: Dietz Verlag, [1867–1890]/1991.
Marx, Karl; Engels, Friedrich. Die deutsche Ideologie. *MEGA I.5*. Amsterdam: Akademie Verlag, [1845–1847]/2017.
Marx, Karl. Manifest der Kommunistischen Partei. *Werke 4*. Berlin: Dietz Verlag, [1848]/2017.

Secondary literature

Anderson, Kevin. Fromm, Marx, and humanism. Rainer Funk, Neil McLaughlin (eds.). *Towards a human science*. Gießen: Psychosozial-Verlag, 2015.
Burston, Daniel. *The legacy of Erich Fromm*. Cambridge: Harvard University Press, 1991.
Chancer, Lynn. Sadomasochism or the art of loving: Fromm and feminist theory. *The Psychoanalytic Review*: 104(4):469–484, 2017.
Chancer, Lynn. Fromm, feminist theory and the psychosocial: from sadomasochism to mutual Recognition. Kieran Durkin, Joan Braune (eds). *Erich Fromm's critical theory*. New York: Bloomsbury, 2020.
Cortina, Mauricio. The greatness and limitations of Erich Fromm's humanism. *Contemporary Psychoanalysis*:51(3):388–422, 2015a.
Cortina, Mauricio. Fromm's view of the human condition in light of contemporary evolutionary and developmental knowledge. Rainer Funk, Neil McLaughlin (eds.). *Towards a human science*. Gießen: Psychosozial-Verlag, 2015b.
Funk, Rainer. *Mut zum Menschen*. Stuttgart: Deutsche Verlags-Anstalt, 1978.
Philipson, Ilene. The last public psychoanalyst? Why Fromm matters in the 21st century. *Psychoanalytic perspectives*:14:52–74, 2017.
Wilde, Lawrence. *Erich Fromm and the quest for solidarity*. New York: Palgrave Macmillan, 2004.

Chapter 3

III To Go to the Roots
Fromm and Marcuse After the *Dissent* Debate

Between 1955 and 1956, Erich Fromm and Herbert Marcuse conducted a lively debate in a series of four articles published in a socialist journal called *Dissent*, which was edited by Irving Howe and Lewis Coser. Howe and Coser had previously commissioned Fromm to write a short paper on "The psychology of normalcy", which appeared in 1954. As of 1963, Fromm was still among the contributing editors of *Dissent*, and his correspondence indicates that he remained in touch with Howe on matters concerning democratic socialists in the US (cf. Howe_Irving_1963–03–01-by). Their shared interest in Jewish tradition may also have provided some common ground. Like Howe and Coser, however, Marcuse taught at Brandeis, which may have given him opportunity for maintaining more frequent contact with them.

Both Fromm's 1954 piece and Marcuse's 1955 article – this one marking the opening round of the debate – were published in similar circumstances. But whereas Fromm's 1954 piece was a withering assessment of consumerism and conformity in post-War America, Marcuse's essay delivered a critique of neo-Freudian and interpersonal psychoanalysis, including the work of Clara Thompson, Karen Horney, Harry Stack Sullivan, Patrick Mullahy, and Erich Fromm. Fromm had certainly cultivated contacts with these people in the recent past, but he felt profoundly misrepresented by "Marcuse's procedure of lumping various 'revisionist' writers together" (1955b:342). He noted that the differences between them were as great as their similarities, and in years to come, sharpened his opposition to their work. In Sullivan, for example, he praised the "recognition of the uniqueness of every person and the respect for human dignity" (u-1949:7), as well as his sensitivity with psychotic patients. But he lamented the fact that "he also believed [...] the American world is the best of all possible worlds and he was not seeing its great problems" (d-1991d-002-eng-draft-04:161). Horney deepened Fromm's opposition to Freud's patriarchal bias, but he thought some of her categories were "superficial", and that she lacked "an adequate concept of society" (1973a:110). In sum: they "didn't analyze social structure" (VID-1963f).

Fromm's objections to being mischaracterized by Marcuse were reiterated much later, in a chapter written in 1969, which stated that "there is no 'cultural' versus 'biological' orientation" in psychoanalysis", and that Fromm's "theoretical concepts differ on fundamental points from those of Sullivan and Horney, just as these two authors differ between themselves" (1990d:1). Indeed, much of Fromm's rebuttal to Marcuse's attack only appeared in the late 1960s through the mid-1970s. By then, Marcuse's ideas were very popular on the Left. By contrast, Fromm's popularity was beginning to wane. He took pains to differentiate himself from authors with whom he had been identified since the mid-1940s.

I Theory

In depicting Fromm and these other analysts as part of a same "school" partaking in a "common attitude", Marcuse (1955:226) was strengthening a larger trend in the reception of psychoanalysis in the 1950s. Fromm exhibited a delayed response to it on print, even though he was quite vocal about it in his psychoanalytic teaching. In 1955, Fromm delivered his first public criticism of Sullivan's model of personality, which he deemed to be a-historical and expressive of an alienated standpoint (cf. Fromm, 1955a). He also wrote that Horney's theories were "more remote from Freud's" than his own, and that "they constitute a fruitful and constructive continuation of Adler's thinking" (cf. 1955e:378). But apart from these remarks, there was little to distance him from Sullivan and Horney et al. at that time. Lumping Fromm together with the other "revisionists" implied that Fromm was aligned not only with *theoretical*, but also with *political* antagonists of Marcuse's.

At first sight, all four papers – two by Marcuse, two by Fromm – revolved mainly around questions of psychoanalytic theory. And I emphasize "theory", not practice here, because Marcuse dismissed any discussion of the "*therapeutical* merits of the revisionist schools" (1955:225) as being outside his sphere of competence. Nevertheless, Fromm's rejoinder was largely written from a clinical perspective, focusing on Marcuse's deviations from Freud and correcting his statements about non-Freudian analysts. We encounter other subjects fleetingly along the way, but they were overshadowed by intense disagreements on libido theory vs. interpersonal relations, and aspects of Freud's metapsychology.

If we only attend to this side of things, then the "Fromm/Marcuse debate" really amounted to a clash between two irreconcilable positions on how to develop and apply Freud's intellectual legacy. Reading it more carefully, however, we find vestiges of another sort of disagreement. When Fromm received the draft for Marcuse's "reply" – the third paper in the sequence – it included a segment which was deleted from the published version. In it, Marcuse wrote:

> "Nihilism", as the indictment of inhuman conditions, may be a truly humanist attitude – part of the Great Refusal to play the game. I cannot

express it better than the editors of this magazine did (vol. II, no. 4:416): "There are times, such as the present, when negativism is the most positive task writers can undertake, when it becomes a form of political and intellectual hygiene. As long as the fish stink – and that, by and large, is what they continue to do – then it is necessary to say: the fish stink. This of course, may not please those who have gone into the fish business".

(d-1956b-eng-type-01)

It was to this version of the text that Fromm presumably wrote his second, brief counter-rebuttal. We can understand Howe's motives for not publishing this segment, which would insult a supporter of his journal. Still, the unpublished passage reminds us that this debate on psychoanalysis appeared in a *socialist* review, and that in 1956, Fromm was still collaborating with Stanley Plastrik and other editors at *Dissent* to organize "a gathering of independent socialists" (Plastrik_Stanley_1956–05–01-by). In couching his objections to Marcuse primarily in psychoanalytic terms, Fromm supposed that he was replying to a paper "in the same field". "I did not think it necessary to take time and enter into a discussion", Fromm wrote in 1968, "since he [Marcuse] based his thoughts on ignorance and distortion of Freud's idea, on distortion of Marx, and a falsification of my position" (e-ME:1). On closer inspection, their disparate claims about Freud and his ideas cloaked disagreements about "positivity" and "negativity", "nihilism" and "optimism" – issues which the original debate merely touched on, but which became more salient later.

Despite growing disagreements on metapsychology, Marcuse and Fromm found common ground elsewhere. Note their common admiration for Ernst Schachtel's (1947) paper "On memory and childhood amnesia". This paper inspired Fromm's revision of the theory of dreams and of the dynamics of repression, as determined by "socially-conditioned filters", and Marcuse regarded it as "one of the few real contributions to the philosophy of psychoanalysis" (1956b:19). Fromm and Schachtel were colleagues at the William Alanson White Institute, and Fromm (1968a) continued to praise Schachtel's (1937) insights on empirical psychology throughout his life. In reading Schachtel's paper on childhood amnesia, we find the hypothesis that

> *The categories (or schemata) of adult memory are not suitable receptacles for early childhood experiences and therefore not fit to preserve those experiences and enable their recall. The functional capacity of the conscious, adult memory is usually limited to those types of experience which the adult consciously is aware of and is capable of having.*

(1947:284)

But whereas Fromm took this claim to be true for adult development in general, Marcuse thought it was "focused on the explosive force of memory, and its control and 'conventionalization' by society" (1956a:19). Perhaps it was – but so, for example, was Fromm's (1947a) concept of the marketing orientation, and its precursor, the idea of an "automaton conformity" (cf. 1941a), which Marcuse formulated in his own language by saying that "the ego submits quickly to the required modes of thought and behavior, assimilating its Self to Others" (1969b:115). It is no wonder then that Fromm (1941a:120) indicated a lecture of Schachtel's, called "Self-feeling and the 'sale' of personality", as one of his sources.

From this point onwards, the number of convergent thoughts and conclusions between Fromm and Marcuse are striking. They disagreed about Zen Buddhism, but were in partial agreement in their attitudes toward existentialism, and in complete agreement regarding behaviorism (cf. Fromm, 1960a; 1973a, 1990e-f; Marcuse, 1964:13). Fromm was a steadfast admirer of *Reason and revolution*, which Marcuse published in 1941. And in *Eros and civilization,* Marcuse adopted a notion of rational authority that was very similar to Fromm's (1936a, 1941a). He wrote:

> Domination differs from rational exercise of authority. The latter, which is inherent in any societal division of labor, is derived from knowledge and confined to the administration of functions and arrangements necessary for the advancement of the whole. In contrast, domination is exercised by a particular group or individual in order to sustain and enhance itself in a privileged position.
> (Marcuse, 1956a:36)

In addition to the preceding, Marcuse's concept of "true" and "false" or "superimposed needs" (1964:7-8) paralleled Fromm's distinction between "artificially stimulated" needs, "irrational passions", and "rational passions" (1955a:334, 1973a). They agreed that "true needs" are rooted in the anthropological "constants" of the species (cf. Marcuse, 1972c), even though Fromm made a clearer distinction between desire elicited by external stimuli and suggestion and character-rooted passions. Marcuse would also eventually come to differentiate between *"emancipatory"* and *"compensatory drives"* (Marcuse, Na.3.374:6) – a noteworthy formulation, since Fromm (1992g) considered the development of the "secondary potentialities" as of a compensatory nature. Similarly, aspects of Fromm's concept of social character show up frequently in Marcuse's writings, though with less differentiation between what Fromm (1941a) considered external sources of influence – "gangs, radio, and television" (Marcuse, 1956a:97) – and the agency of the family, whose "role" Marcuse deemed to be in "decline" (1969b:112).

Finally, Marcuse's (1964, 1969a) reflections on the rise of violence in the US echo Fromm's (1974b) concerns about the increase of necrophilous trends in American social character, and sometimes employed similar examples, albeit formulated in different terminology – "libido cathexis of technology", "attraction to the mechanic", "religion of technology". Finally, judging from one of Marcuse's (1979a:32) last lectures on ecology, the idea that a "radical character structure" is rooted in an affinity to life became common to them both (cf. Fromm 1963b). Indeed, in one of his last planned lectures, Marcuse would even come to define "radical change" as "change of the predominant *character structure*" (Na.3.374:1). There could hardly be a more Frommian formulation.

When responding to the ideas of other thinkers, Fromm's (1962a) inclination was to stress the common ground beneath their different terminologies. But the contentious exchanges in *Dissent* had a lasting impact on both thinkers, even when they were increasingly in agreement with one another. Besides, unlike Fromm, Marcuse was quite taken with the hydraulic metaphor in Freud's model of the mind, and was given to speculating about the displacement and "mobilization" (1969b:115) of certain drives by political and media events. Because the source of these drives was framed in terms of libido-theory, Marcuse saw them and their satisfaction as ends in themselves. Fromm (1970d), by contrast, was not enamored of Freud's metapsychology, and was seldom given to these kinds of conjectures:

> Freud's *homo sexualis* is a variant of the classic *homo economicus*. [...] This social determination by the spirit of the market economy does not mean that the theory is wrong, except in its claim of describing the situation of *man as such*.
>
> (1970d:45)

Despite subscribing to Freud's concept of death instinct – an idea Fromm was critical of – Marcuse was uncomfortable with its tragic implications for social psychology, and revised the theory in a way that brought him inadvertently closer to Fromm. Marcuse followed Fenichel in assuming that, "if quantities of energy can be displaced from the sexual instincts to the ego instincts, then [...] sexual and ego instincts must derive from a common origin. Does not the same hold for eros and destructiveness?" (Fenichel, 1935:369). Marcuse thus affirmed that the life and death instincts spring from a common *quantum* of energy, so that the more there is of one, the less there is of the other: "All additional release of destructive energy upsets the precarious balance between Eros and Thanatos and reduces the energy of the Life Instincts in favor of that of the Death Instinct" (1969b:119). This idea, in Marcuse's own words, "militates against the dualistic conception" (1956a:28) of the instincts, which in Freud's (1924) view, however, was necessary for his metapsychology to cohere[1]. Marcuse's and Fenichel's derivation of the life and death instincts from a single source may both be rooted in a misinterpretation of Freud's remarks in *The ego and the id,* where he speculated that there might be a neutral energy which can be added to strengthen the cathexis of either erotic or destructive drives. Freud (1923) regarded this displaceable energy as desexualized Eros or sublimated energy; hence, not a product of the death drive.

Marcuse's misreading of Freud made it possible to conjecture that the death drive might be extinguished, or subordinated to the life drives: "it is the *failure* of Eros, lack of fulfillment of life, which enhances the instinctual value of death"; "as long as life grows, the former [derivatives of the death instinct] remain subordinate to the latter [sex instincts]", so that in a pacified society "aggression would be subjected to their demands" (Marcuse, 1956a:109,139; 1966b:xix). Comparably, in Fromm's case, destructiveness was the outcome of "the thwarting of life" (1941a:179). However, Fromm (1970h) also insisted on drawing a strong distinction between reactive, self-defensive aggression, which is in the service of life, and destructiveness proper, something which is lacking in Marcuse – or perhaps merely hinted at.

***

In light of the preceding, we can only conclude that there was actually far more common ground between Fromm and Marcuse than the *Dissent* debate suggested. Indeed, this was increasingly the case the more time passed. And if we look for evidence of contacts between them outside their published texts, their relationship appears to be even more complicated! After trading embittered accusations, one might expect a definitive enmity to ensue, but that doesn't seem to have been the case. Not immediately. In 1955 Marcuse wrote enthusiastically to Leo Loewenthal about a panel that Fromm and he participated in. "It was divine: Fromm was very emotional and excited; but the audience (almost a mass assembly) was enthralled by the intellectual Boxing Match" (apud Kellner and Pierce, 2011:101). Fromm explicitly praised Marcuse's work in a number or passages in *May man prevail?* (1961a) and *Marx's concept of man* (1961b).

Of the remaining four letters between them, two were sent between 1963 and 1964, and concern preparations for Fromm's anthology *Socialist humanism* in 1965. Marcuse's (1965) paper partly criticized the main trend of the other contributors' chapters, bearing the title "Socialist humanism?", with a question mark. Still, Fromm published it. In Louis Althusser's case, however, he declined, saying that "since the main point of this symposium is to show a common front, even in spite of a good deal of individual variation between the authors based on the principles mentioned above, your paper would not be in place" (Althusser_Louis_1964–01–08-to). Marcuse was probably not aware of this exchange, but had likely more sympathy for Althusser's theoretical stand, as he recommended that Althusser, Serge Mallet and André Gorz be called for the third Socialist Scholars Conference (cf. l-661123MeMe). Either way, we find Marcuse's letter to Fromm (Marcuse_-Herbert_1963 12–08-by) asking him if he would be willing to review his forthcoming book – presumably *One-dimensional man* – "agreeing or rejecting: this doesn't matter".

So, despite their disagreements on psychoanalysis, Marcuse and Fromm seem to have had a grudging respect for each other up until 1965. They were not close on a personal level, but viewed each other as occasional allies, both politically and intellectually. As we approach 1968, however, the tone shifts. Judging from his notations, Fromm probably did not read the first edition of *Eros and civilization* very attentively. But his copy of the second edition has marginalia for what seem to have been at least three successive readings. He studied this and other writings by Marcuse intensively now, and drafted two lengthy critiques: one as an appendix to *The revolution of hope*, which he later withdrew, and which was originally entitled "Infantilization and despair masquerading as radicalism" (d-1990h-eng-type-01), and a "separate paper" on Marcuse's take on psychoanalysis (d-1990g-000-eng-draft-01:16). Fromm withheld most of what he wrote from publication, publishing only selected passages in different books and essays between 1968 and 1980. In his last interviews, when asked about his attitude toward Marcuse, he remarked that he regarded the philosopher as a "naïve-romantic" (cf. d-1977g-000-deu-type-01) in politics, as a "hedonist" in ethics, a defender of "bourgeois materialism" (1975i:55–7) in anthropological terms, which, all in all, located him in the tradition of "'pornographic' literature […] from de Sade through surrealism down to the contemporary avant-garde of radical writers" (1990g:92).

The reasons underlying Fromm's decision not to publish his commentaries on Marcuse are difficult to discern. When he was negotiating for a new edition of what he considered his "most important papers which had never been published in a book" with Ruth Nanda Anshen, 20 years after the *Dissent* debate, he mentioned his "Controversy with Herbert Marcuse in *Dissent*, The Human Implications of Instinctivistic Radicalism, with a counter-rebuttal, which are papers very much of wide interest today as much as then" (Anshen_Ruth_Nanda_1975–01–21-to; Anshen_Ruth_Nanda_1975–02–18-to). Marcuse, by contrast, seemed to move in the opposite direction. He never retracted his arguments in *Dissent*, nor acknowledged his affinities with Fromm explicitly. Still in 1975, he would be alerting students to the tendency in psychology to try "to become sane in a sick society" (Na.3.327:5). But from the late 1960s on, Marcuse positions were increasingly Frommian. For one, he reacted against Norman Brown's fondness for mythological language, in terms that were curiously reminiscent of Fromm's critique of Marcuse himself, particularly in his portrayals of Orpheus and Narcissus:

> Eros lives in the division and boundary between subject and object, man and nature; and precisely in its polymorphous-perverse manifestations, in its liberation from the "despotism of genital organization", the sexual instincts transform the object and the environment – without ever annihilating the object and the environment together with the subject.
> (Marcuse, 1967a:179)

Here Marcuse sticks to his embrace of polymorphous sexuality, but waxes utopian, relinquishing his earlier attachment to a purely "negative" rhetoric – "the positive is still the negative" (1956b:81); "the politically impotent form of the 'absolute refusal'" (1964:255). He now voiced the idea that critical theory need not refrain from "utopian speculation" (1969a:3) after all. He emphasized that a revolution should be carried by people who represent "a new type of man, a different type of human being, with new needs, capable of finding a qualitatively different way of life, and of constructing a qualitatively different environment" (1970b:7) – a true "change in the 'nature' of man" (1969a:5), which should however "*precede* the revolution" (1969a:18).

Fromm recognized this later change and was "glad" (1990h:129) about it. But he continued to criticize Marcuse's earlier positions, which were not always consistent with his evolving perspective on social change. Indeed, in the *Dissent* debate, Marcuse criticized the post-Freudians because, in their writings, "the social issues become primarily spiritual issues, and their solution becomes a *moral* task" (1955:234). In the late sixties, however, he claimed that "political radicalism [...] implies moral radicalism: the emergence of a morality which might precondition man for freedom" (1969a:10). There should be a new "education of the whole man: *changing his nature*" (Na.3.235:6). He grounded the possibility of revolution in the "organic foundation of morality in the human being", including "an instinctual foundation for solidarity" (1969a:10), much as Fromm regarded "the drive for freedom" as part of "man's basic, natural equipment" (1983d:142), and biophilia as a primary, "biologically given quality in man" (1973a:398). In the *Dissent* debate, Marcuse had denounced Fromm for reviving "all the time-honored values of idealistic ethics as if nobody had ever demonstrated their conformistic and repressive features" (Marcuse 1955:231). Afterwards, he acknowledged that "dialectical materialism contains idealism as an element of theory and practice" (Marcuse 1972a:3) – and even thought that moral conscience could act as "the conscience *of humanity*" (Na.3.219:2–3) in the political process, an idea akin to what Fromm (1947a) called "humanistic conscience".

Of course, there were still relevant differences between the two. Marcuse, ever the Lamarckian, spoke about "cultural needs" which "'sink down' into the biology of man" (1969a:10). Even so, in comparison with the 1950s, he had moved much closer to Fromm. He wanted to work with people who had a "*'biological revulsion'* against cruelty, oppression, brutality, stupidity" (Na.3.235:9) – an idea Fromm (1973a) would hardly have disavowed. As a measure of their silent proximity, we may mention the peculiar fact that in 1968, Marcuse published a lecture he had originally presented in 1956. Here we find him endorsing Fromm's (1955a) humanistic concept of mental health – which was the main focus of Marcuse's objections in the previous year as "essentially unattainable" without "'curing' the patient to become a rebel or [...] a martyr" (1955:231). He explicitly quotes *The sane society*, and goes to say that:

> As a tentative definition of "sick society" we can say that a society is sick when its basic institutions and relations, its structure, are such that they do not permit the use of the available material and intellectual resources for the optimal development and satisfaction of individual needs.
>
> (Marcuse, 1968a:189)

It is no coincidence that this essay was only made public again in 1968, in the book *Negations* – not far from a time when he would be telling students that "a whole generation" was being "educated in the knowledge and goals of a *sick society*", and that a "*'new sanity'*" needed to be achieved (Marcuse, Na.3.235:7,11). Fromm's copy of *Negations* is without any notations, so he was probably unimpressed by or completely unaware of this reference to his work. And so we come to the strange conclusion that Fromm's more substantive reply to Marcuse was not only delayed by 13 years – and even then, mostly withheld from publication –, but also unfolded at a time when they were as close as they would ever be in theoretical terms.

A letter to Marcuse from 1967 gives some indication of the reasons for this startling counterpoint. In it, Fromm outlined a plan for enlisting a number of intellectuals to criticize a recent biography of Marx written by Robert Payne, which Fromm considered to be "a distortion and falsification of Marx's person and theory" (Marcuse_Herbert_1967–12–27-to). Among the 14 names he mentioned to Marcuse was H. Stuart Hughes. But Hughes and Marcuse both gave Fromm similar replies. As chairman of his department at Harvard, and a prominent activist in his own right, Hughes was too busy to oblige, saying "it is better for people like you [Fromm] and me to devote our energies to expressing our own ideas in our form rather than diverting them towards rebutting the ideas of others" (Hughes_Stuart_H_1968–01–16-by) – a strategy Fromm followed with regards to Marcuse in the fifties, to his later regret. Marcuse seems to echo Hughes here, saying: "I don't know whether we should spend time and energy discussing the stuff, but it would, of course, be good if you could place some negative reviews in some of the journals and reviews with large circulation". He thought "He [Payne] and his output are not taken seriously" (Marcuse_Herbert_1968–01–22-by). But the fact that Fromm confided to Marcuse, and not to Hughes, all the people he hoped to involve in this collective undertaking tells us something. It is also telling that both his correspondents turned him down.

This was not the first time that Fromm tried to organize others for the sake of a cause, or the first time he felt frustrated by their lack of engagement. Fromm's repeated disappointments along these lines attest to a deep-seated feeling of urgency and a sense of mission rooted in his childhood upbringing. Raised in an Orthodox Jewish home, his earliest role models for the public intellectual were the Old Testament prophets: men who occupied the public space, and spoke truth to power (cf. 1967b). Incidentally, Marcuse could be found saying that the prophets were "the first radicals" (Na.3.281:1). But Fromm's engagement with this tradition went deeper. It was one source for his life-long effort to reach a wide readership beyond specialist circles, and why he was attuned to swings of opinion among those who *hadn't had* the opportunity – or the desire – to research and clarify their notions of Marx, Freud, or other prominent intellectuals.

Marcuse was also quite attuned to the public and political scene. But the public he addressed was different. Marcuse was interested in providing the then-emerging left-wing movements with justification and a theoretical grounding for their actions. And so we find him as a defender of the "new bohème, the beatniks and hipsters, the peace creeps" (1966:xxi), the "Hippie subculture", the politicized "Blacks", and of course, also the "active minorities" and "the young middle-class intelligentsia" (1969a:35,51). Fromm was less sanguine about the counter-culture and the New Left, and was actively engaging with members of the American political elite. In short, Marcuse was closer to both the academic world and the New Left, while Fromm was concerned with the wider diffusion of knowledge and opinion, but also somewhat enmeshed in what Marcuse and his followers dismissed as "the Establishment". This difference includes also their relation to independent efforts in political education. Marcuse (1969a) was very insistent on the role of the New Left as "educators" of the larger population, and was involved with initiatives such as the *Radical Education Project* (REP), an association founded by the SDS with the "purpose of providing the New Left with an education, research, and publication program" (l-660603RPMe). Marcuse was invited to become a sponsor and accepted the role. Fromm was also included in the initial list of prospective sponsors, and seems either not to have accepted it, or not to have received the invitation.

Also the New Left had to take a stance about the 1968 National Democrat Convention. So it may have angered Fromm when, having signed a public letter with Marcuse in favor of McCarthy's candidacy ("The People's Choice", The New York Review of Books, August 22nd, 1968), he also found him excusing the prevalent practice of calling "public servants or leaders" as "pig X or pig Y" (1969a:35). He was familiar with the fact that "for the anti-authoritarian rebels, the authoritarians and their armed defenders, the police, are 'pigs'" (d-1970f-000-eng-type-01:11). But he didn't believe a complete rejection of electoral politics would be fruitful in the long run. Only after the political climate in the US turned more conservative did Marcuse go back to emphasizing that, when working in a non-revolutionary circumstance, "one must [...] work in and through the institutions" (1972c:4), "organize demonstrations" and "learn the political value of [their] *repetition*" (Na.3.313:6).

Fromm's criticism of Marcuse was very similar to Fromm's criticism of late sixties and early seventies political movements. Not that he confused the two. The papers he withheld from publication sometimes included a fairly nuanced attempt at distinguishing between the different stands – conservative, liberal, and radical – that were at play in American politics. He distinguished between the "traditional patriarchal-authoritarian" lower middle class, the "post-authoritarian" middle and upper classes, and the "anti-authoritarian" radicals, tracing these differences back to the divide between "big cities and rural areas", to "work in large plants and corporations" as opposed to other forms of work (d-1970f-000-eng-typ-001:10–1). He probably had more sympathy for the African American movements than for the student organizations: he wrote "negro violence is a necessary outcome of the misery of black ghetto life" (192l:55), and confided to Lewis Mumford that some of his recent conversations had "confirmed somewhat an expectation I [Fromm] have that a number of the radical Negro leaders are quite capable of seeing things more realistically and rationally [than the SDS] if they speak with people whom they can trust" (Mumford_Lewis_1968-12-08-to). Elsewhere, we find an analysis of the various trends within and alongside the New Left (cf. 1990i). Still, the convergence between his judgment of Marcuse and of radical youth is too great to be missed.

In Marcuse, he criticized the (typically pre-1965) idea of a critical theory "without hope" (Marcuse, 1964:257). He could not foresee that Marcuse would later be telling students that "if you feel only *despair, hopelessness, apathy* – you have given in to the Establ[ishment] propaganda" (Na.3.327:12), and thus wrote also of the late-sixties radicals:

> There is something else they do not understand. You can appeal to people by appealing to their indignation, their ambitions, or even their hate. But you cannot move people to sustained, constructive and truly revolutionary action by any of these emotions. People can be motivated to change only if they have hope.
>
> (1990i:122)

Indeed, in a segment redacted from *The revolution of hope,* Fromm even speculated that it is "characteristic of fascist movements that they owe their existence to common hate, and their success to its mobilization and manipulation" (d-1968a-000-eng-type-05:VI-22–23). He was then still lacking his later differentiation between revolutionary aggression and political destructiveness (cf. 1973a), placing him not too far from Marcuse's own take on "constructive" and "destructive hate" (1968b:s.p.). Of Marcuse, Fromm said that "if one is not concerned with steps between the present and the future, one does not deal with politics, radical or otherwise" (1968a:9) – again, in reference to the ending of *One-dimensional man*, where the idea was presented that "the critical theory of society possesses no concepts which could bridge the gap between the present and its future" (Marcuse 1964:257). Of the radicals, he wrote correspondingly:

> The great prophets, from Isaiah to Marx, also were critics, but they went beyond indignation and did not dwell on despair or hate. Their main effort was to explain, to convince, to warn, and most importantly, to show new ways, to show new alternatives. *The failure of the radical activists lies in the fact that they do not show alternatives.*
>
> (1990i:121)

A third criticism of Marcuse was that he promoted "a straight regression to an infantile pattern", "to the pregenital stage of the infant" – to which Fromm added that "H. Marcuse's appeal to the young seems to rest largely on the fact that he is the spokesman for infantile regression" (1970f:105). He would recall later in life that his attitude towards Marcuse was rather "ambivalent", since "his ideal was that man should become a child, while my ideal is that of the plain maturity of man" (AUD-1980e). Finally, a fourth criticism – namely that "the core of the radicals, both the hippies and the radical activists, show as a rule no knowledge of, no interest in, and no concern with tradition" (1990i:121) – was obviously not extended to Marcuse. After all, they had both undergone a similar cultural education, to the point that Ronald Aronson, a former student of Marcuse's, identified him not only as a professor for "Plato, Aristotle, Kant, Hegel, Marx", but "as someone *of* the tradition" (1971:257–8). Nevertheless, Marcuse criticized students, not for despising tradition, but for their "anti-intellectualism" (Na.3.235:2). In fact, he spoke against it very early on in his correspondence with representatives of the student movement. After Mike Davis reports on what he sees as SDS's main shortcomings, Marcuse replies: "I detect in your report a strong anti-intellectual sentiment, almost inferiority complex" (l-unMeDs). He would later address the same issue publicly in conferences he gave to student associations, whereas Fromm – who also engaged with the youth among his audience – preached that knowledge of the intellectual legacies of the past is the only solid basis to "challenge it and continue it in a critical way, not by repeating it" (AUD-1968a)[2]. Marcuse's later disappointments with the "*interminable* debates on what is Marxist, or Marxist-Leninist, or Trotskist (sic), or Maoist strategy" (Na.3.327:12) eventually led him to a similar perspective.

Meanwhile, Fromm continued to criticize Marcuse's apparent disdain for so-called "traditional values", by which he meant disregard for the "humanistic" axiological notions which he construed as the common ethical ground for humanists all over the world. Since he considered these values – love, justice and reason – as universal, he thought that complete denial and disconnection from them amounted to deep alienation from oneself, and from the capacity to recognize humanity within oneself. In a letter to Lewis Mumford dated January 1969, we read:

> It seems that these people and many of the younger generation and of the technologists believe that [...] the nature of man as he existed in all previous history has ended. In fact, that man is not an entity that could be defined, or even ~~foreseen~~ inferred, with the result, of course, that traditional values no longer have any validity whatsoever. [...] These people seem to confuse the fact that there are many manifestations of man's nature which one can understand in many ways, but the different manifestations do not alter the fact that man is one of the givens, with its own basic structure, conditions of existence and laws for change, flowering and decay. [...] I am afraid that among the young generation there are many who are influenced by this view, and hence who are hostile to any theoretical discourse which deals with man as something real, rather than as "no-man".
> (Mumford_Lewis_1969–01–23-to)³

Of this whole line of thought, we only have an accusation that Marcuse was an "alienated intellectual" in Fromm's (1968a:9) published work. As was the case with Marcuse, Fromm made only a few scattered comments on the negative features of the youth movement: that it was politically and philosophically naïve due to its repudiation of tradition (cf. 1976a); that it was a culture of passivity and regression (cf. 1970f), but also that it aspired to embrace better values, a new life and a new honesty (cf. 1983b). But once again, his correspondence tells a slightly different story. Later in 1969, Fromm wrote another letter to Mumford saying that

> the unrest among the students has also its positive and creative aspects. Actually I think one part of the radicals is motivated by the wish to destroy; another by a deep love for life. [...] But it seems as if the destructive ones over-shout the others.
> (Mumford_Lewis_1969–04–30-to)

Indeed, among the drafts for *The revolution of hope* which were excluded from publication, we find the idea that "there are some [activists] who are mainly filled with hate against the existing order, and who are greatly attracted by violence", but that "it would be a rash and unjustified conclusion to believe that the radical activists consist mainly of such people" (1990i:120).

2 Ethics

Fromm's attitude towards radical American youth was more ambivalent and nuanced than his increasingly harsh attitude towards Marcuse, whom he deemed a man with a "brilliant brain", but of "regressed emotionality" (e-ME:2). Nevertheless, Fromm was also aware that Marcuse had gone out on a limb, and was being threatened, both politically and professionally, in 1968. Evidently, Fromm continued to see Marcuse as a conditional ally in the larger context of American politics, because as his troubles deepened, Raya Dunayevskaya wrote to Marcuse that "Fromm would be for organizing any sort of committee that may be needed in your defense" (l-680714DaMe). To be sure, Fromm was not the only person offering such help (cf. Marcuse, Na.3.995). Still, Marcuse's reply made no reference to his suggestion – or anything else in Dunayevskaya's letter – other than saying: "Thanks for your good note" (l-680724MeDa). The upshot of this exchange? In a letter from a few days later, Fromm now expressed doubt, "whether there would be much of a basis for a fruitful conversation" with Marcuse from then on (Dunayevskaya_Raya_1968–07–31-to). Even so, Fromm withheld the appendix on Marcuse from *The revolution of hope* for fear that it "might help Marcuse's right-wing enemies" (Anderson and Rockwell, 2012:158).

Dunayevskaya tried to persuade Fromm to reverse his decision, but didn't succeed – or did so only partially. In a letter written shortly after, she complained that:

> I do not quite know who is responsible for the extraordinary publicity he has gotten recently, but his influence on the West European youth is greatly exaggerated. It isn't only, as Daniel Cohn-Bendit put it, that there aren't more than a dozen students who have studied his works (unless, he added, it be *Eros and Civilization*), but that they sharply disagree with his politics when they do hear him.
> (Dunayevskaya_Raya_1968–08–10-to)

Fromm asked his most trusted interlocutors about his rival's growing popularity. He was also interested in what other critics of Marcuse had to say. We know that Dunayevskaya sent Richard Greeman's "Critical Re-examination of Herbert Marcuse's Works" to Fromm at his request (cf. Anderson and Rockwell, 2012:161,166), and that Fromm read Alasdair McIntyre's (1970) polemical piece, though McIntyre (1963) had harsh words for Fromm's work, too. From all this, it seems reasonable to suppose that Fromm's conflicts about criticizing Marcuse grew in proportion to his fear that Marcuse was becoming a more influential public intellectual.

Knowing this, we can tentatively infer the processes that yielded the odd juxtaposition between Fromm's stance toward Marcuse in the *Dissent* years and subsequently, in the late sixties. Fromm regarded the 1950s debate as centered on the question of how best to interpret Freud: he replied as someone "in the field", and perhaps didn't think others would take Marcuse's point of view too seriously. He was already alarmed at what he saw as Marcuse's "human nihilism disguised as radicalism" (1955b:349). Later, when

Marcuse's influence was on the rise, he was caught in a web of contradictory impulses. On the one hand, he wanted to win the hearts and minds of the young away from Marcuse, but couldn't endorse many of their attitudes, as his rival did frequently. On the other hand, he didn't want to strengthen the right against Marcuse or the militants whom he appealed to, but thought that radical social change would require very different forms of political organization. He wanted to see McCarthy elected, but didn't want to completely alienate McCarthy's critics on the Left, insuring that a broadly based humanist movement would continue even if McCarthy lost, as in fact happened. So, in the midst of many mounting challenges, Fromm experienced a simultaneous need to fight his rival, and to protect him, whenever possible, from their common enemies. This despite the fact that he now saw Marcuse's "influence" as "*a symptom and a danger*" (d-1990g-001-eng-draft-01:1).

"I believe that his thinking is confused [...] and superficial", he wrote to himself, "and that it confuses young people" (e-ME:1). In the last letter we have from their exchanges, Marcuse wrote that he was "hoping to see you [Fromm] sometime in Europe this year" (Marcuse_Herbert_1968–01–22-by). He did. Fromm was to be the respondent to his paper on a "Reexamination of the concept of revolution" (Marcuse, 1968c) in a Symposium on Marx held by UNESCO in Paris, and did receive a copy of it, but apparently failed to be present (cf. Schaff_Adam_1968–07–04-to). They met later at least two times in the *Salzburger Humanismusgespräche* organized by Oskar Schatz in 1968 and 1969 (1970a; 1970b). We have the proceedings for a portion of their interaction in these meetings. They were polite, but no longer seeking common ground. And yet, similarities persist. As of 1969, Marcuse was insistent on the need to continue acting, regardless of the reaction from the right – "student unrest is *itself the backlash*" (Na.3.219:12–3). By 1972, however, he was warning about an imminent "counterrevolutionary" backlash, and in 1975, defended the movement while criticizing it for having "failed to develop any adequate organizational forms and by allowing internal splits to grow and spread, a phenomenon that was linked to anti-intellectualism, to a politically powerless anarchism and a narcissistic arrogance" (1979b:5) – all qualities that Fromm had criticized from the beginning, and still considered problematic when, a year later, he noted that the movement had been "decreasing", leaving its members "disappointed, apathetic or destructive" (1976a:63).

If Marcuse had a flair for modifying his opinions to suit diverse audiences, or as spirit and circumstances moved him to, Fromm was far more cautious, valuing clarity and consistency. That is why we frequently discover him refraining from public pronouncements on matters where he felt tentative, ambivalent, in danger of alienating or harming potential allies. That is also why he disliked Marcuse's mercurial style, as expressed in his comment that, once Marcuse has "adopted a position that is essentially the one he criticized before", "it is regrettable that he does not even comment on this change in the interests of intellectual clarity" (Fromm, 1990h:129).

Further evidence for Fromm's preference for consistency can be found in his reflections on America in the Cold War years. And it is no coincidence that in 1972, he said that:

> The older generation tends to have a character that is very much shaped by the conventional patterns and by the need for successful adaptation. Many of the younger generation tend to have *no character at all*. By that I do not mean that they are dishonest; on the contrary, one of the few enjoyable things in the modern world is the honesty of a great part of the younger generation. What I mean is that they live, emotionally and intellectually speaking, from hand to mouth. They satisfy every need immediately, have little patience to learn, cannot easily endure frustration, and have no center within themselves, no sense of identity. They suffer from this and question themselves, their identity, and the meaning of life.
>
> (1992s:39)

Here Fromm spoke of character as the expression of congruence between thought, desire, and action. Talking in terms of "values", Fromm thought about something that "guide[s] [...] actions and feelings" (1968a:90); about the inherent relation between passions, which are centered around certain goals, and the realm of *praxis*, of action. Though neither of them ever remarked on this, this way of framing things was not dissimilar to Marcuse's call for a "transformation of values into needs" (1964:233). He was increasingly of the opinion that holding deep convictions, and being able to devote oneself to a certain goal or passion (of a rational or pro-social nature – cf. 1991d), was one of the hallmarks of actually "having character", both in the psychological and in the ethical sense; and that this, in turn, was a condition of successful and trustworthy political action.

For further evidence of Fromm's preference for caution and consistency, note the exclusion of his posthumously published comments on *The art of being* from *To have or to be?*, which was published in 1976. This choice stemmed from his concerns about the effects a text on practices of self-care could have when, by Fromm's own admission, the market for "spiritual commodities" (cf. 1989a:13,17) was on the rise. Incidentally, Marcuse also came to recognize and criticize "withdrawal into a kind of private liberation drug culture, the turn to guru-cults and other pseudo-religious sects" (1979b:5) as a pitfall seducing some among the American youth. This "return into one's self" or "*politics in the First Person*" – "the concentration on the sensibility and feelings of the person", Marcuse felt, "threaten to come into conflict with the organization and self-discipline required by an effective *political praxis*" (Na.3.374:13). But here lies a subtle and important difference. Marcuse had already recognized that drug culture had a potential for weakening the New Left: "sensibility is freed not only from the exigencies of the existing order but also from those of liberation" (1969a:37). And he was initially quite insistent on the irreconcilability of Marxism with Christian doctrine. But eventually, Marcuse came to think of "the great radical heretic movements" (1970b:10) as providing possible models for revolution, and considered that "the revival of the heretic element in religion is today, in my view, on the agenda" (1969c:187). He even included the "heretic movements" as part of a critical education in social history (cf. Marcuse Na.3.235:13). These he saw as being radically different from the escapist and "pseudo-religious" phenomena attracting some youth. On this, Fromm (1992s) would certainly have agreed. He criticized a "naïve" interest in "Oriental religion" (1974a:86), and felt a much stronger sympathy for mystical and heretical sects, as against institutional religion (cf. 1979b). He would also have agreed on the problem with drugs, albeit for different reasons. In one footnote excised from *The revolution of hope* he wrote that:

> the current indulgence in drug consumption [...] creates a short-lived ecstatic experience without bringing about a change in personality [...]. Sometimes these ecstatic experiences are compared to the enlightenment and the sense of union which we find expressed in the Christian, Jewish and Moslem mystics or in the *satori* experience of Zen Buddhism. But they are basically different. These enlightenment experiences are achieved on the basis of a total awakening of the whole personality, of his mind as well as of his heart, and not isolated sensations which look like but are not that sense of union which cannot be achieved by the consumption of certain chemicals. Those who don't see the difference between the "instant Zen" produced by drugs and the state of mind of the enlightened Zen Buddhist or mystic probably have never seen what the latter looks like and hence don't know how to distinguish between genuine union and its synthetic facsimile.
>
> (d-RoHD:III:47)[4]

Now, to the extent that Fromm viewed drug taking (and other aspects of hippie culture) as a form of pacification, he thought it "doubtful that they will survive" (1990g:87). But to the extent that he saw in them an expression of a "religious mass movement" (1990g:86) – in Fromm's (1950a) peculiar sense of religion, as a system providing a frame of orientation and devotion – he actually thought they had some potential. Indeed, we learn from another redacted passage that in his opinion the groups which had a greater chance for survival were those which would be able to reach a "fuller development" of the religious bases of their communion (d-1990g-001-eng-type-01:ad-6). Marcuse, on the contrary, saw in them much more precarious forms of reunion than the properly "political" groups:

there are enough communes which are simply nothing more than an attempt at private, personal liberation, which naturally cannot last and will soon collapse, if the communes do not remain in the political process, in the political education and work jointly with what happens outside and in front of them, they have in general no chance

(Marcuse, 1972c:4).

A culture of "passivity" was thus a problem for Fromm, not for getting in the way of political discipline, as was the case with Marcuse, but in terms of realizing the communitarian aspirations that were found among these same groups. Hence his appraisal of their search for "a new lifestyle" (1976a:91), "a new morality" (1983b:31), "a new honesty" (1983b:33). He could see group sex and sexual freedom as possible expressions of "love of life" (1990g:86), especially outside the "post-authoritarian" middle-class of the times (d-1970f-000-eng-typ-001:11). But he could not see sensualism of any sort as more than an illusory solution, bound to fail:

> To forget oneself, in the sense of anaesthesizing one's reason, is the aim of all these attempts to restore unity within oneself. It is a tragic attempt, in the sense that either it succeeds only momentarily (as in a trance or in drunkenness) or, even if it is permanent (as in the passion for hate or power), it cripples man, estranges him from others, twists his judgment, and makes him as dependent on this particular passion as another is on hard drugs.
>
> (1973a:263).

Indeed, Fromm eventually came to criticize Zen for being too focused on change of perception (1973a:278), and not as deep in its power for character change in comparison to Theravada forms of meditation (cf. Fromm, 2009a). Marcuse (1957) was disinterested in any form of Buddhism, and disparaged drug-taking for dissuading or distracting users from engaging in political action. But what did he see as the "kernel of truth in the psychedelic research"? Precisely "the need for such a revolution in perception, for a new sensorium": "the dissolution of the ego shaped by the established society", which, albeit "short-lived", was based on the fact that "rebels want to see, hear, feel new things in a new way" (1969a:37). His concept of a "new man", he tied to the "potentialities" of the human in general, just as Fromm would; but Marcuse gave a special emphasis to "sensibility and sensitivity" (1970b:8).

Here we find an explanation for the fact that Fromm considered positions Marcuse held before 1965 to represent the actual core of his position, and was unimpressed by (and perhaps even unaware of) the striking similarity in their ideas on important issues as Marcuse's thought evolved. Why? Because regardless of how they interpreted Freud, Fromm and Marcuse had fundamentally different conceptions of "the good life", and accordingly, different conceptions of what constitutes a viable political and social organization. Their divergent views can already be discerned in the *Dissent* articles, where these differences were encrypted in psychoanalytic language and relatively undeveloped. But they figure more prominently in the late sixties, when political circumstances forced the issue out into the open.

Fromm had a hard time with the New Left. "I am one of the few, if you like, radical writers and socialists who is in deep disagreement with the larger part of the New Left and their pseudo-revolutionary and often destructive and unrealistic policies", he wrote to Tristram Coffin (Coffin_Tristram_1974–02–01-to). Marcuse, by contrast, had a much greater affinity with the student movement, because his expectations for the structure of a politically radical movement were quite different. Marcuse wasn't as wary or dismissive of entertaining "utopian" ideas as his "negative" conception of critical theory appeared to imply. Indeed, the last sections of *Eros and civilization* are actually his first statement on the experiential elements he deemed part of an emancipated society. *Eros and civilization* also asserts that "where religion still preserves the uncompromised aspirations for peace and happiness, its 'illusions' still have a higher truth value than science which works for their elimination" (1956:73). And when *One-dimensional man* equates "opposition" and "qualitative difference" (1964:79) in passing, Marcuse is only a step away from the idea that revolutionary opposition should be constituted by the growth of a qualitatively different way of life, including a new morality. "*Redefinition of needs*" would be the "prerequisite of qualitative change" (1964:245), he writes in his earlier formulations, and around ten years later, he says that there should be "a morality of liberation which overcomes, in ourselves, the cynical and brutal morality of the Establ[ishment]" (Na.3.327:8). Fromm himself recognized "some similarities" between his thought and Marcuse's, but still regarded it as "the very opposite of my own position" (e-ME:1). He accused Marcuse of not being clear enough on what the "new needs" and the "new man" would look like (cf. Mumford_Lewis_1969–04–30-to) – but there is reason to suspect that the problem was not only the indeterminacy in Marcuse's writings, but the fact that his and Fromm's (1976a) ideas for a radical social transformation were incompatible.

In the interval between the *Dissent* articles and the late sixties clashes, the most salient reminder we find of the debate in Fromm's writings refers to Marcuse's "negative" denunciation of love and other values. He still felt the need to comment elsewhere, a few years later, that "those who take the problem of love seriously cannot help being social critics" (1959d:131) – nothing like the conformism Marcuse saw in him. That this rebuke stung a little harder than the rest was probably due to the fact that it touched indirectly upon the basic antagonism between his and Marcuse's concepts of "good life". It is not so much, as Fromm (1968a) would have it, that Marcuse was in absolute despair and lacked love of life. He, too, talked about the "*political fight*" as the "fight for life" (1966b:xv). But the "life" they loved was different – this and other concepts point to different experiences, and this experiential realm, alongside the social relations it both presupposes and entails, is where the conflict actually takes root.

This can already be sensed in a comparison between Marcuse's "Eros" and Fromm's "biophilia". There is room, in Marcuse's notion, for sexual enjoyment (cf. 1964), but also for tenderness (cf. 1969a). The experiential *locus* for his concept is still, however, the organism as a subject of *pleasure*, whereas Fromm's biophilia is modeled after the experience of *joy* and vitality, rather than voluptuous sensation. Arguably, these are just poles on a continuum which the notion of Eros as formulated by Freud (1920) can accommodate. Fromm (1966a) was by no means an antagonist of sexual pleasure *per se*. But Marcuse's (1956, 1964) differentiation between simple "sexuality" and "Eros" proper includes not only the idea of a reactivation of the partial instincts and the perversions, but also the notion that the whole body can be a subject of enjoyment, as Freud (1905–24) insisted with reference to pleasure in skin touch, and to the possibility of a circulation of the libido among all the organs. If read with an eye to the partial instincts, Marcuse's position indeed tends to a "Sadean" conception of the body, in which its different portions represent sources for diverse pleasures composed out of different and perhaps dissociated segments. However, in Marcuse's works this coexists with the idea that "Eros" represents an integration of the enjoyment across the whole body – an idea which coincides more or less with the sort of vitality or "emotional intensity" Fromm (1990i) ascribed to life-oriented phenomena and phenomena of abundance.

It doesn't seem that Marcuse's imagination was *so extremely different* from Fromm's as was de Sade's. He was also quite outspoken as regarded his aim of reaching "the liberation of the mind, *and of the body*, from aggressive and repressive needs" (Marcuse Na.3.235:6). There was more room for ambiguity here than Fromm recognized, but this wouldn't have led to reconciliation. They had irreconcilable differences, but their source lay elsewhere. To elucidate this point further, consider a peculiarity in the documents: the copy of the second edition of *Eros and civilization*, which Fromm annotated extensively, is filled with marginalia. But two chapters lack any markings: "Phantasy and Utopia" and "The Aesthetic Dimension". The excerpts he took from the books also indicate disinterest in these segments of the book, which Marcuse deems to be pivotal, while all the more "psychoanalytic" sections – the discussion on Orpheus and Narcissus, the "Philosophical Interlude" – are annotated. Alas, those two chapters – as well as everything Marcuse wrote on art until the end of his life – are probably the best source we have for understanding the root of his conflicts with Fromm! If, after 1965, they both could agree on the necessity of a reorganized moral life, Fromm (1950a) was much closer to what he identified as a universal humanistic *religious* ethos, while Marcuse spoke explicitly about an *aesthetic* ethos (1969a:26).

In fairness to Fromm (1974b, 1991a), he cannot be said to have been insensitive to art. At one point, he likened the role of the psychoanalyst to that of the artist: "the psychoanalyst is not by any means an artist or dramatist, he is no Shakespeare, but he must have the eyes of a dramatist and be capable of capturing the reality of man" (1966j:6). In many of its fundamental aspects, he was in total agreement with Marcuse's (1978) mature aesthetics:

> Great art has the same function as science. It penetrates the common sense picture of man and nature which like common sense thinking is formed and also distorted by society. Art exposes the *essence* of phenomena, their true reality by penetrating the deceptive surface aspects. The artist is by necessity *critical of* the common sense way of seeing and hearing; as far as he is an artist he is a *radical*, because he goes to the roots; he is an *internationalist*, because he touches upon a reality of existence common to all men. If it is the function of science to make man's thought more *critical*, it is the function of art to make man more *sensitive* to all phenomena of life. The scientific and artistic truth both have in common that they go further than conventional thought and perception in touching reality, that is the forces behind the static appearance.
>
> (1965m:4)

Indeed, Fromm briefly studied literature on surrealism and pornography during the years when he was composing his later criticisms of Marcuse with the help of Sarah Sue Wittes' advice (cf. Wittes_Sarah_Sue_1970-04-09-to). He believed that there was a "destructive tendency" that could be followed "from Marinetti's Manifesto of 1909 to those trends in surrealism which are expressed in Breton and eventually in the cadaver-loving philosophy of Marcuse and Brown" (Stone_I_F_1968-03-08-to). From 1968 on, de Sade joined Marinetti in Fromm's (1964a; 1973a) accusations against the apology of sadism and destructiveness. In reading a book by Herbert Gershman on *The surrealist revolution in France* (1969), he noted his impression that the movement was characterized by its "shoking [sic], sadistic, destroying" intentions. In a footnote excluded from his posthumously published text on "Sexuality and perversions", Fromm wrote:

> The most insightful and brilliant study of sado-masochism I find in Susan Somtag's [sic] *The Pornographic Imagination* in her *Styles of Radical Will,* Farrar, Strauss and Giroux, New York, 1969. She characterizes de Sade's interest in the obliteration of personality as being one

from the view point of power and liberty, and with this characterization introduces a viewpoint [...] close to my own concept of sado-masochism.
(d-1990g-001-eng-type-01:13)

He read Sontag's essay with much attention, and more than once, as Sontag contended that "death is the only end to the odyssey of the pornographic imagination when it becomes systematic; that is, when it becomes focused on the pleasures of transgression rather than mere pleasure itself" (1967:62). In the *Story of O*, Sontag saw a "vision of the world" in which "the highest good is the transcendence of personality" – that is, "the extinction of consciousness", "death itself" (1967:55,57). It is an interesting excursion in the world of the arts, and not an accidental one, since surrealism and situationism were part of the political and cultural *milieu* in which Marcuse was read in France. Marcuse could be critical of surrealism, as in the claim that "it has long since become a commodity" (1967b:115). But he displayed a profound interest in the possibility of turning imagination into a political force – "the technician as artist, society as a work of art" (1967c:128); "moral, psychological, aesthetic, intellectual faculties" as "factors in the material production itself" (1972a:3). In fact, he included "surrealism" alongside the religious minorities and socialist groups forming the history of significant political radicalism – a comparison Fromm would have abhorred (cf. Na.3.235:13).

That said, Fromm didn't think of artistic practice, and the sort of relation artists find between themselves, as models for political relations. Sure enough, he recognized the creative process as one in which a certain union may be found between artist and object (cf. 1956a); he discussed the prevalence of narcissism among artists, but also thought narcissism could be checked in the work process (cf. 1964a; 1973a). Think about it: one of his models for a great artist was Pablo Casals, who indeed was one, but why so? – Because, among other things, Fromm (1974b:108–9) admired in him the capacity to sustain effort and find liberation in his regular musical practice of Bach. This trait – which Fromm usually called "discipline" (1973a:271) – is lacking in his image of a personality without a core, without convictions. It is also lacking in what he saw as Marcuse's idealization of the perversions and of polymorphous sexuality, since for him perversions were themselves the fruit of a repressive society (cf. AUD-1970b).

Fromm distinguished between "authoritarian" discipline which is imposed from without, and a state of effort and concentration that is the "expression of one's will" (1956a:78). He said

> without effort we can't attain any of our goals in life, no matter what the advertisements may claim to the contrary. Anyone who fears effort, anyone who backs off from frustration and possibly even pain will never get anywhere, especially not in analysis.
>
> (1974a:84)

and went on to present a combination of "patience and discipline, to learn, to concentrate, to endure frustration, to practice critical thinking, to overcome one's narcissism and greed" (1973a:271) as the requirements for the practice of any *art*. Of course, Fromm (1993c) wasn't merely referring to art in the aesthetic sense, but to "life" itself, or an "art of living". He was enthusiastic for ethical transformation and "devotion to a goal" of personal change and liberation, whose model may be sought in the history of religious practices, some of which Fromm (1992s) admired so much[5].

Despite his intemperate fondness for Freud's metapsychology, Marcuse bridled at all talk of "ego mastery", arguing that it denotes domination, and is inherently or incipiently conformist, like Freud's valorization of "genital primacy". But while Marcuse (1956) spoke emphatically about the "progressive function" of regression, he was not in favor of overthrowing the conquests of the mature ego completely (cf. 1964, 1967a, 1969a). Nevertheless, he found Fromm's emphasis on ethics quite suspicious. Incidentally, the fact that Fromm included the concept of "will" in his notion of discipline touches upon the heart of his idea of human change. Fromm (1955a) included a change in "practice of life" as a requirement *sine qua non* for characterological transformation. This was yet another aspect of Fromm's ideas that Marcuse (1955) deemed "conformistic" in the *Dissent* debate, which amounts perhaps to a certain absolutism his writing retained in the notion of "Great Refusal", and which Fromm disliked for its inability to discern nuance and transition in transformation – both subjective and social. "Refusal", he would later say, "is a sterile act" (VID-1980a). We learn from another redacted segment that Fromm thought both Marcuse and Sartre wrote within the "apocalyptic" tradition of messianism: "give me freedom (socialism, the new society etc.) or give me death" (d-1968a-000-eng-type-01:11). While this is not a fair evaluation of Marcuse's position, especially in later years, it reflects a lacuna in his style of thinking and writing, which was insensitive to the problem of "transition", and thought of "qualitative difference" as a sudden precipitate, not as the product of painstaking and slow modification, as Fromm (1970b) would have it.

As we reach the late sixties, this state of affairs changes slightly. Marcuse never gives up the notion of Great Refusal, nor does he completely do away with the rhetoric and the vocabulary of "negation". He always celebrated "negation" as a principled "rejection" of participation in the established society, coming from people who have become "incapable of tolerating" the existing state of affairs (Na.3.235:6,9). Politically, this develops into a hope that "absenteeism, wildcat strikes, individual and group sabotage" (1972b:27) and other forms of spontaneous "refusal" might pave the way for social change. He thinks capitalism could end with a "diffuse, decentralized disintegration", adding from dispersed "rebellion" in a series of local communities (Na.3.286:10). But he starts envisioning more of a gradient between present and future possibilities, and he wants them, much like Fromm, embodied in people living here and now – "practice here on earth" (Marcuse, 1969c:188), "in the flesh" (Fromm, 1962a:177). The practice he would like to see, however, he tied not to values or to a religious source of inspiration, but to an idea of imaginative freedom, in which social reproduction and the "free exercise of human faculties" would be reconciled in a collective effort to change the environment and sociability alike (cf. 1969a). Marcuse (1970a), too, recovered the ancient, "technical" sense of "art" – but instead of translating it into the ethical suggestion for an art of living, he rather liked the idea that technique could merge with art and the imaginative faculties, and thus open the room for a fusion between phantasy and reality in the very production of the social realm.

Marcuse aimed at achieving a "harmony of the faculties" (1969a:37) – much like Fromm's (1947a) concept of individuation and the development of character involves the integration between intellectual, sensuous, and affective powers. His model for the politically successful agent was thus, for some time, and in some respects, the artist – not, as in Fromm's case, as a passionate disciplined artisan, but as a daydreamer who lived out his daydreams. This may account for the peculiar fact that, after a thorough criticism of behaviorism and operationalism, followed by a conception of technique as embodiment of domination, Marcuse eventually defended the "translation of values into technical tasks" (1964:232): his "imaginative-phantasistic" conception of social reconstruction wished for a collapse of the difference between work and play.

3 Politics

In the *Dissent* debate, Marcuse (1955) had criticized Fromm's and other's treatment of work as "creative work", but from *Eros and civilization* on his own writings oscillate incessantly between the aspiration for an abolition of work, its merger with play, and a more sober position which still recognizes some dualism between "the realm of necessity and the realm of freedom" (cf. Marcuse 1964, 1969d). Fromm (1968a) criticized the view that play and work could be made completely equivalent because he thought that work performed in non-alienated circumstances need not be toil, but can be a vehicle for personal growth (1956a, 1965a, 1970b). Marcuse agreed with Fromm (1991e) in differentiating alienated work from work in general, but may not have grasped that work could be anything other than toil: in Marx, he wrote, "the construction of a socialist society is a creation rather than a production" (1970b:8). For Fromm "production" would hardly have been separated from creation. Rather, it would have been distinguished from "busy-ness" in the sense of a compulsive action, which expends considerable energy but doesn't enhance the agent's well-being.

If Fromm (1955a; 1968a) had for a long time posed the alternative between "socialism" and "robotism", and was increasingly mistrustful of automation and cybernetics, it was only much later that Marcuse wrote – "Men and women can be computerized into robots, *but they can also refuse!*" (Na.3.374:15). But sadly, from the *Dissent* debate onwards, Marcuse remained incapable of distinguishing between Fromm's (1947a) notion of "productiveness" – which is, first and foremost, a production of oneself and others, not of things – from the demand for "productivity" in the industrial sense. This was a mistake. At the same time, Marcuse (1958) was more sensitive than Fromm to the difference between relations of production on a structural level, and the local organization of work – which had implications for their political views on socialism. This was already hinted at in Marcuse's "Reply" from 1956, but never elaborated fully. In Fromm's drafts for his criticism of Marcuse, however, it did not escape his attention (cf. e-ME). He was attentive not only to their differences with regards to Freud, but also with regards to Marx and to politics. If we scrutinize Fromm's study materials, we find that the deepest source of disagreements between them were never fully articulated, not only because Fromm withdrew much of what he wrote from publication, but also because he never finished writing everything he planned. The oldest sketch for his appendix to *The revolution of hope* includes, as topics to be addressed, not only "the distortion of Freud" – which is what he mostly discussed until the end of his life –, but also "Marx", Marcuse's "theory of revolution", and his relation to "decentralization", among other topics familiar from the published writings, such as "hopelessness" (e-ME:1–3).

Now we can pinpoint one of the blindspots of the original *Dissent* debate: centering on what Freud meant prompted Fromm and Marcuse to overlook the extent to which Fromm's anthropology was shaped by the influence of Marx and a number of other relevant sources. The *1844 Manuscripts* are particularly important for understanding his concept of affirmation and of passions (cf. Fromm, 1968h), and in this, once again, his conception and Marcuse's were very close and very distant at the same time. Marcuse (1956, 1958) was close enough to humanistic interpretations of Marx to incorporate the idea of an optimal human development, of the free interplay of human faculties, the problem of overcoming alienation, and many other topics familiar to Fromm[6]. But his *psychology* was less Marxian than Fromm's – or rather, it was comprised of themes and categories that pertain equally to Marx and the German idealist tradition, reformulated within Freudian notions. Fromm reached a different form of integration between these sources, developing a metapsychology of his own.

Fromm's allusions to revolution and decentralization are more important, however. At the end of the day, they had fundamentally different conceptions of what a progressive political movement should look like. Fromm is not correct that Marcuse was strictly against decentralization – not for the late sixties, when the idea occurs that the "centralized bureaucratic communist [...] organization" (1969a:89) should be one of the targets of the emerging political movements. He would even come to say, a few years later, that "decentralization belongs to the essence of socialism" (Na.3.286:11). Fromm was right, however, that Marcuse (1969d) was mistrustful of the idea that a form of "humanistic planning" in Fromm's (1970e) terms would facilitate a revolution in production. Marcuse thought "those who are to exercise the socialist control must have *the new consciousness*, the *new vital needs* and *goals*, the new values" (Na.3.235:12) beforehand, otherwise they risk falling into exploitation again. The main difficulty lay in the fact that Marcuse's political and economic strategies were at odds with each other. Economically, he favored a higher degree of centralization, of "planning" and "collective control of the process of production and distribution" (Na.3.235:12); but he advocated a very decentralized organization for the New Left, "widely diffused, with a high degree of autonomy, mobility, flexibility" (1969a:89). He envisaged "some kind of diffuse and dispersed disintegration of the system, in which interest, emphasis and activity are shifted to local and regional areas" (1969e:124), and at an earlier point, even wrote that "whatever the peace movement has achieved [...] it achieved by its conscious failure to relate, by its break with the other [social] 'sectors'" (l-unMeDs). Still in 1968, he said that "without organization there cannot be an effective movement" (1968d, s.p.), but an emphasis on the need for finding a form of organization "that combines spontaneity and discipline" (1972d:11) is only typical of his later years.

Now, compare this with Fromm's (1968a) proposal of an American civil society organized in terms of groups and clubs – the former as very small, ethically oriented communities aiming at personal and social transformation; the latter, as larger units, variously composed, but brought together by common interests and by a concerted and sustained reactivation of local political participation. Fromm (1955a) was in favor of regular communal gatherings or "town hall" style meetings as part of political life, whereas Marcuse thought in terms of cultural guerilla and a political-strategic dispersion of antagonistic action. Only with the dissolution of the sixties' enthusiasm did Marcuse go back to emphasizing the need for an "organization of direct democracy" – "a strategy of small groups political and psychological in one" (Na.3.327:7) – and the relevance of "winning quantitative strength" (1972c:3–4). Before that, he authorized the New Left as a "vanguard, or leading minorities, or catalysts" (1968e:9) – "the masses always come afterwards!" (Na.3.235:14). He imagined them as the would-be actual leaders of a new society – "this kind of elite is the hope of a free society – those with education, training, and capacity to rule" (1968d, s.p.) – or more modestly as having a "strictly preparatory" role (1968c:15), being the harbingers of the more progressive ideas of the times – "I never proposed that an intellectual elite governs" (1969f:130). Marcuse's proposal would be one for exceptional political action developed by minorities, whereas Fromm's would be a transition from a bureaucratic form of representative democracy into intensive day-to-day political participation by the mass of people.

This is evidenced in Fromm's rather ambivalent attitude towards the feminist and Black movements in the 1970s. While he was uncompromisingly enthusiastic about the relevance of emancipation from racialized and gendered domination, he was rather unhappy with the way the movements actually behaved. "The idea that blacks should unite with women and workers seems to me somewhat naive", he tells Sarah Wittes.

> It seems to me that much of the women's revolution or emancipation is like that of many blacks – a wish to be like the dominant white man rather than to transcend his pattern and to lead a revolution against him.
>
> (Wittes_Sarah_Sue_1971–01–11-to)

The reasons for this estimate were different in both cases. On the topic of women's emancipation, Fromm vacillated between recognition of gendered traits as universally shared by human beings, and the idea that the movement should care for the expression and development of femininity as such, and not for the approximation of women to traces of male dominance as they existed (cf. AUD-1980g). Certainly his attitude partook also of the fact that his political stance was favorable to gender equality, but not to the equality of sexual practices.

As regards identification built around ethnic or national categories, as was the case for some parts of the Black movement, Fromm thought that: "it should be a goal for the black movement to achieve a new synthesis of soul and intellect both for the blacks and for the whites, rather than to admire and to be jealous of a decaying white civilization". He thought this would amount to "establishing identity" in reference to "the present situation of the group and its aspirations for the future", as opposed to founding it in reference "to the past". A sense of identity developed around the sense of present exploitation and marginalization would be politically more trustworthy than one based on ancestorship:

> African identity is a sham first of all because they feel like Americans and not like Africans and, secondly, because the various cultures from which they came are so different that one could not speak of a common root either in language or in culture or in psychology.
>
> (Mumford_Lewis_1968–12–08-to)

His ground for disagreement was, therefore, the feeling that such movements did not reach a degree of universality in their aspirations that would allow them to transcend present-day society. This difference between a *minority* politics in Marcuse's case and a *majority* politics in Fromm's case is intimately related to their different models, in the arts and in religion, for radical social transformation. It leads back to their different relations to McCarthy, as well as to Fromm's more "ecumenical" temperament, as opposed to

Marcuse's individualistic style of thinking up to the early seventies. That said, it is also important to note that Marcuse was gradually persuaded that among the "most urgent *tasks of the left*" was the formation of a "united front" and the "suspension of the ideological skirmishes" (Na.3.310:6). Even so, Marcuse's preaching of "the artist as technician" – of a collapse between imagination and work, so as to live social life as a constructive form of play – would require a more individualistic modus operandi than Fromm's ethical approach, in which communal bonds are strengthened through the aspirations towards a common vision. These are two different forms of organization. Marcuse's notion fluctuates between a stylization of society and a stylization of oneself, whereas Fromm values the constructive efforts of inspired groups for moral reform, which necessarily includes a strong reference to others in its constitution.

Evidence for that can be traced in their different concepts of solidarity. Fromm's (1962a) notion of solidarity was deeply tied to his rejection of nationalism and tribalism, and his desire to cultivate the capacity to embrace cultural differences as local, particular expressions of something universally given to the members of the species. This approach is congruent with his belief that there could be political progress without a descent into violence and chaos. The idea that a new society could emerge, organized democratically in lively groups despite those differences is a morphological correlate of the "humanistic" concept of solidarity: unity in difference. In Marcuse, we find reference both to a "violent solidarity" of the New Left, and to solidarity as "autonomy: self-determination" (1969a:88). Of course, Fromm affirmed that true solidarity does not result in deindividualization, but in context, this proposal in Marcuse's writing is an expression of the difficulty he had in reconciling the risk of fragmentation between the New Left groups, which he would later acknowledge and criticize, and a fear for authoritarian forms of "sticking together" in their wish for political discipline. He and Fromm could agree on the idea of solidarity as "cooperation" in "work and purpose" (Marcuse 1969a:88,91), but beyond the formal definition for this or that word, they were coming at these ideas from very different perspectives on how to engage people to collaborate politically.

This tension had consequences for their conception of how political action should occur. Among Fromm's drafts on Marcuse, we find the isolated sentence: "leads to putsch" (e-ME:3). This annotation suggests that Fromm feared Marcuse's "minority" tactics as possibly leading to a backlash. He regarded the idea of a violent revolution in the US "unrealistic" already in 1955(a), and developed this into the notion that a breakdown of the US political system would have as its consequence a "brutal dictatorship" (1968a:98) – hence one more reason for sticking to the elections. He wrote to Mumford in 1969:

> Psychologically speaking it seems to me the revolutionary tendencies which aim at the violent over-throw of the present system resemble the

fascist model and not that of classical revolutionary concepts from Marx to Lenin. Both Marx and Lenin were deeply convinced that revolution is possible only if you have, if not a majority, at least a large part of the population with you. The idea of the coup by which a small minority which has little support in the total population, can seize power, is typically Nazi and Fascist.

(Mumford_Lewis_1969–04–30-to)

We can only speculate what Fromm would have told Marcuse if he had discussed his paper on revolution at the 1968 Paris Symposium. But we know he was unhappy with what he read, as his markings on the respective paper indicate (side by side with the expression "new needs and new values", he writes: "phraseology"). To be sure, Marcuse's approach was more complex than Fromm acknowledged. For one, Marcuse held the idea that the political minorities should work as anticipators and "catalysts" of a change that would require the participation of the mass and majority of the workers, otherwise it wouldn't happen: "a radical social change is naturally unthinkable without the great majority of the working class" (1972d:11). This went both for the US and on the level of international relations and anticolonial struggles (cf. Marcuse, 1967d; 1969a; 1972a). Still, he had earlier felt the need to justify revolutionary violence as "counter-violence" against the violence of the status quo (cf. Marcuse, 1965a; 1966a), and hence didn't discard the possibility of a political revolution in the strong sense, as Fromm did in the American context. In this respect Marcuse oscillated between rejection – "the situation is not at all revolutionary. It is not even pre-revolutionary" (Marcuse, 1968f:6) – and encouragement – "cultural revolution but not (*yet*) political and economic revolution" (1972a:79). So they could agree on the need for a "cultural revolution" or "renaissance" as something irreducible to political and social revolution, but not on the political means prompting this revolution. Hence another of Fromm's complaints against radical youth: "the concepts of many of them are naïve and they have not even made up their minds whether this is a revolutionary situation in which revolutionary tactics are adequate or not" (Stone_I_F_1968–03–08-to).

Indeed, the difference between their aspirations was already evident in the contrast between *The sane society* and *Eros and civilization*. In the former, Fromm wants to transform passive consumers back into active, engaged and well-informed citizens. In the latter book, Marcuse's blend of Orpheus and Narcissus expresses a mixture of the desire for "pacification of existence" (1964:220) – the satisfaction and quietness of desires – and a heightened valuation of the realm of imagination as a source for well-being. So Fromm and Marcuse are never so close or so distant from each other as in their valuation of the political function of imagination. But whereas Marcuse (1956) privileged *phantasy* and its embodiment in the arts as the model for the political ethos he wished for, Fromm (1947a) privileged the notion of *vision*, of prophetic ascent, as his guideline. Whereas individual "phantasy" presupposes suspending the immediate relations to others and introverting one's interest into the inner world of dreams and daydreams, "vision" implies a directive element to action, as well as coordination of activity with others. In the one case, reality is potentially overbearing: fulfillment of phantasy is increasingly unstable when it passes from a "community of daydreams" (Sachs, 1920) into an attempt at acting together, as it must reconcile – not merely individual desires and tastes, but also a variety of focal points of repression, from which phantasy originally sprung, and which threaten to be overstepped in the act. In the other case, acting on behalf of a "vision" brings the singularity of each one's wishes in greater harmony with shared communal aspirations, but precisely for that reason, its power in feeding collective action is somewhat diminished, the more interest is diverted from the image, back into current existence. Phantasy is defeated by frustration; a vision may be defeated by its success.

Here lies the peculiarity of religious relationships when transposed onto the political realm: they offer a chance that suffering and defeat may strengthen them. Fromm (1970h) himself recognized symbolic attachments and ideals as part of what mobilizes human vital interests, and is protected accordingly. The same effect is not characteristic of aesthetic relationships, based on reciprocal enjoyment. Their aspiration once transposed onto political form is to make political alliance and community coincide in action: the making of a new society should become identical with enjoyment. Disturbances on the capacity to share pleasure and phantasy represent immediate dangers to the existence of the political formation; defeat is easily followed by disinvestment and dissolution of organization. Only where creative collaboration entails other forms of relatedness does it recover the capacity to prompt the relation to continue not only despite, but *because* of adversity.

Fromm's religious model distrusts the fragility of this form of relatedness, which can only survive as long as pleasure is thriving. Correspondingly, each form of organization implies a different relation to authority. Fromm deemed Marcuse's radicalism to be a form of rebelliousness, more than a genuine revolutionary impulse. It formulates the anticipation of a better life in reference to what can be felt, here and now, as relief from burden and fear. To allow ourselves an incursion in the jargon: "the negative" remains tied to "the positive", and does not truly move beyond it. On the other hand, Fromm himself was not exempt from idealization of authority, albeit not exactly in "authoritarian" terms – as can be seen in his relation to those he considered as "Masters of Living". This is but the other side of the difference in their relation to satisfaction – or, more precisely, to the kinds of satisfaction they envisioned. The two aspects are intertwined: Marcuse's hedonism and Fromm's eudaimonism reflect two different forms of dealing with desire and renunciation.

Notes

1 Actually, Fenichel was equidistant from both Fromm and Marcuse on this issue. In discarding the idea of an innate propensity toward death, and in his concepts of life and death, Fenichel was somewhat closer to Fromm's (1962a) mature conceptions: "The young organism is full of prospective potentialities. Every stretch of life it passes through crystallizes out of it 'structure' which makes it 'rigid', limits its prospective potentialities and brings it nearer to the inorganic". They would have disagreed, however, on the idea that the life process is "a course toward death", as Fenichel (1935:371) put it. Fromm agreed that "there is only one certainty in life: that all men die" (1973a:325), but did not reduce the life process to a gradual realization of this end.
2 This recording presents Fromm tackling many of the political issues of his day and being interrupted by a young man who, angered by comments on tradition and the youth communes, proposes that they substitute his "talk" and the "boredom" it provokes for a love-in, where they would "sit and touch each other and love each other". After some heat, the lecture proceeds with Fromm publicly criticizing Marcuse's take on regression and the Great Refusal as forms of an "infantile paradise" (AUD-1968a).
3 Marshall McLuhan experienced a similar fate – Fromm includes him in many of the critical passages which he later withheld between 1968 and 1970. Here's an example: "There are those, like Marcuse, who think that in a materially completely satisfied cybernated (and 'non-repressive') society, there are no more human conflicts like those [...] which are expressed in the Greek or Shakespearian drama or the great novels" (d-1968a-000-eng-type-04:V-20–21). Incidentally, it can be said that despite his openness to certain forms of modernism, Marcuse's (1978) aesthetics became more pronouncedly universalist as years passed – he recognized something of universal and trans-historical in great art, and would thus probably have disputed Fromm's appraisal of his position.
4 Fromm may have written this with Alan Watts in mind. According to his friend Dom Aelred Graham, Watts understood "the hippies" as "a kind of parallel to the early Christians" (1968:7) – a comparison Fromm would have abhorred, as he abhorred Watt's understanding of Zen (cf. d-1991d-000-eng-type-04).
5 Another intriguing way of gauging the relationship between Fromm and Marcuse is in their relation to Alfred Whitehead. It should be remembered that the first occurrence of the notion of "Great Refusal" in Marcuse (1956:146) is derived directly from Whitehead, precisely in a commentary he made on the arts. Later, in *One-dimensional man* (1964:228), he wrote approvingly of Whitehead's idea that "*the function of Reason is to promote the art of life*" (1929:4,8). Fromm couldn't have agreed more – indeed, he seems to have read his copy of this book with great pleasure. He takes note of this reference to Whitehead as he reads *One-dimensional man*, perhaps with some puzzlement in seeing his rival affirm a position so close to his own (cf. e-ME). Other aspects of Whitehead's argument – the distinction between Ulysses' and Plato's "reason" – are on his mind as well when he writes his marginalia on Marcuse's notion of performance principle (cf. 1956:159, Fromm's copy). We need only remember Marcuse's rejection of all "teleological philosophy" in the same book to measure his distance from Fromm.
6 Here, Marcuse's (1956, 1958, 1969d) differences with Raya Dunayevskaya and Gustav Bally on workers' organization and the concept of work are among the most telling indicators, in a comparison with Fromm.

Bibliography

Primary sources – Fromm

Fromm's correspondence

Althusser_Louis_1964–1901–08-to: Fromm to Louis Althusser, January 8th, 1964
Anshen_Ruth_Nanda_1975–1901–21-to: Fromm to Ruth Nanda Anshen, January 21st, 1975
Anshen_Ruth_Nanda_1975–1902–18-to: Fromm to Anshen, February 18th, 1975
Coffin_Tristram_1974–1902–01-to: Fromm to Tristram Coffin, February 1st, 1974
Dunayevskaya_Raya_1968–1907–31-to: Fromm to Raya Dunayevskaya, July 31st, 1968 (apud Anderson and Rockwell, 2012)
Dunayevskaya_Raya_1968–1908–10-to: Dunayevskaya to Fromm, August 10th, 1968
Howe_Irving_1963–1903–01-by: Irving Howe to Fromm, March 1st, 1963
Hughes_Stuart_H_1968–1901–16-by: H. *Stuart Hughes to Fromm*, January 16th, 1968
Marcuse_Herbert_1963–1912–08-by: Herbert Marcuse to Fromm, December 8th, 1963
Marcuse_Herbert_1967–1912–27-to: Fromm to Marcuse, 27th December, 1967
Marcuse_Herbert_1968–1901–22-by: Marcuse to Fromm, January 22nd, 1968
Mumford_Lewis_1968–1912–08-to: Fromm to Lewis Mumford, December 8th, 1968
Mumford_Lewis_1969–1901–23-to: Fromm to Mumford, January 23rd, 1969
Mumford_Lewis_1969–1904–30-to: Fromm to Mumford, April 30th, 1969
Plastrik_Stanley_1956–1905–01-by: Stanley Plastrik to Fromm, May 1st, 1956
Schaff_Adam_1968–1907–04-to: Adam Schaff to Fromm, July 4th, 1968
Stone_I_F_1968–1903–08-to: Fromm to I. F. Stone, March 8th, 1968
Wittes_Sarah_Sue_1970–1904–09-to: Fromm to Sarah Sue Wittes, April 9th, 1970
Wittes_Sarah_Sue_1971–1901–11-to: Fromm to Wittes, January 11th, 1971

Unpublished texts, lectures, interviews by Fromm

u-1949: "The human dignity of the psychotic person. In memoriam Harry Stack Sullivan". Address at the Memorial Meeting for Harry Stack Sullivan, May 17th, 1949, at the William Alanson White Institute.

Drafts, typescripts and study materials by Fromm

d-1968a-000-eng-type-01: typescripts for *The revolution of hope*.
d-1968a-000-eng-type-04: typescripts for *The revolution of hope*.
d-1968a-000-eng-type-05: typescripts for *The revolution of hope*.
d-1970f-000-eng-type-01: typescript for "*The significance of the theory of mother right for today*".
d-1977g-000-deu-type-01: typescripts of a German translation of "*My own concept of man*".
d-1990h-eng-type-01: typescripts for "*The alleged radicalism of Herbert Marcuse*".
d-1990g-000-eng-draft-01: drafts for "*Sexuality and sexual perversions*".
d-1990g-001-eng-type-01: typescripts for "*Sexuality and sexual perversions*".

d-1991d-002-eng-draft-04: transcription of the recordings published as *The art of listening*.

d-RoHD: drafts for *The revolution of hope*. Still without an identifying code.

e-ME: Marcuse Exzerpte: transcription and comments on some of Marcuse's books, especially Eros and civilization and One-dimensional man, presumably taken between 1968 and 1969. Still without an identifying code.

Audio and video recordings

AUD-1968a: "*The myth of paradise*". Pacific Radio (?) – Lecture given around 1968 at a High School in New York.

AUD-1970b: "*Die dialektische humanistische Revision der freudschen Theorie des Menschen*". ORF Salzburg – Lecture at the Österreichischen Rundfunk, Studio Salzburg, on April 13th, 1970.

AUD-1980e: "*Mut zum Sein*". TV interview with Guido Ferrari von RTSI Lugano, 08.03.1980 in Locarno.

AUD-1980g: "*Antworten von Fromm auf Fragen von Boris Luban Plozza*". Brief unpublished interview.

VID-1963f: "*On pyschoanalytic thecnique*". Second part of an interview with Richard Evans in December 1963.

VID-1980a: "*Gespräch mit Erich Fromm*". SWF – Interview with Jürgen Lodemann in Locarno on the occasion of Fromm's 80th birthday. March 1980.

Primary sources – Marcuse

Marcuse's correspondence

l-unMeDs: Marcuse to Mike Davis, undated, presumably early 1965.

l-660603RPMe: REP to Marcuse, June 3rd, 1966.

l-661123MeMe: Marcuse to Louis Menashe, November 23rd, 1966.

l-680714DaMe: Dunayevskaya to Marcuse, July 14th, 1968 (apud Anderson and Rockwell 2012).

l-680724MeDa: Marcuse to Dunayevskaya, July 24th, 1968 (apud Anderson and Rockwell 2012).

Unpublished texts and lectures by Marcuse

Na.3.219: Lectures for the American Civil Liberties Union of Southern California, presumably given May 17th, 1969.

Na.3.235: "What is a 'New Culture' and how are we going to get there". Drafts for two lectures presented at New York University, presumably in 1968.

Na.3.272: "The little idea". Undated typescript commenting on problems of strategy and organization in politics, presumably from the late sixties.

Na.3.281: "The critical spirit". Drafts of a lecture presented at the Leo Baeck Temple in Los Angeles, May 6th, 1970.

Na.3.286: "*Gewalt, Organisation und Erziehung*". Published in a journal called links, s/d.

Na.3.310: ""*Warum radikale Veränderung? Kein Problem in der Dritten Welt*". Drafts for a lecture given in Freiburg, June 20th, 1972.
Na.3.313: "Vietnam Teach-in". Draft of a lecture given at the University of California, San Diego, January 6th, 1973.
Na.3.327: "On students, the university, and education". Drafts for a lecture presented at the Berkeley Campus of the University of California, October 18th, 1975.
Na.3.374: "Radical change". Drafts for a lecture presented at Muir College, April 23rd, 1979.
Na.3.995: a collection of letters in support of Marcuse, as of the threats he faced in 1968.

Drafts, typescripts and study materials by Marcuse

1956b-eng-type-01: typescript of Marcuse's 1956 "Reply", with markings by Fromm. Unlike other Marcuse files, this is held at the Erich Fromm Institute.

Published references

Anderson, Kevin B.; Rockwell, Russell (eds.). *The Dunayevskaya-Marcuse-Fromm correspondence, 1954–1978*. New York: Lexington Books, 2012.
Aronson, Ronald. Dear Herbert. George Fischer (ed.). *The revival of American socialism*. New York: Oxford University Press, 1971.
Fenichel, Otto. A critique of the death instinct. *The collected papers of Otto Fenichel*, first series. New York: W. W. Norton & Co., Inc., [1935]/1953.
Freud, Sigmund. Drei Abhandlungen zur Sexualtheorie. *Gesammelte Werke V*. Frankfurt: S. Fischer Verlag, [1905–1924]/1968.
Freud, Sigmund. Jenseits des Lutsprinzips. *Gesammelte Werke XIII*. Frankfurt: S. Fischer Verlag, [1920a]/1967.
Freud, Sigmund. Das Ich und das Es. *Gesammelte Werke XIII*. Frankfurt: S. Fischer Verlag, [1923]/1967.
Freud, Sigmund. Das ökonomische Problem des Maoschismus. *Gesammelte Werke XIII*. Frankfurt: S. Fischer Verlag, [1924]/1967.
Fromm, Erich. Sozialpsychogischer Teil. Max Horkheimer (ed.). *Studien über Autorität und Familie*. Frankfurt: Dietrich zu Klampen Verlag, [1936a]/1987.
Fromm, Erich. *Escape from freedom*. New York: Henry Holt & Company, [1941a]/1994.
Fromm, Erich. *Man for himself*. New York: Henry Holt & Company, [1947a]/1990.
Fromm, Erich. *Psychoanalysis and religion*. New York: Bantam Books, [1950a]/1967.
Fromm, Erich. The psychology of normalcy. *Dissent*: 1:139–143, 1954a.
Fromm, Erich. *The sane society*. New York: Henry Holt & Company, [1955a]/1990.
Fromm, Erich. The human implications of instinctivist 'radicalism': a reply to Herbert Marcuse. *Dissent*: 2:342–349, 1955b.
Fromm, Erich. Psychoanalysis. J.R. Newman (ed.). *What is science?* New York: Simon and Schuster, 1955e.
Fromm, Erich. Love in America. Huston Smith (ed.). *The search for America*. Englewood Cliffs: Prentice Hall, 1959d.
Fromm, Erich. Psychoanalysis and Zen Buddhism. *Psychoanalysis and Zen Buddhism*. London: Unwin Paperbacks, [1960a]/1987.

Fromm, Erich. *May man prevail?* New York: Doubleday & Company, Inc., [1961a]/1961.
Fromm, Erich. *Marx's concept of man*. New York: Bloomsbury, [1961b]/2013.
Fromm, Erich. *Beyond the chains of illusion*. New York: Continuum, [1962a]/2001.
Fromm, Erich. The revolutionary character. *The dogma of Christ*. New York: Holt, Rinehart and Winston, [1963b]/1992.
Fromm, Erich. *The heart of man*. New York: Harper and Row, 1964a.
Fromm, Erich. (ed.). *Socialist humanism*. New York: Doubleday, 1965a.
Fromm, Erich. *You shall be as gods*. New York: Fawcett Premier, [1966a]/1983.
Fromm, Erich. Science, Art and Peace. *Co-Existence: III–IV*, 1965m.
Fromm, Erich. Marxismus, Psychoanalyse und "wirkliche Wirklichkeit". *Tagebuch*: 21 (9):5f, 1966j.
Fromm, Erich. Prophets and priests. *On disobedience*. New York: Harper Perennial, [1967b]/2010.
Fromm, Erich. *The revolution of hope*. New York: Bantam Books, 1968a.
Fromm, Erich. Marx's contribution to the knowledge of man. *The crisis of psychoanalysis*. New York: Holt, Reinehart and Winston, [1968h]/1970.
Fromm, Erich. *The crisis of psychoanalysis* New York: Holt, Rinehart and Winston, 1970a.
Fromm, Erich. The crisis of psychoanalysis. *The crisis of psychoanalysis*. New York: Holt, Rinehart and Winston, 1970c.
Fromm, Erich. Freud's model of man and its social determinants. *The crisis of psychoanalysis*. New York: Henry Holt & Company, [1970d]/1991.
Fromm, Erich. Humanistic planning. *The crisis of psychoanalysis*. New York: Holt, Reinehart and Winston, [1970e]/1970.
Fromm, Erich. The significance of the theory of mother right for today. *The crisis of psychoanalysis*. New York: Holt, Reinehart and Winston, 1970f.
Fromm, Erich. On the theory and strategy of peace. *On disobedience and other essays*. London: Routledge & Kegan Paul, [1970h]/1984.
Fromm, Erich. *The anatomy of human destructiveness*. New York. Henry Holt & Company, [1973a]/1992.
Fromm, Erich. Psychology for nonpsychologists. *For the love of life*. New York: The Free Press, [1974a]/1986.
Fromm, Erich. In the name of life: a portrait through dialogue. *For the love of life*. New York: The Free Press, [1974b]/1986.
Fromm, Erich. *To have or to be?*. New York: Bantam Books, [1976a]/1981.
Fromm, Erich. Marx and religion. Seyed Javad Miri; Robert Lake; Tricia M. Kress (eds.). *Reclaiming the sane society*. Rotterdam: Sense Publishers, [1979b]/2014.
Fromm, Erich. *Arbeiter und Angestellt am Vorabend des Dritten Reiches*. Giessen: Psychosozial-Verlag, [1980a]/2019.
Fromm, Erich. Affluence and ennui in our society. *For the love of life*. New York: The Free Press, [1983b]/1986.
Fromm, Erich. Who is man? *For the love of life*. New York: The Free Press, [1983d]/1986.
Fromm, Erich. *The art of being*. New York: Continuum, [1989a]/1998.
Fromm, Erich. *The revision of psychoanalysis*. Boulder: Westview Press, [1990a]/1992.
Fromm, Erich. On my psychoanalytic approach. *The revision of psychoanalysis*. Boulder: Westview Press, [1990d]/1992.
Fromm, Erich. The necessity for the revision of psychoanalysis. *The revision of psychoanalysis*. Boulder: Westview Press, [1990e]/1992.

Fromm, Erich. The dialectic revision of psychoanalysis. *The revision of psychoanalysis*. Boulder: Westview Press, [1990f]/1992.
Fromm, Erich. Sexuality and sexual perversions. *The revision of psychoanalysis*. Boulder: Westview Press, [1990g]/1992.
Fromm, Erich. The alleged radicalism of Herbert Marcuse. *The revision of psychoanalysis*. Boulder: Westview Press, [1990h]/1992.
Fromm, Erich. Political radicalism in the United States and its critique. *Fromm Forum*: 25:115–126, [1990i]/2021.
Fromm, Erich. *The art of listening*. London: Constable, [1991a]/1994.
Fromm, Erich. Therapeutic aspects of psychoanalysis. *The art of listening*. London: Constable, [1991d]/1994.
Fromm, Erich. Modern man's pathology of normalcy. *The pathology of normalcy*. New York: American Mental Health Foundation, [1991e]/2010.
Fromm, Erich. The idea of a world conference. *On being human*. New York: Continuum. [1992n]/2005.
Fromm, Erich. Meister Eckhart and Karl Marx on having and being. *On being human*. New York: Continuum, [1992s]/2005.
Fromm, Erich. On the art of living. *The essential Erich Fromm*. New York: Continuum, [1993c]/1995.
Fromm, Erich, Maccoby, Michael. *Social character in a Mexican village*. New York: Routledge, [1970b]/1996.
Fromm, Erich, et al. The People's Choice. *The New York Review of Books* (08/22/1968).
Graham, Dom Aelred. *Conversations*. New York: Harcourt, Brace & World, Inc., 1968.
Kellner, Douglas; Pierce, Clayton. Editors' comments. *Collected papers of Herbert Marcuse, vol. 5*. London: Routledge, 2011.
MacIntyre, Alasdair. Review of The dogma of Christ. *New Statesman* (22/11/1963):748, 1963.
MacIntyre, Alasdair. *Herbert Marcuse*. London: Harper Collins, 1970.
Marcuse, Herbert. *Reason and revolution*. New York: Oxford University Press, 1941.
Marcuse, Herbert. The social implications of Freudian "revisionism". *Dissent*: 2 (3):221–240, 1955.
Marcuse, Herbert. *Eros and civilization*. Boston: Beacon Press, [1956]/1966.
Marcuse, Herbert. A reply to Erich Fromm. *Dissent*: 3(1):79–81, 1956b.
Marcuse, Herbert. Theory and therapy in Freud. *Collected papers of Herbert Marcuse, vol. 5*. London: Routledge, [1957]/2011.
Marcuse, Herbert. Preface. Raya Dunayevskaya. *Marxism and freedom*. New York: Bookman Associates, 1958.
Marcuse, Herbert. *One-dimensional man*. Boston: Beacon Press, 1964.
Marcuse, Herbert. Repressive tolerance. *A critique of pure tolerance*. Boston: Beacon Press, 1965a.
Marcuse, Herbert. Socialist humanism?Erich Fromm (ed.). *Socialist humanism*. New York: Doubleday, 1965b.
Marcuse, Herbert. Ethics and revolution. Richard T. De George (ed.). *Ethics and society*. Garden City: Anchor Books, 1966a.
Marcuse, Herbert. Political preface, 1966. *Eros and civilization*. Boston: Beacon Press, 1966b.
Marcuse, Herbert. Love mystified: a critique of Norman O. Brown. *Negations*. London: MayFly Books, [1967a]/2009.

Marcuse, Herbert. Art in the one-dimensional society. *Collected papers of Herbert Marcuse, vol. 4: Art and liberation.* London: Routledge, [1967b]/2007.
Marcuse, Herbert. Society as a work of art. *Collected papers of Herbert Marcuse, vol. 4.* London: Routledge, [1967c]/2007.
Marcuse, Herbert. The concept of negation in the dialectic. *Telos*: 8:130–132, 1967d.
Marcuse, Herbert. Aggressiveness in advanced industrial society. *Negations.* London: MayFly Books, [1968a]/2009.
Marcuse, Herbert. Destruktiver und konstruktiver Hass. *Die Tat* (12/11/1968):s.p., 1968b.
Marcuse, Herbert. Reexamination of the concept of revolution. *Diogenes*: 16 (64):17–26, 1968c.
Marcuse, Herbert. Student rebels hawk the views of the mild Dr. Marcuse: interview with Bruce Cook. *The National Observer* (07/08/1968):s.p., 1968d.
Marcuse, Herbert. Marcuse: turning point in the struggle: interview with Robert Allen. *The Guardian* (11/09/1968):9, 1968e.
Marcuse, Herbert. Marcuse vows he won't be scared, will teach in Fall: interview with Dorothy Townsend. *LA Times* (07/07/1968):1,6, 1968f.
Marcuse, Herbert. *An essay on liberation.* Boston: Beacon Press, 1969a.
Marcuse, Herbert. The obsolescence of psychoanalysis. *Collected papers of Herbert Marcuse, vol. 5.* London: Routledge, [1969b]/2011.
Marcuse, Herbert. The role of religion in a changing society. *Collected papers of Herbert Marcuse, vol. 5.* London: Routledge, [1969c]/2011.
Marcuse, Herbert. The realm of freedom and the realm of necessity: a reconsideration. *Praxis*:5:20–25, 1969d.
Marcuse, Herbert. On the New Left. *Collected papers of Herbert Marcuse, vol. 3.* London: Routledge, [1969e]/2005.
Marcuse, Herbert. Interview with Harold Keen. *Collected papers of Herbert Marcuse, vol. 3.* London: Routledge, [1969f]/2005.
Marcuse, Herbert. Art as a form of reality. *Collected papers of Herbert Marcuse, vol. 4.* London: Routledge, [1970a]/2007.
Marcuse, Herbert. Marxism and humanity. John C. Raines, Thomas Dean (eds.). *Marxism and radical religion.* Philadelphia: Temple University Press, 1970b.
Marcuse, Herbert. *Counter-revolution and revolt.* Boston: Beacon Press, 1972a.
Marcuse, Herbert. Blue-collar revolution. *New York Times* (08/07/1972):27, 1972b.
Marcuse, Herbert. Möglichkeiten radikaler Veränderung in hochentwickelten industriellen Gesellschaften. *Freiburger Studentenzeitung basis* (07/20/1972):1–4, 1972c.
Marcuse, Herbert. Die verlegenheit des revolutionären Geistes. *Süddeutsche Zeitung* (07/15/1972):11, 1972d.
Marcuse, Herbert. *The aesthetic dimension.* Boston: Beacon Press, 1978.
Marcuse, Herbert. Ecology and the critique of modern society. *Capitalism, nature, socialism*: 3(3):29–48, [1979a]/1992.
Marcuse, Herbert. The failure of the New Left? *New German Critique*: 18:3–11, 1979b.
Sachs, Hanns. The community of daydreams. *The creative unconscious.* London: LLC, [1920]/2013.
Schachtel, Ernest. On memory and childhood amnesia. *Metamorphosis.* New York: Basic Books, [1947]/1959.
Schatz, Oskar (ed.). *Der Friede im nuklearen Zeitalter.* München: Manz Verlag, 1970a.

Schatz, Oskar (ed.). *Die erschrekende Zivilisation.* Wien: Europa Verlag, 1970b.
Sontag, Susan. The pornographic imagination. *Styles of radical will.* New York: Farrar, Straus and Giroux, [1967]/1969.
Thompson, Clara. *Psychoanalysis.* New York: Hermitage House, Inc., [1950]/1951.
Whitehead, Alfred North. *The function of reason.* Boston: Beacon Press, [1929]/1967.

Secondary literature

Bierhoff, Burkhard. *Erich Fromm.* Darmstadt: Westdeutscher Verlag, 1993.
Bierhoff, Burkhard. Triebstrutur oder soziale Beziehungen. Anmerkungen zur Kulturismus-Debatte. Internationalen Erich-Fromm-Gesellschaft (ed.). *Wissenschaft vom Menschen: 2.* München: LIT-Verlag, 1995.
Burston, Daniel. *The legacy of Erich Fromm.* Cambridge: Harvard University Press, 1991.
Jacoby, Russell. *Social amnesia.* New York: Beacon Press, 1975.
Jay, Martin. The Frankfurt school's critique of Marxist humanism. *Social Research*:39(2):285–305, 1972.
Kolakowski, Lezsek. *Main currents of Marxism: vols. 1–3.* Oxford: Clarendon Press, 1978.
Lichtheim, George. [1958]/1974. *From Marx to Hegel.* New York: The Seabury Press.
McLaughlin, Neil. Origin myths in the social sciences: Fromm, the Frankfurt school, and the emergence of critical theory. *The Canadian Journal of Sociology*: 24(1):109–139, 1999.
McLaughlin, Neil. *Erich Fromm and global public sociology.* London: Bristol University Press, 2021.
Rickert, John. The Fromm-Marcuse debate revisited. *Theory and Society*:15 (3):351–400, 1986.
Weber, Michael. Die gesellschaftliche Relevanz des Fromm-Marcuse-Konflikts. Internationalen Erich-Fromm-Gesellschaft (ed.). *Wissenschaft vom Menschen: 2.* München: LIT-Verlag, 1995.
Wheatland, Thomas. *The Frankfurt School in exile.* Minneapolis: The University of Minessota Press, 2009.

Part III

Ontology and the Clinic

This part develops Fromm's anthropological and sociological premises into their most important theoretical consequence: his conception of psychic development. Chapter IV infers Fromm's understanding of psychic determinacies from his psychoanalytic and social psychological notions. It is not concerned with their systematic presentation, but rather with interpreting those concepts which better express how psychic structures form and change. The results of that interpretation are grouped as a series of *ontological* categories or determining relations, which allow us to evaluate some of the contradictory tendencies in Fromm's characterology and normative psychology. Chapter V complements these results with an inquiry into Fromm's *clinical practice*, showing how his ontological premises impact upon, and derive from, his understanding of the goals and technique of psychoanalysis.

Chapter 4

IV Aspects of Ontology (1937–1964)

1 Phenomenology and Economy

When we considered human faculties *as powers*, we dealt with them in abstraction of their effective development – which means in isolation from one another. In abstraction, sensory life bears a determination of its own, and so also emotional and intellectual life. In reality, no sensory act is free from affection or thought. The same is true for other relations between powers. They only behave as autonomous parcels of psychic life if subjective, historical alienation splits them again.

Let us now consider these faculties *as capacities*, in the process of their actualization. Their relations then originate the categories of psychic life. Departing from sensory stimulation in *reproductive perception*, we arouse *affects*. The incision of affects over sensation engenders *generative perception* – phantasy and symbolization with images. This is the domain of *imagination*. The relationship between the affective and intellectual spheres, on its turn, is the domain of *reason*. An affect connected to an idea engenders a *passion* – here, still as a singular passion with a determinate object, as is characteristic for childhood. Once split from ideas, passions decay into *attitudes*. Attitudes are inclinations to a way of desiring, without a determinate object, and forever seeking one. Affective reactions bring conjugated attitudes: from tenderness comes love, from hatred comes destructiveness, from impotence comes sadism. A fixated attitude, meeting again singular ideas as subsequent objects, generates the finite passions of the adult human being. Finally, the relationship between the intellectual and sensory spheres constitutes the domain of *self-awareness*. Values are the sensory concomitants of object relations – the objects effectively orienting conduct, as apprehended in language (by contrast to ideals, which are originated in joining attitudes to images). Values and ideals pertain to the influx of thought over action. They are the last elements in this cumulative structure before its realization in the act – as sensory activity (cf. Fromm, 1941a; 1947a; 1955a).

An affect is a "reaction" to an object; an attitude is a "readiness" for desire; a passion is a "response" to human existential needs. Attitudes occupy a similar position in Fromm as "drives" do in Freud (1915a) after fixated by primary repression. Fromm treats them as equivalent to "object relations". It can thus seem that the difference between *Trieb* and *Einstellung* is lost, but this is not the case. The problem is nominal. Fromm uses the notion of "attitudes" to refer to phenomena in two different levels. Basic, primary attitudes – narcissism, sadism, masochism, everything pertaining to "drives" in Freud – must be distinguished from "character traits" themselves, which are secondary attitudes, derived from those first ones.

For Fromm, attitudes are *conjunctive*: they invest both the subject herself and other objects. "The attitudes toward others and toward oneself, far from being contradictory, in principle run parallel" (Fromm, 1941a:97). Another property is their capacity to *generalize* across the psychic apparatus. They are matricial sources of desire, and fight to determine other psychic processes. The conscious and preconscious modes of "thinking, feeling, and acting" (Fromm, 1941a:276) are all conditioned by attitudes, which for the adult are typically unconscious. Once this process of generalization is consummated, attitudes turn into character *orientations*. We then think of sadism, masochism, narcissism, as readinesses for desire which took hold of the subject's way of being, spreading beyond the affective sphere onto all others. Within this stratification between a core "orientation" and its further manifestations, the notion of "attitude" acquires its restricted meaning, as derivative character trait. However, for a character orientation to be established in the first place, it must succeed in dominating other competing attitudes in the process of character formation (cf. Fromm, 1947a; 1955a).

The double meaning of Fromm's notion of "attitude" reflects the difference between considering character as the product of a previous development, or as an ongoing process. In the first instance, there is a clear hierarchy between the general and the particular – orientations and their derivative attitudes. Then "character traits are to be understood as a syndrome which results from a particular organization [...] of character" (Fromm, 1941a:57). In the second instance, inversely, the degree of generality achieved by an orientation appears as the effect of an ecology of traits, perpetually fighting each other to elevate a certain form of desiring to sovereignty within character. This is expressed in Fromm's definition of social character as a "*syndrome of character traits which has developed as an adaptation to the economic, social, and cultural conditions common to that group*" (with Maccoby, 1970b:16). In the latter case, "syndrome" is a systemic concept, including causes and phenomena are parts of a retroactive process. In the former, it simply groups traits correlated to a common unconscious basis.

The notion of "character" in Fromm includes not only secondary character traits, but also their dynamic sources. It is not anymore a *Cs-Pcs* category, as had been the case with most Freudians, but emphatically *Ucs*, telling us less about the ego, and more about its presuppositions in the id. "Character structure" is then a "system of strivings" – "the specific form in which human energy is shaped by the dynamic adaptation of human needs to the particular mode of existence of a given society" (Fromm, 1941a:276). Singular passions which are not activated only circumstantially, stemming rather from long-lasting attitudes, are called "character-conditioned" or "rooted in the character structure" (Fromm, 1976a:121). These passionate strains are not determined only by their immediate attitudinal source, but by the total set of reciprocal determinations *between attitudes – by the whole structure*, that is.

More concrete than the "character structure" is the "personality structure". In this case, the concept comprehends not only attitudes and their relations, but also the articulations between psychic capacities, as they are permeated by common orientations. Also included are organic determinations – "temperament", which regulates the intensity and rhythm of emotional reactions, and "constitutional traits", inherited dispositions (Fromm, 1947a:51; 1967e:198; 1979a:65; Fromm and Maccoby, 1970b:20). Among the relations between psychic spheres, "reason" is especially worthy discussing. It also bears two meanings. In a more specific sense, "reason" is the effective (historically developed) capacity to think "rationally" – that is, considering things in their own nature, in contradistinction to their pragmatic apprehension by "intelligence". But this "reason" of thought is the fruit of a previous relation: it "flows from the blending of rational thought and feeling" (Fromm, 1968a:42). Correspondingly, every form of undocking between intellectual and affective life produces other modes of thought and feeling. Irrational phenomena acting "contrary" to one's "true self-interests" (Fromm, 1964a:130) also belong to the sphere of "reason" in its broader sense – as the domain of the manifold forms of articulation between affects and ideas. At the level of singular desires, the difference between "primary" and "secondary potentialities" is specified as that between "rational" and "irrational passions" (cf. Fromm, 1973a). This classification is hardly tenable at the genetic or causal level, since all passions are originated in the same way. It is rather a distinction regarding the subjective consequences of different forms of pleasure. It subsumes the *relation to oneself* they imply:

> Rational is all that [...] which furthers the growth and development of a structure. Irrational are all such acts of behavior which slow down or destroy the growth and structure of an entity, whether that is a plant or whether that is a man.
>
> (Fromm, 1991a:72)

The movement of psychic capacities within the personality is what *originates* its structure as such. The total personality or *self* is born out of their integration in the process of individuation, as well as the limitations to this process. Departing from affect (immediate emotional reaction to an object), personality grows into one's "total reaction to his object" (Fromm, 1941a:28; 1947a:104). Through this complex path, contact with the objective world overcomes the previous isolation of human powers between themselves (cf. Fromm, 1955a). Their relations are now the links in a chain leading from the immediate, sensory relation to things to a reaction plentiful of content: behavior informed by character. The act is the last item in a "system of relationships that link an individual to the world" – hence, a *structure* (Fromm, 1983d:42; 1992e:41).

Each phenomenological category addresses one of the *psychic* or *existential needs*. These are specifications of the general striving for sanity. Affects satisfy the need for *relatedness*. Ideas fulfill the need for a *frame of reference* or *orientation* making sense of this world. Their middle-term is the need for *rootedness,* which is satisfied by passions as they orient the subject in the world. Values satisfy the need for *an object of devotion* centralizing one's efforts. Acts satisfy the need for *transcendence*, reaching out effectively toward others. Their middle-term is the need for a *sense of identity,* satisfied by the self-experience resulting from value-oriented action. In a later reformulation, Fromm noted perception satisfies the need for *stimulation* and *excitation*. Relatedness and identity were gathered as aspects of a need for *unity,* and transcendence was specified as a need for *effectiveness* upon the world (cf. Fromm, 1955a; 1968a; 1973a).

In their immediate definition, existential needs may sound redundant: the subject feels because she must feel, thinks because she must think etc. This is not the case. What the concept grasps is the participation of emotional attitudes in all remaining psychic capacities. They are refracted throughout the whole psychic structure, fulfilling a different *function* in each case. In Fromm, a psychic force is the stronger, the greater its participation in preventing psychosis and reproducing structure in its present form. This relation is summarized in Figure IV.1.

There is no process of psychic existence without the relations originating phenomenological categories. The becoming of character and personality is the process of *structuralization* of formerly disparate psychic elements (Fromm, 1968a:94). They come to condition themselves reciprocally in their relations: "all single traits of people are intertwined in quite a definite way and mutually determine each other" (Fromm, 1992e:71). At any advanced moment of this process, we have "character" as a "semipermanent structure of [...] energies" held within a certain "balance of forces", with its own "conflicting tendencies" and "contradictions" (Fromm, 1964:131; 1968a:11; 1974c:118; 1989a:56). "Personality", on its turn, is a secondary set of relations between these same emotional forces and non-affective phenomena. The ontological forms implied in Fromm's concepts are the key elements determining how these relations are formed (compare Thompson, 2020).

2 Mutual Presupposition, Reflection, and Structuration

Fromm's ethics present themselves as a set of norms. We can enumerate some of them: love; reason; truth; creation; hope; interest; awakenness; sensibility; justice; peace; solidarity; security; freedom; lastly, life itself (cf. Fromm, 1962a; 1964a; 1992q). Some of these terms qualify social relations; some of them denote object relations, whereas a third group refers to one's relation to

Aspects of Ontology   129

oneself. Since Fromm believes a good society would try to "develop the human potentialities which are given in the human race" (1992f:82), a hierarchy can be discerned between them. Norms pertaining to social relations (justice, peace, security etc.) are the means and conditions for the fulfillment of inner values: "politics must be judged by moral values, and the function of political life is the realization of these values" (Fromm, 1966a:94). We may therefore choose a pair of those ethical, personal norms as a point of departure for our inquiry.

"Love" is the highest norm in the affective sphere – a "syndrome of attitudes" composed of the intents of care, knowledge, responsibility, and respect (cf. Fromm, 1956a). In the intellectual sphere, "reason" (in particular) is the highest norm (cf. Fromm, 1955a). They determine what Fromm believes is the optimal development in the domain of "reason" (in general). Love and reason are both "modes of comprehension" (1947a:97–8) of their object. Each presupposes the other: neither can achieve excellence without the complementary pair. In the syndrome of attitudes characterizing love, "knowledge" is included – because love, for Fromm (1956a), is desire that the loved object grow in accordance with its nature, and it is not possible to foster its becoming without understanding its singularity. Conversely, knowledge directed to the object's essence is interested in taking part in its development – it is "therapeutically-oriented knowledge" (Fromm, 1962a:151). But this interest coincides with the intimate concern of love – the *affirmation* of the object (Fromm, 1939b:186).

Each norm is entangled in *mutual presupposition* with the other. This is an immediately negative relation – our first ontological form. Without reason, there is no love – since love presupposes knowledge; without love, there is no reason – since understanding the object implies the desire to develop it. All norms in Fromm's critical theory behave like that: they are parts of a "value syndrome" or "system", such that the presence and exercise of each is a condition for the presence and exercise of all others – some having priority (1966a:141; 1968a:91). For Fromm, psychic development is not only limited by the conditions of human existence, but also *self-limiting*, bearing an inner negativity. The manifold possibilities of feeling, thinking, and acting don't combine themselves freely, in an indifferent or infinite permutation. One way of living excludes others; the dominating emotional attitudes select the possible forms of thinking; the forms of thought select the predominating attitudes, and so on.

This negativity is true not only in the relation between norms, but also in their inner determination. Love is a "syndrome" of attitudes because its components form a structure: each presupposes the other. The way the four attitudes are deduced implies a certain hierarchy already. The criterion of "knowledge" appears as a condition for "respecting" the other; "respect" is a requisite for "care", which would otherwise risk degenerating into control. Finally, all previous terms are conditions for the capacity to "respond" sensibly to the object's needs (cf. Fromm, 1956a). This is the reason Fromm qualified psychic and social structures as "totalities" (1947a:234) – just like

Marx (1857–8), who presumed each element in an "organic whole" at the same time poses and presupposes all others.

"Love" is also a good example of the double meaning "attitudes" have in Fromm's works. The "syndrome" of traits would formally have to be derivative of and subordinate to the basic, loving attitude. In reality, it is posed as the set of its conditions of possibility. The syndrome components remain differentiated from each other: they may develop out of distinct relationships, and in unequal measure. But the more they are perfected in their "exercise", the more they converge into a qualitative synthesis (Fromm, 1973a:129–30). The final loving quality is incipiently, but increasingly present in its imperfect forms. This fulfilled quality is what the concept of "love" expresses, now in the form of an accomplished process – a result against whose ideal perfection we can measure the continuum of partial, effective developments of affection in real subjects.

The relationship between concept and thing is here similar to the one Weber (1904) ascribed to ideal types. Fromm (1947a) is clear that the concept's purity does not correspond to the effectively observed phenomenon: a difference remains, such that the idea may be used, by way of contrast, as a cognitive measure of the thing. He believes concrete phenomena can be apprehended by mixing ideal types: "in order to see differences one has first to show them in, so to speak, an ideal form, as if they were separate. In reality they are blended together in various forms" (d-1991d-002-eng-draft-05–08:201). However, Fromm assumes types must reflect the nature of their object, in opposition to the relative arbitrariness Weber allowed in the composition of his own types. This contrast between Fromm's (1941a) realism and Weber's rather overt nominalism escaped his attention.

The psychoanalytic tradition had long employed realist pure types (cf. Jones, 1913). Freud (1937) himself thought the intelligibility of complex phenomena could be derived from the miscibility of conceptual types. In Fromm's works, however, notions such as "love" seem to function also as "ideals" in the sense both Weber and Freud denied their concepts: that of a *telos* to be achieved. This feature is peculiar to Fromm's theory as a normative one. Indeed, Frommian pure types sometimes behave as simple "ideals": abstraction is opposed to the richness of effective life, and theory struggles to submit the existent to its will. However, as Fromm's thought evolves, his treatment of concepts as ideals shrinks. He remains sympathetic to humanistic norms, not in their abstract determination – as principles regulating conduct from above –, but as experiential values: *anticipations* in feeling and intuition of the possibility of a better life, as can be glimpsed in the fractures of ordinary experience. Thus understood, norms are neither descriptions of the way things are, nor dictates on the way things should be. To the anticipation of a better experience in practice corresponds an extrapolation in thought, which provides Fromm's concepts both with their ideality (non-

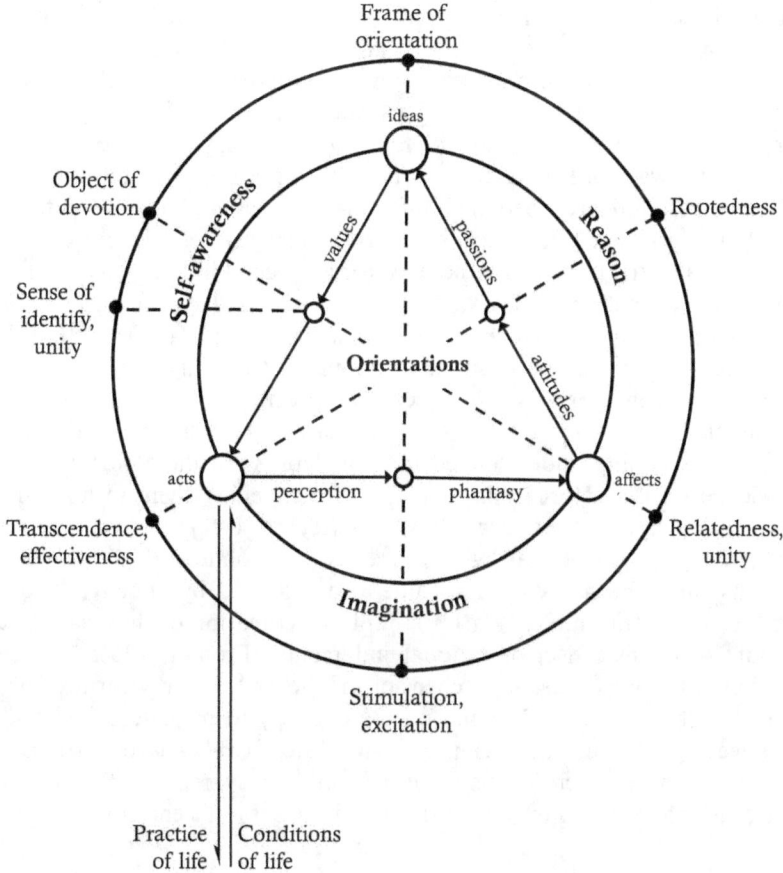

Figure IV.1 Psychic structure and existential needs in Fromm's theory.

equivalence with observed phenomena) and their normativity (immanent value judgment) – without however confusing these two properties.

***

Love's determinations are all within one sphere: care, responsibility, knowledge, and respect are affective motions, germs of acts. Love "presupposes" reason because ideas enable its practical purpose – but what is meant with "knowledge" is foremost the willingness to know. The same is not true for the relation between love and reason: they pertain to different faculties. Reason involves language, unlike attitudes, which are characterized precisely by their split with the intellect. Reason thus "presupposes" love in a different sense: intellectual activity is moved by a force outside its own sphere. In fact, for Fromm (1989a), language is always rooted in affective life, whether it be conscious or unconscious of that. In the first case, both capacities cooperate. In the second, thought is left dull with indifference, or assaulted by passions without knowing. Considered indifferently as norms, love and reason behave as negative, mutual presuppositions. Considered within their phenomenological difference, they display a relation of a new kind: certain ways of feeling correspond with certain ways of thinking.

The correspondences between different attitudes and forms of thought provide us with new ontological categories. Here are a few more examples: on the basis of the feeling of impotence (or a special kind of boredom), there grows, for Fromm, the sadistic attitude, characterized by the wish to "*have absolute and unrestricted control over a living being*" (1973a:322). Which would be the corresponding mode of thought? Certainly not anymore the critical interest in liberating the object's movement. This interest presupposes that living beings cannot be exhausted, that they are not everything they could be, remaining undetermined in their depths. To the contrary, sadistic knowledge wants to force things to speak, compelling them in its wish for certainty. It fixates the terms within which they can be apprehended here and now, refusing their status as living processes (cf. Fromm, 1957a).

On its turn, the narcissistic attitude, characterized by affective "indifference" to others (Fromm, 1947a:110), implies a corrosion of the very capacity to think – a "distortion of rational judgment" (Fromm, 1964a:73). Since affection is the most basic apprehension of the object, every form of objectivity must be based, for Fromm, on the capacity to mediate between ideas and affects. Where affect is lacking, all substrate for *relating* to others is lost. There is no more psychic basis for understanding. Narcissism then corrupts one's sense of reality: only what pertains to the subject's emotional life is

> experienced as fully real, while everybody and everything that does not form part of the person or is not an object of his needs is not interesting, is not fully real, is perceived only by intellectual recognition, while affectively without weight and color.
>
> (Fromm, 1973a:228)

Affect and intellect correspond in refusing to be crossed by difference.

In all the cases above, attitudes and modes of thinking are complementary steps in the same chain of acts. To love, it is necessary to know in depth, and to know in depth, it is necessary to love. To dominate, it is necessary to reduce the other to an "object", and for this to be possible, one must also feel him as submissive. To sustain narcissistic satisfaction, thought must ignore all difference; but precisely because this is established in thought, affect is protected from discovering alterity. The same remains true when we consider the action of psychic mechanisms – with the qualification that here the relation presupposes repression and compromise. If attitudes remain repressed, thought falls into *rationalization:* ideas become means for disguising and justifying gratification. The authoritarian character, dominated by sadistic and masochistic passions, is especially prone to admit an ideology dividing the world between the strong and the weak (cf. Fromm, 1941a). The revolutionary character, on her side, is inclined to choose an egalitarian worldview (cf. Fromm, 1963b). If a *projective* tendency predominantes, paranoid thinking impairs the capacity to distinguish between "possibility" and "probability", taking imaginary conjectures as imminent realities (cf. Fromm, 1961a). Where transference takes hold of perception, the distinction is lost between present and past experience. Thought then reflects this confusion of attributes *parataxically.* Finally, where affect and idea are completely dissociated, thought substitutes effective experience by intellectual rumination or *cerebration* – a *"fetishism of words"* (cf. Fromm, 1960a; 1962a:155)

Both in the immediate relation between attitudes and ideas, and in its mediation through psychic mechanisms, thought is an extension and condition for the satisfaction of the underlying force. However, this does not exhaust the relations Fromm found between the affective and the intellectual spheres. Love, sadism, narcissism, are for him all "modes of socialization" – that is, attitudes (later orientations) formed in the process of interaction between humans, modes of intersubjective relatedness (or withdrawal from it). If we consider, on the other side, the so-called "modes of assimilation" – attitudes and orientations pertaining to the ways of acquiring goods, to the relation to things – we see that ideas don't anymore appear as supports of the act. They appear as *objects* of the corresponding attitudes. For example: characteristic of the receptive orientation is to passively reproduce and assimilate the ideas of others. Those who find satisfaction in exploitation are also gratified in plagiarism. The ones who are capable of productive activity are also more prone to generate new ideas out of their previous knowledge (cf. Fromm, 1947a).

The reciprocal determinations between the affective and the intellectual spheres are therefore of many kinds. They impact here the form, there the content of thought; here what is thought, there the relation to what is thought; here the reception of ideas, there their production. We can group these correspondences into two categories, adding them to our dictionary of ontological forms. Where the attitude determines the content of what is thought, we deal with a substantive, *structuring* determination, which builds relations between different components of the personality. Where the attitude takes the idea as its object, we face a formal, *reflexive* determination. In most cases, it is important to notice, we don't verify a cooperation between capacities, as was the case in the relation between love and reason. To the contrary: the many modes of relation we considered afterwards imply a *split* between what is desired and what is thought. They amount to *ways of not knowing.*

In the relation between love and reason, we had to assume not only the substantive correspondence between an intellectual and an affective purpose, but also the permeability of intellectual activity to its real motivations. Reason presumed the capacity to appropriate what one wants in the very act of thinking. All the correspondences we dealt with later implied the unconsciousness of either aspect in the thought process – be it through interference of psychic mechanisms, or because, according to their nature, the attitudes we were considering restricted the capacity to think. On the one extreme, we have the ideal case in which rational activity achieves an optimal transparency with regard both to the object, and to the thinking subject. On the other extreme, we find cerebration: the absolute lack of communication between affective life and thought. Between the extremes, we find a variety of intermediary relations, in which satisfying the attitude underlying thought demands either ignorance of the object, or of the subject's real motivations. For Fromm (1962a), one thing always comes with the other. Without knowing others, one cannot know oneself. Without knowing oneself, one cannot know others.

Fromm believes each form of feeling engenders a *typical topological constellation*. Attitudes display a correspondence not only with certain forms of thinking, but also with specific distributions of psychic forces between consciousness and unconsciousness. Even if he gives up Freudian metapsychology, Fromm re-elaborates the dynamic, economic, and topological points of view in his own way. He doesn't treat them as independent modes of consideration, insisting that the corresponding determinations are systemically coupled with each other. Instead of typical topical locations for drives, for phantasies, for word-representations (cf. Freud, 1915b), there would be a typical economy of consciousness and unconsciousness according to the *kinds* of drive, the *kinds* of representation predominating in the character system. Instead of a partitioned, but uniform psychic "space", as in Freudian topology, Frommian analysis assumes each kind of passion projects its own topology according to the particularity of its desire. Each passion implies its own *mode of unconsciousness*.

3 Affinity and Generativity

In Fromm's characterology, the quality of passions and emotions has primacy over their intensity. This is reflected in Fromm's concept of "energy", which was generalized into meaning the "desire of the living organism to survive". It remains an abstract or virtual category: "there is no psychic energy 'in general' but only psychic energy channeled in various ways characteristic of a given character structure" (Fromm, 1990d:7–8). This general concept cannot account for the qualitative difference between forms of pleasure, but it still implies the finitude of the organism. To an even greater degree than in Freud (1905–24), who provided libido with partially autonomous sources in the body, in Fromm, "adding energy to one aim" implies "subtracting from another". However, energy is never a starting point in his analyses. The concept only turns up as specifying the relative strength of particular phenomena in comparison to others. No explanation is offered for the passage of general desire into specific modalities, except in the abstract assertion that there occurs a "transformation" of "general human energy" into "specific energy" (Fromm, 1970c:17). Psychic qualia are presupposed as differentiated from the outset, and only afterwards modulated in their combinations with others (cf. Fromm, 1947a).

There follows a different understanding of psychic conflicts and their products. Freud centered his analysis of conflict on the idea that conscious processes can be decomposed into a myriad of independent, partial goals – some of which clash with the demands of repression. Fromm (1973a), to the contrary, centered on the idea that human passions fight not only for circumstantial satisfaction, but also for permanent governance of conduct – that is, of *all* mediations in the personality structure. From this perspective, conflict does not pertain only to the risks of enjoyment (libido against self-preservation or cultural imperatives), but more fundamentally to different ways of enjoying. "The real conflict" happens "between the tendency to self-preservation and optimal development (mental health) and the irrational passions" (Foerster_H_Von_1972–04–29-to). For Fromm, there is already a primary conflict at the unconscious level, to which the conflict between conscious and unconscious demands is superimposed.

Working with pure types, Fromm expressed the contradictions between antagonistic strivings as blends between concepts. He could thus freely color some attitudes with others as the case demanded. This freedom was nonetheless restricted by the assertion that we always find the primacy of one or two attitudes over others. Once an attitude had success in generalizing itself as an *orientation,* "the character of any given person" would usually be "a blend of all or some of these orientations in which one, however, is dominant" (1947a:61). One striving takes the lead, subordinating others, and organizes the use of psychic powers as instruments to its concretion. Since this was an empirical statement, it implied that personality is increasingly unified – not only in ideal types, but also in reality.

In Fromm's writings, character types are indeed formulated as concepts in which the coherence between sensoriality, affectivity, and intellectuality has been maximally exaggerated, such that the personality appears as devoted to a single purpose. For example: the "receptive character" assumes overall a passive position. It "feels that the 'source of all good' is outside" (Fromm, 1947a:62) and waits to receive what it needs from others, out of grace or favor. Its sensory life is reduced to pure consumption. It can only think what it has heard before. Thus a series of secondary character traits develops on the basis of the same fundamental striving: lack of initiative, gullibility, sentimentality, are all specifications of the receptive orientation, each within a different psychic sphere. The "masochistic character", on its turn, enjoys absolute submission, abandonment into a higher power, in whose presence it feels relieved from its responsibilities and from separateness. Its sensory life is oriented to penury and pain; thought is tormented with guilt, easily admitting ideas of obedience, punishment, and submission. Here as well, a series of secondary attitudes develop, such as lack of self-confidence, fatalism, and dependency (cf. Fromm 1941a; 1947a; 1973a).

The relationship between an established orientation and its derivative traits adds to our repertoire of ontological forms. Secondary attitudes develop as specifications of the basic character striving within other psychic spheres. They individuate as partially autonomous colorings of personality, but remain dependent on the primary attitude from which they flow. Orientations are thus *generative* of their traits: once they take hold of character, they set the ground for the proliferation of the corresponding syndrome. The relation is immediately positive. Thus conceived, character has an arboreal structure, with all partial traits leading back to a common root. In Fromm's writings, this unitary representation of the psyche coexists with a tendency toward its dissolution. This secondary tendency is fulfilled only over a long time, remaining mostly implicit to his continued reassertion of older formulations (cf. Fromm 1979b). In the following parts of this chapter, we will discuss some of the key moments effecting these subterranean transformations of Fromm's characterology.

***

Fromm's character typology was originally divided in two segments. The different "modes of relatedness" were separated between those emerging from the process of *assimilation* and those emerging from the process of *socialization*. According to Fromm, there is an *affinity* between certain modes of assimilation and socialization (1947a:113). The last types we mentioned provide a good example. The receptive orientation, in the domain of obtaining goods, would be akin to the masochistic orientation within human relations. Other similar correspondences would be those between the destructive and the hoarding orientations, the narcissistic and the marketing orientations. We would thus have a bicentric model of character, which seems to contradict from the outset the "unitary" mode of integration presumed by pure types. Over time, this contradiction unfolds into a series of important conceptual developments.

The bipartition in two "spheres" of relatedness is always more nominal than effective in Fromm's analyses. Fixating the difference between relations to "objects" and to human "subjects", we make the idea of a character which segments life in two halves, each governing different inclinations. But the concrete description of character types provided by Fromm (1947a; 1964a) does not strictly obey this division. Both the basic strivings pertaining to "socialization", and those pertaining to "assimilation" take hold of the same components of conduct – the modes of feeling, thinking, and acting.

Moreover, the modes of assimilation reverberate expressly over human relations, and the modes of socialization participate in the relation to objects. We saw, for example, that the receptive character is inclined to the same passivity in its relation to material goods and in its expectations of love. The hoarding character spares emotions just as it would spare money, and the masochistic character submits to nature and fate as it would submit to people.

Fromm's description of specific character types results more complex than the categories under which they are ordered. His concrete sensibility is here more advanced than the theoretical formulation. Fromm (1947a) thought character was formed in response to one's conditions and practice of life – but these include given social relations. What matters primarily is not the object of affection, human or otherwise, but the social relation within which it is appropriated. Fromm's classification dissociates both aspects. It rigorously understands subjective phenomena as phenomena of relationship, but suffers from a tendency to introvert the corresponding determinations. Relations are dealt with unilaterally, on the side of a single subject, in abstraction from their fulfillment in exchange with others – as happened also in Fromm's anthropology and sociology. This weakens his capacity to specify practical determinants conceptually.

The genetic interpretation of the concepts of assimilation and socialization serves us better than a purely classificatory interpretation. It allows us to formulate the relation between social and psychic forms in terms cohering better with Fromm's own premises. However, reading them like this implies important changes to their content. Their intended meaning falls apart under analysis. What first appeared as a bicentric concept of character regresses to a higher degree of undifferentiation. The way of "obtaining" satisfaction and the kind of satisfaction desired are reunited in the same act, oriented toward a common circle of objects – but they continue to appear as parallel purposes, under which subsists a diversity within character. The previous duplicity survives in the *relation* between tendencies: the receptive orientation has an *affinity* with the masochistic one; the hoarding orientation has an *affinity* with the destructive one, and so forth.

"Affinity" means that a substantive kinship underlies empirically typical correlations between attitudes. This is for us a new relationship, adding another link to the series of ontological forms we are inferring. All relations we considered thus far abstracted from the actualization of psychic potencies. In the affinities between orientations, this changes for the first time. They imply that permanence within certain social relations reproduces the *conditions* for the emergence of correlated orientations. Thus, masochism does not "generate" receptiveness in the same sense that an orientation generates its derivative attitudes. Rather, remaining within the symbiotic relationship deprives the subject from any means of satisfaction, other than the passive expectation that a powerful other will provide what is wanted. Reciprocally, "receptive" dependency sets forth the conditions for seeking masochistic satisfaction: it makes others available as a masters. We are not anymore within the purely endogenous determination of psychic facts, but rather take a détour through social relations: the object's response must be taken into account. Since Fromm's formulation introverts relationships in their partial moments, this movement is rarely discussed explicitly. However, it is implied by his concepts and their categorial relations.

Between orientations we consider to have an "affinity" there is a relation of *reciprocal implication*. In mutual presupposition, each attitude was immediately negative of others: their development was limited by the absence or presence of other components in the syndrome. Here, each orientation sets forth favorable conditions for arousing others. Unlike the generation of secondary traits by a basic striving, in affinity one orientation does not immediately produce others. It stimulates their reproduction only indirectly, as it seeks satisfaction. The relation is thus mediately positive. Reciprocal implication reestablishes the duality we found in the classification of orientations on new and truer grounds. Where one inclination is present, we find also those it has an affinity with – if not in act, at least in potency.

***

The self appeared before as a *self-limiting* process, with an emphasis on the relations of *repulsion* between certain classes of desire and the corresponding modes of thought and sensation. Now, we understand that there is a relation of *attraction* between different passions. Character has a *positive* conditionality as well: once formed, an inner metabolism replenishes its characteristic needs according to the affinities between orientations, reproducing structure from within. Hence Fromm's *polar* understanding of psychic forces.

4 Convergence and Blends

With the publication of *The heart of man* in 1964, the fragmentation of character into its composing attitudes is completed under the notion of a *convergence* between orientations. Besides pure types determined by a basic, generalized attitude, Fromm now formulates *syndromes of orientations*. He presents two of them: the syndrome of "growth", composed of the orientations to biophilia (love of life), solidarity, and freedom, and the syndrome of "decay", composed of the orientations to necrophilia (love of the dead), narcissism, and incestuous symbiosis (Fromm, 1964a:108,113–4).

The concepts are from the outset problematic. The "syndrome of growth" does not combine analytic units of the same order. "Love of life" should already include "solidarity" – love of nature and of the stranger – as one of its particular cases. Moreover, "freedom" and "independence" cannot really have the character of "orientations" in Fromm (1989a). Subjective freedom is freedom from unconscious compulsion; it refers to a form of relation to desire, not to an intended satisfaction, as the concept of orientation would demand. The "syndrome of decay" doesn't have the same problem:

necrophilia, malignant narcissism, and incestuous symbiosis can all be taken as the most extreme developments of the corresponding attitudes: destructiveness, indifference, sadomasochism, respectively. However, a logical difficulty of a different kind still applies to both concepts.

The concept of character "orientation" already assumes the extension of an attitude onto all psychic faculties. According to its definition, it reaches the most exhaustive diffusion possible within individual conduct – there could be nothing exceeding its degree of generalization. Therefore, it should not be possible to identify "syndromes" of entire orientations. This is another case in which Fromm's formulation clashes with an advanced intuition. What here presents itself as a more general analytic unit – the syndrome – actually expresses the opposite conceptual movement. "Orientations" themselves have now been degraded to a lesser extension, conserving their hold of character only as an *unfulfilled* striving – a purpose only incompletely realized. They preserve, from their attitudinal origin, their character as partial momenta: each "orientation" is just one among others. But their aspiration to the global appropriation of conduct is still present: we don't visualize them only as expectant, acephalous intentions, but as entire chains of psychic acts, refracted through the different human powers. The game of attractions and repulsions between attitudes is now fashioned as an ongoing dynamics – a process which has lost the fixity of pure types, appearing as a struggle between different life conducts.

Opposing or contradictory orientations do not anymore manifest as Freudian compromises, but in a succession of alternated impressions, stratified in time. Fromm's "syndromes" express the opposite movement: a gathering of orientations which collaborate toward a common purpose. In the "syndrome of attitudes", distinct determinations blended into a single qualitative synthesis. In the "syndrome of orientations", this seems to happen again – each group of three orientations is reunited in the final quality of "growth" or "decay". However, there is a significant difference. Growth and decay are not predicates of the subject, like character traits. They are rather qualities *of the vital process*, which is oriented towards diversification and change in one case (growth), and to ossification in the other (decay).

Fromm's understanding of "attitudes" is modified accordingly. This is nowhere as visible as in the case of the forms of "malignant aggression" (Fromm, 1970h:160) – sadism and destructiveness. Fromm saw benign aggression as a neurologically given potency, intending defense of vital interests. Sadism (passion of controlling) and destructiveness (passion of extinguishing life), on their side, were treated as historical drives, based on the *impotence* felt in reaction to damaging conditions of life (1973a:266). Earlier in his writings, Fromm (1941a) had taken sadism and masochism as forms of *symbiotic* relatedness, easing human separation anxiety. They would amount to ways of finding "unity" with others at the cost of individuation – there remaining in the end a partial subject, who gave up freedom for safety.

In this context, Fromm opposed sadism to destructiveness, which consists in a drastic removal from object relations, or "negative relatedness" (Fromm and Maccoby, 1970b:74). Sadism conserves its object so as to control it, whereas destructiveness annihilates it, leading to a new form of withdrawal (comparable to narcissism, which does not seek to deny others' material existence, but ceases to recognize it). The sadistic subject would enjoy a compensation for her feeling of impotence in the exercise of power, whereas the destructive subject would be responding to an experience of almost total paralysis of life, for which she would feel the need to seek *revenge* (Fromm, 1974b:113). Destructiveness would be the product of *unlived life* (Fromm, 1941a:182) – the perversion of the natural impulse to grow into a desire for annihilation and dismembering (cf. Fromm, 1973a).

Fromm never ceased to insist on the essential difference between these attitudes and the corresponding orientations. But his later works reconsidered them as modalities of *aggression*. It is one of the peculiarities of Fromm's psychoanalysis that masochism did not explicitly enter this second grouping, remaining always treated as the passive form of symbiosis. Fromm (1957c; 1973a) retained the emphasis on the clinical correlation between sadism and masochism – where there is one, there is the other. But the concept of sadism was thereafter sectioned between both points of view. As a form of symbiosis, it was the complementary pair to masochism; as a form of malignant aggression, it was the pair to destructiveness. Within this second mode of consideration, the contrast between forms of malignant aggression was considerably weakened. The insistence on their peculiarity started to coexist with a series of intermediary expressions – cruelty, sadistic destructiveness, sadism as an expression of destructive character, hot and cold sadism (cf. Fromm, 1968e; 1970h; 1973a; 1983c). Implied is not a regression of both categories into undifferentiation, but their connection in a continuum, in which the *intensification* of aggressiveness is followed by its gradual transformation into a distinct *quality* – beginning with weaker forms of sadism, and ending in thorough destructiveness.

The two attitudes had always been connected by way of their stemming from similar conditions of life. The same *thwarting of life* conditioning sadism also generated destructiveness – but Fromm (1941a:178) didn't initially specify what would make the difference between one and the other outcome. This community of causes was more strongly emphasized in Fromm's (1968e) later works. Most importantly, the missing explanation was found. The passage from sadistic into destructive aggressiveness is not only a result of outer conditions of existence, but also of inner determinations. It results from the ecology of polar relations between attitudes. While Fromm's (1955a) theoretical formulation was still restricted to the employment of pure types, it was difficult to clarify this relation. With time, the pressure of his rich intuition eroded the rigidity of his earlier conceptualization. It did not do it to the last possible consequences, but enough that more determining relations could be accommodated in his concepts.

The same process also reverberates within the other modes of "socialization". We start seeing differences in gradation everywhere. Only Fromm's late works differentiate more clearly between simple affective "indifference" and fully developed, malignant narcissism, its most extreme corollary (cf. Fromm and Maccoby, 1970b). The milder forms of symbiosis are also differentiated from "incestuous" symbiosis, in which pregenital fixation is markedly intense (cf. Fromm, 1964a). Love, which had previously been directed towards "others" (and oneself) in general, is now radicalized as "biophilia" – love of what is alive, presupposing acknowledgment of life beneath its manifold manifestations (cf. Fromm, 1964a). Finally, destructiveness finds its most radical expression in the absolute perversion of life – necrophilia, or the love of death and the dead (cf. Fromm, 1974c).

To understand how this qualitative gradation develops, let us analyze the orientations composing the syndrome of decay. Narcissism wants to protect itself against everything that would hurt one's self-image (cf. Fromm, 1992g). Fromm (1973a) included narcissistic aggressiveness among the forms of benign violence – but he also thought its vengeful character could serve as a pretext for satisfying destructiveness (cf. Fromm, 1968e). Remaining affectively indifferent, the subject only enters relations with others to the extent that they support her attachment to herself. This creates conditions for a deepening of symbiosis: the self always relies on its confirmation by another, with whom it wouldn't be foreign to develop dependency. Sadism and masochism, on their turn, act as polar hindrances to the development of love (cf. Fromm, 1956a). In paralyzing love, they block the one psychic force that could help disrupt indifference. Conditions for narcissistic withdrawal are replenished. This is also a concomitant result of necrophilic destructiveness, since the annihilation of others throws the subject back into isolation. We saw how sadism is the seed for destructiveness according to its "aggressive" aspect, and we must also remember that extreme masochism erodes the subject's capacity to sustain her own life (cf. Fromm, 1973a). This implies a continued experience of impotence – which is in turn the fundamental condition for the emergence of stronger forms of malignant aggression.

Stepping back from this cursory analysis, we see how the satisfaction of each orientation implies it in the reproduction of all others in the syndrome. As with "affinity", the practical process of their satisfaction induces affection arousing their kin orientations, renewing their causes. Orientations in a syndrome do not converge into a homogeneous quality, as was the case with attitudes, but rather condition each other mutually in their difference. The more they reproduce each other, the more they form a rigid unit – the economy of one form of satisfaction is strengthened by that of all others. This implies a new ontological form. Convergence means that *the quality of orientations is modified* when they are in the presence of others. Narcissism is not the same in the presence or absence of sadism; sadism is not the same in the presence or absence of destructiveness, and so on. From their reciprocal intensification, there derives an *inner gradation* to orientations themselves, which are thus profiled in a succession of staggered forms. For Fromm, "the degrees of evilness are at the same time the degrees of regression" within each "orientation" included in the syndrome (1964a:149). This is an *epigenetic* relation: each orientation is mediately negative of the others, indirectly modifying their nature.

***

With convergence, we complete the necessary relations for a *systemic* concept of psychic determination. The development of each attitude is conditioned – both negatively and positively – by the development of every other attitude. Up to this point, psychic qualities had been split from their measure. Now a synthesis of a different nature is achieved. The passage from one attitude into the other is formulated as a difference in *degree*.

Thinking like this allows us to clarify an idea Fromm (1947a) had developed already in the earlier stages of his theory: that we would find *blends* between strivings, and these would modify the quality of character traits themselves. In empirical observation, orientations would be decomposable in intricate balances of forces, specific to each component of the personality. Thinking, feeling, and acting could express opposing attitudes, as well as develop conflicts within themselves: "the different orientations may operate in different strength in the material, emotional, or intellectual spheres of activity, respectively" (Fromm, 1947a:117). The passions with the greatest *weight* would result victorious. In principle, any number of combinations would be possible between the many "non-productive" orientations, which paralyze the vital process, and between these and the "productive" attitudes, which foster the subject's vitality (cf. Fromm, 1947a). The blends between the productive orientation (love, reason, creation) and its non-productive counterparts were especially interesting, since they prefigured the idea of a gradation of character traits – yet without reaching the staggering of orientations themselves in degrees.

Fromm assumed that the "productive orientation" was capable of reorienting non-productive traits in its own favor. To refer to examples we have already given above: receptive traits such as lack of initiative, gullibility, sentimentality could be turned into acceptance, trust, and tenderness, should productiveness outweigh receptiveness in their composition. Thus, each character trait was conceptualized – contrary to orientations themselves – not as a fully accomplished purpose, but as part of a spectrum: "a point in a continuum which is determined by the *degree of the productive orientation which prevails*" (1947a:116). This allowed a quite malleable understanding of character at the granular level of traits. The problem was that this malleability could not be reached for units of a higher order. An understanding of the meaning and phenomenology of their blends had to be supplemented from clinical and everyday experience, without a clear development within the concept. For some time, Fromm was left with a phenomenology which gave up taking quantitative differences into account, and a psychic economy which gave up the qualitative specificity of phenomena.

This impasse can be understood as a product of three factors: one conceptual, one logical, and one methodological. The conceptual factor was the split between quality and quantity, which occurred as Fromm (1977g) generalized the notion of psychic energy, isolating affects and their derivatives as the exclusive theoretical representatives of the qualitative aspect. The later portion of Fromm's works reconciled in part the two aspects in the gradation between orientations, but didn't achieve *dissolving* the qualitative differentiation of affects between themselves.

The logical factor was Fromm's use of ideal types. They offered three main obstacles. First, pure types abstract and exaggerate, up to their highest coherence, the traits observation finds in incomplete forms. This procedure sublates precisely *differences in degree* into a completed homogeneous quality. Ideal types allow no room for quantitative variation. Secondly, the cognoscibility of mixed and intermediary cases is the clearer, the less types aspire to formulate things in their totality, referring instead to *fragments* or *aggregates* of characteristics – as Freud (1931) himself had already understood. In classic psychoanalysis, pure types had mostly been employed under the assumption that character *traits* were the analytic unit. Fromm kept their use, but expanded their reach into the whole psychic structure. His increasingly rich intuition of psychic qualia had to compete with a formulation accommodating diversity only in the form of fully accomplished totalities. As a consequence, Fromm's characterology had a difficulty in expressing the concrete developmental path of its many character types. Finally, pure types formulated character not as a "system" of relations, but as a "systematic" development of *one* mode of relation at a time. This made it hard to express mixed cases as more than underdetermined juxtapositions of types.

The third, methodological factor, was the kind of empirical inquiry practiced by Fromm. Fromm's characterology developed out of his clinical work, but also in the process of his sociological investigations. Beyond the concept of individual character, Fromm (1962a) developed also that of social character – abstraction of the character traits and orientations common to a certain group. Fromm (1941a) emphasized that this was not a statistical notion. It should rather be taken as a *functional* concept, apprehending not only the roots of character traits in common experience, but also the role these traits had for social reproduction. They were seen as "productive forces" – components of the social activity specific to a class or group. Fromm coupled this formulation with the *hypothesis* that the statistically prevailing traits in a group would coincide with those of greatest functional relevance for the reproduction of the social system (cf. 1992e:65). For a majority of subjects (albeit admitting the most drastic exceptions), the common pressures of culture and practice of life would tend to produce similar character structures, by contrast to which accidents in individual experience would represent minor variations. Most members of a class would "want to do what they have to do" according to their position in the economic, political, and cultural structures (cf. Fromm, 1961a).

The simple prevalence of a trait was thus insufficient for its inclusion as part of "social character" – but Fromm's (1980a) technique for generalization remained a statistical one in all his sociological inquiries. Research identified the distribution of different "orientations" among distinct social classes, age groups, and genders. Theoretical "ideal types" were translated into "factors" in the computation of data, and the miscibility between types was translated into a quantitative relation, a *proportion* between attitudes observed in a given population (cf. Fromm and Maccoby, 1970b). In this context, the postulate of a condensation of psychic activity around one or two dominating orientations acquired a statistical meaning it could never have reached in clinical casuistry. In returning to concrete cases, Fromm transposed onto them the characteristic "unicity" syndromes acquire when considered statistically. This resulted in an oscillation between a differential concept of unity, which understands character (bottom-up) as the set of reciprocal determinations between singular psychic forces, and an identitary concept of unity, which understands character (top-down) as a synthesis of partial forces around a dominating, albeit unconscious tendency.

In the concept of "syndromes of orientation", Fromm (1964a) reached a new compromise, sparing him some of these difficulties, and updating others into a new form. The supposition that the many orientations coexist and reproduce themselves in their multilateral relations came together with the repeated assertion that the "fundamental" problem of character is the strength of biophilia and necrophilia (Fromm, 1964a:38). According to *form*, the second assertion reverts in part the conceptual advancement in the notion of convergence. The governance of conduct is again subsumed to the fight between two particular orientations. According to *content*, however, Fromm's assertion is a step forth. When considered more closely, "biophilia" and "necrophilia" imply more than character orientations in their previous meaning. They contain a necessary reference to life, taking into account not only the attitude's conjunctive malleability, but also the nature of its object. They imply some passions are more adequate to their objects than others.

5 Activity and Contemplation

Let us now consider the implications of our previous discussion. Taking Fromm's concept of psychic energy as point of departure, we couldn't find any mediation explaining how this abstract sum is transformed in affective qualia. The quantitative and the qualitative moments remained at first dissociated. Energy circumscribed the vital process as pure finite potency – but, most importantly, still *inactive* potency. It introjected the forces which would later appear as passionate motions into a virtual point, in a state of repose. To be transformed into any of its particular forms of expression, energy had first to be invited into moving, activated by an outer object – a thesis resembling Ferenczi's (1929) late understanding of the life drive. Only when energy was awakened from its rest by affection could it be "channeled" and "molded" into a specific form, unfolding into an act – or at least its possibility (cf. Fromm, 1941a).

As Fromm's concept of energy loses the character of an autonomous motor, his notion of "force" is modified accordingly. At first sight, the "emotional forces" (1948b:145) composing character are not fundamentally different from Freud's (1915a) drives and their derivatives, except for the origin (organic or psychic) presumed for each. However, Fromm considers also the human faculties to have the character of psychic "forces". In their relation to energy, they are "powers", possibilities – but their development and expression is a necessity. Life's "expressive" moment, which we knew first as the representative of freedom within vital processes, here becomes an imperative: because we have senses, we *must* sense; because we have an intellect, we *must* think. To the degree that intellect, sensation, affection, are experienced as pressing for exercise, they stand as *vital forces* (Fromm, 1955c:98). Here Fromm reintroduces a primordial activity in his concept of the psyche: "energy" is "generated by the active striving of all faculties to attain their objects" (1968h:52), and this activity *precedes* their actualization.

There is therefore an opposition between a reactive understanding of the psyche, which resulted from the concept of "energy", and an active understanding, which derived from the notion of "vital force". This opposition extends to the whole theory of human needs. At first, Fromm (1992e) assumes that the organism is basically *active*: physiological needs are the first imperative impelling the child toward contact with caretakers. The need to survive acts before all others. But Fromm also assumes that the historical passions have a different bodily substrate, being parallel to, and partially independent from, the immediate organic process. Passionate life is constituted, mediated activity. At this level, the organism is seen again as primarily *reactive*, since affection is reaction. Only after character-rooted attitudes and passions are formed does the subject find an enduring motor for action.

Thus considered, psychic life, which needs activity to be fulfilled, must first become capable of that through its relation to others. Human passions remain primarily reactive in nature, whereas human powers are portrayed as inherently active. In the first case, relationship engenders necessity; in the second, necessity compels to relatedness. Fromm takes a step in resolving this antinomy by conditioning the development of all remaining powers to affective development: the exercise of the intellectual and sensory powers presupposes that they be put in motion by emotional forces.

However, this only postpones the problem, since emotional life continues to be dependent on its activation by objects, being generative of desire only on second instance.

Since affection precedes wanting, Fromm's theory remains closer to the objective world than to phantasy. To the extent that objects are lost in memory and repression, psychic and material reality stand in opposition. Contrariwise, to the extent that affects bear a ballast with the circumstances originating them, they represent an adequacy of the vital process to reality – a real, efficient, proportional response of the psyche to its others. For that reason, the concept of "adaptation" is not reducible in Fromm (1941a) to behavioral, "static adaptation". It includes also an unconscious, "dynamic" facet – implying a capacity to respond to the actuality of a certain circumstance in accordance with one's nature.

With the formation of the existential split, affect and its composite categories are also subject to deformation. Then one finds "manifest" and "latent" affects (Fromm, 1989a:70), as well as every sort of falsification of the primary process of reaction. However, at a more basic level, Fromm assumes the adequacy of affects to their arousing objects. For him, the unity of subject and object is not granted in the concept or in desire, but in affection. Regression to purely animal life is not anymore possible (representing in fact, for Fromm, the most mistaken ethical and political life), but it retains its value as an experiential model for what a reconciled life would look like. A "new harmony" of the human being with herself and other beings would still be a "fulfillment on a higher level of what was a Paradise Age on a primitive level" (Fromm, 1991e:69): "in becoming children again we are at the same time not children, but fully developed adults" (Fromm, 1960a:92).

Hence Fromm's *non-theistic mysticism* (1966a:18). He conceives pure experience as beyond expression in words (if also irreducible to sensation), but also cannot admit aphanisis or suspension of subjective organization as permanent resolutions for the existential split. In one place, Fromm (1956a) believes love is the only solution for the problem of human separateness. Elsewhere, he believes "the only answer to life is to want nothing and to mind absolutely nothing, neither life nor even satisfaction nor the approval of certain persons" (Schecter_David_1976–07–05-to). Mistrustful of all transient forms of ego dissolution (trance, drugs), but also of the historically given ego structure, Fromm oscillates between the most contrasting tenets. What they share is the rejection of both ecstasy and asceticism. Neither a partisan of renounce, nor of enjoyment, Fromm ends with an eudaimonism sympathetic to pleasure, but hostile to hedonistic excess. He then finds himself in a pendulum move between a concept of activity oriented to praxis, and a concept of intuitive reconciliation with nature in contemplation (cf. Fromm, 1960a). If the vertebrae organizing Fromm's concepts are a dialectic of necessity and freedom, then the orthogonal axis organizing his norms is a dialectic of contemplation and activity. In religious terms: a dialectic between mysticism and messianism (compare Braune, 2014).

Neither of these dialectics undergoes a definitive development in Fromm's theory. In the first case, because – despite his occasional prophetic enthusiasm (cf. Maccoby, 1996) – Fromm (1947a) believes abolishing human existential dicotomies is impossible. A "new harmony" is not the ultimate perfection of the species, but simply a state in which the conflicts inhering in the human condition may be adequately confronted. He aims for a society in which the inexorable problems of human experience (death, finitude, separation) can be tackled with the aid of an "optimal" development of human powers – without implying an extinction of the tragic element of life. Fromm's mode of expression, given to the construction of ideally completed types, opposes his anthropological sobriety, ever skeptical about definitive resolutions for the schisms of psychic development. If the dialectic of freedom and necessity is not carried to a definitive conceptual resolution, this corresponds simply to the supposition that the cultural process is an infinite one. All new historical solutions "in their turn create new contradictions and now the need for answers" (Fromm, 1992q:100).

It is different with the dialectic of contemplation and activity. Here, Fromm's reflections face a definite theoretical limitation in their subsumption of effective practice to psychic values. Fromm conflates as ways into "oneness" the most different methods (1950a:36). Assuming that all humanisms agree on the highest goals of human experience, he downplays the differences between techniques purporting to achieve these goals (compare Hardeck, 2000). He bridges different philosophical and religious systems with a concept of pure, free activity, which would determine the quality of all emancipated and emancipating action. For Fromm, only those forms of action are "active" in which one's desire is in unity with oneself. If the experience of desire is compulsive or blind, Fromm considers it as a form of passivity: "freedom is the possibility for man to express himself without compulsion, to create something out of himself" (1977a:11). Within this perspective, "activity which fosters self-development" is "not counterposed to contemplation" (1977a:16). Indeed, nothing would prevent contemplation from being the "highest form of praxis" (1976a:80). This may hold true – but only if analysis takes experience in purely psychological terms, abstracting from prescribed practices.

While activity is considered in abstraction from concrete, sensuous action, its concept is preserved in sheer subjective form. This protects it from the toils exteriorization imposes over the contents of human life. Once practice is taken into account again, it cannot help modifying these contents, leading them to irreconcilable contradictions. A valuation of pure experience, after the manner of contemplative mysticism, is radically different from an experience of unity with the object in sensory activity, after the messianic traditions. Both may be seen as seeking to overcome the divide between subject and object, but their results can hardly be equated (compare Funk, 1978). One implies suspending the relation with the object as a way of accessing it thoroughly: in the "state of intense mystical contemplation", "attention is withdrawn completely from the outside world as a potential field of action and is completely focused on self-experience, although the person remains awake" (Fromm, 1949a:45). Re-encounter with the object must then happen by way of topological regression and openness to inner experience. The other implies a thickening of the practical relatedness to the object: "in any kind of creative work the creating person unites himself with his material, which represents the world outside of himself" (Fromm, 1956a:14). Unity is achieved by multiplying the angles through which the object is appropriated, not by withdrawing from them. Differing in the method they employ, these techniques result also in fundamentally different experiences of "oneness". Thus, even if Fromm thinks human change can only be achieved through "exercise in true activity" (1977a:16), his formulations often fall short of a consistently praxiological understanding of norms. He must emphasize the practical fulfillment of norms to turn ethical principles into political forces, but must refrain from emphasizing differences in practice in order to preserve the political unity of humanistic movements.

These unresolved contradictions are reflected in Fromm's concept of "reality". His theory of dreams is paradigmatic. Oneiric productiveness – subtracting deformation by censorship – appears as the model of subjective freedom: "in a certain sense we are free only when we are asleep" (Fromm, 1972a:63). "In dreams, the individual transcends the narrow boundaries of his society and becomes fully human" (Fromm, 1968a:74): they allow acknowledgment of the real relation to the object. Something similar happens with Fromm's concept of "generative perception". Pure phantasy, abstracted from perceptual "reproduction", is for him in the nature of "hallucination" and madness (Fromm, 1947a:89). At the same time, generative perception is treated as a privileged means for recognizing the true nature of things (cf. Fromm, 1959c).

Even though the difference between the "efficacy" of phantasy and effectiveness as such is never lost, the duplicity of the terms points to the naturalistic expectation that, at the basis of psychic reality – that is, within the dynamism of affects – there must subsist an adequacy between human nature and nature in general. On the back side of phantasy, we find reality, and on the back of reality, we find phantasy. Hence the assertion that an appropriate relation to things is double: "the full and productive relatedness to an object comprises this polarity of perceiving it in its uniqueness, and at the same time in its generality; in its concreteness, and at the same time in its abstractness" (Fromm, 1955a:114). In the assertion of a deep coincidence between affects and things, the unconscious recovers in Fromm a vehemently objective character. Thus conceived, it is in fact *real* – "human reality" (Fromm, 1968h:50) –, unnameable to conceptual apprehension, even though it remains potentially given to awareness, and always effective as "unconscious experience".

We may now better understand the correspondences between thought process and attitudes. They occur because both sides of the relation are treated as "modes of comprehension" – ways in which the subject appropriates things subjectively (cf. Fromm, 1992s:143). While distinct according to their phenomenological status, affects and ideas are similar in their character as means through which human beings grasp the world (cf. Fromm, 1990e). The intellectual process is an extension of the primary, affective apprehension of the object, while at the same time resulting from the separation between subject and object. Fromm (1960a) is correspondingly divided between two intellectual postures. On the one hand, he mistrusts the alienating potential of words, seeking a sublation of thought in intuition. On the other hand, he treats apprehension in act and apprehension in idea as complementary movements, each in their own way incomplete. Rational intellection doesn't overcome the existential split. In action, the unfolding of the other's potentialities ultimately exceeds understanding. As an attempt at reconciling the extremes, we find a proposal for unity in practice: departing from negation in thought, Fromm reaches the affirmation of real possibility in the act:

> Love is active penetration of the other person, in which the desire to know is stilled by union [...] In the act of fusion I know you, I know myself, I know everybody – and I "know" nothing. I know in the only way in which knowledge of that which is alive is possible for man – by the experience of union, not by any knowledge our thought can give. The only way to full knowledge lies in the act of love; this act transcends thought, it transcends words. It is the daring plunge into the essence of another – or my own.
> (Fromm, 1957a:195)

Bibliography

Primary sources

Correspondence

Foerster_H_Von_1972–1904–29-to: Fromm to Heinz von Foerster, April 29th, 1972.
Schecter_David_1976–1907–05-to: Fromm to David Schecter, July 5th, 1976.

Drafts, typescripts, and study materials by Fromm

d-1991d-002-eng-draft-05: transcription of the recordings published as *The art of listening*.

Published sources

Ferenczi, Sándor. Das unwillkommene Kind und sein Todestrieb. *Bausteine III.* Bern: Verlag Hans Huber, [1929]/1939.
Freud, Sigmund. Drei Abhandlungen zur Sexualtheorie. *Gesammelte Werke V.* Frankfurt: S. Fischer Verlag, [1905–1924]/1968.
Freud, Sigmund. Die Verdrängung. *Gesammelte Werke X.* London: Imago Publishing, [1915a]/1949.
Freud, Sigmund. Das Unbewußte. *Gesammelte Werke X.* London: Imago Publishing, [1915b]/1949.
Freud, Sigmund. Über libidinöse Typen. *Gesammelte Werke XIV.* London: Imago Publishing, [1931]/1955.
Freud, Sigmund. Die endliche und die unendliche Analyse. *Gesammelte Werke XVI.* London: Imago Publishing, [1937]/1961.
Fromm, Erich. Selfishness and self-love. *Love, sexuality, and matriarchy.* New York: Fromm International Edition, [1939b]/1997.
Fromm, Erich. *Escape from freedom.* New York: Henry Holt & Company, [1941a]/1994.
Fromm, Erich. *Man for himself.* New York: Henry Holt & Company, [1947a]/1990.
Fromm, Erich. Sexuality and character. *Love, sexuality, and matriarchy.* New York: Fromm International Edition, [1948b]/1997.
Fromm, Erich. The nature of dreams. *Scientific American*:180:44–47, 1949a.
Fromm, Erich. *Psychoanalysis and religion.* New York: Bantam Books, [1950a]/1967.
Fromm, Erich. *The sane society.* New York: Henry Holt & Company, [1955a]/1990.
Fromm, Erich. The present human condition. *The dogma of Christ.* New York: Holt, Rinehart and Winston, [1955c]/1963.
Fromm, Erich. *The art of loving.* London: Thorsons Editions, [1956a]/1995.
Fromm, Erich. On the limitations and dangers of psychology. *The dogma of Christ.* New York: Holt, Rinehart and Winston, [1957a]/1992.
Fromm, Erich. Die autoritäre Persönlichkeit. *Deutsche Universitätszeitung*:12 (9):3f, 1957c.
Fromm, Erich. The creative attitude. H.A. Anderson (ed.). *Creativity and its cultivation.* New York: Harper and Row, 1959c.
Fromm, Erich. Psychoanalysis and Zen Buddhism. *Psychoanalysis and Zen Buddhism.* London: Unwin Paperbacks, [1960a]/1987.
Fromm, Erich. *May man prevail?.* New York: Doubleday & Company, Inc., [1961a]/1961.
Fromm, Erich. *Beyond the chains of illusion.* New York: Continuum, [1962a]/2001.
Fromm, Erich. The revolutionary character. *The dogma of Christ.* New York: Holt, Rinehart and Winston, [1963b]/1992.
Fromm, Erich. *The heart of man: its genius for good and evil.* New York: Harper and Row, 1964a.
Fromm, Erich. *You shall be as gods.* New York: Fawcett Premier, [1966a]/1983.
Fromm, Erich. *The revolution of hope.* New York: Bantam Books, 1968a.
Fromm, Erich. On the sources of human destructiveness. L. Ng (ed.). *Alternatives to violence.* New York: Time Inc., 1968e.
Fromm, Erich. Marx's contribution to the knowledge of man. *The crisis of psychoanalysis.* New York: Holt, Reinehart and Winston, [1968h]/1970.
Fromm, Erich. The crisis of psychoanalysis. *The crisis of psychoanalysis.* New York: Holt, Rinehart and Winston, [1970c]/1970.

Fromm, Erich. On the theory and strategy of peace. *On disobedience and other essays.* London: Routledge & Kegan Paul, [1970h]/1984.
Fromm, Erich. Dreams are the universal language of man. *For the love of life.* New York: The Free Press, [1972a]/1986.
Fromm, Erich. *The anatomy of human destructiveness.* New York: Henry Holt & Company, [1973a]/1992.
Fromm, Erich. In the name of life: a portrait through dialogue. *For the love of life.* New York: The Free Press, [1974b]/1986.
Fromm, Erich. Hitler – who was he and what constituted resistance against him. *For the love of life.* New York: The Free Press, [1974c]/1986.
Fromm, Erich. *To have or to be?* New York: Bantam Books, [1976a]/1981.
Fromm, Erich. Vita activa. H.J. Schultz (ed.). *Was der Mensch braucht.* Stuttgart: Kreuz-Verlag, 1977a.
Fromm, Erich. My own concept of man. *Fromm Forum*:17:5–10, [1977g]/2013.
Fromm, Erich. Marx and religion. Seyed Javad Miri; Robert Lake; Tricia M. Kress (eds.). *Reclaiming the sane society.* Rotterdam: Sense Publishers, [1979b]/2014.
Fromm, Erich. *Arbeiter und Angestellt am Vorabend des Dritten Reiches.* Giessen: Psychosozial-Verlag, [1980a]/2019.
Fromm, Erich. On the origins of aggression. *For the love of life.* New York: The Free Press, [1983c]/1986.
Fromm, Erich. Who is man? *For the love of life.* New York: The Free Press, [1983d]/1986.
Fromm, Erich. *The art of being.* New York: Continuum, [1989a]/1998.
Fromm, Erich. On my psychoanalytic approach. *The revision of psychoanalysis.* Boulder: Westview Press, [1990d]/1992.
Fromm, Erich. The necessity for the revision of psychoanalysis. *The revision of psychoanalysis.* Boulder: Westview Press, [1990e]/1992.
Fromm, Erich. *The art of listening.* London: Constable, [1991a]/1994.
Fromm, Erich. Modern man's pathology of normalcy. *The pathology of normalcy.* New York: American Mental Health Foundation, [1991e]/2010.
Fromm, Erich. Man's impulse structure and its relation to culture. *Beyond Freud.* New York: American Mental Health Foundation, [1992e]/2010.
Fromm, Erich. Psychic needs and society. *Beyond Freud.* New York: American Mental Health Foundation, [1992f]/2010.
Fromm, Erich. Dealing with the unconscious in psychotherapeutic practice. *Beyond Freud.* New York: American Mental Health Foundation, [1992g]/2010.
Fromm, Erich. Some beliefs of man, in man, for man. *On being human.* New York: Continuum, [1992q]/2005.
Fromm, Erich. Meister Eckhart and Karl Marx on having and being. *On being human.* New York: Continuum, [1992s]/2005.
Fromm, Erich. Maccoby, Michael. *Social character in a Mexican village.* New York: Routledge, [1970b]/1996.
Jones, Ernest. *The God complex: the belief that one is God, and the resulting character traits. Psycho-myth, psycho-history, vol. 2.* New York: Hillstone, [1913]/1974.
Marx, Karl. Ökonomische Manuskripte 1857-8. *MEGA II.1.* Berlin: Akademie Verlag, [1857–1858]/2006.
Weber, Max. Die Objektivität sozialwissenschaftler und sozialpolitischer Erkenntnis. *Gesammelte Aufsätze zur Wissenschaftslehre.* Tübingen: Verlag von J. C. B. Mohr, [1904]/1922.

Secondary literature

Braune, Joan. *Erich Fromm's revolutionary hope*. Rotterdam: Sense Publishers, 2014.
Cusimano, Franco Antonio; Luban-Plozza, Boris. *Erich Fromm*. Milano: Puleio Edizioni.
Dietrich, Jan. Religion und Gesellschafts-Charakter. Rainer Funk, Helmut Joach, Gerd Meyer (eds.). *Erich Fromm heute*. München: DTV, 2000.
Durkin, Kieran. *The radical humanism of Erich Fromm*. New York: Palgrave Macmillan, 2014.
Funk, Rainer. *Mut zum Menschen*. Stuttgart: Deutsche Verlags-Anstalt, 1978.
Funk, Rainer. *Das Leben selbst ist eine Kunst*. Freiburg: Herder, 2007.
Hardeck, Jürgen. *Vernunft und Liebe*. Berlin: Üllstein, 1992.
Hardeck, Jürgen. Humanismus und Religion: Pluralismus der Wege, nicht der Werte. Rainer Funk, Helmut Joach, Gerd Meyer (eds.). *Erich Fromm heute*. München: DTV, 2000.
Lundgren, Svante. *Fight against idols*. New York: Peter Lang, 1998.
Maccoby, Michael. The two voices of Erich Fromm: the prophetic and the analytic. Michael Maccoby, Mauricio Cortina (eds.). *A prophetic analyst*. London: Jason Aronson Inc., 1996.
Merkur, Dan. *Explorations of the psychoanalytic mystics*. New York: Rodopi, 2010.
Pietikainen, Petteri. *Alchemists of human nature*. London: Pickering & Chatto, 2007.
Thompson, Michael. Fromm's social ontology and the ethical framework of critical theory. Kieran Durkin, Joan Braune (eds). *Erich Fromm's critical theory*. New York: Bloomsbury, 2020.

Chapter 5

V To Touch Reality
Language and Experience in Erich Fromm's Clinics

"It is a peculiar discrepancy that I have in all my writings", Fromm tells David Schecter in 1974: he had

> written very little about the immediate detailed clinical experience when this is one main basis of my thinking and the one in which I find the greatest satisfaction. To understand a dream in a way which is satisfactory to me and to the students gives me still probably more pleasure than any more theoretical endeavour, because I love the concrete and the specific and that which one can see.
>
> (Schecter_David_1974-03-28-to)

Fromm justified this discrepancy saying: "one of the grounds why I never wrote anything about the technique of analysis is that I always had the feeling: I don't know enough, I still need to learn more" (u-1976:28). However, from the mid-1960s on, he had the purpose of writing a systematic treatise on humanistic psychoanalysis, which would have included a section on treatment if finished (cf. Schachtel_Ernst_1965-08-30-to). Fromm didn't accord "technique" a central place in his work, but he opposed the idea that treatment could rely entirely on "individual intuition": "technique is [...] the application of the theory to practice". The art of analyzing would be a compromise between the analyst's singular standpoint and broader principles: "of course the factors, the individual traces of technique depend on the personality of the analyst, his character, his temperament, and many other personal factors, but the general traces of the technique depend on the theory". Pondering the existence and legitimacy of a psychoanalytic technique, Fromm would conclude: "of course there is one and there is not one"; it is "an art, an art is an individual expression; [...] nonetheless [...] there are general laws" (u-1968b:1).

The task of reconstructing Fromm's views on psychoanalytic technique is correspondingly divided in two segments. First, we must discover the theoretical premises giving Fromm's injunctions their particular meaning. Secondly, we must determine their roots in clinical practice. A number of studies and testimonies have already covered a part of this work (e.g. Funk, 2009). They rely either on the memory of Fromm's disciples and analysands, on posthumously published lectures, or on the scarce statements he makes on treatment throughout his works. Here, we shall prioritize sources in which Fromm speaks in the first person about his practical stance. These are centrally the transcriptions of three clinical seminars from 1953, 1968, and 1976, as well as tape recordings from 1966, whereupon Fromm can be heard supervising a case. Clinically relevant statements can be found in a number of audio recordings and videos, in unpublished writings, drafts, and interviews. Fromm's letters with other psychoanalysts also allow us occasional insights into his clinical reasoning.

These documents range from 1952 to 1980, covering a large period after Fromm's break with orthodox technique. Their astounding coherence and relative scarcity authorize emphasizing their similarities over their differences (compare Wolstein, 1981). These and other sources will be used to defend three theses:

1. Fromm has a historical conception of clinical practice. Because suffering is historically mediated, also diagnostic criteria, technical approaches, and nosology vary through time. While the general goals of psychoanalysis are conceived as universal, the means for achieving them depend on the specific historical situation of the analysand.
2. Fromm's theoretical contributions, particularly in social characterology, should be read back in their diagnostic significance. His handling of key praxiological categories, such as transference and resistance, must be understood in reference to his clinical goals.
3. Underlying Fromm's historical conception of treatment is a specific understanding of the relationship between five categories: experience, language, reality, illusion, and truth. They allow us to ground Fromm's clinical stance on his broader ontological assumptions.

I History and Suffering

That particular forms of suffering are of historical nature is immediately implied by Fromm's theoretical premises. According to him, character is formed as the outcome of definite life conditions, which invite the subject into a specific practice of life: "a socio-economic *condition* [...] leads to a certain practice of life and thus shapes man's character" (Fromm, 1961a:69). As she addresses her survival needs, the subject is affected by the beings around her. Affection is also sought as such, since relatedness is a primary need for the human being. Over this mass of affects, there grows an increasingly complex and stable system of attitudes. Each element has its quality and significance modified by its relation to all others. They form a "wholeness" out of the process of their "constant interaction" (Fromm, 1979a:13). The totality thus constituted provides the content for one's practice of life, in which character is either confirmed and reproduced, or pushed towards change.

Historical conditions appear so far as the circumstances out of which character develops. The emphasis falls on the positive aspect: orientations and their traits are actualized, either due to pragmatic necessity, or in repeated affection in relation to certain objects. However, historical factors appear in Fromm also as immanent to the psychic structure, and as fulfilling a mostly negative function – "society has both a furthering *and* a distorting influence on man" (Fromm, 1955a:73). The instances demanding repression are represented both outside and within the psychic structure. "In each society there are social filters which the thoughts and feelings must cross, so that it becomes in general possible to think, feel, or speak them" (Fromm, 1977b:20). Among such filters, Fromm (1962a) counted language, logic, and social taboos. These represented for him the main barriers sustaining the unconsciousness of certain experiences: "What produces repression is in general convention. In other words, it is the thoughts of the social pattern that say that a thought, an experience, should not exist" (u-1968b:11).

Experience has an exceeding quality in comparison to what words can convey: "the full experience exists only up to the point when it is expressed in language" (Fromm, 1960a:62). As historical relations change, new experiences emerge, which take time before they are consistent enough to be formulated in public communication: "the unthinkable cannot be thought, because it lies beyond all external or internal experiences that can be made in a society" (Fromm, 1978b:23). Lies, omissions, and objective blindspots participate in producing a time's hegemonic categories of thought, reproducing the social structure as it presently exists:

> Each culture makes certain assumptions about man and nature which are so generally accepted that there is little awareness of the fact that they have arisen out of the social practice of a culture, and that they are very special assumptions different from those made in other cultures. [...] But what is shared are not only certain views and theories, but built-in categories of perception common to all members of a given culture. [...] They are categories through which all impressions of the outer world are filtered and thus ordered and structured in our perceptions. They are expressed in the practice of life, in language, and logic, and furthermore they determine what is and what is not excluded from our consciousness.
> (d-1976a-000-eng-type-1974–03:1–2).

What cannot be said, thought, or done, includes especially experiential elements that would risk society's current mode of existence: "the truth is [...] a threat to the status quo" (Fromm, 1973a:292). For every particular social class or group, the bulk of unconsciousness is a function of its practical position in life, and the corresponding forms of thought. Repression being among the conditions that sustain suffering, we see how it is to be taken as historically conditioned.

This does not mean that every form of suffering is reducible to historical contingency. For Fromm (1947a), some dilemmas and contradictions inhere in the human condition. However, their accessibility to consciousness, and the way they are treated, are also mediated by culture. In contemporary societies, psychotherapy is one of such cultural instruments for handling suffering. This is the beginning of a historical understanding of therapeutic practices, among which psychoanalysis finds itself.

Fromm didn't think psychoanalysis was the only legitimate method for treatment: "I am convinced", he told his students, "that the analyst should also practice and know how to practice methods of psychotherapy that are not analytic, because if he doesn't, he exposes himself to analyzing patients that would in reality better be treated by other methods" (u-1968b:31). Nonetheless, he insisted in three basic demarcations. First, psychoanalysis should be differentiated from all treatments falling short of reaching the unconscious roots of suffering, like suggestion, counseling, or charlatanism. Second, it should uphold its peculiarity in comparison to methods bringing unconscious material into consciousness through other means, such as meditation or practices of bodily awareness. Finally, it should differentiate between adaptive and radical transformative goals (cf. Fromm, u-1953; Feiner, 1975).

For Fromm, adaptation was not always problematic – but he didn't think psychoanalysis could be legitimized if this was the only therapeutic goal, since purely behavioral modification would suffice for achieving the same in less time. He thought the peculiarity of analysis lay beyond liberation from symptomatic suffering, in a "transtherapeutic" goal: "self-liberation by optimal self-awareness" (Fromm, 1989a:64):

> Analysis can transcend its function, this function of betterment of the infirmity, reaching a point of change of the whole personality in the sense and in the direction of an increase of energy, an increase of well-being, a greater freedom, a greater internal freedom; the development of value, of firmness, of connection, of love greater than what was promised.
>
> (u-1968b:3)

For Fromm (1991a), character analysis had primacy over symptom analysis (compare Biancoli and Luban-Plozza, 1987). Symptoms were treated as contingent expressions of the same structure feeding into characterological suffering: "I say a change in behavior does not necessarily mean a change in structure, but change in structure certainly means change in behavior". Cure was conceived as transformation of the whole character, taking place only when "the basic structure of forces in the person" has been modified (Fromm, u-1953:9,23).

Fromm recognizes the historical conditionality of therapeutic practices in two senses. First, he acknowledges their dependence on economic and political structures, which may impair their capacity to foster radical transformation: "Psychoanalysis opened a market": "a whole market, namely [the promise that] one can cure unhappy people from their unhappiness" (Fromm, u-1976b:55). The same relationship between social class and ideology applies here as anywhere else: "each form of analysis has its own social stratum" (Fromm, u-1976b:76). In the case of Freudian orthodoxy, the necessity to sustain bureaucratic power over the practitioners leads analysis to a dogmatic and ritualistic stance. Patients find in analytic vocabulary a substitute for religion, a frame of reference within which they can orient their lives:

> The great popularity of psychoanalysis in the West, and particularly in the United States, since the beginning of the thirties has undoubtedly the same social basis. Here is a middle class for whom life has lost meaning. They have no political or religious ideals, yet are in search of a meaning, of an idea to devote themselves to, of an explanation of life which does not require faith or sacrifices, and which satisfies this need to feel part of a movement. All these needs were fulfilled by the [Psychoanalytic] Movement.
>
> (Fromm, 1959a:112)

A tacit agreement is formed between the institutional powers and its clients, such that therapy risks losing its transformative quality. "I am maybe used from America to another patient material", Fromm tells in his later years, "namely, people for whom it belongs almost to routine to go in an analysis" (u-1976:37). In the case of heterodox psychoanalysis, Fromm is wary of the same risks his opponents saw in "neo-Freudianism". Like Marcuse, Fromm believes heterodox analysis risks falling into a conformistic position: "the non-orthodox way of analyzing is just as dangerous as the Freudian way" (Fromm, u-1953:7). The main reason for that is economic. With the expansion of the market for psychoanalysis, therapists' status and income becomes dependent on their reputation among patients. Thus arises the fear of frustrating or challenging the client. Again a happy agreement may be formed with the analysand's resistances, such that no substantial change is achieved or sought: "you are trying to look at the situation from the standpoint of anyone who sells something, and who wants a satisfied customer. So you are beginning to falsify, in the first place, your findings" (Fromm, u-1953:32).

Economic factors act upon analysis as external conditions, inviting it into giving up its radical possibilities. Most important for us, however, is the way in which historical factors appear within the analytic situation. Fromm treats analysis not only as a participant in the economic and political structures of its time, but also in its cultural structures. Analysis being centrally a practice based on symbolic exchange, it participates in the general dynamics of communication: "we live in a culture in which language has much more the function of hiding than of communicating" (Fromm, u-1953:31). If practiced without awareness of its cultural position, therapy risks reproducing the same (linguistic, logic, moral) blindspots sustaining repression – particularly those prevailing in the character structure of analysts and analysands alike.

Fromm's criticism of orthodox and heterodox practitioners is extended into the peculiarities of their technical handling. Orthodox Freudian ritualism is conditioned by its institutional situation, but also by its roots in the spirit of authoritarian patriarchalism since Freud's time (cf. Fromm, 1935a). The analysand is often let without response, experiencing a helpless dependence on the authority of the analyst: the setting "artificially infantilize[s] the patient so that more of the unconscious material comes up" (Fromm, 1991a:29). This provides conditions for regression during the analytic hour – sometimes of quasi-hypnotic, dream-like character. Hence the affinity between certain orthodox stances and the authoritarian character. With heterodox treatment, Fromm believes the danger lies closer to the prevalent marketing character in the US of his time: "the language in our time and age has a very similar function of abstractification which money has" (Fromm, u-1953:70). We learn from his clinical seminars that his denunciation of "free chatter" (1991a:117) is directed specifically at the neo-Freudian and humanistic schools, in which he sees a tendency for trivializing free association into superficial conversation, under the banner of a friendlier posture towards the patient. This risks deteriorating therapy into a reinforcement of unconsciousness:

> I think that psychoanalysis is one of the best methods to avoid knowing anything about oneself. I think it is also the best method to know oneself, but certainly there is hardly any method which serves so well the tendency to avoid knowing oneself than psychoanalysis, whether that is Freud's free-association or non-Freudian free association and chatter [...] partly because you don't touch anything which really matters in terms of your experience.
> (Fromm, u-1953:47)

Fromm takes avoidance of truthful association as a duplicate, in the analytic relationship, of a larger trend in North American culture. In trivial talk, Fromm says,

> actually I engage in the same kind of politeness, in the same level of discourse and distance which is characteristic of our usual way of human intercourse, in which instead of reacting directly and spontaneously, we at best hint at things in order not to hurt anybody's feeling.
> (u-1953:30)

It would be part of conversational habits in the US to do away with the tension between publicity and privacy, to avoid contradiction, to remain unaffected. This is hostile environment for true insight: "when you do not let your thoughts and feelings build up pressure, as it were, they do not become fruitful" (Fromm, 1955a:167). If those habits are reproduced within the therapeutic relation, the analyst becomes merely a "sympathetic listener", upon which a significant aspect of unconscious life remains untouched: "there is no sane relation to anything which is reality, and words are used in what seems to me one would consider a pathological form, were it not for the fact that the pathology is cultural, social pathology" (u-1953:32).

Symptoms brought the mark of history as well. Fromm believed, for example, that hysteria of the kind Freud treated was dependent on the "lifestyle" of the 19th century, "the style of big pathos". Its emotional expressiveness had little space left in a world of affective indifference, as was for him the North American 20th century. There, the prevalent "normal" character would have an affinity with schizophrenia, depression – forms of suffering in which the secession between affects and ideas or the "incapacity to feel" (Fromm, 1961a:24) is central:

> The 20th century today has completely lost pathos. [...] Modern man is closer to the schizoid character than to the hysterical one. He feels little, is first of all closed, not communicative, and one can see clearly how here the lifestyle of a society, the cultural lifestyle, which is in turn conditioned through the social function, bears on the change of the symptoms.
> (Fromm, u-1976:33)

Fromm thought it was the task of psychoanalysis to formulate and tackle contemporary problems – the peculiarities of suffering characteristic for the place and time in which it was practiced. Writing to Schachtel on the case of a Basque analysand, Fromm ponders:

> According to Western standards, one would have to assume either a lack of intelligence, or a deeply neurotic inability to act constructively, but the problem which interests me is, whether his attitude is not determined by specific elements in the Basque character, and therefore is not to be interpreted in a way different from what it would have for a representative of modern Western culture.
> (Schachtel_Ernst_1952–10–18-to)

Correspondingly, he asked his students: "what is the trouble in our culture, what is the pathogenic factor in our culture [...] what is the pathogenic factor in twentieth century industrial capitalistic society in Europe or the United States: What are people suffering from here?" (u-1953:64,66). This had implications even at the level of dynamic categories: there would be a cultural particularity to psychic mechanisms themselves. Fromm didn't believe "repression", as it was conceptualized in classic psychoanalysis, was done away with as the belle époque ended. However, in its claim to generality, the concept implied something of the particular characterological constellation of European societies before the First World War (cf. Fromm, 1990g). It was no coincidence that suffering would fall in the sexual sphere back then, and Freud's conceptualization was in line with that: "the whole concept of the unconscious as we find it in Freud [...] has a very direct relation to the cultural and historical situation in which Freud lived, to the problems of that period (sexual repression)" (Fromm, u-1953:64).

Fromm thought the notion of "dissociation" offered a better description of the pathogenic properties specific to North American culture, in which sexuality ceased to be a taboo and passed into a form of consumerism: "our problem is not so much, or not only the problem of the unconscious, something that has been repressed and which isn't there, but it is a problem of our alienation from our own feelings and experiences, of the dimness, vagueness, unreality of what goes on in ourselves" (Fromm, u-1953:64). The problem lay now in the inability to feel fully and deeply; not so much in unawareness of desires, as of their affective roots:

> Psychoanalysis would have to be defined in our day and age not in terms of uncovering the unconscious primarily, but getting in touch with oneself and overcoming alienation from oneself, overcoming the abstractification which has occurred with everything in us and around us. That would be the aim of analytic theory.
>
> (Fromm, u-1953:71–2)

Similarly, an estimate of the tasks of psychoanalysis in other times and places would have to start with an understanding of the peculiarities in the local social unconscious.

Frommian analysis wanted to institute a way of communicating that transcends social blindspots and conventions. Fromm is strict: "the patient must know that in this room that is the analyst's clinic, one does not lie, one leaves behind these conventional topics" (u-1968b:16): "the analyst has to start using a different style, using words which are direct, which refer to reality, which are not hiding anything" (u-1953:40). His recommendation of "directness" and "honesty", of a rather straightforward form of communication, should be understood under this premise (1992g:119). To be sure, Fromm thought directness was integral to any form of deep relatedness:

> Any talk which springs from any sense of reality, from being in touch with reality, [...] any such talk presupposes a particular kind of interpersonal relationship without which the talk is completely abstract. That is to say, not related to any experience in the two persons who talk, and, therefore, nothing is exchanged, and aside from intellectual talk and abstractions, nothing is communicated.
>
> (Fromm, u-1953:71)

This aspect considered, however, directness and honesty should not be taken immediately as general predicaments. Rather, their assertion was meant to counter a particular cultural defect. North American conventions for routine talk were Fromm's model for what an interaction "from periphery to periphery" would look like (1992g:105): "human communication in our culture is such that we touch each other tangentially, from surface to surface, and we say some words about it. [...] That is essentially the communication which we have in our social life (u-1953:44). "Center to center relatedness" stood in specific opposition to it (1962a:152) – but there would be other ways to falsify communication. About Mexico, Fromm thought: "our social convention is insincerity". About Japan, contrariwise: "the Japanese" consider it "a lack of friendliness, in case they are asked something, to soften things and not to tell the truth" (u-1968b:9,12). A communication aimed at affecting and mobilizing the analysand's energies had its place especially while dealing with a society repressing feelings. Other cultural settings, with their corresponding social unconscious, would imply the need for different technical tenets.

Often lacking in Fromm's published outcome, but abundant elsewhere, is the consciousness that technique has to be adapted to the symptomatology of the case. This is particularly evident in Fromm's considerations on psychosis. He recommended not encouraging the patient artificially – but "with the exception of a hopeless depression". "Other techniques are applied" (u-1976:31,35) also for full-blown schizophrenia.

It is perhaps no coincidence that psychotic suffering was paradigmatic of this principle for him. His relational approach was developed as he learned from Frieda Fromm-Reichmann's (1939, 1949) and Harry Stack Sullivan's (1940–45, 1962) innovations in the treatment of schizophrenic and depressive patients. Like them, Fromm believed that, in such cases, "the most potent medicine there is is a human being"(Urquhart_Clara_1970-07-06-to). The fact that Fromm wrote little about psychotic cases (and maybe treated few of them) is another discrepancy in his published output, since the antecedents to his clinical approach developed out of attempts at making severe narcissism available to transferential influence. Even Karl Abraham's (1924) characterology, which was pivotal for Fromm, was not independent from his pioneering studies in the treatment of narcissistic neurosis. The knowledge that even the most withdrawn patients remain open to affection colored Fromm's whole understanding of human relatedness.

"Directness" should not be understood as carelessly emitting an authoritative statement once an interpretation is reached. Fromm thought language, as addressed towards the unconscious, has to respect the ambiguity, the yet-unknown character of the repressed. The patient should not be prevented from developing her own associations, and if the analyst intervened, then her language should preserve the indeterminacy of what is trying to be articulated:

> If you say, "You feel insecure. You feel not wanted", you make a statement which is by far less precise and accurate and less something

to really talk about than what I expressed in this sentence [employing symbolism], because [...] all the defenses of the patient against the insight of this kind of feelings come up by saying and feeling quite correctly, this isn't true and assuming it isn't true. This person at the party doesn't feel exactly not wanted. She is just not entirely sure, which is something quite different.

(Fromm, u-1953:55)

The analyst's formulation should at the same time point to the overall configuration of forces acting in the analysand's character – "it is important to have a frame, not a total one (this is not a very good word), but an integrated frame instead of separated pieces" (Fromm, u-1968b:20). Fromm thought symbolic language was a particularly apt instrument for that: to express an inner experience by symbols is a most precise, specific, and if you please, in that sense, scientific way of expressing a feeling" (u-1953:54). But he also welcomed the possibility of intervening in other ways. The point with directness was for him that the analyst should take full responsibility for what she says. She should not be afraid of making a point, hiding behind timid formulations when arousing conflict would be needed for the development of therapy. A sense of confrontation with oneself was, for Fromm, a hallmark of therapeutic effect: "man reacts in an almost miraculous way, a very interesting one, if he is confronted with the total reality, and if he is confronted in a way that is not a criticism nor an accusation, but also not softness". (u-1968b*:13; cf. Spiegel, 1981)

To institute a different way of speaking in the analytic situation, in general a different way of relating, would allow transcending the culturally prevailing experience. For Fromm, the curative aspect of analysis lies in the capacity to experience what cannot be articulated in words, while having them as midwives and intermediaries in the process:

> Might we not say perhaps that the important thing is the thing which can never be interpreted, that the important thing, the thing which is effective in analysis, is that which cannot be interpreted, but which can simply be experienced, that interpretations at best pave the way, do away with some impediments, but that which can be effective in analysis is never the interpretation.
>
> (Fromm, u-1953:37)

Fromm shared the belief in the relevance of emotional intensity with Karen Horney (1987), another important influence. Both agreed on the relevance of the depth of experience as a therapeutic factor: it should gradually lead the analysand to a higher degree of receptiveness to the ambiguities of emotional life. For Fromm, an analyzed subject would become open to all in herself, both rational and irrational, and make an experience of what a better lived life looks like (cf. VID-1963e). This would be an experience of vitality, of aliveness, of the happiness which accompanies the free exercise of our capacities: "I live in the externalization of my human vital forces; I live lively, I am" (Fromm, u-1977:1). Vitality and growth were the criteria under which he judged the dialogue between analyst and analysand:

> The best I can say about the whole process of analytic technique is that said process must always be characterized by being very alive, precisely because every psychopathology is a lack or absence of life, and for that reason the analyst must give the diseased an example and have a method that is not a [merely mechanic] technique.
> (Fromm, u-1968b:64)

Many of Fromm's indications on the way one should speak with the patient aim at sustaining a sense of movement throughout the course of treatment. His will is that "analysis always move, that it is never stagnant, that it always be about something essential, and that no analytic hour should transcur in which nothing happens" (Fromm, u-1968b:14). Analysis should elicit a living example of what a relation carried in full concentration and activeness feels like – an antidote to psychic death. Instead of Freudian free-floating attention, Fromm recommended a variant he called "concentrated, intense floating attention" (u-1968b:19) as a condition for a deep activation of the analysand – one grounded in her experience of herself as an active subject. This would be the way both for prophylaxis, for a relief from suffering, and for a proper curative effect.

We must read Fromm's comments on his transition out of the Freudian approach under this light. That Fromm felt "boredom" (1979a:40) with his Freudian sessions means that he felt lacking, in the communicational structure suggested by orthodox technique, the means for actually touching life – the one resource with whose help character transformation could be achieved. "I had no living relationship to the patients!", he would complain later in life (VID-1977a). Correspondingly, Fromm's (1955d) only published paper on technique past his Freudian years is a collection of suggestions on what to do if association is stuck: "I behave in an active way to stimulate the patient to talk and react, to respond to significant points in all his situation" (Fromm, u-1968b:12).

As years pass, Fromm comes to defend what he calls an "active technique" (u-1976:13). It was under this heading that Ferenczi (1919–1926) carried his first technical experiments. He tried to find a solution for particularly stagnating resistances, and to accelerate treatment. In Ferenczi's method, the analyst would – contrary to Freudian habit – give specific positive indications, orders, prohibitions, in the expectation that sanctioning one avenue of expression would lead the repressed to displace onto new, more easily analyzable manifestations. Frommian technique is nonetheless more strongly indebted to Ferenczi's (1927–33) later writings – which stem partly from the failure of his earlier experiments with "active technique". Fromm was indeed also worried that the therapeutic process not be extended beyond need, favoring "brief analysis" when the case or the purpose allowed it. With an active method, he said, therapy "becomes certainly shorter" (u-1976:28). He would also not refrain from recommending extra-clinical practices to his analysands – "I invite many patients to learn to meditate" (u-1976b:28). However, he still adhered to the principle that the analyst should not interfere with the patient's life (cf. 1960a). The point lay for him not in the "active prescription" of certain exercises or obligations, but in the *activating* effect of therapy: "the mobilization of the latent energies of a person is actually the central issue of all analytic work" (Fromm, 1991a:108). Analysis should seek to evoke and strengthen the subject's capacity for activity through the aliveness of its own process. In that would reside cure, true transformation.

2 Technique and Vitality

Fromm's handling of analytic technique derives from the principles we articulated above. He expected preliminary interviews to generate a good *prognosis* already after the first hours (cf. u-1968b), even though he would recognize elsewhere how difficult that can be. A preliminary appreciation of the case would allow deciding whether analysis is the adequate method for treatment. If prospects for betterment were little, Fromm considered unreasonable to start (cf. 1991a:104). Judgment should be based on the question: can we expect the analysand's vital forces to collaborate with treatment, or will deadening forces prevail? Malignancy in psychopathology depended for him on this basic balance of forces: "a person who suffers, always suffers from not being able to love life in some way and that is why the person becomes sick" (u-1953:40). The symptomatology of the case would therefore not be the decisive criterion. Fromm recognized how misleading the outward appearance of a case can be. For example: discussing a case bearing all the signs of deep destructiveness, he concludes this was not the deeper reality: "I call this […] a pseudonecrophiliac. He had all the symptoms of necrophilia, but was in reality no deeply necrophilous character. The necrophilous image is in reality a reaction" (u-1976:26).

Following prognosis, Fromm suggested *diagnosis* as an enduring practice, through the whole course of analysis: it is important that "the analyst be elastic, flexible, that he from time to time venture into seeing things totally anew, forgetting what he knows, into seeing the person as if he had never seen her" (u-1968b:64). One should build an ongoing picture of the forces participating in the development of the case, updating it regularly, and asking: "to what degree has the patient gotten better, and to what degree is this betterment due to true discoveries of his unconscious?". This should allow proceeding to "the evaluation of the dynamic structure of his character, comparing the structure before analysis with the point it reached afterwards" (u-1968b:3).

Fromm recommended a radical detachment from all previous conjectures on the case, in favor of a continued penetration into details as they unfold.

Theoretically, this matches the function of analysis as a scientific endeavor – "in psychology we deal with feelings as facts" (u-1953:33). Its peculiarity for diagnosis is connected to Fromm's systemic conception of psychic determination. "Each analysis", he thought, "is an investigation process, and for that reason is based on the principles of scientific investigation; and one of these principles is the process of seeing the whole of an integrated frame" (u-1968b*:18–9). This diagnostic principle also bore therapeutic consequences. According to him, "interpretation is more efficient if it is total than if it is partial", because "man is not exactly a synthesis of separate factors, but lives as a totality which always moves itself, and the knowledge of moving within him [...] is the only knowledge that makes me understand totally how he works" (u-1968b*:8; u-1968b:36).

Fromm's diagnostics are based on a systematic comparison between character traits and symptoms. He doesn't approach symptomatic formations individually, but tries to determine common underlying attitudes behind both, subsequently deducing the probable forces dominating that particular psychic structure. In the one supervision session we have fully recorded, Fromm proceeds precisely like that. Confronted with a case in which the patient displays fears and phantasies related to rape, and even reports a memory of it, he first asks whether the same attitude would be found elsewhere. He realizes the whole complexion of the analysand is one of closure to the world, of withdrawal, concluding that the symptom is probably not derived from one single sexual experience. Rather – he conjectures – the current phobia must be symbolic of the generalized orientation he suspects in the case, which corresponds to a mixture of narcissism and a hoarding attitude (cf. AUD-1966g-1–3).

We see here the practical roots for Fromm's concept of "orientation". It reflects his form of *anamnesis*. Fromm arrives at the notion of generalized attitudes out of this ongoing comparison between different aspects of a subject's life. What theory expresses in seemingly deductive form, deriving concrete singular traits from the overall orientations, Fromm's diagnostics reach inductively. He sustains a constant, ongoing sweeping of the analysand's expressions and activities, out of which relevant recurrences can be identified. From their continued appreciation, there should emerge a gradually unified hypothesis – always open to modification, nonetheless striving for an overall understanding of the forces and points of conflict governing a person's life:

> the intention must always be to find a comprehensive frame [...] and not to lose oneself in a guerrilla war, in which one attacks here, or then there, because this doesn't help the patient, and is in reality no more than a game.
> (u-1968b*:16)

The diagnostic relevance of the notion of "social character" also becomes clear. The truth, for Fromm, is indivisible: one cannot lose insight in one sphere of life without losing it elsewhere[1]. If analysis wants to foster freedom, it needs to be concerned with the analysand's place in the world – not only with the psychic residues of social relations. Fromm thought an apprehension of inner reality could not be dissociated from the understanding of outer reality. As he tells James Luther Adams:

> By and large, psychoanalysis, and in a sense psychotherapy in general, has had a reactionary function inasmuch as it taught people to look at themselves (and not always correctly) and not to look at the world with the same clarity and freedom from illusion. I am deeply convinced also from clinical experience that the two cannot be separated.
>
> (Adams_James_Luther_1976–12–09-to).

The practice of life allowed for and demanded by the analysand's position in the social structure are thus crucial for understanding why her life runs as it does: "I interest myself in analysis way more in getting to know with precision in the first hours, in the first place, where does the patient come from, before I want to know how many sisters he has, how many grandmothers, grandgrandmothers and aunts etc." (u-1976:20).

Orthodox interpretations of symptoms, centered in psychosexual development, were not altogether discarded by Fromm. He treated them as possibilities alongside other interpretations, and required that the clinical process provide evidence for either. Here we find the significance of his systemic approach as primarily *functional*, only secondarily historical (cf. Fromm, 1990f:73–4; Akeret, 1975). His main interest lay in identifying the ongoing functionality of psychic forces. Understanding their biographical origins and crystallization would be a practically useful means, but not a necessary one:

> It almost always pays off very much to know the deep story, because in almost all cases, I understand much better what exists today if I know what occurred to the patient [...] but one must not use in a unilateral way this genetic explanation, and for that reason I overemphasize the critical point that historical interpretation must not be a genetic explanation, but must always be connected with the functional, systemic interpretation.
>
> (u-1968b*:29)

For Fromm, "forces [...] have no interest if however they have no function" (u-1968b*:28). Progress in cure is measured by the question: to what extent is the satisfaction of suffering-related tendencies still a *necessity* for the reproduction of the psychic structure? To what extent have they lost their compulsion? As Fromm emphasized a couple of times in print, changes in functionality can only be engendered gradually, with a modification of the total psychic economy of which they are a part. The decisive criterion for change lies not in the vicissitudes of singular points of conflict, but in the overall structure of which they are a part.

Fromm (1957a) attributed great therapeutic efficiency to "core to core" relatedness. Besides allowing affective motion, it would also have a peculiar effect: the *shared recognition of psychic processes as real*. Fromm believed a big part of the suffering-inducing aspects of repression lay in its capacity to suspend acknowledgment of one's experiences *as real*: "self-deception, deception and lies are in reality one of the existing pathogenic factors" (u-1968b*:18). Bringing isolated aspects of experience into shared language would be an instrument to acknowledge them as shared realities – as existent, and present in the lives of others as well: "a word transforms itself into a reality only when directed to another person" (u-1968b:7). A humane, concentrated communication would have both prophylactic and therapeutic effects, fostering the readiness for change.

A number of Fromm's technical predicaments aimed at making this reality-effecting process possible. Relevant, for him, was that the analyst be able to hold a non-judgmental attitude: "many times", he thought, "the reality of an attitude that gives trust, hope, strength and energy to the patient, is perhaps one factor, or the most important factor of therapy" (Fromm, u-1968b:54). The analyst's personality and an attitude of deep concentration would be key for overcoming the anxieties involved in derepression (compare Tauber, 1959). Much as Fromm recommended in politics that values should be practiced "in the flesh", so also in therapy:

> a love for life [...] is indeed the main quality which the analyst should have [...] and I would say indeed that the analyst must be able to be at least somewhat more related than other people, somewhat more direct, somewhat more spontaneous.
>
> (u-1953:32,40)

Fromm's lectures suggest a peculiarly aggressive posture toward *resistance* (cf. Bacciagaluppi, 1988). Not that he didn't recognize the need to give treatment its time – especially, as we have seen, in cases of deep psychic vulnerability. One should "make it easy for the patient that the resistance be not so strong", for "the strength of resistance depends a lot on the analyst" (u-1968b:60–1). However, as a general rule – to be adapted according to the situation – Fromm suggested that the analyst actively elicit resistance by sharing his reaction to what the patient says, instead of waiting for points of resistance to emerge and dissolve spontaneously. "I want to tell you what I listen, what I have listened", he tells his analysands, and he knows: "upon that, one will find an enormous resistance" (u-1976:10). This is related to the general principle of avoiding stagnation: "one can transform the attitude of resistance of the patient in an attitude of movement, of dialogue, of something that always moves" (u-1968b:61). It is also related to the function ascribed to language in the clinic. The analyst's words, in their warm frankness, are meant to make it impossible to circumlocate conflicts – which is after all one of the effects of resistance. A truthful reaction is, for Fromm, an instrument to arouse the recognition of what was unconscious as real:

> In general people believe that if one must say something to the other person that is a bit hard, that can hurt him, that can produce resistance etc. [...] the idea is to do it step by step. Well, this is a very common and current method; but if one wants to wake up someone to reality, this method doesn't apply, because here we speak of a very interesting and important quality of man, namely: man has the special faculty of responding to reality.
>
> (u-1968b*:8)

To bring the analysand into confrontation with unavoidable issues would be an essential part of the analytic process. The condition for that would be that the *interpretation* – or, as Fromm would prefer it, the reaction to the patient – be true. While not completely discarding the idea that the clinical material must be deciphered, he preferred the idea that the task of the analyst is "simply describing" (u-1953:53): "what for me corresponds to traditional interpretation is in reality to see the fact" (u-1968b*:25). Addressing the phenomenology of the case correctly would counter the tendency to substitute careful observation for theoretical speculation, allowing to grasp its essential determinants: "to see means to penetrate him or her in a timeless manner and to be 'in' the person", he tells Clara Urquhart (Urquhart_Clara_1964-06-29-to). A truthful word, under appropriate conditions, touches the reality of feeling and moves it. Inappropriate conditions may also be given – "there are many reasons why the total truth does not always have this [liberating] effect" (u-1968b*:15). Then words may do nothing immediately – but their effect lingers on unconsciously and paves the way for further change.

As regards the psychic mechanism for achieving analytic insight, Fromm formulated it as *empathy*, to which should be coupled a *therapeutic desire* (u-1968b:56). Fromm's concept of empathy is perhaps a bit misleading, as it denotes two different processes at once. One of them is identification: listening to others allows one to emulate their experience within oneself, and hence to understand what is probably at stake behind their behavior:

> Indeed, much can be said about me, about my character, about my total orientation to life. Such insights can be gained by observation, together with trained theoretical thought or by direct insight penetrating the outer shell down to the roots by empathic intuition. This insightful knowledge can go very far in understanding and describing my own or another's psychical structure. But the total me, my whole individuality, my suchness that is as unique as my fingerprints are, can never be fully understood, not even by empathy, for no two human beings are entirely identical. This is the limitation of even the best psychology. But in the process of mutual relatedness, the other and I overcome the barrier of separateness, inasmuch as we both participate in the dance of life.
>
> (d-1976a-000-eng-draft-01:98)

In this sense of the word, "if one cannot experience it, go through it, if you please, in homeopathic doses, one cannot really see what the patient is talking about, and one cannot convey it to the patient" (u-1953:52). Empathy would be an act of "controlled imagination", in which "tact, sensitivity, intuition" (u-1953:38) participate jointly.

The other meaning of empathy is as a process of deep alterity: one must abandon oneself completely into the uniqueness of another psychic structure. It is then a process of "playing in the other" (u-1968b:45) – what matters is "what one experiences in the other" (AUD-1975h). Each determination of the concept refers to a different presupposition of core to core relatedness. Identification points to the undifferentiated, general human material which is common to any two members of the species, and provides the basis for mutual understanding. Alterity points to the fact that this same material has been organized in a singular form for each of us: "no two persons and their dynamics are ever the same" (1961:169). Since Fromm believes the task of analysis is to grasp this singularity, one must be able to refrain from oneself, venturing in the analysand's experience in its otherness. Taken together, both aspects achieve "sharing" as Fromm wanted it: we listen to the peculiarity of others, but in doing that, we listen to ourselves: "to be aware of suffering is to be aware of the deepest that we have in common" (AUD-1967a); only in understanding evil in oneself does one understand it in the other (cf. AUD-1961b).

Alterity incurs also in Fromm's handling of *transference*. He considered this process one of the pillars of analytic treatment: "transference is a microscopic method of observation of man's relations towards the world"; it is "the mirror in which we can observe the whole emotional structure, and especially the irrational one, which exists within the patient" (u-1968b:51). However, Fromm more strongly emphasized its capacity to act as resistance (cf. Freud, 1926). He understood deep unchecked phantasizing as an unnecessary obstacle: "it is not necessary that the patient develop such an ardent transference". Rather, "it is preferable to use the transferential material in relation to others" (u-1968b:29,55), releasing the therapeutic relation from being thoroughly saturated with phantasy material. Lingering on the transferential relation for too long without confronting it with reality would induce one of the biggest dangers of analysis: "it makes the patient dependent" (u-1976:29), alienating her responsibility for herself (cf. 1991a:119). It may also happen that "the transference is used by the patient and also by the analyst as a substitute of real trust" (u-1968b:38). The analyst should thus walk on two tracks, offering herself both as the object of transference, and as a real human being – but the latter should increasingly take precedence over the former in the course of treatment.

Fromm's (u-1968b) treatment of *countertransference* was similar. It followed the same principles, with an emphasis on its capacity to corrupt the courage to think and speak the truth. All sorts of motivations could participate in that: fear of the analysand, lack of trust in oneself, sexual desire, narcissism. Brought together in practice, Fromm's treatment of resistance, transference, and countertransference corresponded to what he thought was the basic principle effecting character change. We saw that shared acknowledgment of the reality of one's experience was for him the crucial *therapeutic* aspect in the relation: it brought relief, and produced a trust that would, of itself, mitigate resistances. Its *transtherapeutic* aspect lay in fully experiencing what emerges into consciousness. This would produce a lively conflict within the subject: "the effect of conscientization, the effect of transforming the unconscious, is solely based on the fact that there is a conflict, that there is a person [...] that can struggle with the unconscious material" (u-1968b:6; cf. Epstein, 1975). Fromm wanted to avoid that lifting repression transcur in a dream-like atmosphere: this would attenuate the effectiveness of the experience and the responsibility towards it:

> cure, the effect of analysis, depends on two factors: that the infantile material comes out, [...] but also that at the same time it is a relation, a real situation, in which the patient as a man, as an adult, can fight with the child-man, with the irrational man.
>
> (u-1968b:53)

The prophylactic and relieving effect of analysis depends on ensuing consciousness of repressed material as shared reality (relationship to the analyst). Its capacity to prompt change depends on the reinscription of the repressed as real (relationship to oneself). Both aspects are reunited in the notion we examined before, that consciousness of emotional experience effects a liberation of energies: "the curative effect of confrontation with internal or external reality is that our force of reality is based on our contact with reality, our human energy" (AUD-1965a). A lively therapeutic relationship would result in the activation of the wish to live, and to live better. This would amount in part to a fearful reaction: conflict with oneself mobilizes the will to survive and a readiness for practical change. It would also engage our impulse to activity beyond survival, freedom beyond necessity.

Among the means and objects of analysis, Fromm (1960a) maintained the importance of *free association*, albeit recognizing its tendency to engender new forms of resistance. The analysis of *slips*, contradictions in discourse, involuntary gestures and other details of expression remained significant, but no psychic formation had more relevance for him than *dreams*. He considered them "the most important instrument we have in psychoanalytic therapy" (1991a:121). Of course, an overproduction of dreams could just as well function as resistance, as Freud (1911b) had already noted, and interpretation could function as rationalization (cf. Fromm, 1991a:123). However, the richness of insight to be expected in dreams was, for Fromm, unparalleled by insight based on phenomena of waking life. In sleep, he wrote, we achieve freedom from the restricting social categories orienting the tasks of self-preservation. Censorship notwithstanding, sleep phenomena would be the closest to a pure expression of life's tendency to transcend the purposes of survival:

> During sleep man rests; that is to say, he is free from the obligation to work and defense. But this means also he is free from the necessity to perceive the world as it has to be perceived in work and defense; he is free from being impressed by common sense and common nonsense, which influence him during his waking life. He is free to perceive the world in its reality without the distortions of social clichés and purposes. He can see it as he really sees it, and not as he is supposed to see it if he wants to adjust to a group.
> (Fromm, 1991h:138)

Fromm (1951a) insisted in a stronger differentiation between association over and translation of the dream than Freud (1901). Interpretation should not slip into such a fragmentary understanding of the latent material that no message could be extracted: an "optimal interpretation" should be preferred to a "maximal" one (Fromm, 1991a:136). Fromm opted for a concise and direct translation of the whole dream, addressing its core experience, instead of allowing interpretation to get lost in the immense chain of intermediary ideas one finds in the latent thoughts. This rather "centralizing" tendency in dream analysis corresponds to the one we verified in Fromm's diagnostics, whose method was to bring together different aspects of the patient's life.

The process of analysis, according to Fromm, "is one which never ends" (u-1953:56). *Termination* of treatment should occur when there are enough signs that deep character change has been established. If this is not possible, a combination of recovery from symptoms and a stable prognosis should suffice:

> When to finish analysis? One can say that there is a case, an optimal case, when there is a true change. The true change is a transformation of the nuclear energies of character. In other words, that in the energies of man there is a change in distribution, let's say, that the passivity, the hatred, the envy, the lack of productiveness change into more productiveness, more love for life, more energy, more clarity etc. etc. In this case, all his friends know he has changed. The second aim is a more restricted one, and it is the conventional aim of the disappearing of the symptoms, from which one is cured – the symptoms will not present themselves anymore.
> (u-1968b:63)

Therapeutic experience should then be continued in self-analysis: "analysis is successfully ended when a person begins to analyze himself every day for the rest of his life" (Fromm, 1991a:188). Either through meditation or through the use of other techniques, it would be important to listen to oneself and confront one's conflicts throughout life. Analysis would then have provided the analysand with a structure for self-knowledge – "one can usually [...] have enough experiences of the ground mechanisms from his treatment" (u-1976:49) – and a particular openness to life and oneself: "seeing the truth is an attitude. To see reality and see through lies in an attitude" (u-1976:44).

3 Truth and Reality

In Freud (1912–13), the notions of material and psychic reality meant to discriminate between the effectiveness proper to outer objects and those of the imagination. Psychic reality meant the effectiveness of phantasy – of everything representational – over the subject. Knowledge of material reality and acknowledgment of the falseness of imaginary phenomena remained a property of ego-bound reality check, attached to consciousness (cf. Freud, 1911a). In Fromm, to the contrary, "most of what is real is not conscious, and most of what is conscious is not real" (AUD-1966f). Awareness is mostly the realm of illusion; unconsciousness is the dwelling of unknown truth. Fromm's emphasis on emotional experience thus culminates in its equation with inner reality: "my character structure, the true motivation of my behavior, constitutes my real being" (d-1976a-000-eng-draft-01:101). Conversely, being is the "world of feelings" (u-1976:46).

Fromm's concept of the unconscious distances it from its imaginary-mnemonic aspect, bringing it closer to a notion of a-representational reality: "the reality of our experience" (u-1953:77). This duality had been present not only in Freud (1938b) himself, but also in the works of other psychoanalysts. Fromm isolated and developed the objective moment. For him, subjectivity is not lost; unconscious experience remains irreducible to the body – but it acquires a vehement concreteness, whose apprehension constitutes all true processes of awareness: we capture the unconscious only in "a state of intense awakeness" (1989a:37). Language is for Fromm negative of experience, while illusion is negative of reality (particularly of inner, affective reality). Each is to its other as being less than it, abstracted from it, existing in secession from its roots: "if we use language to express inner experiences, then to a large extent [...] we refer to an abstract concept which denotes a reality with which we are not in touch" (Fromm, u-1953:70). As a consequence, Fromm arrives at a *negative* concept of truth. Much as mysticism is for him the outcome of negative theology (cf. 1992s), also awareness begins with the negation of illusions: "the process of waking up from illusions is the condition of freedom and of liberation from suffering" (1979a:x). This, he believes true in the history of science, in politics – and also in the clinic (cf. 1979a).

In the sphere of objective outward phenomena, truth retains for Fromm (1955a) the propositional value of tackling the essence of what is and denying that which is not. In the "subjective objectivity" of unconscious experience, developing a relation to what is repressed coincides with living through it, admitting it into awareness and traversing it. Truth is then the *effect* of dissolving false ideas and desires – in therapy, the dissolution of resistances obstructing an immediate apprehension of reality (cf. 1992g:118):

> Insight into reality has in fact a totally special and unique, liberating and resolving effect over people. However, people often fight against it and show resistances, because these insights many times bring them in contradiction to other people, first of all with public opinion, which concerns illusions, and not the insight into real relations. Truth has always become dangerous.
>
> (Fromm, u-1975:7)

This is the reason Fromm's concept of the unconscious has such a great affinity with the notion of *unconscious knowledge*.

> Unconsciously we know everything and yet we don't, because it is indeed very painful to know and at the same time there is nothing more exhilarating which doesn't even exclude pain than to know, than to be in touch with reality.
>
> (Fromm, 1992g:85)

Awareness amounts to seeing "what is real inside or outside of myself" (AUD-1966f). Language is the vehicle for that: not as determining the experience, but by making it available to shared acknowledgment and awareness: "the human *is* only inasmuch as he is with others" (Fromm u-1974:7). What comes forth in the process of lifting repression is something one always knew, always suspected, but never had the courage to admit to oneself: "the analyst touches upon reality which the patient knows and has always sensed" (u-1953:65). Fromm's technical stance is correspondingly summarized in the formula: *to touch reality with words*. "You touch reality, which means you say the truth" (1992g:84) – and "saying the truth is nothing more than to describe the total reality [...] in a most complete or total, in a most frank and exact way" (u-1968b:14; cf. Spiegel, 1981).

***

Fromm's understanding of psychoanalysis is thus summarized in his notion of *truth*. "The medicine of the analyst is truth" (u-1968b*:24).

Repression is, conversely, "repression of the truth" (VID-1977a; cf. Kwawer, 1975). This conception, as well as the relationships it presupposes – between language and experience, between illusion and reality – leads back to a number of different sources, without being reducible to either. Here, we will emphasize four of them.

Ferenczi's (1927–1933) late work is one of Fromm's templates. Fromm's recommendation of an attitude of frankness without authoritarianism was already part of Ferenczi's recipe: he wished to avoid a repetition of the traumatogenic aspects of parent-child relationship within the analytic relationship. Ferenczi was among the first to develop the idea that therapy is not finished without a full character analysis. After his first experiments with active technique were over, he was led to the position that admitting repressed desires and memories as real is a condition for full recovery. Removing doubt over whether associations were of phantastic, mnemonic, or present character would be just as important as having them occur, lest the analysand would lack decision on how to integrate the unconscious material. This was later followed by the idea that denying the reality of an actually occurring event has a traumatogenic effect, and by an exploration of the infantile roots of the habit of lying.

Ferenczi wanted to explore alternative ways to avoid stagnation and further the psychoanalytic method beyond the treatment of symptoms. His modifications of technique eventually led him to an alternation between relaxation and activity as governing the therapeutic relationship, with very similar results as those favored by Fromm. On the other hand, many of his patients were brought back to hysteriform symptoms – with that, also to the necessity of reincorporating knowledge from Freud's and Breuer's early cathartic method. Centering therapy on the apprehension of unconscious processes as real led to discharge-like, affectively saturated manifestations, whose resemblance with Fromm's "reality of feeling" is unmistakable.

Groddeck's (1917–34; 1925–27) notion of the id was also among Fromm's sources. It brought together the subjectivity of life with the objective lawfulness of the soul. For Groddeck, contrary to Freud, the id comprehended the relationship between body and psyche in all their strata. Freud (1938a) pointed in that direction in speaking of a primordial "id-ego", but the conceptual emphasis in his writings fell always on their later differentiation as a point of conflict. In Groddeck, contrariwise, the concept prefigures the notion of "self", as Fromm (1941a) and other analysts would later develop it. Groddeck considered the ego a form of "manifestation" of the id, not a differentiation from it. Unlike the "self", however, Groddeck's id is not conceived as a psychic entity, but as a psychosomatic one, whose expressions freely transit between body and psyche. This led him to the rather extreme formulation that all organic diseases were available to psychotherapeutic methods. Fromm could not agree with this: "I don't say that the problem of infirmity in general, of somatic infirmity, resolves itself in mobilizing vital energy" (u-1968b:22). He restrained himself to a psychological formulation, in which the body participates mostly as a support for gestural expression, and psychosomatism is considered as a particular class of relation between mind and organism. Fromm nonetheless retained a conceptual peculiarity typical of Groddeck's – namely, the great emphasis on psychic processes as *vital processes* seeking an unfolding of life (or its restriction).

We get a glimpse at the deep coincidence and the deep disagreements between their conceptions if we remember that Groddeck was a strict determinist in philosophical terms, but at the same time employed the expression "the undetermined" (*Das Unbestimmte*) as an alternative for "id" (*Es*). This amounts to an interesting contradiction in his reasoning, which Fromm resolves with a few displacements. He would frontally disagree with Groddeck that "id", the whole, was so thoroughly deterministic that there would be only destiny as the inner compulsion of our lives. But he would agree in treating psychic processes as developments out of a yet-unfulfilled treasure of potentialities – in this sense not-yet-determined –, of which we could have no exhaustive knowledge (cf. Fromm, 1957a). To this treasure would correspond an "innate striving for health" (Fromm, 1991a:93), which analysis should free from its obstacles – another idea shared between both thinkers ("Nasamecu"). Fromm could thus find a compromise between the opposing tendencies in Groddeck: life contents retained enough determinacy that they could be recognized in their regularity; but they retained enough indeterminacy that freedom could be sought in their actualization. The lawfulness of psychic processes was dissociated from the rather formal aspect it has in Freud (1901), in reference to psychic mechanisms, and reinscribed as a property of the developmental tendencies of psychic contents themselves.

Besides the theoretical and technical approximations between Fromm, Ferenczi and Groddeck, he remained an admirer of their personal qualities. In a late interview, he recalled them as two of the most innovative psychoanalysts after Freud, adding as an explanation to why this would be the case:

> One simple answer which comes to mind firstly is that they both were not intellectuals. In contrast to most other analysts who are intellectuals and mostly concerned with the manipulation of theories, Groddeck and Ferenczi were human beings, who empathized with the person they wanted to understand and I would say who felt in themselves what the so-called patient was telling them; they were persons of great humanity and for them the patient was not an object but a partner. It is very characteristic, for example, for Ferenczi, that when a patient left a session Ferenczi would tell him "thank you" because this was not a matter just of courtesy or even in that respect

it would be very rare, but an expression of his feeling, of sharing with the patient.

(AUD-1978c)

This capacity to bring intuitive penetration and theoretical understanding into unity, Fromm admired also in *Spinoza*'s (1677) mature formulation of the mind. Both share an understanding of psychic processes in terms of a lawfulness of content, not of form. The *Ethics* stipulate a relationship between body and mind in which psychic phenomena are subject to a regularity of their own, without either being reducible to an emanation of the body, or being completely apart from it: "the mind is the idea of its actually existing body". Affects are understood as grounded in affections, rooted on a reality beyond their phenomenal being. This conceptualization left a deep trace in Fromm's understanding, as we can see in the relations between what Spinoza calls the three primary affects – joy, sorrow, and desire. A productive ambiguity entails in the Spinozan definition of these terms. On the one hand, concrete desires, directed at particular objects, stem from the affects aroused by them – a peculiarity of Spinoza's psychology which is true also for Frommian theory, and emphasized by Fromm in his marginalia to the *Ethics:* "emotion → desire" (e-N380). So far, desire is "the essence itself of man in so far as it is conceived as determined to any action by any one of his affections". But there is also another conception of desire in Spinoza, sometimes captured under the notion of "appetite", as "the very essence or nature of man in so far as it is determined to such acts as contribute to his preservation". Here, to the contrary, affects appear as derivatives of this truly primary desire: to affirm what pertains to one's essence. Desire is then, by comparison, "appetite which is self-conscious", retaining a reference only to the mind, whereas appetites as such include a reference both to the body and the mind. The first definition is deeply related to primary psychic reactivity in Fromm, whereas the second is a source for his understanding of primary activity.

Since Spinoza's psychology is articulated around the difference between potency, actuality, and the potency to act, it provides Fromm with a description of the different degrees of reality to be found in phenomena, as they remain undetermined or pass into action: "there are realities more or less real" (Fromm, u-1968b:45). Affects being the ideas of a body's diminished or expanded power to act, they prefigure Fromm's understanding of primary self-awareness and reflexivity. Spinoza's theory is such that truer ideas must follow from a truer disposition of the body – that is, from a relation in which the subject is in a position to actualize her potency, and hence to become "more real" (more perfect) than she was before. Truthfulness of ideas and truthfulness of the real psychic process underlying them go hand in hand: they are correlate aspects of the fulfillment and affirmation of one's essence. Fromm would thoroughly agree.

Finally, we should not forget the influence of the mystics, particularly *Meister Eckhart* (2009), over Fromm. If Spinoza prepares a psychology in which a theory of truth is attached to a theory of human development, Eckhart helps delineate mystical experience as bearing precisely the vehement concreteness implied by Fromm's notion of experience. As Thomas Merton puts it, in agreement with a previous letter by Fromm:

> I think what you are really saying is that true mysticism does not know God after the manner of an object, and that is perfectly true. God is not experienced as an object outside ourselves, as "another being" capable of being enclosed in some human concept. Yet though He be known as the source of our own being, He is still das ganz Andere.
> (Merton_Thomas_1954–10–02-by)

In Eckhart, we find at the bottom of self-experience (formulated in theological language) the "source of all being" – God as such –, whereas Fromm (speaking in non-theistic language) reaches the conclusion that depth experience is the experience of being: "I am what I do", "I am what I am", or simply, "I am" (Fromm, 1989a:120). While the development of Eckhart's experience through time cannot be easily reduced to general formulations, one of the lines of continuity in his thought is the idea that the potencies of the soul lead in introspection to a region where they cease to behave as in common consciousness, dissolving into something imponderable for ordinary language. This peculiarity of mystical expression is integral to Fromm's notion of the unconscious. It gives experience a definite momentum in having therapeutic primacy over elaboration in words.

Note

1 Only towards the end of his life did Fromm come to doubt this idea. In discussing Rousseau's personality with Sarah Wittes, he writes: "Incidentally, you raise a very interesting and puzzling problem: how a man who was so puzzled with regard to his personal relations could be so clear and lucid with regard to the political situation. I cannot help feeling that what you remark is true although I have always maintained that the two go together and that in matters of insight one cannot be blind in one eye only. But apparently this is not so and I shall have to revise my ideas about this" (Wittes_Sarah_Sue_1977–01–25-to).

Bibliography

Primary sources

Fromm's correspondence

Adams_James_Luther_1976–1912–09-to: Fromm to James Luther Adams, December 9th, 1976

Merton_Thomas_1954–1910–02-by: Thomas Merton to Fromm, October 2nd, 1954
Schachtel_Ernst_1952–1910–18-to: Fromm to Ernst Schachtel, October 18th, 1952
Schachtel_Ernst_1965–1908–30-to: Fromm to Schachtel, August 30th, 1965
Schecter_David_1974–1903–28-to: Fromm to David Schecter, March 28th, 1974
Urquhart_Clara_1964–1906–29-to: Fromm to Clara Urquhart, June 29th, 1964
Urquhart_Clara_1970–1907–06-to: Fromm to Urquhart, July 6th, 1970
Wittes_Sarah_Sue_1977–1901–25-to: Fromm to Sarah Wittes, January 25th, 1977

Unpublished texts, lectures, interviews by Fromm

u-1953: "*The goals of psychoanalysis*". Transcript of lectures given at the Willkie Memorial Building, New York, and sponsored by the New York William Alanson White Institute in 1953.

u-1968b: "*Conferencias clínicas del Dr. Fromm*". Instituto Mexicano de Psicoanálisis. Transcript of clinical lectures given in Mexico between February and March, 1968.

u-1968b*: source documents for the above lectures, with a different page numbering.

u-1974: "*Anti-autoritäre Bewegung, die Maschine als Mutter und die Suche nach politischen Alternativen*". Transcript of a conversation between Fromm and the theologian Hans-Eckerhard Bahr.

u-1975: "*Wahrheit und Lüge. Hans Lechleitner im Gespräch mit Erich Fromm*". Transcript of a TV–Interview in ARD on June 19th, 1975. So far not published.

u-1976: "*Seminar zu Theorie und Praxis der psychoanalytischen Therapie mit deutschen Psychoanalytikern der DGP aus München (Professor Riemann)*". Transcript of a seminar on psychoanalytic theory and practice in Locarno, 1976.

u-1977. "Haben oder Sein. Ein Gespräch mit Paul Assal". Segments of an interview with Paul Assals about To have or to be? in Locarno on March 18th, 1977.

Drafts, typescripts and study materials by Fromm

d-1976a-000-eng-draft-01: drafts for *To Have or to Be?*, written between 1974 and 1976.

d-1976a-000-eng-type-1974–03: drafts for *To Have or to Be?*, written in 1974.

e-N380: marginalia to one of Fromm's copies of Spinoza's *Ethics*.

Audio and video recordings

AUD-1961b: "*Der moderne Mensch und seine Zukunft*". WDR – Lecture in 1961 in Düsseldorf, recorded by the Westdeutschen Rundfunk.

AUD-1965a: "*Psicoanálisis*". Lecture given in Mexico City or Cuernavaca, probably in 1965.

AUD-1966f: "*The automaton citizen and human rights*". Pacific Radio (?) – Lecture given at the American Orthopsychiatric Association's 43rd Annual Meeting in San Francisco on April 13th, 1966.

AUD-1966g-1–6: "*Clinical Seminar conducted by Erich Fromm, organized by Ruth Moulton*". William Alanson White Institute, New York, May 26th and 27th, 1966.

AUD-1967a: "Interview of Richard Hefner with Erich Fromm on You Shall Be as Gods". Pacific Radio – Recorded April 1st, 1967. Broadcast: WBAI, January 1st, 1969.
AUD-1975h: *"Antwort auf A. Auer, Gibt es eine Ethik ohne Religiosität? und Schlussowrt von Auer"*. Symposium on the occasion of Fromm's 75th birthday, "Psychoanalytic theory and therapy". Lecture on May 26th, 1975 in Locarno.
AUD-1978c: *"Erich Fromm: Interview with Gérard Khoury – part 3"*. Part three of an interview given to Gérard Khoury on December 2nd, 1978 and in February, 1979 in Locarno.
VID-1963e: *"On pyschoanalytic theory"*. First part of an interview with Richard Evans in December 1963.
VID-1977a: *"Gespräch zu Haben oder Sein?"*. SWF – Interview with Micaela Lämmle und Jürgen Lodemann in Locarno; production of the Südwestfunk Baden-Baden. Broadcasted on March 1977.

Published sources

Abraham, Karl. Versuch einer Entwicklungsgeschichte der Libido auf Grund der Psychoanalyse seelischer Störungen. *Psychoanalytische Studien zur Charakterbildung.* Stuttgart: S. Fischer Verlag, [1924]/1969.
Eckhart, Meister. *The complete mystical works of Meister Eckhart.* New York: The Crossroad Publishing Company, 2009.
Ferenczi, Sándor. *Bausteine II.* Vienna: Internationaler Psychoanalytischer Verlag, [1919–1926]/1927. See the papers corresponding to the date.
Ferenczi, Sándor. *Bausteine III.* Budapest: Verlag Hans Buber, [1927–1933]/1939. See the papers corresponding to the date.
Freud, Sigmund. Über den Traum. *Gesammelte Werke II-III.* Frankfurt: S. Fischer Verlag, [1901]/1961.
Freud, Sigmund. Formulierungen über die zwei Prinzipien des psychischen Geschehens. *Gesammelte Werke VIII.* London: Imago Publishing, [1911a]/1955.
Freud, Sigmund. Die Handhabung der Traumdeutung in der Psychoanalyse. *Gesammelte Werke VIII.* London: Imago Publishing, [1911b]/1955.
Freud, Sigmund. Totem und Tabu. *Gesammelte Werke IX.* London: Imago Publishing, [1912–1913]/1940.
Freud, Sigmund. Triebe und Triebschicksale. *Gesammelte Werke X.* London: Imago Publishing, [1915]/1949.
Freud, Sigmund. Hemmung, Symptom und Angst. *Gesammelte Werke XIV.* London: Imago Publishing, [1926]/1955.
Freud, Sigmund. Abriss der Psychoanalyse. *Schriften aus dem Nachlass.* London: Imago Publishing, [1938a]/1955.
Freud, Sigmund. Ergebnisse, Ideen, Probleme. *Schriften aus dem Nachlass.* London: Imago Publishing, [1938b]/1955.
Fromm, Erich. Politik und Psychoanalyse. *Gesamtausgabe, Band I.* Stuttgart: Deutsche Verlags-Anstalt, [1931b]/1999.
Fromm, Erich. Die gesellschaftliche Bedingtheit der psychoanalytischen Therapie. *Gesamtausgabe, Band I.* Stuttgart: Deutsche Verlags-Anstalt, [1935a]/1999.
Fromm, Erich. Zum Gefühl der Ohnmacht. *Gesamtausgabe, Band I.* Stuttgart: Deutsche Verlags-Anstalt, [1937a]/1999.

Fromm, Erich. *Escape from freedom*. New York: Henry Holt & Company, [1941a]/1994.
Fromm, Erich. Individual and social origins of neurosis. *American Sociological Review*:9:380–384, 1944a.
Fromm, Erich. *Man for himself*. New York: Henry Holt & Company, [1947a]/1990.
Fromm, Erich. *The forgotten language*. New York: Holt, Rinehart and Winston, [1951a]/1960.
Fromm, Erich. *The sane society*. New York: Henry Holt & Company, [1955a]/1990.
Fromm, Erich. Remarks on the Problem of Free Association. *Psychiatric research report*: II:1–6, 1955d.
Fromm, Erich. On the limitations and dangers of psychology. *The dogma of Christ*. New York: Holt, Rinehart and Winston, [1957a]/1992.
Fromm, Erich. *Sigmund Freud's mission*. New York: Grove Press, Inc, [1959a]/1963.
Fromm, Erich. Values, psychology, and human existence. A. Maslow (ed.). *New knowledge in human values*. New York: Harper and Row, 1959b.
Fromm, Erich. Psychoanalysis and Zen Buddhism. *Psychoanalysis and Zen Buddhism*. London: Unwin Paperbacks, [1960a]/1987.
Fromm, Erich. *May man prevail?*. New York: Doubleday & Company, Inc, [1961a]/1961.
Fromm, Erich. *Beyond the chains of illusion*. New York: Continuum, [1962a]/2001.
Fromm, Erich. *The heart of man*. New York: Harper and Row, 1964a.
Fromm, Erich. *You shall be as gods*. New York: Fawcett Premier, [1966a]/1983.
Fromm, Erich. Marxismus, Psychoanalyse und "wirkliche Wirklichkeit". *Tagebuch*: 21(9):5f, 1966j.
Fromm, Erich. Scientific research in psychoanalysis: an editorial. *Contemporary psychoanalysis*:2:168–170, 1961.
Fromm, Erich. Consciencia y sociedad industrial. *Ciencas politicas y sociales*: 43–44:17–28, 1966p.
Fromm, Erich. The crisis of psychoanalysis. *The crisis of psychoanalysis*. New York: Holt, Rinehart and Winston, [1970c]/1970.
Fromm, Erich. Interview with Ignacio Solares: El hombre necesita algo mas. *Revista de revistas: 1* (2. 6. 1972):5–9, 1972d.
Fromm, Erich. *The anatomy of human destructiveness*. New York. Henry Holt & Company, [1973a]/1992.
Fromm, Erich. In the name of life: a portrait through dialogue. *For the love of life*. New York: The Free Press, [1974b]/1986.
Fromm, Erich. *To have or to be?*. New York: Bantam Books, [1976a]/1981.
Fromm, Erich. Interview with Alfred A. Häsler: Das Undenkbare denken und das Mögliche tun. *Ex Libris*: 22:513–519, 1977b.
Fromm, Erich. My own concept of man. *Fromm Forum*: 17:5–10, [1977g]/2013.
Fromm, Erich. Das Undenkbare, das Unsagbare, das Unaussprechliche. *Psychologie heute*: 5:23–31, 1978b.
Fromm, Erich. *Greatness and limitations of Freud's thought*. New York: Harper and Row, Publishers, [1979a]/1980.
Fromm, Erich. Die vision unserer Zeit. *Mitteilungen aus dem Literaturarchiv der Stadt Dortmund*: 7:29f. 1980g.
Fromm, Erich. *The art of being*. New York: Continuum, [1989a]/1998.
Fromm, Erich. The dialectic revision of psychoanalysis. *The revision of psychoanalysis*. Boulder: Westview Press, [1990f]/1992.

Fromm, Erich. Sexuality and sexual perversions. *The revision of psychoanalysis.* Boulder: Westview Press, [1990g]/1992.
Fromm, Erich. *The art of listening.* London: Constable, [1991a]/1994.
Fromm, Erich. Modern man's pathology of normalcy. *The pathology of normalcy.* New York: American Mental Health Foundation, [1991e]/2010.
Fromm, Erich. Is man lazy by nature?. *The pathology of normalcy.* New York: American Mental Health Foundation, [1991h]/2010.
Fromm, Erich. Man's impulse structure and its relation to culture. *Beyond Freud.* New York: American Mental Health Foundation, [1992e]/2010.
Fromm, Erich. Dealing with the unconscious in psychotherapeutic practice. *Beyond Freud.* New York: American Mental Health Foundation, [1992g]/2010.
Fromm, Erich. The relevance of psychoanalysis for the future. *Beyond Freud.* New York: American Mental Health Foundation, [1992h]/2010.
Fromm, Erich. The search for a humanistic alternative. *On being human.* New York: Continuum. [1921]/2005.
Fromm, Erich. Meister Eckhart and Karl Marx on having and being. *On being human.* New York: Continuum, [1992s]/2005.
Fromm, Erich. Maccoby, Michael. *Social character in a Mexican village.* New York: Routledge, [1970b]/1996.
Fromm-Reichmann, Frieda. Transference problems in schizophrenia. *Psychoanalysis and psychotherapy.* Chicago: University of Chicago Press, [1939]/1959.
Fromm-Reichmann, Frieda. Intensive psychotherapy of manic-depressive psychosis. *Psychoanalysis and psychotherapy.* Chicago: University of Chicago Press, [1949]/1959.
Groddeck, Georg. *Von Menschenbauch und dessen Seele.* Frankfurt: Stroemfeld Verlag, [1917–1934]/2010.
Groddeck, Georg. *Die Arche I-III.* Frankfurt: Stroemfeld Verlag, [1925–1927]/2001.
Horney, Karen. *Final lectures.* New York: W. W. Norton & Company Inc., 1987.
Spinoza, Baruch. *Ethics.* New York: Hafner Publishing Company, [1677]/1949.
Sullivan, Harry Stack. *Conceptions of modern psychiatry.* Washington: The William Alanson White Institute Foundation, 1940–1945.
Sullivan, Harry Stack. *Schizophrenia as a human process.* New York: W. W. Norton & Company Inc., 1962.

Secondary literature

Akeret, Robert. Reminiscences of supervision with Erich Fromm. *Contemporary Psychoanalysis*: 11:461–463, 1975.
Aramoni, Aniceto. Fromm el amigo, el terapeuta, el hombre universal. Salvador Millán, Sonia de Millán (eds.). *Erich Fromm y el psicoanálisis humanista.* Mexico City: Siglo Veinteuno Editores, 1981.
Bacciagaluppi, Marco. Erich Fromm's views on psychoanalytic "technique". *Fromm Forum*:11:5–13, [1988]/2007.
Biancoli, Romano; Luban-Plozza, Boris. Erich Fromms therapeutische Annäherung oder die Kunst der Psychotherapie. Lutz von Werder (ed.). *Der unbekannte Fromm.* Frankfurt: Haag und Herchen, 1987.
Buecheler, Sandra. Erich Fromm's place in the interpersonal tradition. *Fromm Forum*:22:7–20, 2018.

Chrzanowski, Gerard. The mystery paper of Erich Fromm. Paper presented at the Washington School of Psychiatry, available at the EFIT. 1994.
Crowley, Ralph. Tribute on Erich Fromm. *Contemporary Psychoanalysis*: 17(4):441–445, 1981.
Derbez, Jorge. Fromm en México: una reseña histórica. Salvador Millán, Sonia de Millán (eds.). *Erich Fromm y el psicoanálisis humanista*. Mexico City: Siglo Veinteuno Editores, 1981.
Epstein, Lawrence. Reminiscences of supervision with Erich Fromm. *Contemporary Psychoanalysis*: 11:457–461, 1975.
Feiner, Arthur. Reminiscences of supervision with Erich Fromm. *Contemporary Psychoanalysis*: 11:463f, 1975.
Funk, Rainer (ed.). *The clinical Erich Fromm*. New York: Rodopi, 2009.
Gojman, Sonja. The analyst as a person: Fromm's approach to psychoanalytic training and practice. Michael Maccoby, Mauricio Cortina (eds.). *A prophetic analyst*. London: Jason Aronson Inc., 1996.
García, Jorge. Erich Fromm in Mexiko: 1950–1973. Internationalen Erich-Fromm-Gesellschaft (ed.). *Wissenschaft vom Menschen: 3*. München: LIT-Verlag, 1995.
Krassoievich, Miguel. *Technique in the psychoanalytic method of Erich Fromm*. Mexico City: Demac, 2007.
Kwawer, Jay. A case seminar with Erich Fromm. *Contemporary Psychoanalysis*: 11:453–455, 1975.
Landis, Bernard. Erich Fromm. *WAW Newsletter*: XV(1):10, 1981a.
Landis, Bernard. Fromm's approach to psychoanalytic technique. *Contemporary Psychoanalysis*: 17(4):573–581, 1981b.
Millán, Salvador. Die Entwicklung der Mexikanischen Psychoanalytischen Gesellschaft und des Mexikanischen Instituts für Psychoanalyse. Internationalen Erich-Fromm-Gesellschaft (ed.). *Wissenschaft vom Menschen: 3*. München: LIT-Verlag, 1992.
Millán, Salvador. Erich Fromm in Mexico: a point of view. Internationalen Erich-Fromm-Gesellschaft (ed.). *Wissenschaft vom Menschen: 6*. München: LIT-Verlag, 1995.
Ortmeyer, Dale. Reminiscences of Erich Fromm. Typescript available at the EFIT. 1997.
Rickert, John. Erich Fromms Institut in Mexiko. Lutz von Werder (ed.). *Der unbekannte Fromm*. Frankfurt: Haag und Herchen, 1987.
Saavedra, Víctor. *La promesa incumplida de Erich Fromm*. Mexico: Siglo Veinteuno Editores, 1994.
Schechter, David. On Fromm. *WAW Newsletter*: XV(1):10, 1981.
Silver, Catherine. Erich Fromm and the making and unmaking of the sociocultural. *The Psychoanalytic Review*: 104(4):389–414, 2017.
Silver, Catherine. Fromm's socio-psychoanalytic conceptualization of the clinical encounter in relation to the social third. *Fromm Forum*: 24:115–124, 2020.
Spiegel, Rose. Tribute. *Contemporary Psychoanalysis*: 17(4):436–441, 1981.
Tauber, Edward. The sense of immediacy in Fromm's conceptions. S. Arieti (ed.). *American Handbook of Psychiatry II*. New York: Basic Books, 1959.
Tauscher, Petra. Erich Fromm als Analytiker in Berlin. Lutz von Werder (ed.). *Der unbekannte Fromm*. Frankfurt: Haag und Herchen, 1987.
Wolstein, Benjamin. A historical note on Erich Fromm: 1955. *Contemporary Psychoanalysis*: 17(4):468–480, 1981.

Part IV

Critique and Praxis

In the previous part, we studied Fromm's ontological premises and their clinical application. Here we will deduce their *ethical* and *political* consequences. Chapter VI investigates the inner workings of Fromm's normative humanism. It examines a series of contrasting tendencies within his ethics, each of which results in a different way of grounding value judgments. These tendencies are reported back to Fromm's conception of psychic determination, as we search for the most coherent alternative between them. This allows a subsequent assessment of the *logical* structure assumed by his critical theory. Fromm's understanding of the theoretical functions of affirmation and negation is derived from their practical correlates in two of his main spheres of activity – the psychoanalytic clinic and humanistic politics.

Chapter VII complements theoretical results with an investigation of Fromm's conduct as a political agent and public intellectual, in a series of endeavors between the 1950s and the 1970s. It enquires into the social psychology of humanistic movements, establishing the correspondences and contradictions between practice – as prescribed by Fromm's theory – and praxis – as was actually possible for him and his allies within their historical circumstances.

Chapter 6

VI Aspects of Logic and Ethics (1964–1980)

1 Reflexivity

The period following from 1964 to 1976 – the interval between the publication of *The heart of man* and of *To have or to be?* – culminates in a new reformulation of Fromm's characterology. Instead of "syndromes of orientation", we now find character conceptualized in terms of *modes of existence*, centered around a new alternative: "being" or "having" (cf. Fromm, 1976a). At first sight, the change may look unsubstantial. The syndrome of attitudes characterizing the "mode of having" combines aspects Fromm had described since the 1940s as typical of the "hoarding" and "marketing" characters. It is a "property-structured existence" (Fromm, 1976a:97), devoted to the possession of the ego, of material goods, of emotions and memories. The traits pertaining to the "mode of being" recover with some modifications what was previously described as the "productive" and "biophilic" orientations, as well as the more general "syndrome of growth". In being, we would find a state of openness, of immersive experience in the present moment – a life of *"process, activity, and movement"* (Fromm, 1976a:13). On closer inspection, however, these new formulations contain important advancements in comparison to their predecessors.

The main novelty is that the two modes do not refer to the topical relation between unconscious orientation and conscious attitudes, but rather to the total relation between consciousness and unconsciousness. We must remember that, for Fromm, the notion of "existence" refers precisely to the passage of psychic "potentialities" into acts – with that, into effective qualities in the subject. "Being" presumes the ever renewed exercise of psychic powers. Thus, a mode of "existence" is a way of relating to one's latent powers through time. It is a determinate *articulation* between awareness and the unconscious – a form of their structural juncture. Fromm reaches a psychoanalysis of the *transit* between consciousness and unconsciousness.

The mode of "having" is the conceptual representative of psychic paralysis, of the effort for remaining identical to oneself, and reproducing the conditions for this identity. It results in the formation of a fixed ego, who owns itself and is hostile to change. The permeability of consciousness to the unconscious is here at a minimum. Contrariwise, the mode of "being" corresponds to a mode of relation of the psyche to itself in which it is optimally *capable of changing*. Topologically, this coincides with a highly developed *openness* of consciousness to unconscious processes, allowing the continued discovery and appropriation of one's underlying psychic reality. The notion of "being" thus absorbs the category of "process". This can be understood as a compromise between the "active" and the "contemplative" axes in Fromm's works. Two distinct models of subjective change are subsumed under this understanding of "being": on the one hand, the experience of our essentiality, of the transience of conscious phenomena once we reach deep, meditative stillness; on the other hand, the dense flux of emotions in praxis.

The categories of "being" and "having" appear as parts of a larger series which includes also the notions of "preserving", "coveting", and "using" (Fromm, 1960a:36). Why should then Fromm counterpose "being" only to one of these four terms, instead of referring to the whole ensemble? The reason is that the hoarding appropriation of goods displays the greatest clinical and sociological correlation with the incapacity for change. At this stage in the development of his thought, Fromm had already reached concluded that different forms of malignant aggression derive from their intensification in degree. He could thus see the "hoarding character" (Fromm's version of the old Freudian anal character) as the initial term in a series that would end in the harshest necrophilic traits. Notice how here the distinction between relatedness in assimilation and in socialization is left aside:

> This hypothesis suggests that the development: normal anal character → sadistic character → necrophilous character is determined by the increase of narcissism, unrelatedness, and destructiveness (in this continuum there are innumerable shadings between the two poles) and that necrophilia can be described as *the malignant form of the anal character*.
> (Fromm, 1973a:387)

Let us now generalize this way of reasoning onto the whole ensemble of categories of which the two main modes of existence are a part. We then see that each term in the series corresponds to one of the old "modes of assimilation". "Being, having, preserving, coveting, and using" are summaries of the basic orientations for the "productive, hoarding, receptive, exploitative, and marketing" character types. However, there is a big difference in conceptual form. What was previously formulated in terms of specific attitudes (to receive, to exploit etc.) is now posed in the form of a global relation between consciousness and unconsciousness. Where the "modes of assimilation" thought mainly of the subject's relation to an object, the "modes of existence" refer to the subject's relation to herself. Not one's desire, but one's *relation to desire*, is now at the center of the concept.

Indeed, Fromm's experience of the psyche is increasingly drawn to these inner folds of subjectivity. "Being" and "having" are the formal prototypes of a more general category in Fromm's psychology: the *reflexivity* of the psychic process – its capacity to relate and react to itself. The modes of existence are the final terms in the long process of dissolution experienced by Fromm's original bipartition of character between modes of assimilation and socialization. Instead of classifying object relations in their immediacy, we now have a generalized appreciation of the circularity of the psychic system: its structure conditions its own capacity (or incapacity) to change over time.

2 Self-Awareness and Conscience

Reflexivity pertains to a series of categories in the sphere of *self-awareness*. We will now examine the most important among them in their ethical significance. We shall remember that self-awareness was for Fromm the domain of the relation between the *intellectual* and the *sensory* spheres. The term is misleading. In Fromm, self-awareness does not always denote an *effective* awareness of oneself, but primarily the psyche's capacity to react to itself – in which both conscious and unconscious moments may be included. Its closest correspondence in Freud (1900–30; 1938) would be his understanding of cenesthesia in the id, or simply the concept of unconscious thought processes. In Hegel (1817–30), it falls closely, not with egoic *Selbstbewußtsein,* but with the more primitive *Selbstgefühl*. In Fromm, self-awareness is freed from its immediately intellectual forms and demonstrated in its pre-verbal activity. Indeed, the capacity to become conscious of any psychic process already presupposes this former, unconscious reflexivity, according to which the psyche apprehends its own inner movements. It thinks with affects, and is affected by itself. According to its intellectual aspect, self-awareness thus means knowledge that one knows something – self-apperception. According to its sensory aspect, it means self-apprehension – reflexive reaction of the psychic process to itself.

Sensory self-apprehension is prior to intellectual awareness of oneself. Let us then begin with an examination of this side of the relation. The duality between action and reaction is resumed in Fromm's concept of *sensation*. As a psychic sphere, sensation is at the same time passive and active. It refers simultaneously to perception and to the act in which something is perceived (sensuous activity). Fromm calls it a "physical [...] and sensory" sphere, but also the sphere of "action" (Fromm, 1955e:379; Fromm and Maccoby, 1970b:71). Up to this point, psychic activity and reactivity were split between the "vital forces" of human powers, and the "emotional forces" based on affects. Now they are gathered in a single category. This is pregnant with consequences for us. Depending on the appreciation one has of the relation between these moments, self-awareness stands in a different determination with behavior. In the one case, action determines character; in the other, character determines action.

We will reach a clearer understanding of this problem if we take into account that the subjective duality contained in "sensation" is also formulated objectively, in the opposition between "conditions of life" and "practice of life". "Conditions of life" are everything that affects the production and reproduction of life – social relations and culture included. As a concept, it displays no ambiguity. The same cannot be said about *practice of life*. It will be taken as a more abstract or more concrete concept, depending on how we interpret it. If we follow Fromm (1992e) in assuming that physiological needs are the entry point into social relations, the consequence is that the subject stands in a practical relation to others *before* her psychic structure is constituted. She acts first, and later, in reaction to the relations thus established, unfolds the whole psychic chain leading to character formation. Conversely, if we follow Fromm (1947a) in assuming action expresses one's passions, practice can only be represented as following *after* a character structure is formed.

According to its position in Fromm's system, we are forced to consider life practice each time in either of its meanings, without resolving their discrepancy. In its most *abstract* sense, "practice of life" appears as prior to character, indeed as its objective support. Action is primarily determined by material demands, as well as by certain rules of conduct within the corresponding relations of production. As such, it is initially pragmatic, merely "adaptive" behavior. Only at a second moment does it acquire the character of a meaningful, psychically determined chain of acts. This view is implied by Fromm's *functional* appreciation of character – especially of social character. Character's biological function is then to make possible action without constant "conscious deliberation". Its social function (or of those traits which are related to production) is to displace individual energies toward the "social process" (Fromm, 1941a:102,281; 1947a:59). Practice of life thus appears as geared mainly toward physical survival.

Contrariwise, if we take one's practice of life as a resultant of character, it appears as responding primarily to the tasks of psychic survival and expression. Thus considered, it is not anymore the empty, purely reactive behavior it had prior to character formation, but rather its most *concrete* result and summation. The primary objects and experiences which led to psychic structuralization appear as lost in time and repression, and character emerges as an autonomous system of strivings, acting to preserve its existing structure. It may still be treated according to its psychological function – to organize a subject's forms of satisfaction and prevent her from falling in psychosis – but the expressive aspiration to freedom is now also a possibility.

It is not a coincidence that this duality falls exactly within Fromm's understanding of the sensory sphere. Praxis is the central mediating factor between subject and object. In the notion of practice of life, more than in any other, life is posed as a structured process, including both the "furthering" and the "hindrance" of our psychic potentialities. For most modes of production, the more character is structured by the demands of production, the less it becomes "productive" of itself (cf. Fromm, 1944a). Entangled in irrational passions, it remains attached to the satisfaction of attitudes whose consequence is an interruption of psychic life. Contrariwise, if conditions for a free exercise of human faculties are given, character shows the propensity to preserve structure in the act of changing it, expanding the reach of one's powers:

> the opposite of the concept of ego is the concept of I or self. This "I" is nothing fixed, nothing static. It exists only in the here and now as the center of my system of productive activity and experience, of relating, of feeling, of seeing. There is nothing to be conserved in the "I" – but there is hope. [...] the hope for something more intense, purer, more potent.
> (d-RoHD:I:1:11)

Social relations and object relations are thus reunited in the problem of character change. Character is a living process, a beam of evolving relations which must change together for transformation to be possible. It is a unity which must reproduce itself in the act, in each practical relation in which it is involved. Where it enters relations activating new potencies, it risks its own change. Being dependent upon one's practice of life, its reproduction or modification is fundamentally conditioned by the possibility of *acting in a new way* – one must "change routinized behavior" and "practice" new attitudes for them to sediment (Fromm, 1974a:86; 1989a:119). However, depending on the way we understand "practice of life" itself, we reach very different comprehensions of the route for a new praxis. If we take action in its abstract sense, as immediate adequacy to practical demands, the emphasis falls on *conditions of life* as determining character. Behavioral, "static adaptation" precedes affective, "dynamic adaptation". It follows that the main condition for subjective change would be the transformation of the social relations in which the subject takes part. After all, they are the main anchor reproducing one's mode of existence. Contrariwise, emphasizing action as anchored on character structure results in the idea that one's strivings must be changed *before* a new practice of life can emerge.

Under these premises, the problem of subjective change becomes that of the *characterological consequences of the act*. We are then interested in the degree to which a different praxis creates conditions for the emergence of a new subjectivity – and conversely, the degree to which an inner change is a presupposition of changes in behavior. This opens a correlated problem: that of understanding the position of *will* in Fromm's system. Fromm's analytic training disposes him to mistrust all attempts at change based purely on conscious deliberation – yet traces of a voluntaristic conception are not wholly absent from his writings. There remains the idea that, since it is the objective support of character formation, practice of life may be modified by "willing one thing" (cf. Fromm, 1989a). Life may then be "practiced", deliberately exercised, just like the artist practices her technique. Fromm tries to resolve the tension between the contemplative and the practical axes with an "art of living", in the ancient meaning of the term – "*a system of objectively valid norms constitutes the theory of practice (applied science) based on the theoretical science*" (Fromm, 1947a:17).

The duality we've been developing then makes itself felt to the last consequences. If taken in its abstract sense – the precedence of action over desire – practice of life leads to the primacy of the object in determining the facts of subjectivity; but it also opens room for the idea that action, once it deviates from its own characterological presuppositions, can function as a motor of change. Since singular, situational desires are possible, a practice without a corresponding characterological basis may also induce it *post factum*, unfolding previously weak or inactive forms of reaction – "latent systems which until then have remained dormant" (Fromm and Maccoby, 1970b:22). We are left with a concept of change based on willpower: once one learns which would be the psychic ideals to achieve, one can practice the means through which they are cultivated. Here, Fromm's (1989a) model are liberatory practices of religious ascent – especially non-ascetic forms of mediation. He introverts in individual effort the measures certain salvific practices developed within their corresponding institutional relations. "Concentration", "discipline", "patience", "effort", are then the precepts through which a certain degree of liberation may be achieved (Fromm, 1956a:vii,85–6).

On the contrary, if we take the concrete notion of practice of life as a point of departure – precedence of desire over action – the relationship is inverted. At first, we have the appearance of a primacy of unconscious reality in determining action. We deal mainly with psychically determined acts, such that little room is left for will to find any freedom in relation to passions, other than through suppression or accidental circumstance. Here Fromm introduces a distinction between "rational" and "irrational will" (1973a:475), recognizing that the disposition over motor skills may also have the passive character he ascribed to irrational phenomena. But then social life acquires a decisive importance: changing the objective constellation in which the subject finds herself appears as the privileged means for acting upon her fixed mode of existence. We become interested in opening space for indeterminacy in psychic life. Norms don't appear anymore as established virtues to be achieved, but as small fractures within one's experience, pointing to the possibility of a better life. The way to fulfill these norms is not prescribed beforehand. Rather, they act as orienting signs in an unknown path, singular to each one's life.

We then have the peculiar result that, in both ways of interpreting the problem, the diagnosis and the proposed form of intervention are mismatched. If determinative primacy is given to the object, the path toward character change emphasizes the subject's willful action – an active posture up and against one's restricting circumstances. If determinative primacy is given to the subject, the path toward change emphasizes the objective world. In the first case, Fromm suggests disciplined devotion to the fulfillment of certain given norms – freedom through activity. In the second case, norms are discovered in the process of becoming, of experimenting and confronting change. This second formulation of character change is not based on negative will, but rather on affirmative *insight*. It relies on the capacity to listen to oneself and discern, within one's experience, the voice pointing to the possibility of well-being – in which a contemplative moment in unmistakable.

Taking a step back, we can now see that the duplicity of our results is prefigured in the very category of self-awareness. According to its intellectual side, it implies the capacity to determine action on the basis of emotionally invested ideas: willful action. However, according to the sensory side, it implies self-apprehension and self-orientation based on the *quality* of what one experiences. This second determinacy is the source for Fromm's insistence in coupling his psychodynamics with a more detailed phenomenology. A capacity for reflexive self-orientation seemed to him essential in creating conditions for freedom. For that reason, he included *sensibility* – "capacity for joy and sadness" – among the essential determinations of an enduring "well-being" (Fromm, 1960a:36). "One has to know one's own self in order to understand what the interests of this self are and how they can be served" (Fromm, 1947a:134).

***

The different routes to character change we considered so far are represented in Fromm's theory by two opposing appreciations of *norms*. Change through willful practice is coupled with the *ideals* one aspires to achieve. Change as the fruit of insight, on its turn, is based on experiential *values* – "anticipations of our most valuable goals" (Fromm, 1951a:181) or glimpses of our possible ways into becoming. Fromm's tendency is initially to speak of notions such as "freedom", "love" etc. as "ideals". Over time, we hear more and more about "effective values" (Fromm, 1976a:124) – not the proper "ideal" guidelines of conduct, but rather those "real objects" to which passions are attached, such that they work as effective determinations of how people "act" (Fromm, 1976a:122; 1992k:48). Values should not be mistaken with the "objects" of "object relations". They are the aspects of experience which *accompany* these relations, being concomitant with them: one's "object of devotion" is "the basis for all his effective – and not only proclaimed – values" (Fromm, 1973a:260). In the rapport to values, Fromm expects to find "not only intellectual elements but elements of feeling and sensing which are expressed in the relationship to the object of devotion" (1955a:65). All psychic faculties collaborate in their fulfillment. For that reason, effective values stand in deep relation to one's *sense of self* (cf. Fromm, 1955a). Values are the subjective counterparts to one's global self-experience, and thus lead us to the next of our reflexive categories.

Self, as the summary of psychic structuralization, is the term expressing the variability of *effective* self-awareness as a function of the relation to others. It resumes the transit between consciousness and unconsciousness as correlate to a subject's real relations: the juncture between psychic functions changes together with desire. Devotion to different objects is therefore coupled with different global self-experiences: "the experience of self [...] has various forms, depending on which aspect of the personality is felt to be the ground of its identity" (u-NYPL-7.4.7132:4). This may be illustrated negatively if we remember that, in one particular case – that of the "marketing orientation" – Fromm (1947a) believes that the resulting character structure is marked precisely by lack of a stable nucleus of strivings. Desires acquire an evanescent character, adapting to what others demand in different situations. This is "a self-system in which I am, I experience myself as a reflection of others" (d-1991d-002-eng-draft-04:160). Fromm thought the blend of marketing and receptive orientations which characterized social life in post-war America tended to produce personalities "without [...] well-founded convictions" – correspondingly, with *"no character at all"* (Fromm, 1976:63; 1992j:39). Seeking an understanding of this assertion will help us clarify the different positions "ideals" and "values" occupy within the self, as well as their contrasting practical and ethical significance.

For Fromm, a "conviction" is opposed to mere "opinion", a belief determined by conditioning or suggestion: "only those opinions which are rooted in the character structure of a person, behind which there is the energy contained in his character – only those opinions *become convictions*" (Fromm, 1963b:148). Thus formulated, the distinction refers to the *reception* of certain ideas: "character structure decides what kind of an idea a man will choose and also decides the force of the idea he has chosen" (Fromm, 1963b:148). An understanding of the relations we are inquiring will be facilitated if we turn our attention toward the *production* of ideas. We then see that Fromm presumes them to be *expressions* or *carriers* of experience, however deformed by unconscious psychic mechanisms. For him the origin of thought lies in experience – particularly in its emotional aspect, even though sometimes the idea of "intellectual experience" (1951a:7) also occurs in his texts:

> The boundary between awareness of feeling and expression of feeling in words is very fluid. There is the completely non-verbalized experience, and close to it the experience in which a word appears like a vessel that "contains" the feeling and yet does not contain it, for the feeling is constantly flowing and it overflows the vessel. The word-vessel is more like a note in a musical score, which is a symbol for a tone but not the tone itself. The feeling may be still more closely related to the word, but as long as the word is still a "living word", it has done little harm to the feeling. But there comes a point where the word becomes separated from the feeling, i.e., also from the speaking person, and at this point the word has lost its reality, except as a combination of sounds.
>
> (Fromm, 1989a:80)

In its origin, language would have a poetic-expressive function. Its quality as being for others develops only secondarily, in the process of communication. To "communicate", thinks Fromm, "naturally language has to *abstractify*" – "abstract from the unique concrete phenomena, which permits me to cover numerous objects of similar kinds with one word" (1991e:52). Contrariwise, in relation to the speaker, the word is a sign for a unique experience, with an "entirely subjective meaning" (1979a:15). In his appreciation for this expressive and singularizing function of language, Fromm gave preference to symbolic communication in dreams and in art, in which he saw a compromise between the two terms. "Poetry, music, and other forms of art are by far the best-suited media for describing human experience because they are precise and avoid the abstraction and vagueness" (1968a:11); "the poet expresses the experience which the average person senses but is unconscious of; by giving it form he is able to communicate the experience to others" (1990f:59). Symbolic language would thus be the one "adequate to describe real experience" (1964a:106). The sign's "referent" is resumed as emotional reality – affect, form of apprehension of the object. The more this emotional basis is lost, the more language becomes an instrument of alienation.

Fromm extended the same reasoning to ideals. He valued in them the capacity to symbolize and express the hope and aspirations motivating the struggle for a better society, but was mistrustful of their role as imperatives on the way things should be. He warned about their propensity to deteriorate into ideology, breaking their connection with experience and emptying themselves into alienated forms. Fromm thought alienated ideals behaved in a falsifying, repressive manner – but this should be distinguished from their effectiveness as symbolizations of concrete, really lived experience:

> The ideology serves to bind people together, and to make them submit to those who administer the proper use of the ideological ritual; it serves to rationalize and to justify all irrationality and immorality that exist within a society. At the same time the ideology, containing in itself the frozen idea, as it were, satisfies the adherents of the system; they believe themselves to be in touch with the most fundamental needs of man, with love, freedom, equality, brotherliness—because they hear and say these words. And at the same time, however, the ideology also preserves these ideas. While they become rituals they nevertheless remain expressed; they can become living ideas again when the historical situation enables man to awaken and to experience again as real that which had become an idol.
> (Fromm, 1961a:124)

This description allows us to specify the difference between ideals and values. Both of them are subjective representatives of norms, but each stands in a distinct relation with their unconscious attitudinal basis. *Ideals* are conceptual vessels for something which is actually of *imaginary* nature. They express attitudinal strivings as phantasies of fulfillment, investing concepts with an image abstracted from its origins in sensation. They are born as extrapolations from living experience, and remain susceptible to degrading into "mere words", abstracting from the emotional soil from which that image originated. Because of the capacity of ideals to become vehicles of repression, Fromm came to displace the basis of his normative theory toward the experiential content behind them. *Values* don't bear an imaginary character, referring instead to the effective object of passions. They capture in language the experiential concomitants to object relations. Instead of losing themselves in the phantasistic projection of a fulfilling future, values stick to the *real* (sensory) relation to the object. They capture one's experience of oneself as a concomitant to one's relatedness to others, moving us to seek the quality of satisfaction we re-encounter in relating to certain objects. The difference is clear: ideals are abstracted derivatives of object relations, whereas values express one's self-experience in the course of these relations. They bear the reflexive character we are interested in investigating (cf. Fromm, 1947a).

The difference between both normative forms finds a compromise in Fromm's concept of *vision*. Extracted from the Jewish prophetic tradition, the term incorporates aspects of both other phenomena. It is treated alternately as ideal, as phantasy, as concept (cf. Fromm, 1979a:106; 1991e:69). Visions share with ideals their character as images, of anticipations projected out of germinal experiences. Contrary to ideals, however, they must partake in proper conceptual determinations. They are of ethical and political interest only if they are "rational visions", which "can be realized" (Fromm, 1980g:29). The content projected by phantasy is thus already in a metabolism with intellect, being carved out in reference to *real* possibilities – not merely imaginable ones. Visions share with values their character as effective orientations to action. However, in them the coincidence between living experience and concept takes a step back. Visions express more than what was in fact experienced, expanding it in the image of what *could be* – halfway between the dream and the daydream. At the same time, they retain a connection with reality in the memory of their non-identity with given existence. They then act in their *difference* with this existence, both criticizing it and being criticized by it. Visions become lighthouses, orientations for social reconstruction – but not anymore in the immediacy of remembered experience, as was the case with values.

Fromm's normative psychology is thus not a theory of how subjects *should be*, but it oscillates between distinct relations to what *can be* – to the category of possibility. In some places it abstracts and inflates, from effective experience, the image of a fulfilled change, orienting action to its concretion (ideal). In other places, it remains attentive to the unaccomplished character of these experiences, displacing normative orientation toward the subject's sensibility and self-apprehension in the process of living (value). In yet other cases, Fromm prefigures a dialectic of experience, posing norms as a relation between phantasy and effectiveness (vision). In all three instances, the relation between concept and inner experience is the crucial one – but only *values* express this inner experience as reflexive, self-experience. This is the reason they, and not the other forms, are at the core of one's sense of self.

To go back to our earlier model in this discussion – to say that someone "lacks character" as she "lacks conviction" amounts to saying that the subject stands in a weak relatedness to herself and her own experience. Unconscious self-apprehension does not develop into its conscious appropriation – correspondingly, one's global experience of oneself is weakened. This is the reason Fromm refers the "marketing orientation" to a *loss of self*, a reinforcement of alienation. Reduced to her own ego, the subject feels set apart from herself. Desires are pulverized in the ignorance of what is good or bad for her. Her acts feel like they are initiated from outside, not from her own core. No transit develops between consciousness and her latent potentialities, and she is left with an impoverished existence (cf. Fromm, 1955a). The most fulfilling alternative to this state of affairs would lie in accomplishing *unity*: not simple identity with oneself, but differentiated, multifaceted relation between one's inner and outer differences – "within oneself and with the natural and human external world" (1973a:262).

***

Thus far, we explored two categories of great ethical significance: practice of life, as the objective vehicle for character change, and the norms which may orient this practice. Out of the many oppositions we discovered within each category, a particular connection deserves our attention. Understanding praxis as expressive of character structure derived the idea that change starts with a modification of our objective position in the world, allowing us insight into ourselves. Later, we discovered the main content of this insight is given by a series of affirmative values, which express our self-experience in the course of relatedness to others. We thus achieved a concept in which reflexive psychic forms take the lead in allowing character change.

This line of reasoning will be completed in examining the psychic instance in which experiential values are gathered. *Conscience* represents a fold or reflex determination of simple consciousness. For that reason, Fromm (1947a) connects it to the domain of self-awareness as well. He distinguishes – once again in the form of miscible ideal types – two contrasting determinations of moral life. "Authoritarian conscience" has an ascetic and repressive character, being oriented by guilt before unaccomplished obligations. "Humanistic conscience", on its turn, compels one to feel guilty, not in disobeying others, but in disrespecting oneself, in acting against one's own integrity and desire:

> The other source of guilt feeling is man's own conscience; he senses his gifts or talents, his ability to love, to think, to laugh, to cry, to wonder and to create, he senses that his life is the one chance he is given, and

that if he loses this chance he has lost everything. [...] He cannot help feeling guilty for the waste, for the lost chance.

(Fromm, 1955a:205)

Humanistic conscience is the accomplished figure of the capacity for adjudicating self-apperception – the ability of discerning, in experience, what is good or bad for oneself and others. It is easy to see how "ideology" falls with the repressive function of authoritarian conscience, whereas one's orientation by experiential values approximates the function of humanistic conscience of leading the subject toward her own good.

Fromm (1947a) understands these two forms of conscience as parallel determinations of moral life, weaker or stronger according to the case. However, their origin is not given as identical. Fromm believes the authoritarian conscience is acquired in the same way as the Freudian (1924) super-ego – introjection of the parental imago with the dissolution of the Oedipus complex. However, distinct processes are offered for explaining the origin of autonomous conscience. In some cases, Fromm traces it back to the incorporation of the mother imago, as if introjection would differentiate a psychic segment capable of fulfilling the functions of care. Each structure would then correspond to a different power structure – patriarchal and matriarchal, respectively – and humanistic conscience would amount to "*motherly conscience*" (Fromm, 1955a:47). In other passages, however, Fromm poses it as an immediate response of the psychic organism to itself – a reflex gesture approximating synderesis or moral cenesthesia (cf. Fromm, 1983d).

We saw before that certain forms of anxiety, powerlessness, separation, helplessness, express one's relation to oneself as a function of primary relation others. In the sphere of humanistic conscience there emerges a secondary class of reflex affects, expressive of one's relation to oneself once the whole of personality is already formed. These affects are concomitant to or expressive of vital processes – forms of *affective knowledge* (Fromm, 1947a:158). For Fromm, "happiness" and "depression" are of such a nature, together with guilt of the kind we discussed above. These are all indexes resuming the general quality of the vital process, "*a reaction of ourselves to ourselves*" (Fromm, 1947a:159). If "humanistic conscience" is not given with birth, it appears at least as aspiring to a spontaneous development, concomitant with the structuralization of personality. Where it appears to be inactive or weakened, the problem is not to develop it, but to "learn how to listen to it" (Fromm, 1947a:161). The argument insinuates a "natural moral sensibility" (Fromm, 1983d:142–3).

For Fromm (1949c), the process of psychic formation is centered on social relations – especially the early experiences amidst the family, with its affective atmosphere, its social character and pedagogical methods. However, his later writings sometimes displace the determination of the "experiential values" guiding his critical theory onto nature – love, solidarity, freedom, would be drives "inherent in human nature" (Fromm, 1965h:xv). We saw many prefigurations of this naturalistic tendency before: first, in the presumed agreement between the reality of affects and the object's reality; then, in humanistic conscience and its reflex affects. These categories lead back to the assumption that the psyche knows what is good for itself: "our own internal voices guide us in directions that are compatible with the physical and psychic potential of our particular organisms" (Fromm, 1983d:23).

The ambiguity of Fromm's ideas on the origins of humanistic conscience and values – natural or social – is also on occasion replicated in his relation to so-called non-productive attitudes. In the majority of instances, the receptive, exploitative, and other basic attitudes are treated as responses developed within social relations – but there do also occur passages where they are treated as necessary stages in childhood development. In this case, they are seen as primarily propelled by the inner movement of bodily and psychic development, being fixated by social experience only on second instance:

> The first years in the child's life are necessarily a period during which the infant is not capable of taking care of itself, to form the surrounding world according to its wishes under its own powers. It is forced either to receive, to snatch, or to possess because it cannot yet produce. Thus, the category of having is a necessary transitional stage in the child's development. But if possessiveness remains the dominant experience in the adult, it indicates that he has not achieved the goal of normal development to productivity but has become stuck in the experience of having, because of this failure in his development. Here, as with other orientations, what is normal at an early stage of evolution becomes pathological if it occurs at a later stage.
> (Fromm, 1989a:110)

There remains always a potential contradiction between the equanimous character of human traits as simple characterological possibilities, on the one hand, and Fromm's insistence on the determinacy of a *telos* of psychic development based on the concept of "human nature" – between historical and biological determinations of the species, that is. This touches upon the central problem of knowing whether a normative theory grounds its value judgments on natural or historical, general or singular terms. Politically expressed, this problem means: to what extent must historical action be oriented by its specific circumstances, and to what extent must it (or can it) rely on a transcending point of view – in Fromm, the "standpoint of reason and humanity" (1963b:158).

3 Differentiation and Freedom

Fromm's solution for the problem of grounding his ethics consists in collapsing both sides of the opposition in one: the "general" aspiration of every psychic structure is to become "singular" – that is, to individualize. Much as the life process is one of "structured growth", he assumes, also psychic life wills to weave its elements in an articulation allowing to crystallize the results of previous experience, as well as to further diversify its own capacities. In the concept of the given human potencies is included the totality of alternatives of a subject's development, as forces pressing to be put in use. Thus considered, however, each potentiality is equivalent to any other. They represent antagonistic *teloi,* all of which nonetheless remain distinct from the others, expressing possible "differentiations" of the subject. No immanent ethical criterion is given by which we could judge some as better than others.

Determining "difference" (individuality) as a valuing criterion is thus not enough to sustain an antirelativistic position – and Fromm (1947a), from the ethical standpoint, is strictly antirelativist. The valuation of some attitudes and orientations over others can only be justified under Fromm's metapsychological premise: that the content of desire and the form of psychic organization (therein included one's relation to desire) are mutually conditioned. For Fromm, the vital process *poses part of its own conditions,* precisely in the form of the structure acquired up to a certain point in its evolution. What is then expressed as an immanent striving for love, for freedom etc. is the formulation, in substantive terms, of a hypothesis that would better be expressed in relative terms. Namely: that the contents dominating the psychic process condition the relation of this process to itself – and with it, the concrete form it assumes, with the corresponding capacity for change and sense of self.

The key to Fromm's ethical stance is then the supposition that desires – psychic vehicles of the vital process – behave not only as partially autonomous units of meaning, but also as *functional* units. In other words: they have implications for the constitution of this very process *as process,* as becoming, being its ends and its means at the same time. Indeed, this is the unavoidable consequence from the fragment of ontology we reconstructed before: what one desires and experiences today conditions what one may desire and experience tomorrow. Cause and effect are reintegrated at the same level. The psychic "structure" is conceived as evolving from its own inner conditions as well. In contrast to Fromm's apparently static concepts, there rises a concept of psychic determination which is emphatically transversal in time. Psychic development is then understood as an intricate chain of polarizations between elements which, according to their quality, turn the psychic structure more or less capable of changing – more or less capable of actualizing itself as non-identical to itself. Each character constellation will strengthen or weaken its "flexibility" and "regenerative power" (Fromm and Maccoby, 1970b:23).

The nucleus of Fromm's ethics is occupied by *freedom* – after all, also an "essential quality of life" (Fromm, 1964a:32). *Differentiation* as a process and the capacity to keep changing are more highly valued than already constituted difference. Thus, Fromm's concept of "liberation" is divided in two mutually conditioning segments, each corresponding to one of the groups of ontological forms we identified. The relation to objects and external conditions, Fromm (1941a) develops under the notion of "negative freedom" – "freedom from fear, from need, from oppression and violence" (Fromm, 1960b:69); from political authority and tradition (cf. Fromm, 1955a). He sees the process of political and cultural change as an increasing removal of obstacles to spontaneity: satisfaction of basic organic and psychic needs, and above all the abolition of the objective bases of repression – that is, of "outer domination" (Fromm, 1989a:7). Thus far, freedom is independence – not being hindered by others in exerting what one wants (cf. Fromm, 1941a). But this relation to external obstacles – absence of an impediment – is not enough, according to Fromm, to produce effective freedom. For that to be possible, working within the subject's relation to herself is also necessary – such that she will find herself capable of and up to exercising her faculties according to her own impulse.

This "positive freedom" – freedom to pose oneself and dispose *in practice* of the possibilities opened by political and cultural transformation; to "act of one's own free volition" (Fromm, 1939b:185) – is the most complete, affirmative expression of a principle we tracked before in many of its partial prefigurations: the "expressive" moment of life; free "activity"; the "sense of self" developed into an experience of differentiated unity with oneself (cf. Fromm, 1941a). Here, both sides of the concept are joined in a more specific relation: negative freedom, in relation to others, is *possible* freedom; positive freedom, in relation to oneself, is *effective* freedom:

> Freedom that is not arbitrariness but the possibility to be oneself, not as a bundle of greedy desires, but as a delicately balanced structure that at any moment is confronted with the alternative of growth or decay, life or death.
> (Fromm, 1976a:157)

Fromm's whole normative program is based on this concept of freedom. If they are abstracted from each other, both facets of the concept lead to untenable positions. A unilateral emphasis on the "negative" aspect redounds in politicization at the expense of the subjective dimension – a political equivalent to the inclination toward "activity", in abstraction from contemplation. On the other hand, a unilateral emphasis on "positive" freedom results in spiritualization, a totally interiorized concept of character change – corresponding to the "contemplative" moment, if taken in isolation. Even though these dissociated tendencies sporadically occur in Fromm's writings, the specificity of his conception and its most fruitful conclusions are to be found in the passages where both sides are taken in unity. We then reach a bond between subjective change and social change. The objective meaning of inner liberation is the search for enlarging one's experiential possibilities, and requires struggling against irrational authority and domination. The subjective meaning of outer liberation is to make one's free relation to oneself *practicable*. Both aspects are then reunited in a single movement.

Considered subjectively, the more the psychic process feeds irrational passions, allowing them to feedback into themselves, the more it acquires a compulsive character and loses its freedom. We then have the most absolute reification, incapacity to change:

> Every evil act tends to harden man's heart, that is, to deaden it. Every good act tends to soften it, to make it more alive. The more man's heart hardens, the less freedom does he have to change; the more is he determined already by previous action. But there comes a point of no return, when man's heart has become so hardened and so deadened that he has lost the possibility of freedom, when he is forced to go on and on until the unavoidable end which is, in the last analysis, his own physical or spiritual destruction.
> (Fromm, 1966a:81)

On the other hand, the more an ecology is formed which favors rational passions, the less the subject is free *not to* change: the regressive tendencies atrophy, and cease to act as efficient forces in the conduct of life. Finally, where both tendencies clash in a balance of forces, different alternatives are left open for psychic life. The dissolution of essential differences between attitudes into differences in degree, which is characteristic of the last phases in Fromm's characterology, reappears now as a *gradation* of inner, positive freedom:

> The proportion will be different in each person, and also the degree of repression versus the degree of awareness of the archaic orientation. There are people in whom the archaic side has been so completely eliminated, not by repression but by the development of the progressive orientation, that they may have lost the capability of even regressing to it. In the same way there are persons who have so completely destroyed all possibilities for the development of a progressive orientation that they too have lost the freedom of choice – in this case, the choice to progress.
> (Fromm, 1964a:122)

Since polar psychic forces fight to establish an economy of traits and passions from which they feed and stabilize, and this economy always circulates through objects and conditions of life – we end with a concept of the psychic process such that one's freedom is conditioned by that of all others. The occlusion or openness of consciousness to the unconscious, of subject to desire, may now be seen as resulting from intersubjective *circuits of acts* (cf. Fromm, 1976a:107). As a consequence:

> freedom is not a thing or a substance. It is a state of mind, a way of being in the process of living; it is different for each person and it is different in each moment in life. And every act which debilitates the person's vitality and

integrity diminishes her marginal freedom. And every act which strengthens them, increases it.

(Fromm, 1972d:6)

The whole process of a subject's action through time has a cumulative effect over her own conditions for freedom, as well as others'. The act is not related to others only according to its immediate objective consequences, but also as posing the subjective conditions for every subsequent act. The individual life process thus appears as a chain of "decisions" – passional decisions, that is, either conscious or unconscious – which enhance or weaken one's vital possibilities. The political process, correspondingly, appears as a decision between alternatives leading to common vitality or rigidification. Fromm (1964a) calls this theoretical stance *alternativism*.

Alternativism adds an important element to our understanding of normativity in Fromm. His preference for love, solidarity, reason and other such values is not grounded only in the assumption that they create inner conditions for an optimal openness to unconscious processes. Equally important is the assumption that they incline the subject to reaffirm the freedom *of others* as well. Fromm (1947a) assumes, according to the determination of the "productive" attitudes, that they seek not only one's own conditions for growth, but also those of others. Conversely, he believes the non-productive attitudes have paralyzing or destructive consequences for everyone:

> Power over people is the very opposite of productiveness; as a matter of fact, it paralyzes and eventually kills all productive abilities in both the one who has power and the one who submits to it. On the other hand, any form of social organization which excludes the possibilities of persons or groups having power over others will of necessity stimulate and reinforce productiveness in all its members.
>
> (Fromm, 1942b:317)

This property finds its highest expression in love "of life" and "of death" as such – biophilia and necrophilia. Here we see how meaningful it is that the processes of self-awareness are partly displaced onto the unconscious in Fromm. The alternative between biophilia and necrophilia implies not only the prevalence of rational or irrational passions, respectively, but also the subject's capacity to relate to herself *as* a living being, in need of free expression. In this assumption is implied a reflexive determination, which exceeds the "conjunctive" character of attitudes as such. It presupposes one's vital and moral self-apperception – as well as a new and important attribute: it's *transitivity* with one's experience of others. Biophilia is different from simple love in its capacity to communicate the affective acknowledgement of one's own living nature with that of the other.

Necrophilia, conversely, is distinguishable from simple destructiveness in its orientation to objects which bear the quality of death.

The vital process, as a process referred to and dependent on others, happens always between psychic subjects, and is thus reciprocally furthered in biophilia. Contrariwise, sadistic desires wish to reduce the other to a "thing", suspending his vital process; destructiveness wants to annihilate living structures. Fromm's ethics are accordingly compelled, not to an affirmation of human singularity as such, but to an affirmation of those differences which he understands as capable of *mutual affirmation*. His ethical program leads not to an equivalent openness to all forms of individuation, but especially to those which are able to recognize and affirm, in oneself and in others, their unfulfilled potentialities – their life.

***

The process of acknowledging the inner potentialities of life is formulated in Fromm's concept of *humanistic experience* (1962a:178). The subject's becoming, the dissolution of repression, the overcoming of illusions and stationary forms of satisfaction – all would lead to the capacity to assimilate in oneself the many partial figures of humanity: "the infant, the child, the adolescent, the criminal, the insane, the saint, the artist, the male, *and* the female" (Fromm, 1960a:106). These may appear to any subject as an "other", but they are all equally constitutive of humanity – symbolic ciphers of its variegated potentialities and experiential positions. The basis for a peaceful and affirmative conviviality with difference would thus not lie in its reduction to an abstract common denominator – the "concept" of the human, or any equivalent – but rather in the progressive, *concrete* assimilation of the many partial figures of non-identity – the many aspects of experience which deviate from one's ego as constituted so far. Hence Fromm's (1963f) concept of "humanity" as concrete, not abstract: universality emerges as unity of partial differences, not as subsumption under a basic identity. "Man, only by developing his own individuality fully, could come to the experience of his own humanity – and that means, of all humanity" (Fromm, 1992m:68).

According to its concept, this process should include all psychic inclinations Fromm deemed "regressive". It would then represent a crossing and elaboration of those modes of self-apprehension – separation, powerlessness, anguish etc. – which may lead to the desire to "escape from freedom", withdrawing from the possibility of positive freedom (cf. Fromm, 1941a). Fromm expected this process to lead to a dissolution of regressive tendencies: "the evil desire will melt away and disappear under the light and warmth of enlarged consciousness" (Fromm, 1959e:87). Being able to fully experience the basic affects responding to the human condition should lead to the gradual emergence of more adequate "solutions" in response to it – that is, modes of relatedness and of desire better apt to reconcile human life's expansive impulse with its split nature.

Since this impulse and this split are represented as belonging to different spheres – one, the immanent activity of "vital forces", simple potency of freedom; the other, the basis of human passions in the scope of psychic needs – Fromm is led to introject the many possible character developments as *teloi* given with human nature. The more the facts of individuation, which were initially derived from the social process, are imputed to the constitutional necessities of the human being, the more the process of psychic singularization is grafted back into the organism. Fromm then speaks of a "basic personality", constitutionally given, such that it would be necessary to discover in a character structure "which of the traits [...] are part of the original nature and which are acquired through influential circumstances; furthermore, which of the acquired qualities conflict with the genetic ones and which tend to reinforce them" (Fromm and Maccoby, 1970b:20; Fromm, 1979a:65). In this perspective, Fromm's humanistic motto – *"to become what we potentially are"* – coincides with the task of discovering, for each individual, *"what this person was meant to be"* (1960:36; 1992g:112). The repertoire of potentialities given in the beginning of life doesn't anymore appear as an indeterminate set of equivalent alternatives, but as predetermined or disposed in a certain direction.

This strain of thought in Fromm's ethics leads to an immanent, *naturalistic* eudaimonism. In this view, the characterological results of the process of individuation are represented as latent necessities, preceding their real development, and requiring from the outset a determined developmental path. They appear, in other words, as *ends in themselves*. We are led to intuit a general figure of "good life" as a *telos* immanent to life. We measure the varied forms of life deviating from this model as deformations of the vital process in its confrontation with social conditions. This impels the search for change to seek resources not in experience itself, but in the opposition between effectiveness and ideality.

Under these conditions, one problem is left unsolved. We must represent singularity as given within the undifferentiated human "potentialities". This means representing it as efficient before its concretion, presupposed to its real position – which results in dissociating Fromm's ethics from his ontology. The possibility of an immanent, universal value judgment is retained – but norms and their realization are treated as biologically given, not as evolving from social affection. The concretion of values is seen as moved by a predetermined inner impulse, such that social relations can only appear as obstacles or vehicles for their fulfillment – but not as *posing* anything new, as Frommian characterology would require. Everything pertaining to other forms of becoming is expelled from the essential process of life, and portrayed as the fruit of accident – of one's relations to bad conditions of life. The "irrational" is then understood as "lack of the rational"; deviations from an optimal development are taken as partial, incomplete forms: "lack of integration" of the self (Fromm, 1942a:309). Such the impasses of Fromm's (1947a) "humanistic ethics" – a theoretical equivalent to treating norms of living as "ideals of human relatedness" (Fromm, 1963c:169).

On the other hand, if we don't take valued attitudes as ends in themselves, but in their systemic sense – as mutually referred elements and conditions of the living process – we have completely different results. This way of reasoning originates a second, *sociological* strain within Fromm's ethics. In this case, the emphasis falls not on the realization of certain characteral qualities, but on the *function* these qualities fulfill in psychic economy – both in terms of the satisfaction of psychic needs, and in terms of the striving for freedom. We understand that some constellations of qualities are more satisfactory because they are *means* for freedom, protecting one's capacity to keep changing. We then interpret every characterological answer to the human condition as a response which poses its own problems – certain forms of satisfaction, of suffering and disquietude (cf. Fromm, 1962a). We deal with psychic becoming as an infinite process, to the same extent that the historical multiplication of human forms of manifestation is (potentially) infinite. The valuing criterion is resumed in the *experiential quality* taken by the life process. The subject's self-experience becomes a provisional guide, orienting psychic development according to circumstance. This is the stance taken by Fromm's (1966a) later "biophilic ethics" – the theoretical equivalent to treating norms of living as "effective values", instead of ideals (compare Funk, 1978).

From the point of view of Fromm's ethics, we can thus understand the self in two different ways. Taking a naturalistic stance, "productiveness" appears as a spontaneous impulse, an immediate datum at the earliest point in the chain of ontogenesis, and every "non-productive" form is seen as resulting from the simple negation of that primal spontaneity. Each subject stands in a negative relation to time. Optimal development is already given in intent at the earliest developmental point. Everything happening later is a matter of postergating or advancing its actualization according to the adequacy of external conditions. The "totality" of the self is objectified and prefigured in the original dispositions and vital forces of the organism, and emphasis falls on its confrontation with the "environment" – the family "breaks" or "weakens" the child's "will", and from this point on, "the courage to act spontaneously" is increasingly lost (Fromm, 1941a:234; 1947a:155). We think transcendentally and negatively, aiming at the dissolution of obstructions to the best possible experience of human life.

On the other hand, if we take a sociological stance, the self appears as a result – the provisional product of a certain constellation of forces. Time is now understood as an immanent factor to the *formation* of the psychic structure. It is necessary that each of its elements, in their simple, immanent development, be taken to a certain degree of saturation, exhausted in its given forces, fulfilled in experience and in its practical exercise. Only within this *duration* will certain changes become – not only possible, but also *necessary* according to the relations established therein. Attitudes are marked by a functional value within the whole structure, which is either exhausted or strengthened over time. We think immanently and affirmatively, aiming at the *saturation* of the experience proposed by a certain caracterial constellation:

we try to bring each individual development to its last consequences, to the point of a metamorphosis in character.

Once again, these opposing theoretical tendencies produce a middle-term in Fromm, which we may call a *pedagogical* strain within his ethics. We then understand that, even though they are endowed with a predetermined, immanent directionality, potentialities of any kind must be fed to grow. They are given first as inactive "dispositions" (Fromm, 1977b:17). Primacy in character development is again ascribed to the objective world, which fulfills the role of "stimulating" or "destimulating" the development of certain forms of relation. Vital forces act, but they don't act alone: appropriate object relations will either "cultivate" or "dry up" one's inner dispositions (Fromm, 1973a:333; 1974b:90). They will do it in a more or less coherent way with what the subject "is meant to be" according to her organic inclinations: "education should help men become as they were born" (Fromm, 1977b:17–8). Having achieved a good balance between the naturalistic and the sociological stances with regards to Fromm's ontology, this theoretical third way nonetheless fails in upholding criteria for a universal ethics such as Fromm intends it. The distinction between "primary" and "secondary" potentialities is broken, since now "destructiveness" and other perversions of life may also appear as strong genetic dispositions. The constitutional determinacy of character doesn't always incline subjects to the good life, and thus "becoming what one is meant to be" does not result in a tenable ethical principle.

Upon examination, the more coherent of the three couplings between ethics and ontology remains the "sociological" one. The best possible balance between the theoretical tendencies at stake is found when we treat the process of subjective formation as open, unfinished, demanding time – and constitutionally indeterminate. We then seek to determine which character structures offer the best possibilities for the *continuation* of their own becoming. The basis for a normative psychology is here not anymore in the natural predetermination of the self. It is also not in a simple valuation of indeterminacy or inactuality. Rather, judgments of value center on the experiential quality resulting from each stage in subjective becoming. They orient further development on the basis of one's reaction to one's own life process and objective situation. This process is then acknowledged in its restlessness and indeterminacy – but in an intent of *progressive determination*. Each constituted totality appears as incomplete – a finite singularization of human forces, crossed by the infinity of the general, or what is still possible. At the same time, the many alternative ways of being do not fall in ethical indifference, since we dispose of an immanent criterion for evaluating them. This position leads us to understand politics as a work with the nuances of experience. The task of "critique" is then to enlarge the scope of what is experientiable consciously, using the enhanced sensibility thus acquired as an instrument to orient the subject's path in life, as well as for evaluating the life practices fostered by different social structures. Correspondingly, a normative psychology is not interested in fixating an ideal psychic structure, but rather in studying variants of structuralization as *modes of its movement in time* – that is, as a function of its inner ecology of traits, in their interaction with practical conditions.

The sociological tendency in Fromm's ethics still presupposes a "moderate" naturalism of its own: it assumes the adequacy of affection to its objects, as well as the adequacy of a subject's self-apperception in responding to her own life process, at least at the unconscious level. The "strict" naturalism implied by the biological teleology we examined before would lead us to think that subjective liberation corresponds to overcoming the primary negations to which one is subject in social life, opening space for the "spontaneous" expression of previously hindered forces. This "moderate" naturalism of the affects allows a different interpretation. Character formation is seen as marked by an insufficiency, a lack in the relation between its constitutive components – a *limitation* of what one could experience and practice. Further development is then not immediately equivalent to a "negation of the negation" – psychic unclogging following from the erosion of resistances, the overcoming of repression etc. It is accomplished only with the acknowledgment and affirmation of the previously suspended vital forces, which now ask for passage into new forms. Thus, when emphasis is given to life's own affirmative aspect (growth), the process of character change is conceived preferably as reverting or sublating negations, understood as exogenous to life itself. To the contrary, when emphasis is given to life's inner negativity (structure), character change coincides with the affirmation of psychic vital aspirations in social practice.

4 Affirmation and Negation

We shall now join the results of our inquiry into Fromm's ethics with our previous conclusions concerning his ontology and anthropology. Translating the main stages of psychic development into logical terms will allow us to express the core of Fromm's approach to critical theory in the form of its basic *logical structure*. Let us recall that "affirmation" and "negation" were the residual terms expressing the most distant and abstract experiential layer discussed by Fromm: the point in which psychic powers, taken as "vital forces", appear as pure activity – but an activity of entirely formal character, since it only develops in the effective contact with objects (cf. Fromm, 1968h). The presence of these potencies was in the beginning as pure impellence to the object: want of feeling something, being affected by something, thinking about something – not more than that. The need for physical survival threw the subject into its relations with others, beginning with the infantile experience of care, and extending into adult cooperation. But the expansiveness of human powers added a second layer to this encounter. The impellence to things, as it remained unsatisfied, became a risk for the subject, which was threatened with falling apart into madness, should she not find the means to develop object relations. The vital forces' aspiration to freedom was thus mediated by the aspect of necessity, which the concept of "existential needs" expresses in its negativity: without effective relations to an other, the subject disintegrates.

Since the consummation of every potency finds in the *act* its most accomplished form, the psyche was moved to its own exteriorization. This experience resulted in the consolidation of "objective alienation" – the formation of an ego, and the more or less intense split between affect and intellect. The pure affirmativeness of life thus led to a first experience of negation, in the form of the need for an other. This appeared as the feelings of separateness, of powerlessness, of helplessness. These affections inscribed in the subject the basis for everything Fromm would have deemed as "irrational passions". They did not appear as an immediate result in this process, but were established as necessary, specified possibilities to every subsequent movement of life – true potentialities.

As long as we were considering the first stage in the above development, we represented others as the bearers of all "negativity". Life appeared as appetite for its own position – immanent pressure of vital "possibility" to realize itself through all lanes and all lives. The power to break or interrupt this process was concentrated on the other side of the relation, and amounted to a selective or determinative act. In the condition of "potency", the multiplicity of vital experience was reunited in a virtual point, but left suspended in prefiguration. With the beginning of object relations, this abstract multiplicity was enriched and impoverished at the same time. It passed into the concreteness of existence, but not in its totality – rather as a "choice" among its own possibilities. When we consider the second stage in the development, object relations are already established, and a different understanding follows. Life appears now as marked by an immanent negation, underlying all structure it may come to form. The expression of "potentialities" is not anymore immediately free, but a response to this basic lack of the living being. There it acquires the character of a "need", in the simple negative sense this term has when we speak of "existential needs".

Notice that this analysis of Fromm's basic concepts led us to a position which partly clashes with his assertions in other levels. For Fromm (1947a), "secondary potentialities" are secondary in their dependence upon harming *conditions* of life – exception being made only when his later texts recognize their occasional presence in the form of genetic dispositions. For us, it derives from the argument above that "secondary potentialities" are secondary only to life's abstract, immediate affirmativeness. We had to identify the very want for objects – as is characteristic for human vital forces – as an anthropologically ubiquitous source for the painful affects exciting irrational passions. In Fromm's account, the origin of hatred would lie in the lack of a "good enough" object. In our account, his conceptual scheme allows a parallel conclusion: it derives from the inner lack which is imprinted in the psychic structure by every and any object. In other words: experiences of powerlessness, helplessness etc. must themselves be divided between those unavoidably rooted in universal, anthropological conditions, and those rooted in historical, accidental conditions (cf. Fromm, 1947a). Fromm's classification of the phenomena emerging from these painful affections tends to obscure this difference. It is not directly at the level of the "cause" of passions that they can be discerned as "rational" or "irrational", but at the level of their consequences for subjective development.

We can now clarify the duality between psychic activity and reactivity as resulting from the negation of the primary, formal activity of vital forces. Affect represents the incorporation of the object into the inner constitution of the act, after the human powers have faced their own insufficiency. At the same time, we reached the parallel conclusion that this primitive relation between a subject who is becoming and her world was followed by a specifically intellectual repercussion. The split between subject and object was followed by the "split" between "rational thought and felling" (Fromm, 1960d:204; 1968a:42). This second result duplicated, in the developing subject, the negative operation it had previously undergone. It extended negation into an aspect of one's being for oneself, not only for others. If we gather both sides of the process in their simultaneity, as aspects of a single movement, we are finally able to derive the "reflexivity" of the psychic structure. "Self-awareness" doesn't anymore belong immediately to consciousness. It is displaced onto the unconscious infrastructure of experience. The painful affects of helplessness, powerlessness etc. which accompanied this process, are themselves reflex gestures – self-apprehensions or reactions of the psychic process to itself. In these affects, the psyche *knows* itself as different from itself in the process of *becoming* so. The nucleus of the Frommian unconscious is formed from this knowledge, and the emotional currents it liberates.

Negation within a relation in which the other is for the subject unfolds, therefore, in a relation in which the subject is an other for herself. This is the formal law governing the birth of subjectivity till the end of childhood. From this point on, the "affirmative" aspect of life returns always, and only, colored by its negation. The "potency" of infinite multiplication of life is reduced to a relation between an actuality – in which that potency was effected as partial, determined – and the persistence of the formal activity of vital forces, which continue to seek expression. For this reason, the ontological categories we discerned within Fromm's characterology are never marked by absolute immediacy: they all stem from *relations* between phenomena. They represent further moments unfolding the earlier process of subjectivation. Their character as immediately negative (mutual presupposition) or positive (generativity) corresponds to the secondary autonomy unconscious psychic life acquires after it has been impressed by and split from the object. Their character as mediately positive (reciprocal implication) or negative (epigenesis) corresponds to their continued dependency on others, which is reasserted and rediscovered with every re-encounter in the world of objects.

The whole process of personality formation now appears as a "response" to the existential spilt – as an attempt at recovering the lost, simple "unity" of immediate affirmativeness (vital forces in abstraction) by developing a new, mediated unity (psychic capacities in actual relationship). The work of affects, attitudes, passions, is then to seek an overcoming of the basic negation which gave birth to the subject. Hence the concept of "structured" growth. The inner diversity of life has to be stratified in time, taking its inner contradictions into account. Each concrete development confirms its correlate psychic processes, but is at the same time the contradiction of others.

***

Having the above in mind, a critical theory must begin with the aspects in which the psychic economy of affirmation and negation leaves it *open to change*. One such important aspect is thought. Let us notice that language remains the only point in which the "systemic" character of personality formation is not expressed in the form of a bilateral relation between psychic forces. For Fromm, experience is the soil from which concepts grow; powerful emotional currents participate in selecting which ideas we generate and believe – but unconscious experience is not itself *constituted* by language. In its expressive function, language remains a precarious instrument: "the concept, or the symbol, is only an approximate expression of the experience" (Fromm, 1966a:16). As it enters the realm of communication and abstracts from its emotional origins – so goes Fromm's (1962a) account – language crystallizes in a set of culturally prevailing categories, moral and logical imperatives, filtering which aspects of one's inner reality reach consciousness. This reality may be touched by words, but it is not made *from* them – unlike words themselves, which are born from one's emotional life. Language thus determines the *path* of the psychic process, but not its *content*.

On the other hand, culturally prevalent patterns of thought are themselves one of the main forces relating a subject to others. According to Fromm (1978b), these patterns originate in social relations, and express the horizon of experience characteristic for a certain social structure. The human relations and forms of experience which are blocked by this structure correspond, in intellectual life, to unthinkable, unspeakable, inexpressible thoughts. These form the "social" nucleus of the unconscious – the areas of repression common to a certain group, underlying variations in individual biography (cf. Fromm, 1966p). A society's horizon of expression is thus "time-conditioned" (Fromm, 1979a:22): it tends to a historically determined, socially conformist restriction of each individual's possible experiences.

The first task in fostering change is thus to "think the unthinkable" (Fromm, 1973a:485). Critical theories, in Fromm's understanding, are interested in making subjects *capable of experiencing* those aspects of reality which common language doesn't incorporate. Their first movement is the *negation* of false consciousness, "negation of illusory thinking" (Fromm, 1979a:2). The first measure one takes in attempting to develop a repressed experiential layer is to break its immediate forms of hindrance, which are given with the categories of consciousness in its present form of organization:

> With regard to contemporary societies, it is certain that our conscious mind, that is, the social filter itself, can be liberated to a high degree through a function which is also a process of the human mind, that is, *critical thought* – the critical and interrogating attitude, and specifically one which interrogates the structure, the function and the ideology of a certain society. In the same process of critique or inquiry, the categories or schemes of the conscious mind lose something of their strength and rigidity; thus, the thoughts of the critical mind become conscious, when they would otherwise remain unconscious.
>
> (Fromm, 1966p:13)

This negative, critical penetration into reality is a component to many of Fromm's experiential models. Here we will abstract from his religious sources and discuss two others more closely – psychoanalysis and humanistic politics.

In clinical work, disillusionment corresponds to the work of confrontation with resistance and the erosion of repression. At this stage, the work of change appears as purely negative: the movement of "attitudes" appears as negated by the ego structure, and the task of lifting them from repression, as suspending this negation. This constellation subsists as the treatment's progress originates new transitory symptoms, acting outs, and other expressions of compromise upholding the unconsciousness of the psychic conflict. Here, life appears as provided with tendencies for well-being and health: "'Curing' means removing the obstacles that prevent them from becoming effective" (1947a:x). The pressure of the repressed for springing up acts as an unconscious support for the therapeutic alliance – so long as transference doesn't function as resistance.

The success of this purely negative, unobstructing gesture, leads nonetheless to a movement which, in Frommian vocabulary, we can only describe as *affirmative*. Should the repressed finally break into consciousness after all the undertows and anxieties of working-through, the experience it engenders is quite remarkable. It is not reducible to relief, being rather in the nature of a subjective quake, which reverberates the reorganization of one's inner structure of forces. Freud (1916–17) would have spoken about the liberation of the energy invested in countercathexis. Fromm (1973a) would have agreed. He would make, with Reik (1935), the experience of a "surprise", a "shock" in the act of reincorporating what remained unconscious thus far, emphasizing the revivifying effect of analysis (cf. Fromm, 1960a; 1991a).

In contradistinction to many other points, here Fromm's thought condensed an intuition profoundly marked by the rhythm and timing of clinical work. For him, the clinical process could only be understood as double-sided: the former "negative" gesture of perforation through false consciousness derives, as its result, an "affirmative" moment, paving the way for a movement of the analysand's "vital forces". This leads neither to a new determinacy of character, nor to its simple indeterminateness. Rather, it results in changing the *mode* of determination of life in its process – its mode of existence. One's relation to the unfulfilled aspects of character is modified, allowing a further determination of the personality with greater freedom. The subject reaches the *possibility* of being in new ways – of transitioning between distinct experiences without fixating either of them. These peaking moments of the therapeutic process gave Fromm the experiential model for deep human change in general. For that reason, both his clinical and his political action were identically conceptualized – as simultaneously negative and affirmative (cf. Fromm, 1970k; compare Durkin, 2020).

Let us now examine the characteristics of this clinical model of liberation. Fromm's representation of the closure of perlaboration in a sudden act corresponds, in the best of possibilities, to a special case among the forms and effects of clinical work, with a peculiar character of paroxism of the psychic conflict. We know how often these achievements are succeeded by a retreat of psychic elasticity or a worsening of suffering – be it by way of negative therapeutic reaction, or other forms of regeneration of the balance of forces sustaining the conflict. We must then clarify their significance in Fromm's thought. Despite his emphasis on the emotional process, Fromm's method for reaching this psychic paroxism still emphatically involved the passage of the repressed through language – indeed, it required the full experience of the insufficiency of language in grasping the unconscious. Fromm remained close to Freud's and Breuer's (1893) handling of catharsis in *purpose*, approximating Ferenczi's (1929) neocatharsis in *method*. He was less focused on the liberation of affect as such, and more in the "confrontation with inner reality" it presupposes. Even if his portrayal of clinical success privileged a paroxistic form rather single-handedly, his main line of practice did not especially rely on the relief brought about by spontaneous ab-reaction. Fromm's paroxistic model of insight should be taken as the culmination of what is usually a very long process of crossing through the partial components of repression.

Another important aspect must be taken into account. Sudden insights are characteristic of particularly well-carried onsets against *topical* points of repression. They occur in association or interpretation once a specific element or complex of repressed ideas reaches consciousness. However, Fromm extended the significance of this experiential model beyond its singular occurrences in the analytic process. They were for him among the purest anticipations of a better life. The corresponding liberating reaction, which combines feelings of relief, surprise, awakenness, and emptiness (cf. Fromm, 1960a:72), was for him a condensed icon of the qualities a thoroughly-carried analysis would tend to install *permanently,* as a basic coloration of the life process. The corresponding vitality and emotional intensity would then be the phenomenological correlates of the primacy of life and freedom as ethical goals. Aliveness would be concomitant to an optimal openness between consciousness and the unconscious (cf. Fromm, 1980g).

In the act of reintegrating the repressed, the subject has a taste of what a better life would feel like. He:

> experiences the first glimpses of joy and strength that he sometimes attains. And only then a decisive new factor enters into the dynamics of the process. This new experience becomes the decisive motivation for going ahead and following the path he has charted. Until then, his own dissatisfaction and rational considerations of all kinds can guide him. But these considerations can carry him only for a short while. They will lose their power if the new element does not enter – experience of well-being – fleeting and small as it may be – which feels so superior to anything experienced so far, that it becomes the most powerful motivation for further progress – one that becomes stronger in and of itself the further progress goes on.
>
> (Fromm, 1989a:120)

In clinical insight, consciousness acquires an orienting criterion for the continuity of the analytic process, as well as for extra-clinical processes of change. The experience cannot be undone. Each breakthrough conditions all the remaining path: "there is no first or second step; there is only the constant practice in productive activity and tolerance of uncertainty" (d-RoHD: V:1:136). The significance of insight lies therefore not only in the ("negative") relief of suffering, but all the more in the fact that such experiences are generative of ("affirmative") *values* in Fromm's sense. They are paradigmatic acts of self-apprehension, strengthening one's relatedness to oneself and others.

As a result, the subject develops a particular affective "responsiveness" (Fromm, 1960a:66) to herself. To that is coupled a greater capacity for change: affective processes, unhampered by repression and suppression, may now unfold in consciousness as *finite*. A strengthened openness to inner reality coincides with openness to material reality:

> By becoming less of a stranger to himself, the person who goes through this process becomes less estranged to the world; because he has opened up communication with the universe within himself, he has opened up communication with the universe outside.
>
> (Fromm, 1960a:107)

Psychic "growth" is thus resumed in the process of reception and development of our inner differences, as they are activated in our encounters with others in the process of living.

The main conceptual representatives of norms in Fromm's theory – ideal, value, vision – may also be seen as modeled in part after this seminal experience of vitality, as it occurs in clinical work. Their meanings are better understood in their differences with the analytic situation. Since in Fromm's account of cure one's effective self-apperception is of such great importance, his concept of "value" is phenomenologically closer to the analytic act than any other. However, one important difference remains. In the clinic, revitalizing self-apprehension is at its peak when transferential relatedness is at its lowest. The erupting vitality one finds there is in a deep sense a result of one's self-experience – it appears as the vital process's reaction to itself, not as concomitant to present object relations, as the concept of "effective values" would require. Indeed, insight into object relations may be seen as the necessary antecedent form to pure self-experience – its typical manifestations being closer still to the elaboration of suffering than to its dissolution in aliveness. The difference increases even more when we take the other two notions under comparison. According to their concept, "ideals" express the fulfillment of life-furthering tendencies in imagination. These tendencies are indeed the main forces leading to analytic paroxism – but the corresponding representation is typically missing in the analytic act. Lifting repression may arouse sensory activity in many ways, but it is not followed by an immediate anticipation of satisfaction in phantasy. More commonly, it will be coupled with reminiscence, a particularly meaningful expression, a symbolic visualization – one among many forms of apperceiving the repressed. The concept of "vision", on its turn, reunites the therein separated aspects within a single formation. It tries to bring the representation and its experiential concomitant together. Each in their way, the three categories abstract and dissociate attributes which, while being *capable* of joint occurrence, are not given in their suggested articulation in the clinical *situation* serving as Fromm's model.

***

All these ambiguities considered, the idea is formed of a typical arc, which the analyst repeats many times in the treatment of each analysand. Departing from a real conflict and the suffering tied to it, de-repression slowly clarifies the nature of the contradictions at stake. Consciousness reaches a certain degree of penetration in the reality of its relations to oneself and others. The analysand is brought to a position of greater awareness and acknowledgment of the problems she faces, of lesser propensity to their avoidance. At the same time, she is put in better conditions to confront and solve them (cf. Fromm, 1955a). Thus conceived, the analytic process provides a miniature model of subjective transformation: beginning with the negation of illusions, it culminates in affirmative self-experience, enhancing one's capacity for freedom.

Only one aspect is missing. The analysand is left with the task of seeking a change in "practice of life" which would allow her to *preserve and extend* the well-being foreshadowed in clinical experience. This part of the work doesn't happen within the analytic dyad, but only as she acts outside the clinic:

> No amount or depth of psychological insight can ever take the place of the act, of the commitment, of the jump. It can lead to it, prepare it, make it possible—and this is the legitimate function of psychoanalytic work. But it must not try to be a substitute for the responsible act of commitment, an act without which no real change occurs in a human being.
>
> (Fromm, 1957a:199)

Crucial for us is that this arc – starting with suffering, passing through an experience of enlightenment and liberation, leading finally to a modification of conduct – is the same Fromm recognized as characteristic for *political* emancipation. There as well:

> *The beginning of liberation lies in man's capacity to suffer,* and he suffers if he is oppressed, physically and spiritually. The suffering moves him to act against his oppressors, to seek the end of the oppression, although he cannot yet seek a freedom of which he knows nothing. If man has lost the capacity to suffer, he has also lost the capacity for change.
>
> (Fromm, 1966a:75)

Transposing his psychoanalytic and religious experiences onto the political realm, Fromm assumed there would be a basic consubstantiality between the processes of liberation in the clinic and in political life. Conversely, political forms made their way into Fromm's clinical practice. His therapeutic conduct was in part shaped by the gestures he considered effective in "mobilizing energies" in the political situation. There, Fromm (1966a) wanted to awaken people to the tragedy of their own lives, moving them to participate actively in the struggle for a better life. In the clinic, correspondingly, he wanted to pinfold the passions in a confrontation with their own reality, suspending the laxity with which they are usually dealt:

> I believe the problem of cure lies in the following: that the patient confronts the irrational archaic part of his personality with his own sane, adult, normal part and that this very confrontation creates conflict. This conflict activates forces which one has to assume if one has the theory that there exists in a person – more or less strongly and, I think, again that is a constitutional factor – a striving for health, a striving for a better balance between the person and the world. *For me the essence of analytic cure lies in the very conflict engendered by the meeting of the irrational and the rational part of the personality.*
>
> (Fromm, 1991a:29)

Accordingly, Fromm's (1964a) concept of "alternativism" was applied to both fields. Clinically, the term was introduced under the assumption that the deepest confrontation with oneself happens when we recognize the possible alternatives to our actions and being. Politically, the idea emerged that the task of critique was to confront people with the real consequences of the different political paths available. The emotional correlate to this intellectual posture was, in both cases, a sense of urgency – Fromm talks about directing oneself to the analysand's "emergency energies", about recovering her "sense of shock" (1991a:29,95). Here the prophetic ascendancy of his conduct is unmistakable. Its origin is not analytic, but political and religious. Its model lies in the *interpellation* by the political or intellectual leader, by contrast to interpretation, construction, and other modes of intervention characteristic of the Freudian prescription book.

Fromm's formulation of political leadership is tainted with an analytic sensibility, just like his approach to analysis draws from the experience of political and religious appeal. The task of a leader interested in emancipation would be to address truth in common suffering. She as well, like the analyst, would have to be able to dispel illusions and touch the real needs of subjects. In Fromm's model, both practices partake in the problem of activating people – drawing them to a sense of urgency and a will to act upon their life circumstances. Indeed, he took this moral form of engagement as a model for efficient mobilization in general. In classic free association, the repressed comes to meet language, and as a result its relation with the subject is changed. In Fromm's model, words go after the repressed as the representatives of reality:

> Confronting reality creates momentary anxiety; it makes one feel unsure for the moment. This "resistance" against the reality one does not want to see is often strong enough to make the effort ineffective, even if this effort refers to the relevant, to the totality, and even if it is radical and not an "installment" of the truth. But anyone with some experience with this problem knows the often unexpected and sometimes seemingly miraculous reactions of people when they are shown reality objectively, without fanaticism or fear and with the intention of being helpful to them. There occurs, indeed, a "moment of truth" in which something happens which is quite unexpected, very sudden, and hardly to be described in terms of time. A person suddenly sees and senses that "this is it". In fact, he has the feeling that he has always known it, or he wonders how he could have been so blind not to have known it. It is like awakening from a dream, or from half-slumber.
> (Fromm, 1990i:124)

At first sight, everything seems to move according to the same law. Political action starts with the negation of illusions, just like the analytic process. Fromm's formulations imply that the subsequent movement of liberation will also remain identical in both domains. However, once we jump into the political situation, the functions under examination cannot work in the same way as in the psychoanalytic clinic. Acting upon the same human material, analysis and political mobilization are not identical in method. They coincide in needing to understand which are "the conditions by which men are deeply touched". But their purposes are different: "appealing to the hearts and minds" (Fromm, 1990i:123) and seeking character change are neither identical goals, nor engender identical experiences.

The difference at stake may be illustrated in referencing Fromm's analysis of the biblical psalms he characterized as "dynamic". In these psalms, according to his interpretation, hope and happiness burst forth precisely after the moment of greatest grief and despair (1966a:163–5). The similarity with his account of political mobilization is striking. Even more significant is its contrast with the paroxistic model deriving from the analytic setting. Here, the suddenness of a change of heart is not the precipitate of a long, laborious process of perlaboration. It is rather an immediate reaction – a reversion of one's despair into action. The experience of *cure* stands to mobilization through *appeal* as the painstaking therapeutic transformation of character stands to religious conversion or spontaneous remissions. Fromm considered the latter "genuine", if rare models of "life affirmation" and a "basic change" in one's economy of forces (1973a:297). The difference in path is, however, not without consequence for the final result in each case.

The formula for Fromm's critical theory – the joint action of the affirmative and negative functions – expressed a fine trait of clinical experience in logical terms. It referred originally to the point in which affects are reported back to their bodily substrate, dissolving in a deep subjective repercussion. The same unity of the affirmative and negative moments cannot be upheld in political praxis. The sudden, "dynamic" reversal of suffering into hopeful action is not anymore identical to psychic liberation as the result of working-through – *because effective values don't emerge spontaneously in the public arena, as they do in one's free self-experience:*

> criticism remains futile and historically ineffective if it is not related to at least the attempt to raise those questions which in turn might lead to an answer, and if not to an answer at least to pointing to the direction in which the answer lies. [...] You can appeal to people by appealing to their indignation, their ambitions, or even their hate. But you cannot move people to sustained, constructive and truly revolutionary action by any of these emotions. People can be motivated to change only if they have hope. They can have hope only if they have a vision; they can have a vision only if they are shown alternatives, and they can have alternatives only by a tremendous effort of thought and imagination – not by a concentration of all energies in protest and indignation.
>
> (Fromm, 1990i:121)

As Fromm himself acknowledged, "a rational, realizable vision is no gift, but must be worked out through an ever clearer and more critical insight into the individual and social reality of man" (1980g:30) – an insight we better conceive as the fruit of collective effort and collaboration (cf. Fromm, 1960b). Here, the distance between clinical and political practice unavoidably grows. The task of articulating subjects around a diagnosis of their common suffering does not lead, in mass movements, to an immediate affirmative moment, but rather to a mediated *attempt at affirmation*. This difference is summarized in the contrast between "values" and "visions" as representations of norms. In clinical work, anticipatory "values" emerge at the crucial moments of insight into the unconscious – but as an expression of the subject's relation to herself. These glimpses of joy and hope "must be free [...] from any interference of the analyst in the life of the patient, not even that of the demand that the patient gets well" (Fromm, 1960a:87). They are made possible by "core to core relatedness" in analysis, but are reactions of the living being to herself, expressing a new self-relatedness – which in turn prepares her for a new relatedness to others. In this state, they are in the nature of singular phenomena – the highest subjective representatives of the "contemplative" axis in Fromm's works.

The realization of such values in *common* action already presupposes a negotiation between the specificity of individual passions and the desires of others. The main interest is then not in the immediate fulfillment of one's vital, "expressive" needs, but in finding a mode of social organization which makes this fulfillment *practicable*. For this reason, a "political vision" does not anymore correspond to the subject's organic response to her process of liberation. Common values are here forms of political relatedness and presuppositions of its organization in collective action. In political work, articulating a common "vision" of good life is only possible through the "interference" of others – not least of all because the passions supporting change must be activated and channeled by the political formation toward a common goal. A vision is, after all, an "appeal to action" (Fromm, 1968a:vii) – the highest subjective expression of Fromm's tendency toward "activity".

Fromm's formula for critique must then be taken with a grain of salt. "Affirmation" is not of the same character when treated in psychological and political terms – lack of identity in practical conditions leads to irreconcilable differences in operation. Fromm's aspiration to transpose clinical and political experiences onto a single form – as implied by his vocabulary and some of his theses on suffering and change – ultimately cannot hold. However, this does not result in a simple falsification of Fromm's premises, but rather in their further qualification and development.

We find the seeds for a more precise formulation of his logic within Fromm's own vocabulary. Affirmation in the clinical setting and in political struggle are distinct according to their mediate or immediate character – but they share in the quality of their own *incompleteness*. The paroxistic experience of vitality in the clinic must be fulfilled by practice outside the analytic relationship. Political practice is aimless without a firm grasp of the experiential qualities one wants to fulfill in common life. Thus considered, the immediate, clinical affirmation of life and the struggle for its mediated political realization work as the complementary sides of a unity. This corresponds to the highest possible speculative development of Fromm's concept of freedom. Before, we treated "negative freedom" mainly as the fight against social constrains, whereas "positive freedom" was sided with the spontaneous expression of one's life. Now, enriched by their concrete development within the practical spheres Fromm took as models for his critical theory, both sides of the concept unfold within themselves. Positive freedom also implies an inner negative moment – freedom "from the bondage of irrational passions" (1951a:247). Correspondingly, negative freedom implies a positive moment – it supposes one's capacity to disobey, "to resist pressure" and "follow [...] rational intention" (1964a:131; 1991a:89). As a consequence, Fromm's ethics of freedom must understand both the active and the contemplative aspects in liberation as *mutually presupposed* in their difference (compare Bronner, 1994).

In Fromm's (1950a) formulation of salvific practices and mystical experience, these two axes couldn't be satisfyingly reconciled: they were treated in ideal identity in their pursuit of "oneness", abstracting from the practical differences between alternative methods for their fulfillment. Fromm's subsumption of "critique" to a common logic in different spheres of activity risked the same problem – but he found a way out in acknowledging the lack of identity between the personal and political strivings for freedom. In his understanding, neither should be subsumed to the other: they are only effective if they remain different, correcting each other as parallel processes:

> Any attempt to overcome the possibly fatal crisis of the industrialized part of the world, and perhaps of the human race, must begin with the understanding of the nature of both outer and inner chains; it must be based on the liberation of man in the classic, humanist sense as well as in the modern, political and social sense. The Church still by and large speaks only of inner liberation, and political parties, from liberals to communists, speak only about outer liberation. History has clearly shown that one ideology without the other leaves man dependent and crippled. The only realistic aim is total liberation, a goal that may well be called *radical* (or *revolutionary*) *humanism*.
>
> (Fromm, 1989a:7–8)

Formulating what a good society should look like presupposes the subject's sensibility to herself – her *capacity to desire her own good,* and consequently that of others: "what does one experience of the essence of the other? What does one experience from his characteristics, his sufferings, his joys? [...] What does one see from him? This is true sensitization" (u-1974:9). Conversely, an anticipation of the good life can only grow amidst the social process, and to the extent that it allows this experience. Thus conceived, (singular) experiential values correct the tendency for (general) political visions to deteriorate into ideologies. They guarantee the subject's rootedness in herself and her deep responsiveness to others, safeguarding her against a full identification with the political process. Political visions, on their hand, renew and realize one's self-experience as part of one's relation to others, taking it out of its isolation, and channeling it toward a common life practice. Each instance is the other's negation. In their mutual criticism, they make a common affirmation of life possible.

Bibliography

Primary sources

Unpublished texts, lectures, interviews by Fromm

u-NYPL-7.4.7132: "The self". Unpublished book chapter on the concept of "self", maybe written for *Man for himself*.
u-1974: "*Anti-autoritäre Bewegung, die Maschine als Mutter und die Suche nach politischen Alternativen*". Transcript of a conversation between Fromm and the theologian Hans-Eckerhard Bahr.

Drafts, typescripts, and study materials by Fromm

d-1991d-002-eng-draft-04: transcription of the recordings published as *The art of listening*.
d-RoHD: drafts for *The revolution of hope*. Still without an official identifying code.

Published sources

Ferenczi, Sándor. Relaxationsprinzip und Neokatharsis. *Bausteine III*. Budapest: Verlag Hans Buber, [1929]/1939.
Freud, Sigmund. Die Traumdeutung. *Gesammelte Werke II-III*. Frankfurt: S. Fischer Verlag, [1900–1930]/1961.
Freud, Sigmund. Vorlesungen zur Einführung in die Psychoanalyse. *Gesammelte Werke XI*. Frankfurt: S. Fischer Verlag, [1916–1917]/1969.
Freud, Sigmund. Der Untergang des Ödipuscomplexes. *Gesammelte Werke XIII*. Frankfurt: S. Fischer Verlag, [1924]/1967.
Freud, Sigmund. Ergebnisse, Ideen, Probleme. *Gesammelte Werke XVII*. London: Imago Publishing, [1938]/1955.
Freud, Sigmund; Breuer, Joseph. Über den psychischen Mechanismus hysterischer Phänomene (Vorläufige Mitteilung). in: Sigmund Freud. *Gesammelte Werke I*. London: Imago Publishing, [1893]/1952.
Fromm, Erich. Selfishness and self-love. *Love, sexuality, and matriarchy*. New York: Fromm International Edition, [1939b]/1997.

Fromm, Erich. *Escape from freedom*. New York: Henry Holt & Company, [1941a]/1994.

Fromm, Erich. Faith as a character trait. *Psychiatry*: V:307–319, 1942b.

Fromm, Erich. Individual and social origins of neurosis. *American Sociological Review*:9:380–384, 1944a.

Fromm, Erich. *Man for himself*. New York: Henry Holt & Company, [1947a]/1990.

Fromm, Erich. Psychoanalytic characterology and its application to the understanding of culture. *Fromm Forum*:12:5–10, [1949c]/2008.

Fromm, Erich. *Psychoanalysis and religion*. New York: Bantam Books, [1950a]/1967.

Fromm, Erich. *The forgotten language*. New York: Holt, Rinehart and Winston, [1951a]/1960.

Fromm, Erich. *The sane society*. New York: Henry Holt & Company, [1955a]/1990.

Fromm, Erich. Psychoanalysis. J.R. Newman (Ed.). *What is science?* New York: Simon and Schuster, 1955e.

Fromm, Erich. *The art of loving*. London: Thorsons Editions, [1956a]/1995.

Fromm, Erich. On the limitations and dangers of psychology. *The dogma of Christ*. New York: Holt, Rinehart and Winston, [1957a]/1992.

Fromm, Erich. Psychoanalysis and Zen Buddhism. *Psychologia, Kyoto*: 2:79–99, 1959e.

Fromm, Erich. Psychoanalysis and Zen Buddhism. *Psychoanalysis and Zen Buddhism*. London: Unwin Paperbacks, [1960a]/1987.

Fromm, Erich. Let man prevail: a socialist manifesto and program. *On disobedience*. New York: Harper Perennial, [1960b]/2010.

Fromm, Erich. The prophetic concept of peace. *The dogma of Christ*. New York: Holt, Reinhart and Winston, [1960d]/1992.

Fromm, Erich. *May man prevail?* New York: Doubleday & Company, Inc, [1961a]/1961.

Fromm, Erich. *Beyond the chains of illusion*. New York: Continuum, [1962a]/2001.

Fromm, Erich. The revolutionary character. *The dogma of Christ*. New York: Holt, Rinehart and Winston, [1963b]/1992.

Fromm, Erich. Medicine and the ethical problem of modern man. *The dogma of Christ*. New York: Holt, Reinhart and Winston, [1963c]/1992.

Fromm, Erich. Humanismo y psicoanálisis. *La prensa medica Mexicana*:28:120–126, 1963f.

Fromm, Erich. *The heart of man: its genius for good and evil*. New York: Harper and Row, 1964a.

Fromm, Erich. Foreword II. *Escape from freedom*. New York: Henry Holt & Company, [1965h]/1994.

Fromm, Erich. *You shall be as gods*. New York: Fawcett Premier, [1966a]/1983.

Fromm, Erich. Consciencia y sociedad industrial. *Ciencas politicas y sociales*: 43–44:17–28, 1966p.

Fromm, Erich. *The revolution of hope*. New York: Bantam Books, 1968a.

Fromm, Erich. Marx's contribution to the knowledge of man. *The crisis of psychoanalysis*. New York: Holt, Reinehart and Winston, [1968h]/1970.

Fromm, Erich. Introduction. Ivan Illich. *Celebration of awareness*. New York: Doubleday and Co., 1970k.

Fromm, Erich. Interview with Ignacio Solares: El Hombre Necesita algo mas. *Revista de revistas: 1* (06/02/1972):5–9, 1972d.

Fromm, Erich. *The anatomy of human destructiveness*. New York. Henry Holt & Company, [1973a]/1992.

Fromm, Erich. Psychology for nonpsychologists. *For the love of life*. New York: The Free Press, [1974a]/1986.
Fromm, Erich. In the name of life: a portrait through dialogue. *For the love of life*. New York: The Free Press, [1974b]/1986.
Fromm, Erich. *To have or to be?* New York: Bantam Books, [1976a]/1981.
Fromm, Erich. Interview with Alfred A. Häsler: Das Undenkbare denken und das Mögliche tun. *Ex Libris*:22 (5):13–19, 1977b.
Fromm, Erich. Das Undenkbare, das Unsagbare, das Unaussprechliche. *Psychologie heute*: 5:23–31, 1978b.
Fromm, Erich. *Greatness and limitations of Freud's thought*. New York: Harper and Row, Publishers, [1979a]/1980.
Fromm, Erich. Die Vision underer Zeit. *Mitteilungen aus der Literaturarchiv der Stadt Dortmund*: 7:29f, 1980g.
Fromm, Erich. Who is man?*For the love of life*. New York: The Free Press, [1983d]/1986.
Fromm, Erich. *The art of being*. New York: Continuum, [1989a]/1998.
Fromm, Erich. The dialectic revision of psychoanalysis. *The revision of psychoanalysis*. Boulder: Westview Press, [1990f]/1992.
Fromm, Erich. Dealing with the unconscious in psychotherapeutic practice. *Beyond Freud*. New York: American Mental Health Foundation, [1992g]/2010.
Fromm, Erich. Political radicalism in the United States and its critique. *Fromm Forum*:25:115–126, [1990i]/2021.
Fromm, Erich. *The art of listening*. London: Constable, [1991a]/1994.
Fromm, Erich. Modern man's pathology of normalcy. *The pathology of normalcy*. New York: American Mental Health Foundation, [1991e]/2010.
Fromm, Erich. Man's impulse structure and its relation to culture. *Beyond Freud*. New York: American Mental Health Foundation, [1992e]/2010.
Fromm, Erich. What I do not like in contemporary society. *On being human*. New York: Continuum. [1992j]/2005.
Fromm, Erich. The disintegration of societies. *On being human*. New York: Continuum. [1992k]/2005.
Fromm, Erich. A new humanism as a condition for the One World. *On being human*. New York: Continuum. [1992m]/2005.
Fromm, Erich; Maccoby, Michael. *Social character in a Mexican village*. New York: Routledge, [1970b]/1996.
Hegel, Georg. *Enzyklopädie der philosophischen Wissenschaften im Grundrisse, III*. Frankfurt: Surkhamp, [1817–1830]/1986.
Reik, Theodor. *Der überraschte Psychologe*. Leiden: A. W. Sijthoff's Uitgeversmaatschappij N. V., 1935.

Secondary literature

Braune, Joan. *Erich Fromm's revolutionary hope*. Rotterdam: Sense Publishers, 2014.
Bronner, Stephen. Fromm in America. *Of critical theory and its theorists*. London: Routledge, [1992]/2002.
Dagostino, Vicki; Lake, Robert. Fromm's dialectic of freedom and the praxis of being. Seyed Javad Miri, Robert Lake, Tricia Kress (eds.). *Reclaiming the sane society*. Rotterdam: Sense Publishers, 2014.

Durkin, Kieran. *The radical humanism of Erich Fromm*. New York: Palgrave Macmillan, 2014.
Durkin, Kieran. Mapping Fromm's critical theory. Kieran Durkin, Joan Braune (eds). *Erich Fromm's critical theory*. New York: Bloomsbury, 2020.
Funk, Rainer. *Mut zum Menschen*. Stuttgart: Deutsche Verlags-Anstalt, 1978.
García, Jorge. Erich Fromm's humanism and the stranger. *Wissenschaft vom Menschen: 6*. München: LIT-Verlag, 1995.
Jay, Martin. The Frankfurt school's critique of Marxist humanism. *Social Research*: 39 (2):285–305, 1972.
Maccoby, Michael. The two voices of Erich Fromm: the prophetic and the analytic. Michael Maccoby, Mauricio Cortina (eds.). *A prophetic analyst*. London: Jason Aronson Inc., 1996.
Schaar, John. *Escape from authority*. New York: Basic Books, Inc., 1961.
Thompson, Michael. Normative humanism as redemptive critique: knowledge and judgment in Fromm's social theory. Seyed Javad Miri, Robert Lake, Tricia Kress (eds.). *Reclaiming the sane society*. Rotterdam: Sense Publishers, 2014.

Chapter 7

VII To Fill the Hearts of Men with a New Spirit

Politics in Erich Fromm's Thought and Action

"I have been a socialist since my student days forty years ago", Fromm writes to Adam Schaff in 1962, "but have never been active until the last five years, when I have been very active in helping to form an American peace movement, on the left wing of which I find myself" (Schaff_Adam_1962-05-08-to). Indeed, the late 1950s watch Fromm take a definite turn towards political engagement – as a political organizer, mediator, and commentator.

This chapter provides a characterization of Fromm's political activities. They are not without their ambiguities, as evidenced by Fromm's own emphasis on his ineptitude for political action – coexisting with the claim that he was "an extremely political person" (1974b:115). In one of his last interviews, he puts it simply: "I think theoretically, and I say what I think". He downplays his activism in favor of Eugene McCarthy as a minor event; and when the interviewer, Guido Ferrari, confronts him with his engagement against nuclear war, he replies: "I absolutely don't call that political, since it is simply, I would like to say, human activity: to prevent the destruction of men. But in reality one can already say that this is a political activity" (AUD-1980e).

Fromm's late self-understanding is so skeptically modest for several reasons. One of them is an increasing disappointment with his political endeavors, particularly in the 1970s – the same decade when his emphasis on the curative value of "disillusionment" is at its peak (Fromm, 1979a:x). Without giving into despair or resignation, Fromm is increasingly aware of the difficulties involved in organizing people even for transient tasks. Already in 1969 he would think back about his Socialist Manifesto of 1960(b) with a sense of confusion: "I have always been puzzled why 'Let Man Prevail' has been baught [sic] by so many people, and yet the number of people within the Socialist Party who would stand for its ideas is so small" (Gulotta_-Larry_1969-08-22-to). Confronted with a political suggestion from Clara Urquhart, he replies: "I am of course in full agreement with your ideas [...] The trouble is that, maybe having been made skeptical by my experience [...], I cannot see any way to accomplish it" (Urquhart_Clara_1970-05-25-to).

Eleven years later, he would have reached a deeper reevaluation of his own role in politics. This is particularly apparent when we confront Fromm's rather skeptical attitude in the 1970s with documents from the early 1960s, when his political engagement seemed much more encouraging and effective. "I made a number of speeches for the socialist party", he tells Karl Polanyi in 1960 – "and I was glad to see the very favorable response of the students" (Polanyi_Karl_1960–11–08-by). Still four years later, he is enthusiastic about his lecture touring:

> work was compensated by the feeling that my lectures met fertile minds [...] the audience, and especially the young generation gave me the impression of freshness, openness, and hope, and of being really eager to hear somebody who had not too many illusions and yet faith.
> (Urquhart_Clara_1964–11–05-to)

Fromm's relationship to the student movement came to change in the late 1960s. Indeed, his evolving sense of politics reflected the ongoing historical process (cf. Heale, 2001). He wrote Urquhart in 1972: "we are witnessing a historical period coming to an end with ever-increasing convulsions and signs of dissolution" (Urquhart_Clara_1972–03–21-to). This is something he experienced not only as an observer of global politics, but also in the shifting efficacy of his own strategies. Remembering back his course of experience as simple "human activity" was a token of recognition that the core motivation for Fromm's political action – the ethical nucleus he formulated as "radical humanism" – was increasingly displaced away from the core of political disputes.

1 Humanism as Political Formation

Fromm's political engagement reached a peak in the mid-1960s, but this was not the first time he took issue with public matters. It began with his transition from being a Zionist into becoming a critic of it:

> I was a Zionist from the age of 18 to about 22 and quite active in the Zionist Youth movement. [...] I left the movement with a declaration which went something like this: "I cannot stand your nationalism and I believe you are not basically different from the Nazis".
> (Fulbright_J_W_1976–02–11-to)

Years later, in 1948, he articulated with Leo Baeck, Hannah Arendt and Albert Einstein to write a letter and a petition for a cooperation of Jews and Arabs in Palestine (cf. Fromm, 1990t). It was published in the New York Times on April 18th, 1948, with the objective of drawing public attention to Jewish intellectuals and leaders who disapproved of war and terrorism in Palestine. The ad calls "each group and particularly its leaders" to "uphold standards of morality and reason in their own ranks rather than confine themselves to accuse their opponents of the violation of these standards". It appeals to the "fundamental spiritual and moral principles inherent in the

Jewish tradition and essential for Jewish hope". Much of Fromm's later political rationale is prefigured here. The problem addressed is international in nature, and it is on the basis of moral and spiritual values, especially as represented by leading cultural figures, that he hopes to foster political change.

A similar endeavor happens in 1955, again around the subject of war. Fromm (d-1990u-003-eng-type-01) participates in writing a draft called "Citizens for Reason", with the aim of warning the presidency and the wider public against the risks of atomic war. A key issue is the recognition of the Communist government in China as legitimate. He involves Daniel Bell, Lewis Mumford, Stephen Siteman and other intellectuals in trying to perfect and sign the draft. Here as well we find a template for the problems Fromm will face later in life. He is disappointed with the group's capacity in mobilizing others: "It is, indeed, most surprising that we have only about ten signatures to a statement which seems to correspond to a large and growing sentiment in America" (Bell_Daniel_1955–04–22-to).

He also finds it difficult to redact a document reconciling the number of signatures, the prestige of the names involved, and the mass reach of the argument. "I wanted to write a statement which expressed the truth in a clear and uncompromising fashion. At the same time, I felt there was an urgent need to mobilize as many people as possible, for the purpose of influencing the senators and the President", he writes Mumford (Mumford_Lewis_1955–05–14-to). By that time, so many versions of the text had been disapproved that Fromm was afraid the effort would be lost. "I believe that if we continue changing the statement, we shall never get anywhere, and even lose some of the signers who had been willing to sign the statement as it was", he tells Daniel Bell earlier that year (Bell_Daniel_1955–04–22-to). He was right. Fromm ends up lamenting to Siteman: "we have to acknowledge the fact that our action cannot be carried out" (Siteman_Stephen_1955–05–26-to).

Fromm will eventually find himself on the other side of the situation, trying to be persuaded to sign documents he feels insecure about. When Abraham Muste asks him in 1965 to add his name to a "Declaration of Conscience", he refuses throughout a series of attempts to convince him that the text is reasonable. After it is published, Fromm reflects:

> When I see the names of so many friends with whom I feel completely one, I begin to wonder whether I was wrong in my criticism. Yet, even thinking about it now, I just have the same feeling that I could not defend the document.
> (Muste_Abraham_J_1965–10–21-to)

The next year, when Bertrand Russell invites him into signing an "Appeal to American Conscience" attacking the Vietnam War, Fromm responds: "your appeal is formulated it seems to me lack in a completely objective attitude, and it seems that indignation got the better of judgment [...] and will fail to appeal to the very people it is meant to appeal to" (Russell_Bertrand_1966-10-08-to). This is the case even if he thinks that "in the Vietnam War, the United States have way more guilt than any other country" (u-1968b:14).

In the course of such negotiations, Fromm gradually experiences the difficulty in reaching what he considered "the most important thing" in politics: the subordination of ideal disagreements to common principles and collaboration; "the sense of human and spiritual solidarity among all who believe in the dignity of man and of his soul, regardless of all doctrinal differences" (Merton_Thomas_1954-10-27-to). There is a conflict between Fromm's theoretical self-understanding, the form of mobilization he feels is most appealing, and the constellations of interest governing actual political developments. In order to start understanding this conflict, let us first explore how Fromm's search for common values was lived through in his concrete relations to other humanists.

"Mysticism and humanism belong together", Fromm writes in agreement with Thomas Merton in 1954 (Merton_Thomas_1954-10-27-to). In practice, this means: the criteria for political unity have to be experiential, not ideological. Fromm favored commonality of feeling and attitude over commonality of thought. This was a particularly prominent trace in his dealings with theistic humanists, who were among his main political collaborators:

> those who worship the "living God" will have no difficulty in sensing that they have more in common with the "unbelievers" than they have in what separates them; they will have a sense of deep solidarity with those who do not worship idols and who try to do what the believers call "God's will".
>
> (1968a:146)

An essential aspect of the humanist currents Fromm championed is their attempt at grounding *political alliance* on *shared moral concern:*

> Regardless of one's religious or political creed, what all those who are concerned with man have in common is not the question whether God is dead, or what is democracy, but that man and his conscience do not die in the process of his brutalization.
>
> (d-1990r-003-eng-type-01:7)

Remarkably, Fromm determined political alliances between different humanistic stances in *negative* terms. Collaboration would amount to a "common fight against idolatry" (1966a:41,178): "to me, the denial of idol worship is, so to speak, the religious point which can unite us all, while we may deviate in any positive picture" (Merton_Thomas_1954-12-08-to). This formulation stands in opposition to Fromm's emphasis on the affirmation of common experiences orienting the vision of a better society – joy, hope, faith. In contradistinction to the formula we gave above, this affirmative tendency posits *common ethical commitments* as a foundation for *political communities*. Nothing illustrates this better than Fromm's proposal for organizing civil groups and clubs in 1968, in the context of Eugene McCarthy's presidential run:

> By the "Clubs" I refer to clubs of 100 to 300 people which would be more than political clubs but develop self-education, debate, social and political action on a grass roots basis within the general aim of the humanization of society. The "Groups" would be the very dedicated quasi-religious group of people who would try to transform their personal lives in the direction they want man to be in a more humane society.
> (McCarthy_Eugene_1968-08-12-to)

Whereas in Fromm's theory both tendencies stand in unity, in reality they blossom into a myriad of practical contradictions.

"Even though we disagree on theological matters, I am sure you know that my interest in politics is a direct outcome of the significance of religious, or if you prefer, spiritual matters", Fromm writes Merton in 1961 (Merton_Thomas_1961-11-23-to). He would like to see political groups organized by appeal to "reason and conscience" (Bell_Daniel_1955-04-22-to), mobilized by a sense of mutual recognition and support. In therapy, Fromm (u-1968b) ascribed a deeply transformative power to experiencing one's feelings as shared realities. In politics, he wanted subjects to sense that their concerns are confirmed in the feelings of others: solidarity without identification. The recognition by others that one's feelings are justified would activate the subject, capacitating her to fight against commonly acknowledged dangers. Fromm opposed rationalistic attitudes, also called humanistic, whose distance from him is illustrated in his break with the American Humanist Association in 1973:

> In recent years my doubts about the program and principles of the association have been increasing. These misgivings, however, reached a critical point when I heard that Dr. Skinner had been chosen 'humanist of the year'. [...] I consider his book one of the most anti-humanist in spirit.
> (Chambers_Bette_1973-05-10-to)

Many of Fromm's practical associations would have been impossible without suspending doctrinaire differences. Of course, any collaboration between representatives of different creeds requires tolerance between intellectually irreconcilable positions. However, building political relatedness out of a shared *moral* attitude is not a matter of necessity. It represents one among other ways of producing political unity – such as Marcuse's option for an aesthetic bond between subjects. Humanism as Fromm wants it is a particular kind of political formation – a way of bringing people together toward action, with its own potentialities and pitfalls.

***

Let us now identify the emotional undercurrents bringing Fromm and his allies into relation. Venturing into their correspondence, we find a series of recurring affections, essential to humanistic political relations. It remains Fromm's peculiarity to reaffirm friendship with his allies in terms of a feeling of unity beyond disagreements in creed. Commenting to Hildegard Goss-Mayr on an encounter with Karl Rahner, he writes: "I find Rahner's way of thinking and his whole attitude very close to my own, even though we differ very much in doctrine" (Goss-Mayr_Hildegard_1963–11–28-to). With Merton: "I feel from all you say that even though we speak often in different words, the faith is the same" (Merton_Thomas_1962–01–30-to). Similarly, in communication with Adam Schaff: "I often think of you and feel that in spite of great differences in our views and in our life history there is a great deal that we have in common" (Schaff_Adam_1964–03–09-to).

Reaffirming communion in feeling brought Fromm and his friends into *relief from solitude*. He found deep consolation in meeting people with whom he agreed emotionally. He tells Mumford on several occasions: "your books and your person become almost a necessity if one does not want to be overcome by feelings of isolation" –

> here I feel something we have so deeply in common and yet share with so few other people. […] This is a sense of comradeship which is very precious to me, especially in a world in which we have very few companions walking the same way.
> (Mumford_Lewis_1968–12–08-to; Mumford_Lewis_1973–12–05-to)

Similar confessions abound. After Karl Polanyi writes him a reflection on his life, Fromm returns to him with a token of gratitude for his "expressing a sense of friendship which I always felt and feel, in spite of the fact that we have seen so little of each other, secondly because of what you write" (Polanyi_Karl_1960–04–14-to). Similarly, Clara Urquhart writes him: "sometimes it seems that the only thing that is important – is that there are people like you to keep the flames of humanism burning, until the storms of the present world changes have given way to a new birth…" (Urquhart_Clara_1964–06–19-by).

In times of deepest trouble, both personal and political, these relations developed a peculiar political *enthusiasm* – an intervention against affective paralysis, which humanists cultivated both in their attempts at mutual support, and in self-care. Where we find Fromm subject to feelings of isolation, of doubt, of despair, his reactions are strikingly elated. "I have never felt as desperate with regard to the chances of ending the cold war, […] and I only express my feelings of urgent hope that your attempts will succeed", he tells Merton in 1961 (Merton_Thomas_1961–11–23-to). Compare this account of the birth of the concept of biophilia, in a letter to Clara Urquhart:

The other night I wrote a kind of appeal which is centered around the love of life. It was born out of a mood of despair which made me feel that there is hardly any chance that atomic war will be avoided, and sudden insight in which I felt that the reason why people are so passive toward the dangers of war lies in the fact that the majority just do not love life. I thought that to appeal to their love of life rather than to their love of peace or to their fear of war might have more impact.
(Urquhart_Clara_1962-09-29-to)

Here we find once more the reciprocity between Fromm's therapeutic and political views. Depression in a sub-clinical level (boredom, indifference to life) was for him a major characteristic of mid-20th century US society (cf. Fromm, 1973a). For that reason, he believed that a progressive motion in society would depend on the capacity to devote energies to a common vision – "vitality can only be ignited by means of a new vision towards which all energies direct themselves" (Fromm, 1980g:29). Political action would be the best prophylaxis: "depression deprives one, so to speak, of the appetite and zest for new things, and yet it is precisely the vision of something to which one devotes oneself fully which combats depression" (Urquhart_Clara_1966-09-12-to).

Fromm's sense of politics was correspondingly tied to a *sense of urgency* – "the idea obviously being that in a burning house we have to fight the fire and nothing you do would be of any use if the house burns down" (Wittes_Sarah_Sue_1968-12-01-to). *Anguished anticipation* was another essential aspect in humanistic political relations. We feel it behind Fromm's identification of prophets and critical intellectuals as "warners" (VID-1979b). This is as much an aspect of Fromm's (1950a; 1968a) sense of "concern" as the attitudes he overtly emphasized – the capacity for hope, the readiness to respond emotionally and act. After all, didn't he think curative, "emergency energies" were "mobilized only when the whole organism is confronted with a real danger" (Fromm, 1973a:89; 1991a)? Didn't he believe one of the aims of analysis was to "transform anxiety into fear" – to convert anguish before a seemingly unavoidable danger into something the subject can confront (AUD-1965b)?

Fromm discouraged fixating confidence or despair in matters political: "optimism and pessimism do not help with the most important questions in life", he tells Boris Luban-Plozza (AUD-1980g). But we see his life swung by the same currents of hope, fear, paralysis, as would be the case for any other political movement. On the way to the 1968 primaries, Fromm writes McCarthy: "Like a few other people, I was deeply depressed by the cleverly and timed out coup of President Johnson" (McCarthy_Eugene_1968-04-13-to). Not that he would have liked to stimulate unrealistic panic. Fromm was no partisan of catastrophic apocalyptic anticipations, valuing instead a sense of realism in estimating political alternatives. "The function of warning is not the function of threatening", he recalls (AUD-1980g). For years, he insisted against the political common sense of his times that Russia had no expansionist interest, being no threat to the US or Europe (cf. Fromm, 1961a). When ideas of climatic disaster started gaining prominence, he preferred to consult other specialists first on their plausibility (cf. Wald_George_1970–01–22-to). His editorial interventions display him as allergic to alarm without evidence (cf. Lens_Sidney_1964–02–06-to; Bottomore_Tom_B_1964–01–20-to). Indignation – an affect easily associated with "moral concern" – he discarded as a mistrustful basis for action (cf. Fromm, 1967e). He would even on occasion insist that political calculation could learn from the cold objectivity sought by military strategy (cf. Muste_Abraham_J_1966–11–21-to), reminding his friends that not emotional response as such, but its relationship with intellectual activity, is what constitutes reason: "one word about listening to one's heart: most people go by their hearts and come to very wrong conclusions. If reason and heart disagree one must examine what might be wrong with the emotional process" (Urquhart_Clara_1967–06–17-to).

We learn by Fromm's own admission that his feelings sometimes waned in the wrong direction. As the "Citizens for Reason" venture is given up, he tells Mumford:

> I felt at the time that there was immediate danger of getting into a war over Quemony and Matsu, and that anything that could be done which would avert this catastrophe ought to be done. [...] The facts show that I was wrong in my expectations.
> (Mumford_Lewis_1955–05–14-to)

Years later, in the aftermath of McCarthy's loss in the 1968 election, he writes:

> I suddenly felt I could help to save the world by going all the way to campaign for McCarthy, and the book [*The revolution of hope*] was essentially written in the expectation that whether McCarthy would win or lose it would help to mobilize the forces behind him for constructive and important purposes. While, of course, there may have been a slight chance in the spring that McCarthy could make it, I over-estimated it, not so much in my thinking as in the feeling, and I acted on an impulse which prevented me from seeing also his shortcomings with full clarity.
> (Mumford_Lewis_1969–01–23-to)

The limit between irrational alarm and consequent anticipation was hard to discern. At the core of Fromm's political anxieties was the risk of atomic war – not only in times of urgent crisis, as with Cuba in 1962 (cf. Fromm, 1963h), but also regarding a number of other issues in foreign and defense policy:

> By the present policy of continued armament and support of economically and politically reactionary regimes, we shall lose the battle for the minds of men in Africa, Asia and Latin America. Or, more probably, we shall help to blow Western man and his civilization to pieces. If this fear is hysterical, then let us have more of it.
>
> (Fromm, 1961i:12)

Throughout the 1960s, Fromm thought "an armament race" would "most likely lead to a nuclear war by error or folly, thus destroying democratic civilization as we know it" (d-1990j-003-eng-type-01:2). The 1970s show us a man who has survived his worse political nightmares. He grows skeptical of his feeling, but also of the prospects for the immediate future. During the Nixon presidency, he tells Urquhart: "hope is at a low ebb now, but that does not mean that faith needs to be at a low ebb too" (Urquhart_Clara_1972–03–21-to).

It is not in Fromm's temperament to imprison future possibilities in the impasses of the present. He defends a hope that is "impatient and active, looking for every possibility of action within the realm of real possibilities", and only recognizes surrender into despair as "rational" if there "would be the knowledge that no possibility can be seen" (Fromm, 1973a:484–5). Rational faith in politics remains, for him, the act of "rely[ing] on experience that gives us the conviction that things could be different" (AUD-1962g). However, his personal estimate of the room of political possibility increasingly shrinks as years pass. He could not help feeling beaten down by the times. Asked by Gérard Khoury whether he sees a contemporary horizon for a socialist revolution, he responds:

> I don't. So I think there is almost no reason for hope except faith, which is a different story. I, for instance, have a faith that unless the human race destroys itself before, eventually it will arrive at a state – not of perfection – but of a tremendous development.
>
> (AUD-1978c)

"One can believe", he tells Luban-Plozza a couple of years later. But he thinks few people have any faith – and "without belief in the future of man, man has no future" (AUD-1980g).

How different from his statements in 1968, when Fromm (1968a:15) was enthusiastically hoping for McCarthy's victory: "Hope is the mood that accompanies faith. Faith could not be sustained without the mood of hope. Hope can have no base except in faith"! How hopeful those times, twenty years before, when he would write to Mumford, not without a tint of *pride*: "I entirely agree with you that indeed we are the early Christians of another era" (Mumford_Lewis_1960–08–16-to)! As the world turns, humanistic associations, including many of the ones Fromm was personally involved with, start facing bigger and bigger impediments. In the 1960s, he said of countries like Yugoslavia, Czechoslovakia, Poland, and Hungary: "while I do not think that these countries represent truly socialist countries, I believe that they are very different from the Soviet system" (Bottomore_Tom_B_1964-01-20-to). Still in 1980, he recognized Yugoslav socialism as the one that got the closer to his own ideals (cf. AUD-1980e). But as early as 1974 he found himself writing to Toma Granfil, then Yugoslav Ambassador, urging the country to stop persecuting his friends, the Marxist scholars from the *Praxis* school (cf. Granfil_Toma_1974-11-15-to). Fromm is at first not altogether happy with the public reaction to Watergate, and feels the political mood to be astonishingly contagious: "the numbness of conscience and emotional response is a frightening fact. One can observe it in oneself, that sometimes one reacts more slowly or less intensely than one would have ten years ago" (Fulbright_J_W_1973-09-02-to). Only when the scandal develops a clear public reaction does he feel satisfied (cf. u-1972). Even the moon landing a couple of years before was for him so very discouraging: "It seems to me it was the final abdication of man, and the official beginning of the worship of the machine – a foretaste of the world as it might develop" (Urquhart_-Clara_1969-08-04-to). With an increasingly fragile health, and coming from a series of aborted political attempts, Fromm felt his room for action shrink more and more.

2 The Social Psychology of Humanistic Movements

We may now bring together the modes of affection we isolated above, evaluating them in their political significance, as the emotional material peculiar to humanistic political formations. The fluctuations humanist relations undergo – between expressions of pride and of idealization, of compensatory enthusiasm and consolation, of despair and hope – are rooted in the division we found before, between a negative, shared moral concern, and a positive, common ethical commitment. Their characteristic affective motions flow from this objective counterposition.

***

The reliance of humanistic alliances on shared *concern* leads back to their roots in anguish – ultimately, in self-preservation. This provides them with their immediate *content*.

Fromm is opposed to the cultivation of irrational anxiety and guilt. He considers them to be paralyzing feelings, fostering submission. He is, however, favorable to experiencing real political dangers for what they are. As he puts it to Adam Schaff: "man is willing to adjust to the social order, driven by his self-preservation, yet [...] there is also a second level of preservation which leads to revolutionary movements and revolutionary thinking, because of conflicts within the social order" (Schaff_Adam_1965-01-13-to). Each subject in a humanistic formation, such as envisioned by Fromm, must be able to experience their relationship to political events and social circumstances as arousing concern for the preservation of life. We are therefore faced with a triangular structure, in which the bond between subjects is mediated by their reference to a common object. This is the source for the feeling of *relief* we find in some of Fromm's letters. It expresses the liberation political agents achieve in having their suffering acknowledged by others. What Fromm feels as moods of *despair* and *hope* in politics is another effect of the same structure. They develop as subjects incorporate the reactions of others as constituents of their own feeling.

That political concern is *shared* implies that the social relation acknowledges political dangers and reactions to them not only as objectively common, but also as subjectively mutual. This is their *formal* peculiarity.

Acknowledgment of common concern was enough to account for the swings of mood, for affective tension and relief within humanistic relations. These were expressions of the fact that the relation to political circumstances became mediated by the relation between political agents. Now, inversely, the relation between subjects appears as mediated by their relation to their political circumstances. In sharing, what happens to others is experienced as happening to oneself; their fate is felt as being one's own. Each finds their relation to their own lives as confirmed by the other. Thus its conscious manifestations are not anymore purely cathartic or negative, but rather feelings of *encouragement,* of enhanced potency. It is upon this predicate that humanistic relations try to generate the capacity for political action. When this mutuality of experience is brought into self-awareness, we can speak of *solidarity* in Fromm's terms.

Finally, that such a shared concern should be of a *moral* nature implies that something other than the will to live is also at stake. The relations we have sampled above provide enough evidence that they revolve not only around self-preservation, but also around aspects of narcissism. This provides them with their mediated *content.*

Much as Fromm has written against narcissism in politics, it infiltrates the relations around him in a number of different forms. He is partly aware of that, as in commenting to Merton:

> as to your question on the difference between humanistic conscience and narcissism, I think you touch one of the most important and at the same time difficult problems. Undoubtedly we see that self-sacrifice can be just as much an expression of narcissism as self-aggrandizement.
> (Merton_Thomas_1954–12–08-to)

He later comes to appreciate the duality of historical religions in this respect: their intended spiritual function is to break down narcissism, and yet religious group narcissism is ubiquitous (cf. AUD-1963b; AUD-1965c). In humanistic formations, a particular sign of narcissistic relatedness is political *enthusiasm*. This affect is less typical of times of hope and political victory than of attempts at overcoming depression. We must see it as helping repress despair, compensating for it, and retrieving the capacity for political action only on second order.

The counterposition inhering in humanistic relations – between their immediate content (self-preservation) and a mediate one (narcissism) – leads to an important fissure within the corresponding political formations. As these forces are subsumed to a common form, they become part of the historical *material* allowing political work. Each aspect leads to a distinct form of *mobilization*.

To the extent that political relations remain based on anguish and the will to survive, they relate subjects as acknowledging a problem they have in common. This acknowledgment facilitates their way into action in making it possible to elaborate the reality of their suffering and the alternatives to it. Subjects share their wish to live, and to live better. However, satisfaction of this wish is left out of the political relation. As long as they remain based on shared *concern*, political alliances behave negatively toward their object. They are in no position to evolve into a common, positive practice of life. For this to be possible, subjects must agree on a common life conduct – whereby reintroducing doctrinaire differences is unavoidable. One's vital forces are not consummated as pure attitudes, but only in determined forms of action, for which symbolic mediation is necessary. Without this, common values remain stuck in their ideality. Their realization falls without Fromm's ecumenical conception. The affirmative moment – the wish for a better life – is thus the content and presupposition for humanistic political alliances – but it cannot be realized *within* them. Alliances continue only as long as their goal is frustrated.

The mechanism behind this form of mobilization must be a form of transient *introjection*. One must be able to bring sparks of the other's experience into oneself, to reproduce them and affirm them – but without holding to them as one's own, since there is no common positive practice emerging out of it, except in the attempt at negating common political circumstances. The relation strengthens the subject's capacity to act – but cease collaboration, she is left alone. This sustains her autonomy, but at the cost of an acute consciousness of her unfulfilled aspirations. Fromm's enduring sense of *loneliness* corresponds in part to this structure. Political efficacy comes at the cost of an enduring separateness between allies, which punctuates the joy of solidarity.

Grounding political relatedness on shared narcissism corresponds to an attempt at overcoming this separateness. We met two expressions of this tendency among Fromm's relationships – first in the *idealization* of one's political allies, later in the *pride* of sharing values with them. In our documents, idealization incurs mostly in the evaluation of others, which are now experienced as examples and living testimonies of moral strength. If this is carried through *projection*, mobilization is based on the authority of the idealized object to command one's will. Contrariwise, if idealization results from *transference,* it grounds action on personal devotion: love for the cause is born out of love for the object. Acting together, these two mechanisms result in what Fromm (1990a) would have called "idolatry". The source for one's action falls on the other's side. Thus structured, humanistic formations are shaped as chains of idealization. Each subject is for the others the representative of their ideals, and finds in others the representatives of her own.

Pride implies a third alternative. Narcissistic satisfaction is shared, but subjects now stand as equals before each other. They understand themselves as partaking in the same moral qualities, whereby *identification* may be established. Their relation is grounded on the common possession of their ideals, and they are capacitated to act under the premise of protecting these ideals. This leaves humanistic formations vulnerable to sectarian configurations of the kind Fromm (1961a) would have called "fanatical". They owe a part of their persuasion to their capacity for reverting secrecy and exclusiveness into satisfaction for their members – an important gratification, especially for minoritarian positions. The function is still fulfilled that each subject becomes a support for the action of others. Their sense of separateness is overcome, but at the cost of having to sustain the fiction of their ideals (and the risk of deep disappointment) as the means for mobilization. Hence Fromm's emphasis on action as exemplary manifestation of character:

> it is one of the essential points of humanism [...] to consider not only what people say and think, but also what the human reality behind these thoughts is. [...] Usually the criteria for such differentiations are positions and acts outside the ideology itself.
> (Schaff_Adam_1963–10–05-to)

Fromm's works display little evidence of a wish for haughty religious elitism. If it was ever present in his life, he must have developed quite a strong reaction against it, since both his public and private communications are sound in rejecting group narcissism – the best example here being Fromm's deep rejection of Jewish nationalism (cf. Fromm, 1964a; 1966a). However, both his works and his personal conduct confirm a tendency for idealization. We glimpse his political pride in rare, but astonishingly strong statements, whenever his prerogatives are hurt. His appraisal of many a political ally in terms of their "personal integrity" (Coffin_Tristram_1974–03–26-to) is matched by the great offense he could take on disputations of his own commitment:

> At a time when former radicals find it opportune to change their views for the safe haven of adjustment, such suspicions are easily aroused and the most important quality which I pride myself on, namely not to have

> adjusted my views, either to please the Left or the Right, in other words my personal integrity, is questioned.
>
> (Coffin_Tristram_1974-02-01-to)

Fromm's appeal to the suspension of intellectual differences is thus a form of practical compromise, and a necessary one. It amounts to the fact that political alliances require finding unity between the practitioners of different life conducts, whereas the establishment of ethically-based communities presses for immediate identity and compatibility in conduct. We find the most important theoretical expression of this problem in Fromm's concept of solidarity. Like empathy, solidarity is defined in two very different, apparently irreconcilable ways. On the one hand, "suffering and sorrow are what we share and the deepest ground of human solidarity" (Adams_James_Luther_1978-04-28-to). On the other hand, the concept expresses the fulfillment of humanistic experience: solidarity should emerge where there would be love for the stranger – that is, openness to all that is human, to difference within and outside oneself (cf. Fromm, 1955a; 1964a).

The duality of these definitions corresponds to the different significance solidarity has when considered in ethical and political terms. As a *politically efficient* factor – an affection activating subjects and helping coordinate action – solidarity is based on a negative moral agreement, for which shared suffering is the basic presupposition. As an *ethically efficient* factor – a foundation for social relations within a political community, especially if organized democratically – it works differently. It has to acknowledge and affirm the diversity of human expressions within the community, but may give up the task of coordinating action. This amounts to the difference between collaborating toward a change in common *conditions* of life, and collaborating within a common *practice* of life. Not coincidentally, Fromm referred solidarity to suffering more often in discussing political emancipation, whereas openness to difference recurs when he discusses the "need for rootedness" – which includes the relationship of the singular subject to the social world around her (cf. Fromm, 1955a; 1966a; compare Wilde, 2004).

3 Humanism and the Way of the World

Let us now examine the vicissitudes humanistic relations faced in confrontation with objective political circumstances. These confrontations multiply in Fromm's life as he establishes himself as a notorious public intellectual, reaching a wide global readership (cf. McLaughlin, 2021). His status as a writer opens the door for a number of initiatives of various political characters – from philanthropy to antiwar conferences (cf. Macdonald_Nancy_1973-12-29-to; Pauling_Linus_1961-02-23-to). Fromm's correspondence is filled with invitations to integrate the board of supporters in petitions, political societies, scientific committees, conferences – a number of which he accepts. His signature lends these endeavors credit and respect.

Fromm's intellectual reputation is also his bridge into a connection with members of the US Congress, sided sometimes with David Riesman and Michael Maccoby. Notorious among these are William Fullbright and Eugene McCarthy, but also a number of other senators and representatives, who eventually ask his advice regarding international relations and the development of the cold war (cf. Bowles_Chester_1960–06–21-by). A significant portion of Fromm's publications is targeted directly at the political class, *May man prevail?* being the most significant example:

> The book had a peculiar fate. It was widely read and even in the last few years a few thousand copies are sold every year. But I am afraid it was little read by the very people whom I had mostly in mind as readers, members of the Senate and the House.
> (Fulbright_J_W_1974–09–07-to)

In the meantime, Fromm's involvement with the US Socialist Party, his occupations with the National Committee for a Sane Nuclear Policy (SANE), the Fellowship of Reconciliation (FOR) and other branches of the pacifist movement lead him to refine his experience as a lecturer for political audiences (cf. Hassler_Alfred_1971–07–15-by; Keys_Donald_F_1966–07–28-by). Touring through universities, Fromm gets in touch with student organizations, with the feminist and Black movements. These experiences are parts of his political education in the course of practice (cf. Thomas_Norman_1963–08–12-to)

Fromm's position as an intellectual guarantees him a relative freedom with regards to local political constraints in social movements and in the state. At the same time, his attempt at addressing different strata of political life leaves a mark in the rationale for his praxis, especially regarding matters of political method (compare McLaughlin, 2001). Fromm's political stances can only be understood as an effort to reconcile the contradictions therein contained with a stable, principled ethical position. Where his writings present a fairly developed reflection on *matters of principle* for socialists and pacifists, an analysis of his actual political conduct reveals under which premises he acted in the society of his times, and what he saw as ways to effect change within the corresponding structures – that is, his take on *matters of strategy* and *tactics* (cf. Fromm, 1963h).

For Fromm, one must "distinguish between two principal topics – one of principles, and one of tactical considerations" (Schaff_Adam_1963–10–05-to). This implicit political theory, which we learn from Fromm's biographical data and social relations, is an important complement to his overt political theory, as formulated in print. Nothing speaks louder in this respect than the occasions in which Fromm articulated a strategic plan for the Left, such as in

The revolution of hope. The original edition of the book included a draft to be sent back to Fromm regarding the possibility of organizing "groups" and "clubs" (cf. 1968a). In a letter written in 1970 to Sarah Wittes, Fromm laments that: "The response was not too encouraging, because I found very few people who show enough independence, activity and insight to organize groups. [...] I can be more helpful by my theoretical work than by becoming an organizer of groups myself" (Wittes_Sarah_Sue_1970-03-09-to). This had been Wittes' own view, as she initiated correspondence with Fromm a couple of years before, censoring him for venturing outside his field of expertise (cf. Wittes_Sarah_Sue_1968-11-18-by). At the time, he justified taking part in praxis out of a feeling of urgency: "It often appears to me that the situation is so grave that what little my influence would be worth in terms of contributing to the humanistic movement, it is worth more than my theoretical contributions" (Wittes_Sarah_Sue_1968-12-01-to). Over the years, however, we see him bending toward her opinion that the best venue for his energies would be the production of ideas.

This particular stance allows us to read back other of Fromm's political frustrations. An interesting case in point is his attempt, around 1966, to promote a World Conference, reuniting both theistic and non-theisitic humanists, with the purpose of discussing matters of war and the survival of humanity. Fromm (1992n) discusses this possibility with Merton, Urquhart, Mumford, and many others. He wants the reunion to be called by the Pope – which leads to the conference never happening: "We must now accept that the Pope will do nothing" (Urquhart_Clara_1966-12-29-by). For some time more, Fromm tries to find a replacement for the aborted conference: something as an "International Forum for the Survival of Man" could be promoted (Urquhart_Clara_1967-05-28-by). The idea occasionally morphs into a plan for institutionalizing a "Bureau for Factfinding" (Urquhart_Clara_1967-07-12-to) – an idea not unlike Fromm's (1968a) later propositions for the "Voice of American Conscience". "The question" now, he writes Schaff, "is how one could arrange a sufficiently impressive committee of artists, scientists, writers etc." (Schaff_Adam_1966-12-30-to). Both suggestions remain unaccomplished (cf. Urquhart_Clara_1967-07-11-by).

The process leading to the failure of these initiatives is as interesting as the concept behind them. Fromm writes effusively to his collaborators to diffuse a draft calling the conference – a method similar to the one used in the "Citizens for Reason" venture. We see along the way how Fromm's correspondents in humanism take issue with the structure he proposes. A typical reaction is Siegmund Warburg's – a banker who is mistrustful of having the conference called by a religious authority, and suggests centering the conference on representatives of the sciences (cf. Warburg_Siegmund_G_1966-10-31-by). A similar conflict of interest had already been a topic between Fromm and Adam Schaff as they tried to form the board of editors for a humanistic journal. Their attempt at reconciling their interests (a weightier Marxist or nontheist panel) with those of Ruth Nanda Anshen, who was much more sympathetic to theistic humanism, led them to a dead end. As Fromm summarizes it to Urquhart:

> Professor Schaff [...] had doubts about having too many theologians, and especially Catholics on the board of editors. [...] I think the theologians should not have a majority, as it were, but I definitely feel the Catholic humanists, like the Protestant humanists, are very important.
> (Urquhart_Clara_1963–10–01-to)

Four years later, the matter is still being discussed, and revolves mainly around the conditions each party imposes for their own participation. Schaff insists particularly on having Roger Garaudy compose the board of editors, as he had done during Fromm's editing of *Socialist humanism* (cf. Bottomore_Tom_B_1963–09–28-to). Fromm is increasingly demotivated, as they cannot find support from another editor, and Anshen does not comply with Schaff's demands (cf. Schaff_Adam_1967–01–10-to).

Some people were more enthusiastic than others about Fromm's ecumenical approach. Thomas Merton opens his correspondence with Fromm emphasizing precisely this point:

> it seems to me important that all who take to heart the value and the nobility of the human spirit should realize their solidarity with one another, and should be able to communicate with one another in every way, in spite of perhaps great doctrinal divergences.
> (Merton_Thomas_1954–10–02-by)

However, similar conflicts abound whenever Fromm participates in rather personal selection processes, such as he would later recommend for the constituency of a "Supreme Cultural Council" (1976a:179). In many such cases, his capacity to persuade his collaborators to suspend their differences is at a low.

Fromm's tolerance to doctrinaire divergence aimed at consolidating larger majorities, both immediately with the signatories of a text, and in terms of the expected public reaction to it. When Abraham Muste invites him into composing a "Plan for a Commission of the World Community", Fromm responds enthusiastically, but worried with the preliminary suggestions for building up the group:

> My only doubt is whether the proposed names are not so heavily loaded on the pacifist side that the others, like Toynbee might not wish to participate. [...] Could one find some people who are not pacifists or socialists, but who are concerned with the world, who would join the commission?
> (Muste_Abraham_J_1965–08–31-to)

Unfortunately, not all issues in associating with others could be reduced to intellectual divergences. An example is Fromm's own unwillingness to have a piece of his published with David Siqueiros. "As is generally known", he writes, "he participated in the first murder attempt against Trotsky while the latter was living in Mexico [...] (I personally would not even want to published [sic] with him)" (Urquhart_Clara_1962-01-05-to). Reputational and moral issues would be only one among many other problems tearing political organization apart.

Another case in point is Fromm's attempt at eliciting a humanistic movement in 1968. While the clubs and groups he proposed were a general model for political renewal, he thought McCarthy would be a particularly apt leader to organize them into a larger movement. "The question again", he writes the candidate in 1968, "is when to start all this, and whether you would take the leadership of this movement in case you should not be nominated" (McCarthy_Eugene_1968-08-12-to). He was not so attached to McCarthy that he would not consider carrying the task further without him: at a later point, he asks William Johnson and Michael Maccoby whether they would agree in contacting the candidate, asking for anticipations on his interest, or lack thereof (cf. Johnson_William_1968-09-04-to). Such a movement should be feasible without control of the state: it would aim at reorganizing civil society into politically active groups, not on submitting them to a government, even if a "humanistic" one.

Fromm had some success in spreading this idea among his collaborators, as we find a document signed by William Johnson, Ivanhoe Donaldson and Michael Maccoby proposing an "After November Committee" to be working after the elections, "whatever the[ir] outcome", promoting

> the creation of decentralized groups or centers where individuals would meet regularly with the purpose of exchanging information, for study and analysis of events, and for increasing the consciousness of the members. These groups would be autonomous, without bureaucratic or centralized control.
>
> (Johnson_William_1968-10-08-by)

The committee remained, however, centered around McCarthy, and died with his lack of initiative. Fromm's biggest disappointment lay not so much in the fact that McCarthy lost the elections, but in noticing how he withdrew from the task of leading a political renewal after his defeat. He kept his correspondence with McCarthy for some more time, only eventually to resign from trying to animate him into this position again. He would tell Mumford the next year: McCarthy "made it so particularly clear that all hopes about which we had often talked – that he would participate in a movement – were of no interest to him" (Mumford_Lewis_1969-01-23-to).

***

In a number of other ventures, acting with the same instruments, Fromm had at least partial success. The 1948 draft mentioned above is a case in point. However, the situations we are discussing now display some of the recurring obstacles Fromm's political conduct met. Generalizing from a comparison between them and other similar endeavors allows us to formulate the limitations of his political means.

The first element standing out is Fromm's difficulty in acting as an organizer in practice. By his own admission, Fromm didn't have the temperament for political leadership (cf. 1974b). "I had never the wish to become a politician", he tells Gérard Khoury in 1978 (AUD-1978a). While he played a leading role in a number of other endeavors (i.e. the foundation of SANE and several psychoanalytic associations – cf. Hardeck, 2005), the rules governing the development of social movements and of scientific institutions are partly different, and he would not find success in each case. Another side of the problem rests on Fromm's rather fragile health, especially from 1966 on. His politically most active years partly overlap with an increasing need for rest and self-care. "I am not really sick, the point is simply that I did much too much and it depleted my energies", Fromm writes Riesman in 1968 (Riesman_David_1968–07–05-to) – and it would be far from the last time in the remaining 12 years of his life that he would strain himself to the limits of his health. Personal factors considered, however, there remains one crucial factor: it is mainly on moral grounds that Fromm expects to achieve mobilization. Where appeal to shared sensibility is possible, Fromm is in his element. Where he finds himself is in competition with interests of any other kind – power, money, management of reputation – his appeal is considerably weakened.

McCarthy's campaign illustrates that well. Two elements are of particular interest. First: the very differentiation between "clubs" and "groups" implies Fromm's acknowledgment, however dim, that the "quasi-religious" attitude he championed would not easily provide a general basis for political reactivation. He expected an ample basis for agreement only from a negative relationship to political events, not from the positive commonality of ethical values. However, without previous participation in ethical communities, subjects are not available to share moral concerns. Fromm's method of organization couldn't rely on the same basis as his method of mobilization. As he puts it to Mumford: "I entirely agree with you that if McCarthy had found it in himself, after the Chicago terror, to express the moral revulsion all decent people felt, he would have polarized the sentiment of the country" (Mumford_Lewis_1969–01–23-to). And yet, he ran many times against the verification that moral revulsion was seldom present, and rarely enough to produce more than transient cooperation.

In 1955, struggling with the difficulties around the "Citizens for Reason" statement, Fromm writes to Merton: "In all these weeks in which I did practically nothing but try to find people to sign the declaration, and talked with them about the danger of war, I rarely spoke to anyone who was really deeply concerned" (Merton_Thomas_1955-04-13-to). In 1968, noticing the dissipation of the movement around McCarthy, he comments: "I am afraid one has to admit that this constituency has dispersed, and very little has remained" (Mumford_Lewis_1969-01-23-to). Coalitions during an electoral campaign are not, after all, long-lasting moral allegiances. They also don't lead of necessity to the foundation of self-organized, ethically-oriented communities. This brings us to the second point: the discrepancy between Fromm's trust on the capacity of moral concern to motivate agents spontaneously, and his increasing admission that humanistic movements lacked leadership. As he puts it to Tristram Coffin: "If there were one leader with great stature I think there could be a point of crystallization in America which would amount to a kind of renewal of energies and hope, but this leader is missing up to now" (Coffin_Tristram_1974-10-25-to).

If anything in Fromm's thought and character was offhand with the problems of politics, it was not out of incapacity to recognize the power of competing interests. Still around the topic of McCarthy, he writes: "I believe there are a few political leaders, and they are very rare indeed, who are not – or who are very little motivated by vanity or greed for power, but by a sense of mission" (Mumford_Lewis_1969-01-23-to). His social psychology includes the difference between true ideals and rationalizations, between conviction and the wish for power (cf. Fromm, 1961a). Also in matters of tactics, we are not without example that Fromm was able to address the pragmatic side of politics. Discussing the apparent contradictions in a speech by Barry Goldwater, he writes:

> The fact is that any good tactician in his place would do precisely what he did – first to win power in the party by appealing to the fanaticism of the right wing, and after he had gotten that far, to make a second step to discount his previous statements, and make statements of a liberal nature which are to win the liberals and those between them and the right wing.
> (1964k:16)

He would hold similar arguments in interpreting other political statements (cf. Fromm, 1961g; 1964i). For one: Fromm saw Henry Kissinger's dealings with Israeli foreign policy rather skeptically: "my suspicion remains that Kissinger's policy to kill two birds with one stone was more due to his own wish for maximum success than to his insight" (Riesman_David_1975-02-01-to). And yet, the same writer who insisted so much in the difference between words and facts, between behavior and motivation, would ground some of his most exuberant political demands – not on common interests, but in "the stimulation of an idealistic mood, [...] a new wave of genuine idealism and, for many, a religious attitude" (d-1990m-003-eng-type-01:3). The same man that saw Israel so critically also criticized the same state for believing "that only might and the decision of arms can regulate unsolved conflicts", with "no confidence in the spirit, in the warmth of the human heart to which one can appeal" (Fulbright_J_W_1973–11–19-to).

Fromm's last years are marked by an impressive attempt at developing a renewed realism. "Who has an interest in truth?", he asks in one of his last interviews (1980b:18). At the root of this question are not only his scientific commitments – truth in thought –, but also his arduous learnings in politics. His disappointments led him to an increasingly modest estimation of the reach of humanistic politics – even though he never gave them up. To the end of his life, Fromm would believe that a group which cannot commit to its values out of true human interest – truth in experience and practice – is not a viable political formation. An ideal which is not lived "in the flesh" was also, for him, an ideal which has "no reality" (AUD-1966e). Presupposing this appraisal of communitarian realization of values, indeed institutionally-based social rewards must be felt as alien, risking estrangement and the downfall of the desired movement. Where attachment to experiential values is not greater than interests of other kinds, Fromm's appeal meets a dead end: "I am more and more appalled by the moral apathy one finds" (Merton_Thomas_1960–11–03-to).

Symbolic of such impasses is Thomas Merton's reaction to the 1955 initiative on peace. His commitment to humanist values, both in religion and in politics, is beyond any doubt: he and Fromm remained in friendly correspondence to the end of Merton's life in 1968. However, as regards joining the "Citizens for Reason" appeal, he tells Fromm:

> I am certainly glad to have my personal attitude on the matter known, but I do not want to involve my monastery or my Order in anything that looks like a stand on some particular detail of political policy with regard, for instance, to China or Formosa.
> (Merton_Thomas_1955–03–18-by)

Merton's case is quite peculiar for the immediacy with which his decision is affected by institutional constraints: the rather immediate power of censorship he ascribes to his superiors, being a monk, as he was (cf. Merton_Thomas_1962–02–16-by). But the problem is identical when Fromm deals with politicians, intellectuals, and leaderships in other fields. About the same theologians whose integrity as humanists he held no doubt, he would also say: "They are, indeed, bound by their organizations, and hence cannot express, or even think, entirely without the tendency of not leaving the dogmatic frame of reference of the church" (Schaff_Adam_1963–10–05-to). It is peculiar to Fromm's tendency for idealization that his dealings with McCarthy led him to such "great disappointments", and enduring ones (Riesman_David_1975–03–05-to), despite the fact that this man was not less bound by interest than any other.

We saw before the inner contradictions humanistic formations faced in trying to sustain moral mobilization. Here we deal with their clash against radically different forms of organization. Fromm is deeply disappointed when such matters of presumable common concern as the survival of mankind are not enough to cross through competing political interests. He feels quite unmotivated by others' lack of response. The more he is overburdened with the task of animating people into action, the more he withdraws: "At any rate, if there are not enough people with an active interest in it it will have to be dropped, since I cannot possibly organize this myself" (Riesman_David_1967–08–19-to). Fromm comes to a sharp experience that the form of mobilization he favored didn't easily hold up its strength as a principle of organization.

4 Strategy, Tactics, and Principles

Thus far, we identified a basic conflict between Fromm's moral form of mobilization and its ethical presuppositions, and another between Fromm's religious model for political relatedness and the world of power and interest. We recognized institutional constraints – social forms not based on ethical commitment – as an enduring point of resistance against humanistic initiatives, limiting them from without. Let us now approach the same question from within, developing the motivations for Fromm's venturing into the world of political institutions. After all, much of his political practice was addressed at the same organizations he otherwise criticized: churches, the state, the press. This will lead us to a more complex picture than the one we have now.

The same three examples from 1966 and 1968 will again be useful. This time, we won't be interested in their "success" or "failure", but in the intention and reasoning behind them. We may begin by recovering the problem of finding adequate *leadership*. At least two different intents are involved here. First, the attempt at providing a model for social-characterological change. The Pope and Eugene McCarthy figure in each case as personalities whose charisma, creed and authority Fromm would trust in drawing people toward a new political vision:

> what would recommend the idea of the Pope to me is that his role would not be essentially that of Head of the Church, but as a temporal head of state who, however, has great moral authority and who, like his predecessors, has shown great responsibility and activity in matters of peace.
> (Adams_James_Luther_1966–10–14-to)

A new conduct of life should be represented in character and action by the participants in a humanistic movement, and particularly by their leaders. A socialist leader would have to bear a character structure pointing beyond the social limitations of his times (cf. Fromm, 1963b). Had Fromm not been so disappointed with their capacity for self-organization, he might have expected to see some of the best women and men of his time shining in local political life. The primacy of experience over thought meant for him that *ethical exemplarity* was a central political principle.

Examples of the above abound. Fromm's appreciation of men as different as Daitero Suzuki and Shlomo Rabinkow would coincide in expressions such as: "He was an authority purely by his being, and never because he promised approval or threatened disapproval" (Fromm, 1967a:87); "he was a man without titles, without positions, without a craving for prestige or recognition, a man for whom life was entirely the process of being, and not that of having" (Fromm, 1987a:99). Fromm's impressions of other intellectuals and leaders were often based on the same principles. He thought the choice of contributors for his edited book from 1965, *Socialist Humanist,* should not be based only on theoretical brilliance, but also "to some extent according to what they represent as human beings" (Schaff_Adam_1963–11–08-to). He disliked Walter Benjamin's theorizing, but admired his "absolute integrity" (Markovic_Mihailo_1975–07–16-to). Adorno's complicated style was for him a proof of lack of conviction (cf. Dunayevskaya_Raya_1976–10–02-to). Sartre and Jung, he saw as mere opportunists (cf. Urquhart_Clara_1963–10–01-to; u-1976:68).

Fromm also extended his appraisal of ethical exemplarity onto the challenges of activism. Questioned during a lecture on how to persuade people to join a political movement, he replies: "Just do it! When you talk to people, be yourself, be mindful of the difference between truth and fiction, be aware of what makes you afraid of conviction" (AUD-1962i). It was of utmost importance for him that the members of a political organization could convince of the viability and truthfulness of their ideas by force of their own example. He tells an interviewer:

> I think that the new man, in case he develops himself the way I conceive it, will not let himself be known by his uniform, his costume or his hairstyle, but in the way he speaks, the way he goes, the way he looks, that is, in his whole personality – and this personality makes an impression.
>
> (u-1974:14)

Hence the importance of "groups" in his 1968 definition: they should act both as models and proofs of the possibility of a different life. He was convinced that this could be effected even by smaller numbers of truly committed people:

> This doesn't happen in books, it happens only in a living tradition, in men who still understand these values. And I believe that what is today decisive is that groups exist which develop and transmit these values not only theoretically, but in their existence, as an experience. It plays no role if these groups are small.
>
> (u-1974:14)

The second aspect involved in trying to articulate with established leaders was, however, the attempt at reaching a mass organization. It was the problem of numbers, of *majority formation*. Commenting on the Watergate case, Fromm says:

> what we are lacking are voices which speak clearly, outline a comprehensive program, can be understood by millions of people, can awake hope, and above all reach enough people. We lack a great figure who would have the capacity to do all this in a way which could seize the minds of millions of people and silence the rest into shame.
>
> (u-1972:1)

Fromm's interest in his dealings with Left theologians lay mainly in the fact that "they are the intellectual leaders of a movement in the church which definitely puts the interest of man – and that means, also, of peace – above all dogmatic considerations" (Schaff_Adam_1963-10-05-to). For similar reasons, he established contact with a number of people who were directly involved in the practical reorganization of the faithful into communities (cf. Adams_James_Luther_1958-04-25-by). Fromm rightly intuited these communities as the condition of possibility for political alliances as he wanted them:

> Christianity, even in its institutionalized and alienated form, did not give up the biblical texts, the prophetic texts, the gospels, and the fantastic thing is that through all these centuries, even up to this day, again and again these gospels and the prophetic texts became alive in many revolutionary forms where generally Christianity came to life again. That happens mostly in the Christian sects in the middle-ages, after the reformation, and it happens today again, especially in Latin American countries.
>
> (AUD-1977g)

If "matters of principle" and "matters of strategy" should be differentiated, then Fromm's relationship to purported humanistic leaders was based on both aspects. On the side of principles, he thought they were the highest representatives of common ethical values. On the side of strategy, however, he thought of them and their institutions as *channels* for the diffusion and reactivation of those values. Since institutional faith offered a previous organization of the faithful into formed communities, Fromm saw in them a *latent infrastructure* for political change – and a major way of overcoming his difficulties in bringing people together. While the *goal* of a radical movement would lay in producing a new constellation of social relations, a new practice of life – the *means* for doing so would require a deep engagement with the available historical organizations.

Better yet if these traditions were already activated by force of their own inner development: in 1966, the Catholic Church was still experiencing a renewed liberal phase after the Second Vatican Council, and enjoying a prestige Fromm would have liked to mobilize in the interest of peace. "I feel that the church never had such a responsibility as now when the human race is in danger of such acts and such brutalization", he tells Thomas Merton in 1961, shortly before Vatican II (Merton_Thomas_1961–11–23-to). As for McCarthy, Fromm believed he was effective in reactivating the human interests of a good deal of the US population: "he is not a man of the machine, in attracting the allegiance of a large sector of Americans" (Mumford_Lewis_1969–01–23-to). Mobilizing these leaders in his favor would have meant an access to thousands of people. Their institutions would serve as means for greater political capillarity, and for the socialization of political subjects into new character structures: an organized progressive expression of faith "would make an impression on people", he thought (Merton_Thomas_1961–11–23-to). Preformed communities, once reached and activated towards humanistic aspirations, would figure as transitioning powers between present and future – organs produced by a previous organization of society, capable of carrying it into a new structure: "one does not achieve anything with destruction [...] to the contrary, one can only build from the healthiest elements, both economic and humane, that one finds beforehand in a society" (VID-1975g).

This explains the permeability of many of Fromm's writings to Biblical language, even if by the 1960s he had already abandoned his earlier Jewish faith for decades (i.e. Fromm, 1965j; 1968f). Writing and speaking in the language of a certain tradition would be a way of mobilizing the potentialities in the human material provided by previous history. The attempt at forming majority consensus quickly led into the problem of rhetorics, of the form of addressing people. At stake for Fromm was "a real battle for the mind and hearts of the people" (u-1972:1) – for which the capacity to speak in the right language would be decisive. He privileged a clearly understandable style above any aesthetic and theoretical purposes. "After all", he tells Sidney Lens, "you want to convince people who are not from the very beginning already convinced of your position" (Lens_Sidney_1964–02–06-to). More than once, in discussion with his correspondents, Fromm brings up the argument whether a simplification in style would not help reach a wider public. Regarding Schaff's *History and truth*, he says: "the same ideas could, of course, be expressed in a more popular form, but that would be in many ways a different book" (Schaff_Adam_1971–01–25-to). Advising Sarah Wittes on the publication of her dissertation on Rousseau, Fromm thought she should make the point straight and clear, without any academic "heaviness" (Wittes_Sarah_Sue_1970–04–09-to). He was not interested in Lacan's way of abstracting, and even Ernst Bloch's prose annoyed him (cf. Riesman_David_1976–02–12-to; Markovic_Mihailo_1975–07–16-to). He preferred James Luther Adams' style, "which deals with profound problems in such a simple and straightforward way which shows that you care enormously for the reader" (Adams_James_Luther_1976–12–14-to). Meister Eckhart was his chosen one in style and substance – an author he has "read again and again and love as perhaps no other writer" (Auer_Alfons_1974–04–01-to).

This brings us into another aspect of Fromm's activity: his role as editor (and as a mediator between editors and writers). Fromm took it as part of his craft not only to formulate ideas, but also to publicize them as broadly as possible. His connections in the publishing world were of course not without interest in the diffusion of his own ideas. Discussing the unfavorable stance many official lines of Marxism took against psychoanalysis, he asks Adam Schaff whether his own brand of humanistic psychoanalysis should not be introduced in the Eastern European satellite countries: "I think it would be logical if the Socialist countries would build up a psychoanalysis oriented not along the lines of mechanistic materialism of Freudian analysis, but on lines similar to mine" (Schaff_Adam_1966–08–30-to). At this point, the peculiarity of the relationship between political allies dissolves into their dealings as intellectuals, not specifically as representatives of humanism. However, the fact remains that Fromm had eminently political criteria in his remaining editorial choices.

Fromm's interest in circulating strongly academic prose was way lesser than in the case of texts addressing a mass audience. He had an important role in selecting the material to be published by the Fondo de Cultura Economica, an important editorial endeavor in Mexico. He preferred writers whose prose could help *shape public opinion*. About *Socialist Humanism*, for example, he writes his contributors that: "it is more important to have the book published soon in a cheap [paperback] edition, so that it can get into the hands of students and intellectuals" (Schaff_Adam_1963–04–21-to) – which ended up not happening (cf. AUD-1966e). He insisted on the importance that each paper in the book "appears in a form which has an optimum of clarity and does not discourage the reader by abstruseness which makes him feel this is not for him" (Dunayevskaya_Raya_1964–04–15-to). He was interested in having Paulo Freire's method for the alphabetization of peasants disseminated in an important Mexican newspaper: "it is an important issue, since the government functionaries read El Nacional, and the publication of this paper would be a very convenient form of calling the attention of these people to your method" (Freire_Paulo_1968–01–12-to). In a years-long letter exchange, he assists Adam Schaff with the US translation of *Marxism and the human individual* (cf. Schaff_Adam_1968–12–28-to). Mihailo Marković, Gajo Petrović and others all reach for his favor to circulate translations of their writings (cf. Petrovic_Gajo_1963–02–08-to). Raya Dunayevskaya holds a conversation for years in an attempt to have Fromm help her publish a German translation of *Philosophy and Revolution* (cf. Dunayevskaya_Raya_1974–05–30-by). He tries to involve publishers in releasing a translation of Danilo Dolci's poetry (cf. Sherwood_A_1979–06–14-by). Even Marcuse asks Fromm whether he would write a review of *One-Dimensional Man* (cf. Marcuse_Herbert_1963-12-08-by).

Fromm's connections to literary reviews and big newspapers were more important than his connections to scientific journals. Even in his own field, he says in 1975, "I have no connections with psychoanalytic journals except Contemporary Psychoanalysis, which is published in New York" (Dunayevskaya_Raya_1975-07-08-to). In matters political, he ponders the desirability of a venue for publication against how large or small the audience would be; and even when he writes scientific reviews (or is reviewed), reaching a large readership is clearly more important than peer recognition. He thanks Riesman for writing a review of *The anatomy of human destructiveness* "for the New Republic rather than more leisurely for a scholarly magazine, since without any doubt, for purposes of promotion a good review from you would be much more effective than publication in a widely read magazine" (Riesman_David_1973-11-02-to). Conversely: "when I am not writing [...] the [scientific] literature doesn't occupy me in special. I read much in the domains where I think I really have to learn" (u-1976:50).

We occasionally see Fromm taking the trouble of circulating pieces of news which didn't get enough attention in the USA (cf. Fromm, 1962e). To have the public *informed* about the relevant political facts would be for him no lesser goal than having them interpret such facts under a humanistic framework: "the only thing that one can do [...] is to give information, truth, and constructive ideas or to put it differently, to enlighten people, rather than to obscure them by meaningless talk or straight lies or unbaked ideas" (Coffin_Tristram_1974-10-25-to). Good quality, clear information would be a necessary condition for a democratic renaissance (cf. Fromm, 1976a). Hence his idea of an institution responsible for filtering and distributing facts as a supplement to the regular press, repeated in many of the proposals we saw before. As he puts it in a letter to Riesman: "a group of people who would make it their business to dig out these facts and send them around, even if they went only to many individuals, could do, in my opinion, something important" (Riesman_David_1967-08-19-to).

Style and form mattered; but Fromm was also worried with the problem of generating *credibility* for certain ideas and authors. Reputation was essential for him. "The general inefficiency to move things and to undertake anything with concerted effort and according to a plan, is, I believe, just as undermining to democratic structure as the distrust in the moral qualities of politicians", he tells Coffin in 1974 (Coffin_Tristram_1974-06-28-to). Discussing the possibility of encouraging a lowering in consumption and the standard of living in the US, he tells Riesman:

> The question is only who can present the case in such a convincing form as to create a new mood? [...] is there a sufficient bulk of genuinely responsible political and cultural figures who may disagree on many

questions of politics but who could make a convincing case for the need for an entirely new orientation and appeal to the powerful needs in man which often show in times of crisis, to give up his selfishness for the sake of a common vision.

(Riesman_David_1975-02-01-to)

Fromm wanted to make an impression for the consistency and plausibility of the socialist and pacifist causes. He sought to protect the public image of the institutions and intellectuals representing them. His *Socialist Humanism* should was to be a testimony "that the renaissance of Marxist humanism is a world-wide phenomenon" (Schaff_Adam_1962-05-08-to): "this is meant first of all to impress readers who are not specialists in Marxism, in the United States, with the vitality of humanist socialism" (Dunayevskaya_Raya_1964-04-15-to). Conversely, fighting the influence of political antagonists who were getting public attention became a central concern. We saw some such cases in Fromm's reaction to Marcuse, as well as his dislike of Robert Payne's biography of Marx. The situation recurs a number of other times. From the same principle follow his interventions against Ernest Jones' views on Ferenczi (cf. Fromm, 1958a), to which effect he articulates with Clara Thompson, Izette de Forest, and Michael Balint. He is later bothered with Alexander Solzhenitsyn, whom he mistrusts as a nationalist "reviving the cold war" (Maccoby_Michael_1975-07-23-to) – and who, most dangerously, "from the various reports in the press", "has great influence" (Coffin_Tristram_1975-07-21-to). He writes his opinion to the New York Times after consulting Noam Chomsky and some of his other political correspondents. Where there is no conflict around the content of a petition, there still recurs the question of calculating which would be the ideal public face of the endeavor (cf. Chomsky_Noam_1975-08-20-by).

***

Fromm went increasingly skeptical of the use of force as means for political change. "The older I get the more I doubt the value of violence, even in the best of causes", he writes Urquhart. "Its main effect is to arouse violence on the other side, and it all ends in brutality and blood-shed. I even doubt that things which cannot be accomplished without violence can be accomplished at all" (Urquhart_Clara_1964-07-02-to). Even non-violent extrapolations of the law should for him be carried only carefully: "breaking the law is too serious a business to be used in gestures" (Cousins_Norman_1968-01-15-to). Only towards the very end of Fromm's life does he clearly affirm the necessity of "a completely successful socialist revolution" (AUD-1978c), arriving at a "classless society" (Fromm, 1979a:135) – an expression timidly recurring through his later writings, but which was characteristic in his earlier, Freudian phase (cf. Fromm, 1931b). Fromm's formulation of the revolutionary character insisted that it should remain close to democratic forms and methods (cf. Fromm and Maccoby, 1970b). Correspondingly, in his actual political practice, he tried to achieve change through the available institutional means – or else, by producing new institutions within the frame of legality. His increasing skepticism regarding institutional interest was combined with a trust on the basic capacity to steer government, church, and other associations from within – activating their inner conflicts and strengthening progressive forces against conservative ones:

> Somebody may argue that by supporting morally the progressive movement in the church, one is actually helping the church to change, and thus to strengthen it. But I do not believe this argument is valid [...] by the closer contact of these elements of the church with humanists of other camps, theological thinking itself will be exposed to significant criticism.
> (Schaff_Adam_1963–10–05-to)

We know how much Fromm abhorred anti-intelllectualism in politics. This is because he saw tradition as a treasure of possibilities for social change, both reactionary and progressive (cf. Fromm, 1950a). His take on ancient Judaism is paradigmatic. He wrote *You shall be as gods* with the intention of demonstrating that the Old Testament "has one core, which is a revolutionary one" – "the liberation from social oppression" – "without, of course, ignoring that there are at the same time nationalistic, Xenophobic and reactionary elements which form the opposite trend to the progressive one in the Old Testament" (Schaff_Adam_1965–01–13-to; Schaff_Adam_1966–03–21-to). Even though the book was only published in 1966, Fromm speaks of it as "the first book I wrote" (AUD-1967a), since he had intended to publish on the Old Testament since the 1930s. As a passing, but crucial moment in the development of the book's concept, we discover he was worried with countering conservative religious movements in 1950s US. We have allusions to Fromm's rejection of business-minded religion in a number of smaller writings (cf. Fromm, 1950b). He writes Merton:

> if I follow the kind of religious propaganda, as it is made by Billy Graham, Rev. Peale, and I hope you do not mind if I mention also Bishop Sheen, I am shocked by the blending of alleged religious teaching with the profoundly irreligious spirit of the modern business world.
> (Merton_Thomas_1954–12–08-to)

Two years later, he reports to Angelica Balabanoff the intention of writing about "the really revolutionary ideas of the Old Testament in their psychological and philosophical significance for modern man, and with that to effect against the hypocritical 'Religious Revival' movement, which is popular in America" (Balabanoff_Angelica_1956–10–25-to).

Fromm saw the reactivation of moral sensibility as a condition of possibility for the long-term success of any radical proposals. Without acknowledging suffering and its causes, no real change would be possible: "there is only one hope to stop the wave of violence, and that is to become sensitive once more to all that is alive" (d-1990r-003-eng-type-01:7):

> it is very important to work precisely on that moral kernel which still exists […]. The day when more people awake to the fact that under the surface they are dissatisfied and not happy will be a day I believe in which important and constructive social changes can be made if there are people with the vision and practical sense to formulate them and to translate them into legislation.
> (Coffin_Tristram_1974–02–12-to)

Thus he recommended Lyndon Johnson that he take into account the "legitimate discontents" expressed by conservatives, bringing them into the framework of the democrats' policy:

> There is a widespread feeling among many people who are not necessarily reactionaries, who feel sincerely shocked by the results of a mass society, by the lack of individualism, by lack of any philosophy which is or substitutes for religion. From the standpoint of Johnson's campaign, it might be important if the President did not leave this kind of approach to Goldwater, but on the contrary, if he would make it his own. By that I mean that he should make one or two speeches saying that the country suffers from uniformity, materialism, from the loss of the virtues of individualism and initiative, and so on, and then continue: these dangers can not be overcome by returning to the past or by preaching hate, but by developing the resources of the country to such a point that we overcome the dangers and find our traditional virtues in new forms. Such speeches would do something to take away the issue as one of the great Goldwater assets.
> (Fromm, 1964k:16)

Fromm saw the objective basis for political majority formation in the existence of forms of suffering which are common to many social classes and political factions. His diagnosis of the political situation in the late 1960s USA was primarily class-centered (cf. d-1970f-000-eng-type-01), but at the same time he believed characterological suffering was increasingly patterned after middle-class life practice – "the most alienated class today are the intellectuals and the middle-class" (u-1976:38). The first condition for political success would be transforming common discontents into shared concerns. His affinity with the peace movements derived from his biophilic ethics, but also from the expectation that avoidance of war and the survival of the species should be topics with an utmost force for social generalization. Besides class solidarity, there is another element which is important for the working class as well as for many groups in the rest of the population, namely the question of war and peace [...] in the United States the real line is drawn not so much between different political views, as it is with regard to the problem of peace and disarmament.

(Balabanoff_Angelica_1962-01-21-to)

Fromm's immediate purpose (to be differentiated from his long-term goals) would be to form a humanistic *center*. He was interested in articulating the political discussion around basic humanistic premises, shared both by Left and Right, so that the political process could evolve from there on toward a more radical stance. Fromm is explicit that his strategy for the McCarthy campaign is not to articulate a Left camp, but rather a general humanistic camp: "I believe the Americans who want to put mankind back in the saddle are to be found beyond all traditional lines of ideologies – among conservatives, humanist Catholics and Protestants, humanist Marxists, and humanist liberals" (McCarthy_Eugene_1968-04-13-to). The greatest urgency lay in establishing consensus on a diagnosis of social problems – on which are the problems politics need to tackle: "voicing the questions, the essential concerns of the average American, and analyzing in the answers what the real facts are" (Coffin_Tristram_1974-06-28-to). Effecting the solutions various humanistic schools offered for political problems would only be possible after public discussion had reached an agreement on shared moral difficulties.

Considered in their capacity for sustaining *mobilization*, humanistic political formations imply a particular articulation between ethical and moral relatedness. The positive aspect appears at the same time as presupposed to the negative one and sublated in it. Humanistic alliances need to overcome the boundaries of particular political and religious communities, but cannot be formed without their previous existence. This resulted from our analysis of Fromm's political relations with humanists. Here we find a peculiar inversion: in the rationale of Fromm's public interventions, ethical commitment appears as presupposing shared moral concern. Formal agreement on the problems to be tackled becomes the way into experiencing common values; political alliances become the means for engendering political communities. This inversion corresponds to the main purpose in Fromm's public intellectualship: fostering political *organization* – bringing subjects into political relations in the first place. A good example is Roger Hagan, who collaborates with Fromm in the *Committee of Correspondence*, and writes David Riesman full of gratitude: "activism, and behind it commitment, and behind that an ethical base, are all new to me. They have come to me as a result of working with you and of reading Erich Fromm" (Hagan_Roger_1959-07-16-by).

The opposition between our initial results and these is of great practical consequences. Each corresponds to a different moment in the life of a political formation. Common ethical commitments appear as presupposed to shared moral concerns if we must explain the *origin* of humanist political formations. In this case, we follow the transposition of ethical relations onto a specifically political form: previously existing communities are gathered in a broader alliance. Conversely, shared moral concerns appear as presupposed to a common ethical orientation if we take the political formation as seeking its *reproduction* within each particular community. Then it acts as a socializing force: the political form induces the relations it once expressed.

5 The Powers that Be and the World to Come

Fromm's template for action is summarized in the assertion: "what matters really is to move the big powers to change their policy" (Warburg_Siegmund_G_1966–11–04-to). Of course, endeavors such as McCarthy's campaign targeted the hold of state power. Fromm's connections in the House of Representatives and the Senate pointed towards that as well. However, in the majority of cases we examined, his main goal was *influencing public opinion* at large. As he puts it to Fulbright: "As long as there is a public opinion that counts – and I am optimistic enough to believe that it still counts in America to some extent – what you have to say must be said" (Fulbright_J_W_1976–02–11-to). The end goal would be "to win over as many people as possible since the decision-makers in turn are influenced by the mood of the country" (Thomas_Norman_1962–10–17-to).

Once Fulbright loses the elections of 1974, Fromm suggests he might "exercise indirectly a great influence by articulating the concerns of reason and realistic humanism, which has an echo in large sectors of the American population, and thereby would have also an influence on governmental action" (Fulbright_J_W_1974–06–10-to). This brings us into another point of conflict in his political rationale. We have seen the tensions he faced in managing the opposition between a minority ethics and a majority political formation, between alliances based on moral reaction and the real course of power and interest. Now we can read back the instances we already know with another opposition in mind: that between state and civil society.

Fromm oscillated between treating each as the subject of political action. This stemmed of necessity from his choice of political means. The goal of establishing a democratic, humanist socialism envisions civil society – that is, really existing human beings in their social activity – as the ultimate object of concern. "To be an end in oneself, never a means to anybody else", is how Fromm defined his notion of justice (1941a:263). Rejecting the use of violence except in the most drastic circumstances, Fromm tried to achieve this purpose by steering the direction of presently existing political and religious institutions. However, having institutions as his purported means of influence demanded an inversion of means and ends in his short-term efforts. As the subject of transient interventions on particular political problems, civil society appeared only as the object of politicians' fears and considerations as they make their decisions. The population acts here mainly as a mass of voters, whose opinions should constrain the developments within the state – not yet as the final subject of politics, as a fulfilled socialism implies.

A good illustration of this conflict are Fromm's suggestions for using his sociopsychoanalytic method – otherwise intended as an instrument for science – for pragmatic purposes. One of the constants in his intellectual endeavor were "empirical investigations studying the forces underlying mass behavior" (Fromm, 1948b:147). Now these investigations should be put to political use. This was the case in his Mexican village study, since one of the purposes of the book was to research alternatives for economic development in rural Mexico (cf. Fromm and Maccoby, 1970b). But immediate political interests had no lesser priority. At one point he suggested to Abraham Muste that the experience acquired during political campaigns be reverted to the use of the peace movement: "we in the peace movement could use the knowledge gained for our propaganda [...] What I had in mind, really, is a psychological study of the views of people, their attitudes, and their deeper motivations underlying these attitudes" (Muste_Abraham_J_1962–10–17-to). He offered a similar suggestion to McCarthy: "I believe it would be helpful it during the campaign a social psychological study was made which tried to find out which ideas are close to the heart of the voters" (McCarthy_Eugene_1968–08–12-to). Michael Maccoby (1969) did develop some of the statistical studies Fromm (1964a) proposed on the distribution of biophilous and necrophilous trends among different political fractions. He wished to strengthen his predictive power in politics, and to refine his instruments for moral sensitization. First and foremost, they would be of interest for the state, or those aspiring to its control.

Fromm's political methods are even farther removed from civil society when it comes to international relations. Even though most of his efforts were targeted at influencing US politics, this did not mean he took this society as his ultimate object of concern. Fromm understood US social and psychological structures as the most developed expressions of tendencies ubiquitous to contemporary capitalism. "All the countries in Europe and America develop themselves in the same direction", he writes in 1956, "and the example of the United States shows the problems which other countries are already confronting, and which they will face in greater measure in a short time" (1956d:5). He seems to have believed so to the end of his life: "the development that is valid for America imposes itself slowly in Western Europe as a consequence of our industrial mode of production" (u-1976:38). Not that he didn't see the importance of local variance against global trends:

each Latin American country approaches its own problems, consequence of its particular socioeconomic and political structures. These specific traits mix themselves with the general traits of capitalism, and it is this mixture, particular to each country, that needs to be studied to arrive at a complete understanding of the social and psychological problems of each Latin American country.

(1956d:6)

Both because of the immanent tendencies of capitalism, and the dominance the US had in world politics, Fromm thought influencing national politics represented a shortcut for intervening over the globe. Disputing US public opinion meant for him disputing a part of the world's fate.

An illustration of this principle is a modality of action we have not mentioned yet, but recurs throughout Fromm's life: his trying to rescue political prisoners and vulnerable citizens. The better documented case here is a years-long attempt at freeing Heinz Brandt from imprisonment in East Germany – to which effect he articulated with Peter Benenson, Bertrand Russell, Urquhart and others, eventually succeeding in Brandt's liberation (cf. Russell_Bertrand_1966–08–19-to). Since this endeavor is already well discussed in the literature (cf. Friedman, 2013), I will emphasize only its similarities with other, lesser known cases. In trying to secure the liberation of political targets, Fromm followed an identical rationale, and used the same resources as in other political interventions – public opinion and the prestige of intellectuals and leaders.

In Brandt's case, this strategy is embodied in the intention to publish a book about the man to arouse public attention and put pressure on the DDR government (cf. Urquhart_Clara_1963–11–01-by). The same happens when Fromm is worried about the persecution of Dom Hélder Câmara in Brazil. He writes McCarthy in December 1969, a year after the elections, that Ivan Illich "has received a list of 11 people, with his name as the last, with the announcement that they would all be killed in the order of the list. The first two (two priests) were found tortured to death, and there is a great probability that the rest, including Dom Hélder, will follow". Important for us is Fromm's conclusion:

> I am entirely convinced of his [Illich's] idea that the only thing one can do in an attempt to save Dom Hélder's life, is to make him as well known as possible in the United States, because that might somewhat impress the Brazilian dictators.
>
> (McCarthy_Eugene_1969–12–29-to)

To this effect, Fromm invited McCarthy to write a preface for a publication of Hélder Câmara's writings in English. Ruth Anshen had originally commissioned Fromm himself for the task, but after discussing the situation with Illich, he decided to transfer this responsibility to McCarthy – a Catholic of public relevance –, in the expectation that this would have greater public effect. Anshen disagreed with him. The discussion extended itself over months, and the book was eventually published with a text by McCarthy (cf. Illich_Ivan_1970–09–08-to). As for the Arch-Bishop, he survived until 1999.

Hélder Câmara's is a particularly developed instance of a behavior Fromm displays in yet other cases. Still in 1970 he discusses with Illich the possibility of rescuing "a Brazilian Left-wing journalist who has been in prison for some time, is now released and under police surveillance and in danger of being re-arrested at any moment" (Illich_Ivan_1970–09–08-to). He participates also in much less urgent situations, trying to find job positions for other intellectuals and relatives of his friends. These cases need not distract us from what the Brandt and Dom Hélder stories share: namely, the attempt to help the destiny even of singular political agents indirectly, from abroad, by means of influencing US public opinion.

Here lies the last essential tension in Fromm's political program: that between the national and the international scopes of action. The risk of atomic war, as well as conflicts such as those in Palestine and Vietnam, mobilized his greatest efforts. Fromm gave utmost primacy to the promotion of peace and survival over other political questions. As a consequence, he prioritized international relations over domestic ones. This required a subsumption of capitalist production to broader political interests: a peaceful status quo could be reached "only if we subordinate private business interests to a total policy of peace and freedom" (d-19901-003-eng-type-01:4). But it also meant a subordination of domestic class struggle and revolution to foreign affairs.

Fromm's style of reasoning in international matters was tailored around the relation between heads of state. National class and status conflicts were subsumed to broader constellations of forces. Civil society was considered not in terms of its inner social differentiation, but in terms of its capacity to support the rise and fall of governments: "if a government is defeated too often it will fall. That holds true by and large for democratic governments as well as for the Russian government. So Kruschev did fall" (Fulbright_J_W_1970–07–18-to). His position regarding the removal of troops in Vietnam is a case in point. While in terms of principle he would have been favorable to the immediate cessation of the bloodshed, in strategic terms, he thought this would not resolve the geopolitical problems at stake:

> the Peace Movement made a great mistake in talking about withdrawal of our troops [...]. One of the things which attracted me particularly to McCarthy was that he always talked about the political solution in Saigon as the decisive point and not about the withdrawal of our troops.
> (Maccoby_Michael_1972–07–04-to)

Avoiding war was so central to Fromm's political calculations that he was eventually brought into conflict with his remaining political stances. In particular defense issues, Fromm was a pacifist. He argued for unilateral atomic disarmament, later bilateral and universal disarmament, as a means for avoiding escalation (cf. Fromm, 1960c, 1975a):

> The continuation of the arms race is the necessary accompaniment of the continuation of the cold war. The arms race will most likely lead by accident, misunderstanding or folly to the outbreak of nuclear war, which will mean, at the very best, the end of civilization as we cherish it in the West. Hence universal, inspected disarmament must be striven for, as long as it is still time.
> (d-1990j-003-eng-type-01:10)

However, the best short-term scenario he could think of was not based on extinguishing US and USSR hegemony over the globe, but its consolidation in a tolerant conservative alliance – even if this came to the detriment of national progressive politics:

> I dislike a conservative police state like the Soviet Union for its contempt for the spirit, and human reason. I must confess I also do not like the Soviet-American understanding, because it is a deeply reactionary alliance [...]. But in spite of this, I am deeply convinced that when the life of humanity is at stake there is almost nothing that justifies risking the holocaust.
> (Fulbright_J_W_1973–11–19-to)

"The aim must be to end the cold war by mutual concession in secondary points which do not violate the vital interests of either side" (d-1990q-003-eng-type-01:7), he thought. Fromm tried to persuade politicians that fear of USSR expansionism was unwarranted; that revolutionary rhetoric had no substance in its actual foreign policy, working only as ideological cement for inward social relations. The USSR would actually be interested in avoiding an escalation of conflicts (cf. Fromm, 1961a; 1961g). Ever a socialist, Fromm wanted to achieve a "stateless society" (1960b:61) – but he favored peace under a conservative nation-state to a revolution risking nuclear catastrophe. The risk was too high. He did so only reluctantly, but nonetheless maintained that this would have been the best compromise for the times:

> An agreement between the United States and Russia will constitute an agreement of two conservative powers which one might like as little as one would have liked an alliance between the United States and Czarist Russia. But considering the fact that the overriding concern of man today is the avoidance of war, a Russian-American understanding is a

necessity, because it is the condition for the ending of the arms race, and hence for ending the probability of a nuclear holocaust. Such an understanding leaves also the hope that the uncommitted nations, especially the former colonial nations, will adopt forms of democratic socialism which put them neither in the Russian or Chinese camp, nor in the camp of the United States or her allies.

(d-1961h-eng-type-01:3)

Working within the institutional framework of his time, Fromm took the existence of the state for granted, and conceived a realistic peace policy as one limiting territorial expansionism. He was much more concerned with the possibility of a renewed German expansionism than with the USSR (cf. Fromm, 1966h). Commenting on the political tensions since Berlin's division between the Western and the Eastern blocs, he wrote:

there is no other way to ending the arms race, than by American-British recognition of the Oder-Neisse line, as part of a peace treaty with East and West Germany which stabilizes the *status quo*. This is regrettable for all genuine friends of freedom, yet any other course leads to the destruction, not to the liberation of Central Europe.

(d-1990o-003-eng-type-02:12)

Fromm's (1963g) theory acknowledged the domestic grounds for war and expansionism. He repeatedly emphasized their socioeconomic motivations, and based his appreciation of Germany on the same principles:

There are no real conflicts between the Soviet Union and the Western bloc (aside from the mutual suspicions arising from the arms race), except the German problem. Germany is the latest of the highly industrialized European countries, eager for territorial expansion, in search of raw materials and markets. This expansionist tendency led to the First and to the Second World Wars. It is a mistake to believe that the militarism of the Kaiser, or the evilness of Hitler were the "causes" for these wars. Both the Kaiser and Hitler were front men for the explosive mixture of German industrial strength plus military skill. The same forces still exist in Germany, sparked by an increasing nationalist feeling about the "stolen territories" and unification, this time fronted by democratic politicians.

(d-1990j-003-eng-type-01:8)

Political power had nonetheless a certain ascent in Fromm's reasoning, in comparison to capital. He thought "the struggle for control of foreign territories is primarily one caused by the fear of losing one's ear power, if the opponent gains control of other territories". He didn't consistently translate territorial conquest in its economic interest, reducing it sometimes to an interest in maintaining power prestige. As a consequence, he thought "there are no basic conflicts of economic interests between the two blocs [...]. The only real conflict exists with regard to the fear of each bloc: that the other will bring new territories under its control" (d-1990q-003-eng-type-01:4).

This vacillation on the economic function of expansionism had important consequences for Fromm's calculations. He overestimated the degree of autonomy foreign policy could achieve in a government's decisions. In some cases, as that of Germany, he sought to curb national economic interest by fostering a global balance of forces turning military action unlikely. Fromm applied the same line of reasoning to China, which he saw as likewise expansionist:

> It is a fallacy to believe that our alternative today is between Soviet Communism, and American Capitalism. The real conflict lies today between the expansionist countries under the leadership of China, and the conservative countries represented by the United States and the Soviet Union. However, if an agreement is reached between the United States and the Soviet Union, and furthermore, if China is given a seat in the United Nations and becomes a part of a general disarmament pact, there is reasonable hope that the aggressive wing of the Chinese Communists will be superseded by the more peace-minded one – because of the fact that a world without armament will offer China economic possibilities which make military expansion unnecessary.
>
> (d-1961h-eng-type-01:5)

Here we see again the same principle as before: intervention on US foreign policy is an instrument for affecting power relations elsewhere. Only now the object is the balance of political forces within other states. Fromm wanted to induce a geopolitical constellation allowing the rise of pacific fractions of the dominant classes, as illustrated by these comments on the German question:

> [by the] recognition of the present frontiers, we shall bring about the downfall of Khrushchev; the reactionary forces in Russia will accuse him of having tried to arrive at a detente with the United States and having failed. On the other hand, if the Soviet Union should shift to a tougher policy, the "tough" forces here will accuse the Administration of having been unrealistic and soft, of having permitted itself to be deceived by Khrushchev. Such a development may lead to the ascendancy of the war-minded forces in the Soviet Union and of the Goldwater forces in the United States. What this would mean for the chances for peace hardly needs to be spelled out.
>
> (Fromm, 1964h:61)

***

Fromm (1960b) had no nostalgia for colonialism. He tells Fulbright:

> if one compared the suffering which one of the great human achievements, the modern industrial world, has caused to colonial people, and up to not so long ago to workers, they certainly were not less than what the Chinese did and probably much more.
>
> (Fulbright_J_W_1974–12–17-to)

The best representative of his stance in this respect is his criticism of Israel (cf. Jacobs, 2015). For years, he had been in disagreement with the very premises for the existence of Israel as a state: "they founded their state on the property of former inhabitants of the land to which they had neither a legal nor a moral right" (Bottomore_Tom_B_1967–07–12-to). He was deeply impressed by Israeli violence through the decades – "Israeli terrorism against British and Arabs in the years 47 and later, was of such dimensions that it surpasses the Arab terror" – and thought "the Palestinian demand for a state of their own" was "legitimate" (Riesman_David_1975–01–08-to). In the course of the 1970s, he came to see the nature of violence against Arabs as racist and colonialist. "The resolution calling Israel a racist state has very good grounds" (Fulbright_J_W_1976–02–11-to), he tells Fulbright:

> one of the great historical facts of this period is [...] the approaching end of patriarchal superiority over women, and the end of the white hegemony over the rest of the world. Israel has taken the function of being a last bastion for colonialism at the very moment when colonialism is folding up.
>
> (Fulbright_J_W_1974–12–17-to)

He was moreover deeply distrustful of Israel's foreign conduct: he thought "the main ace the Israelis have is the continuation and increase of the cold war" (Fulbright_J_W_1970–07–18-to).

Fromm welcomed the colonial revolutions as "the most fundamental fact in this century". He thought they need not be carried in the form of "violence, wars and bloody revolutions", but could be done as "planned economic developments with the help of the rich nations" (d-1990m-003-eng-type-01:2). US foreign policy was brought into question again. Fromm wanted the US government to support colonial revolutions of a democratic kind, including socialist ones. He could offer no argument within the interests of the state, much less of domestic capital with international aspirations, except an ideological one – the preoccupation with "the battle for men's minds". Indeed, he counted on the victory of socialism in the ex-colonies, should they be left to their own self-determination:

> We must accept the fact that the underdeveloped countries will not choose between Communism and capitalism, but only between various types of socialism: the Russian totalitarian managerialism; the Chinese anti-individualistic total mass Communism; and various forms of decentralizing, humanistic socialism, as presented in a wide gamut ranging from Yugoslavia to Burma and India.
>
> (Fromm, 1961i:12)

He was left with the argument that endorsing the self-determination of ex-colonies would be an instrument to avoid that the Chinese model of revolution might become hegemonic and prompt violence – as he thought was China's interest:

> What is really necessary if we are to prevent China from gaining the sympathy of the whole colonial world is that we stop supporting reactionary regimes all over the world, that we support regimes that represent the economic and social aspirations of the majority of their populations (even if they are socialist regimes), and that we cooperate with the Soviet Union in the attempt to channel the great colonial revolution which cannot be stopped into peaceful and constructive paths.
>
> (Fromm, 1965k:13)

Besides containing war, Fromm wanted to reach international conditions allowing greater independence for the countries adopting socialist models he endorsed, like Yugoslavia. "American support for neutralist, democratic socialist regimes among the former colonial nations; support for the Tito, Nasser, Nehru third force" would be ideal (d-1990j-003-eng-type-01:11). "As soon as the cold war would end", he thought – "and that means as soon as both sides recognize the existing *status quo* [...] Russia would be in a position both economically and politically to permit a greater degree of liberalization in the satellite countries" (d-1990k-003-eng-type-02:4–5). Here again, he tried to achieve global influence through American politics. Acceptance of neutrality would provide the conditions for a development of democratic socialism, and at the same time diminish the risk of war:

> An economically strong democratic New Europe, with no ambitions to hold on to colonial possessions, or to regain lost territories, can become one of the strongest forces for peace and democracy. An alliance between the United States and such a democratic New Europe could welcome a neutral bloc of socialist-oriented nations, as represented today by the group led by Tito, Nehru and Nasser.
>
> (d-1990o-003-eng-type-02:18)

The development of the cold war didn't favor Fromm's expectations. He faced a strong conflict between the internal, political conditions for the emergence of democratic socialisms, and the geopolitical conditions necessary for their economic survival. Fromm's political line was torn between the pragmatic necessities of risk management, and the hope that humanism would gather enough momentum in each country to allow a self-determined socialist transition. He could not reconcile pacifism and socialism. His works and engagement show him running through the most opposite lines and parties, torn by the necessity of bringing together what political reality sets apart, and setting apart what politics bring together.

Bibliography

Primary sources

Fromm's correspondence

Adams_James_Luther_1958–1904–25-by: James Luther Adams to Fromm, April 25th, 1958
Adams_James_Luther_1966–1910–14-to: Fromm to Adams, October 14th, 1966
Adams_James_Luther_1976–1912–14-to: Fromm to Adams, December 14th, 1976
Adams_James_Luther_1978–1904–28-to: Fromm to Adams, April 28th, 1978
Auer_Alfons_1974–1904–01-to: Fromm to Alfons Auer, April 1st, 1974
Balabanoff_Angelica_1956–1910–25-to: Fromm to Angelica Balabanoff, October 25th, 1956
Balabanoff_Angelica_1962–1901–21-to: Fromm to Balabanoff, January 21st, 1962
Bell_Daniel_1955–1904–22-to: Fromm to Daniel Bell, April 22nd, 1955
Bottomore_Tom_B_1963–1909–28-to: Fromm to Tom Bottomore, September 28th, 1963
Bottomore_Tom_B_1964–1901–20-to: Fromm to Bottomore, January 20th, 1964
Bottomore_Tom_B_1967–1907–12-to: Fromm to Bottomore, July 12th, 1967
Bowles_Chester_1960–1906–21-by: Chester Bowles to Fromm, June 21st, 1960
Chambers_Bette_1973–1905–10-to: Fromm to Bette Chambers, May 10th, 1973
Chomsky_Noam_1975–1908–20-by: Noam Chomsky to Fromm, August 20th, 1975
Coffin_Tristram_1974–1902–01-to: Fromm to Tristram Coffin, February 1st, 1974
Coffin_Tristram_1974–1902–12-to: Fromm to Coffin, February 12th, 1974
Coffin_Tristram_1974–1903–26-to: Fromm to Coffin, March 26th, 1974
Coffin_Tristram_1974–1906–28-to: Fromm to Coffin, June 28th, 1974
Coffin_Tristram_1974–1910–25-to: Fromm to Coffin, October 25th, 1974
Coffin_Tristram_1975–1907–21-to: Fromm to Coffin, July 21st, 1975
Cousins_Norman_1968–1901–15-to: Fromm to Norman Cousins, January 15th, 1968
Dunayevskaya_Raya_1964–1904–15-to: Fromm to Dunayevskaya, April 15th, 1964
Dunayevskaya_Raya_1974–1905–30-by: Dunayevskaya to Fromm, May 30th, 1974
Dunayevskaya_Raya_1975–1907–08-to: Fromm to Dunayevskaya, July 8th, 1975
Dunayevskaya_Raya_1976–1910–02-to: Fromm to Dunayevskaya, October 2nd, 1976
Freire_Paulo_1968–1901–12-to: Fromm to Paulo Freire, January 12th, 1968
Fulbright_J_W_1970–1907–18-to: Fromm to Fulbright, July 18th, 1970

Fulbright_J_W_1973–1909–02-to: Fromm to Fulbright, September 2nd, 1973
Fulbright_J_W_1973–1911–19-to: Fromm to Fulbright, November 19th, 1973
Fulbright_J_W_1974–1906–10-to: Fromm to Fulbright, June 10th, 1974
Fulbright_J_W_1974–1909–07-to: Fromm to Fulbright, September 7th, 1974
Fulbright_J_W_1974–1912–17-to: Fromm to Fulbright, December 17th, 1974
Fulbright_J_W_1976–1902–11-to: Fromm to Fulbright, February 11th, 1976
Goss-Mayr_Hildegard_1963–1911–28-to: Fromm to Hildegard Goss-Mayr, November 28th, 1963
Granfil_Toma_1974–1911–15-to: Fromm to Toma Granfil, November 15th, 1974
Gulotta_Larry_1969–1908–22-to: Fromm to Larry Gulotta, August 22nd, 1969
Hagan_Roger_1959–1907–16-by: Roger Hagan to David Riesman, July 16th, 1959
Hassler_Alfred_1971–1907–15-by: Alfred Hassler to Fromm, July 15th, 1971
Illich_Ivan_1970–1909–08-to: Fromm to Ivan Illich, September 8th, 1970
Johnson_William_1968–1909–04-to: Fromm to William Johnson, September 4th, 1968
Johnson_William_1968–1910–08-by: Johnson to Fromm, October 8th, 1968
Keys_Donald_F_1966–1907–28-by: Donald Keys to Fromm, July 28th, 1966
Lens_Sidney_1964–1902–06-to: Fromm to Sidney Lens, February 6th, 1964
Maccoby_Michael_1972–1907–04-to: Fromm to Michael Maccoby, July 4th, 1972
Maccoby_Michael_1975–1907–23-to: Fromm to Maccoby, July 23rd, 1975
Macdonald_Nancy_1973–1912–29-to: Fromm to Nancy MacDonald, December 29th, 1973
Marcuse_Herbert_1963–1912–08-by: Herbert Marcuse to Fromm, December 8th, 1963
Markovic_Mihailo_1975–1907–16-to: Fromm to Mihailo Marković, July 16th, 1975
McCarthy_Eugene_1968–1904–13-to: Fromm to Eugene McCarthy, April 13th, 1968
McCarthy_Eugene_1968–1908–12-to: Fromm to McCarthy, August 12th, 1968
McCarthy_Eugene_1969–1912–29-to: Fromm to McCarthy, December 29th, 1969
Merton_Thomas_1954–1910–02-by: Thomas Merton to Fromm, October 2nd, 1954
Merton_Thomas_1954–1910–27-to: Fromm to Merton, October 27th, 1954
Merton_Thomas_1954–1912–08-to: Fromm to Merton, December 8th, 1954
Merton_Thomas_1955–1903–18-by: Merton to Fromm, March 18th, 1955
Merton_Thomas_1955–1904–13-to: Fromm to Merton, April 13th, 1955
Merton_Thomas_1960–1911–03-to: Fromm to Merton, November 3rd, 1960
Merton_Thomas_1961–1911–23-to: Fromm to Merton, November 23rd, 1961
Merton_Thomas_1962–1901–30-to: Fromm to Merton, January 30th, 1962
Merton_Thomas_1962–1902–16-by: Merton to Fromm, February 16th, 1962
Mumford_Lewis_1955–1905–14-to: Fromm to Lewis Mumford, May 14th, 1955
Mumford_Lewis_1960–1908–16-to: Fromm to Mumford, August 16th, 1960
Mumford_Lewis_1968–1912–08-to: Fromm to Mumford, December 8th, 1968
Mumford_Lewis_1969–1901–23-to: Fromm to Mumford, January 23rd, 1969
Mumford_Lewis_1973–1912–05-to: Fromm to Mumford, December 5th, 1973
Muste_Abraham_J_1962–1910–17-to: Fromm to Abraham Muste, October 17th, 1962
Muste_Abraham_J_1965–1908–31-to: Fromm to Muste, August 31st, 1965
Muste_Abraham_J_1965–1910–21-to: Fromm to Muste, October 21st, 1965
Muste_Abraham_J_1966–1911–21-to: Fromm to Muste, November 21st, 1966
Pauling_Linus_1961–1902–23-to: Fromm to Linus Pauling, February 23rd, 1961
Petrovic_Gajo_1963–1902–08-to: Fromm to Gajo Petrović in February 8th, 1963
Polanyi_Karl_1960–1904–14-to: Fromm to Karl Polanyi, April 14th, 1960
Polanyi_Karl_1960–1911–08-by: Fromm to Polanyi, November 8th, 1960

Riesman_David_1967–1908–19-to: Fromm to Riesman, August 19th, 1967
Riesman_David_1968–1907–05-to: Fromm to Riesman, July 5th, 1968
Riesman_David_1973–1911–02-to: Fromm to Riesman, November 2nd, 1973
Riesman_David_1975–1901–08-to: Fromm to Riesman, January 8th, 1975
Riesman_David_1975–1902–01-to: Fromm to Riesman, February 1st, 1975
Riesman_David_1975–1903–05-to: Fromm to Riesman, March 5th, 1975
Riesman_David_1976–1902–12-to: Fromm to Riesman, February 12th, 1976
Russell_Bertrand_1966–1908–19-to: Fromm to Russell, August 19th, 1966
Russell_Bertrand_1966–1910–08-to: Fromm to Russell, October 8th, 1966
Schaff_Adam_1962–1905–08-to: Fromm to Adam Schaff, May 8th, 1962
Schaff_Adam_1963–1904–21-to: Fromm to Schaff, April 21st, 1963
Schaff_Adam_1963–1910–05-to: Fromm to Schaff, October 5th, 1963
Schaff_Adam_1963–1911–08-to: Fromm to Schaff, November 8th, 1963
Schaff_Adam_1964–1903–09-to: Fromm to Schaff, March 9th, 1964
Schaff_Adam_1965–1901–13-to: Fromm to Schaff, January 13th, 1965
Schaff_Adam_1966–1903–21-to: Fromm to Schaff, March 21st, 1966
Schaff_Adam_1966–1908–30-to: Fromm to Schaff, August 30th, 1966
Schaff_Adam_1966–1912–30-to: Fromm to Schaff, December 30th, 1966
Schaff_Adam_1967–1901–10-to: Fromm to Schaff, January 10th, 1967
Schaff_Adam_1968–1912–28-to: Fromm to Schaff, December 28th, 1968
Schaff_Adam_1971–1901–25-to: Fromm to Schaff, January 1st, 1971
Sherwood_A_1979–1906–14-by: Fred Sherwood to Fromm, June 14th, 1979
Siteman_Stephen_1955–1905–26-to: Fromm to Siteman, May 26th, 1955
Thomas_Norman_1962–1910–17-to: Fromm to Norman Thomas, October 17th. 1962
Thomas_Norman_1963–1908–12-to: Fromm to Thomas, August 12th, 1963
Urquhart_Clara_1962–1901–05-to: Fromm to Clara Urquhart, January 5th, 1962
Urquhart_Clara_1962–1909–29-to: Fromm to Urquhart, September 29th, 1962
Urquhart_Clara_1963–1910–01-to: Fromm to Urquhart, October 1st, 1963
Urquhart_Clara_1963–1911–01-by: Urquhart to Fromm, November 1st, 1963
Urquhart_Clara_1964–1906–19-by: Urquhart to Fromm, June 19th, 1964
Urquhart_Clara_1964–1907–02-to: Fromm to Urquhart, July 2nd, 1964
Urquhart_Clara_1964–1911–05-to: Fromm to Urquhart, November 5th, 1964
Urquhart_Clara_1966–1909–12-to: Fromm to Urquhart, September 12th, 1966
Urquhart_Clara_1966–1912–29-by: Fromm to Urquhart, December 29th, 1966
Urquhart_Clara_1967–1905–28-by: Urquhart to Warburg, May 28th, 1967
Urquhart_Clara_1967–1906–17-to: Fromm to Urquhart, June 17th, 1967
Urquhart_Clara_1967–1907–11-by: Urquhart to Peter Benenson, July 11th, 1967
Urquhart_Clara_1967–1907–12-to: Fromm to Urquhart, July 12th, 1967
Urquhart_Clara_1969–1908–04-to: Fromm to Urquhart, August 4th, 1969
Urquhart_Clara_1970–1905–25-to: Fromm to Urquhart, May 25th, 1970
Urquhart_Clara_1972–1903–21-to: Fromm to Urquhart, March 21st, 1972
Wald_George_1970–1901–22-to: Fromm to George Wald, January 22nd, 1970
Warburg_Siegmund_G_1966–1910–31-by: Siegmund Warburg to Fromm, October 31st, 1966
Warburg_Siegmund_G_1966–1911–04-to: Fromm to Warburg, November 4th, 1966
Wittes_Sarah_Sue_1968–1911–18-by: Sarah Sue Wittes to Fromm, Nov. 18th, 1968
Wittes_Sarah_Sue_1968–1912–01-to: Fromm to Wittes, December 1st, 1968
Wittes_Sarah_Sue_1970–1903–09-to: Fromm to Wittes, March 9th, 1970

Wittes_Sarah_Sue_1970-1904-09-to: Fromm to Wittes, April 9th, 1970

Unpublished texts, lectures, interviews by Fromm

u-1968b: "*Conferencias clínicas del Dr. Fromm*". Instituto Mexicano de Psicoanálisis. February to March, 1968. Written transcription.

u-1972: "*Erich Fromm Quote – After Watergate*". Unknown whether and where this quote was published.

u-1974: "*Anti-autoritäre Bewegung, die Maschine als Mutter und die Suche nach politischen Alternativen*". Transcript of a conversation between Fromm and the theologian Hans-Eckerhard Bahr.

u-1976: "*Seminar zu Theorie und Praxis der psychoanalytischen Therapie mit deutschen Psychoanalytikern der DGP aus München (Professor Riemann)*". Transcript of a seminar on psychoanalytic theory and practice in Locarno, 1976.

Drafts, typescripts and study materials by Fromm

d-1961h-eng-type-01: "*Russia, Germany, China: remarks on foreign policy*". Printed and distributed as a manuscript.

d-1970f-000-eng-type-01: typescript for "*The significance of the theory of mother right for today*".

d-1990j-003-eng-type-01: "*Remarks on a realistic foreign policy*".

d-1990k-003-eng-type-02: "*Khrushchev and the cold war*". Unknown whether this paper was published in English.

d-1990l-003-eng-type-01: "*Is there an alternative to the policy of force?*" First published under this title as typescript 1961 in the Committee of Correspondence – Newsletter.

d-1990m-003-eng-type-01: "*The United States' global responsibility*". Written as typescript entitled "Memo on Foreign Policy" in 1965.

d-1990o-003-eng-type-02: "The future of the New Europe". The typescript, written in 1961, was maybe a draft for a chapter in Erich Fromm's *May Man Prevail?*.

d-1990q-003-eng-type-01: "*Alternatives to Nuclear War*". Typescript of a lecture given in 1961.

d-1990r-003-eng-type-01: "*The war in Vietnam and the brutalization of man*". Fromm's speech for the SANE Garden Rally on December 8th, 1966.

d-1990u-003-eng-type-01. "*Citizens for reason*". Drafts written in 1955.

Audio and video recordings

AUD-1963b: "*The psychological roots of war and destruction, part 3*". Pacific Radio (?). Recorded at 92nd Street YMCA, New York City, 18 April 1963; Broadcast: WBAI, 20 October, 1963.

AUD-1962g: "*Democracy*". Feature of the Series "Erich Fromm on Sigmund Freud" at the Pacific Radio, no. 6. Recorded at San Bernardino by John Handner. Broadcast: KPFA, 7 Decemeber, 1962.

AUD-1962i: "*A New Humanism as a Condition for the One World*". Pacific Radio (?) – Lecture given at April 4th, 1962 at Sherwood Hall in La Jolla, California.

AUD-1965b: "*Presentacione on a social psychoanalytical topic*". Presumably given on October 29, 1965 in Mexico City.

AUD-1965c: "*Psychology of nationalism*". Pacific Radio (?) – Lecture introduced by Dan Lyles, given at the American River Junior College, Sacramento, 12 October, 1964; broadcasted by KPFA, February 1st, 1965.

AUD-1966e: "*Discussion to the lecture: The renaissance of humanist socialism*". Pacific Radio (?) – Los Angeles, June 1st, 1966.

AUD-1967a: "Interview of Richard Hefner with Erich Fromm on You Shall Be as Gods". Pacific Radio – Recorded April 1st, 1967. Broadcast: WBAI, January 1st, 1969.

AUD-1977g: "*Fromm is recording privately his thoughts on existentialism*".

AUD-1978a: "*Erich Fromm: Interview with Gérard Khoury – part 1*". Part one of an interview given to Gérard Khoury on December 2nd, 1978 and in February, 1979 in Locarno.

AUD-1978c: "*Erich Fromm: Interview with Gérard Khoury – part 3*". Part three of an interview given to Gérard Khoury on December 2nd, 1978 and in February, 1979 in Locarno.

AUD-1980e: "*Mut zum Sein*". TV interview with Guido Ferrari von RTSI Lugano, 08.03.1980 in Locarno.

AUD-1980g: "*Antworten von Fromm auf Fragen von Boris Luban Plozza*". unpublished interview.

VID-1975g: "*Entwürfe für eine Gesellschaft von morgen*". TV discussion broadcasted by the Südwestfunks Baden-Baden. Symposium on Fromm's 75th birthday, "Psychoanalytische Theorie und Therapie".

VID-1979b: "Interview von Heiner Gautschy mit Erich Fromm". DRS – For the Talkshow series "Unter uns gesagt", recorded in Hotel Adler-Post in Hinterzarten; broadcasted on September 7th, 1979.

Published references

Fromm, Erich. Politik und Psychoanalyse. *Gesamtausgabe, Band I*. Stuttgart: Deutsche Verlags-Anstalt, [1931b]/1999.

Fromm, Erich. *Escape from freedom*. New York: Henry Holt & Company, [1941a]/1994.

Fromm, Erich. Sexuality and character. *Love, sexuality, and matriarchy*. New York: Fromm International Edition, [1948b]/1997.

Fromm, Erich. *Psychoanalysis and religion*. New York: Bantam Books, [1950a]/1967.

Fromm, Erich. Dianetics – for seekers of prefabricated happiness. *Fromm Forum*: 2:7–8, [1950b]/1998.

Fromm, Erich. *The sane society*. New York: Henry Holt & Company, [1955a]/1990.

Fromm, Erich. Palabras a la édicion española. in: *Psicoanálisis de la sociedad contemporanea*. México: Fondo de Cultura Económica, 1956d.

Fromm, Erich. Psychoanalysis – science or party line? *The dogma of Christ*. New York: Holt, Reinhart and Winston, [1958a]/1963.

Fromm, Erich. Let man prevail: a socialist manifesto and program. *On disobedience*. New York: Harper Perennial, [1960b]/2010.

Fromm, Erich. The case for unilateral disarmament. *Dedalus*: 89(4):1015–1028, 1960c.

Fromm, Erich. *May man prevail?* New York: Doubleday & Company, Inc., 1961a.

Fromm, Erich. Communism and co-existence. The nature of the totalitarian threat today: an analysis of the 81. Party Manifesto. *Socialist Call*: 28(4):3–11, 1961g.

Fromm, Erich. Paranoid or hysterical thinking. *The New Leader* (5/29/1961):10–12, 1961i.

Fromm, Erich. Dissenting Voices in Germany. *Council of Correspondence* (07/1962):16–19, 1962e.

Fromm, Erich. The revolutionary character. *The dogma of Christ*. New York: Holt, Rinehart and Winston, [1963b]/1992.

Fromm, Erich. *War within man*. Philadelphia: American Philadelphia Service Committee, 1963g.

Fromm, Erich. United States foreign policy after Cuba. *Council of Correspondence Newsletter* 23:8–21, 1963h.

Fromm, Erich. *The heart of man*. New York: Harper and Row, 1964a.

Fromm, Erich. Foreign policy after the test ban. *The Correspondent*: 30:58–62, 1964h.

Fromm, Erich. Detente Through Firmness. *The Correspondent*: 31:6–9, 1964i.

Fromm, Erich. Legitimate Discontents. *The Correspondent*: 32:16, 1964k.

Fromm, Erich. Are we sane? in: W. D. Nunokawa (ed.), *Readings in abnormal psychology*. Chicago: Scott and Foresman, 1965j.

Fromm, Erich. Summary for the opposition. *The Correspondent*: 34:13, 1965k.

Fromm, Erich. *You shall be as gods*. New York: Fawcett Premier, [1966a]/1983.

Fromm, Erich. Is Germany on the march again? *War/Peace Report*: 6:3f, 1966h.

Fromm, Erich. Memories of Dr. D.T. Suzuki. *The Eastern Buddhist*: II:88f, [1967a]/1967.

Fromm, Erich. Do we still love life? *Love, sexuality, and matriarchy*. New York: Fromm International Edition, [1967e]/1997.

Fromm, Erich. *The revolution of hope*. New York: Bantam Books, 1968a.

Fromm, Erich. The condition of the American spirit: are we fully alive? *Newsday*, Garden City (01/13/1968), 1968f.

Fromm, Erich. *The anatomy of human destructiveness*. New York. Henry Holt & Company, [1973a]/1992.

Fromm, Erich. In the name of life: a portrait through dialogue. *For the love of life*. New York: The Free Press, [1974b]/1986.

Fromm, Erich. Remarks on the Policy of Detente. in: *Detente. Hearings before the Committee on Foreign Relations, US Senate, 93rd Congress, 2nd Session*. Washington: US Government Printing Office, 1975a.

Fromm, Erich. *To have or to be?*. New York: Bantam Books, [1976a]/1981.

Fromm, Erich. *Greatness and limitations of Freud's thought*. New York: Harper and Row, Publishers, [1979a]/1980.

Fromm, Erich. Marx and religion. Seyed Javad Miri; Robert Lake; Tricia M. Kress (eds.). *Reclaiming the sane society*. Rotterdam: Sense Publishers, [1979b]/2014.

Fromm, Erich. Interview with Robert Neun: Wer hat Interesse an der Wahrheit? *PTT-Zeitschrift* (04/1980):8f, 1980b.

Fromm, Erich. Die vision unserer Zeit. *Mitteilungen aus dem Literaturarchiv der Stadt Dortmund*: 7:29f. 1980g.

Fromm, Erich. Reminiscences of Shlomo Barukh Rabinkow. Leo Jung (ed.), *Sages and Saints*. Ho-boken: Ktav Publishing House, [1987a]/1987.

Fromm, Erich. *The revision of psychoanalysis*. Boulder: Westview Press, [1990a]/1992.

Fromm, Erich. For a cooperation between Jews and Arabs. *New York Times* (04/18/1948). 1990t.

Fromm, Erich. *The art of listening*. London: Constable, [1991a]/1994.
Fromm, Erich. The idea of a world conference. *On being human*. New York: Continuum. [1992n]/2005.
Fromm, Erich; Maccoby, Michael. *Social character in a Mexican village*. New York: Routledge, [1970b]/1996.

Secondary literature

Friedman, Lawrence. *The lives of Erich Fromm*. New York: Columbia University Press, 2013.
Hardeck, Jürgen. *Erich Fromm*. Darmstadt: Wissenschaftliche Buchgesellschaft, 2005.
Heale, M. *The sixties in America*. Edinburgh: Edinburgh University Press, 2001.
Horvat, Branko. A new social system in the making: historical origins and development of self-governing socialism. Branko Horvat*et al.* (eds.). *Self-governing socialism, vol. 1*. White Plains: International Arts and Sciences Press, Inc., 1975.
Jack, Homer. Die Friedensbewegung und Erich Fromm. Lutz von Werder (ed.). *Der unbekannte Fromm*. Frankfurt: Haag und Herchen, 1987.
Jacobs, Jack. *The Frankfurt school, Jewish lives, and antisemitism*. Cambridge: Cambridge University Press, 2015.
Joach, Helmut. Gelebter Humanismus und politisches Engagement. Rainer Funk, Helmut Joach, Gerd Meyer (eds.). *Erich Fromm heute*. München: DTV, 2000.
Klasic, Hrvoje. Titos's 1968 reinforcing position. Gorana Ognjević, Jasna Jozelić (eds.). *Revolutionary totalitarianism, pragmatic socialism, transition, vol. 1*. New York: Palgrave MacMillan, 2016.
McLaughlin, Neil. How to become a forgotten intellectual: intellectual movements and the rise and fall of Erich Fromm. *Sociological Forum*:13 (2):215–246, 1998.
McLaughlin, Neil. Optimal marginality: innovation and orthodoxy in Fromm's revision of psychoanalysis. *The Sociological Quarterly*: 42(2):271–288, 2001.
McLaughlin, Neil. *Erich Fromm and global public sociology*. London: Bristol University Press, 2021.
Wilde, Lawrence. *Erich Fromm and the quest for solidarity*. New York: Palgrave Macmillan, 2004.
Wilde, Melissa. *Vatican II*. Princeton: Princeton University Press, 2007.

Conclusion
Toward a Political Sociology

Throughout this book, practical determinants in Fromm's thought and action were derived from theoretical considerations. The argument ventured into historical examinations only to the extent allowed by conceptual analysis at each stage of the discussion. In doing so, we derived a series of praxiological categories, translating between Fromm's ideas and their experiential sources. In this chapter, our main conclusions are recapitulated under those categories. The contents, contradictions, and blindspots in Fromm's thought are considered in their relation with the form of clinical practice and the political movements he endorsed.

1 Psychological Presuppositions to Political Life

We started with a peculiarity in Fromm's later style – a resistance to formalization, whose effect was a contradiction between a static mode of abstraction, and a processual concept of vital phenomena. This peculiarity hampered the expression of Fromm's conception of psychic determination – a fragment of *ontology*. His was a materialism seeking the immanence of form in matter: each psychic force projects a particular topology, according to its polar nature. Fromm's psychodynamics were correspondingly characterized by a primacy of qualitative over quantitative aspects, and by a systemic understanding of psychic processes. However, unlike his economy and topology, they were still formulated in Freudian terms. For that reason, Fromm's ontological categories remained mostly presupposed to his psychoanalytic and social psychological concepts.

Between 1937 and 1976, these concepts suffered a series of transformations. We understood them as attempts at bridging the gap between the qualitative and the quantitative sides of the psychic process, following Fromm's rejection of libido theory. Because ideal types only allowed portraying character as a fully developed unity, and because social research operated at a higher degree of abstraction than analytic casuistry, empirical character was initially thought of as dominated by one or two basic strivings. Behind this unitary formulation, Fromm articulated a series of relatively marginal notions, which advance beyond his overt theoretical stance. From them we inferred the ontological forms composing his systemic concept of psychic determination.

Out of the relations *between primary attitudes*, we extracted the category of *mutual presupposition*: each of the elements under comparison is a condition for the development of all others. They stand in an immediately negative relation to each other, limiting their capacity to fuse into the perfected quality the syndrome wills to achieve. In the relations *between orientations and attitudes,* we found an immediately positive relation. The orientation is *generative* of its subordinated attitudes; character traits subsist only as they keep flowing from their unconscious source, specifying the use of human powers as instruments for its fulfillment. Unlike mutual presupposition, generativity presupposes structuralization. We found two corresponding classes of determinations in the relation between *attitudes and ideas*: a formal, *reflexive* one – to take ideas, feelings, sensations, as objects of satisfaction – and a substantive, *structuring* one – the content of the idea, feeling or sensation corresponds to that of the attitude.

All the previous categories expressed endopsychic determinations. Relations *between orientations* were more complicated. They presumed a détour through social relations, such that seeking the satisfaction of one tendency reactivates the conditions engendering others. The affinity between orientations posited a mediately positive relation between them – their *reciprocal implication*. Each is a potential consequence of the other, due to their shared conditions of existence in social life. The convergence of orientations into syndromes completes this line of reasoning, positing a mediately negative, *epigenetic* relation between them. Orientations act upon others in their practice. Each is for the others an agent of change, staggering and specifying them in a continuum of graduated qualities. A similar gradation is formed in the relation *between secondary attitudes,* as they establish *blends*. The same character trait may be bent towards one or the other extreme, as the proportion between contributing forces changes. Motivations for feeling, thought, and action may be contradictory or concurrent, as they draw their energies from distinct attitudinal sources. Unlike converging syndromes, blends of desires remain an endopsychic determinacy, without requiring mediation by the object's response.

According to this systemic concept of psychic structure, the whole is negatively presupposed to its parts, and each part is positively presupposed to the whole. The whole is formed by the concrete constellation of its singular components, but it is also a latent aspiration within each of them. Polar forces repel their opposites, constraining their growth, and coalesce with their kin, necessitating them in order to be fully born. Character syndromes fight to reproduce themselves as viable forms of satisfaction in their relation to changing practical constellations. Each basic attitude fights a strategic dispute against others for the decisive amounts of energy in governing conduct. Psychic conflict is primarily in the unconscious polarity between alternative ways of being, secondarily in the clash between drives and self-preservation or morality. Character structure results as an evolving totality – a multilateral conditionality of its components in their movement.

We understood the attempt at giving voice to this conception as the source for Fromm's late interest in systems theories. He remained close to them in his interest for a self-referential, circular, and process-oriented notion of causality, but rejected their conceptual formalism. As a critical theorist, he shared the aspiration for a normative social science, but distinguished his stance by giving primacy to emerging affirmation, as opposed to position or negation. His approach clashed with other formulations of object-relations and interpersonal psychoanalysis by its adherence to historical materialism, and by its negative understanding of language. Finally, we found his peculiarity among other Marxisms in his critical approach to the problem of freedom from the point of view of the unconscious. It follows from Fromm's ontology that the movement of character structures is from the outset conditioned by its relations to others. This has an important political consequence: freedom and unfreedom are anchored in social relations; subjective and social change are mutually dependent upon each other.

2 Goals

Fromm's *anthropology* started with life as demanding structured growth, both bodily and psychic. All the categories pertaining to life were moments in a dialectic of necessity and freedom. In the human species, general psychic energy was specified in two forms of activity: self-preservation and free expression. Imagination, reason, and self-awareness were given as determinacies of self-preservation, helping coordinate action. They also resulted in the need to guarantee one's sanity by relating to others. Psychic survival being a condition for physical survival, it prompted the formation of society. The preservation of society became the condition for that of its members. In the determination of vital expressiveness, psychic energy developed within human powers. We discovered their primary differentiation in three faculties – sensory, affective, and intellectual – whose exercise is an immediate imperative. Action multiplied their relations as capacities and led to psychic structuralization. Favorable or unfavorable conditions of life led to different results in the operation of the corresponding potentialities – primary or secondary. Effecting these potentialities led human powers to realization in historical existence.

The movement of life extended for Fromm into an economy of affirmative and negative moments in human ontogenesis. Life's affirmative impulse was represented first by human powers as vital forces. However, their want of objects led to an introjection of negation within the subject, resulting both in objective alienation – the split between subject and object – and a correlated dissociation between the intellectual and the affective spheres. This existential split developed into an existential contradiction – a basic disquietude motivating human change. It was followed by the experiences of powerlessness, separation, helplessness, anxiety. This complex of painful self-affections appeared as human life's earliest forms of self-awareness, and came to constitute the nucleus of the Frommian unconscious. Their latency instituted irrational passions as objective potentialities within character. The primary polar logic counterposing attitudes to their opposites thus unfolded into a secondary one, of compensatory character. Desires may act as forces repressing their own motives – the affects one wants to remain ignorant of. The opposition between psychic activity and reactivity resulted from the partition of the affirmative and negative moments between immediate vital forces and their modification by affection. Primary reflexivity developed as the relation to objects modified the subject's relation to herself. Freedom and unfreedom both resulted as anthropologically determined possibilities.

Fromm based his *ethics* on these anthropological premises. Freedom and the capacity for change were given as its highest norms, being understood as the human specification of the moment of vital growth. Their experiential concomitants were resumed in the quality of vitality. These ethics provided the basis for Fromm's *clinical* goals. He proposed an "activating technique", capable of eliciting aliveness in the analysand. The analyst should provide the stimulus and the reassurance to have previously unconscious experience acknowledged as shared reality through language. From this principle derived Fromm's rather aggressive posture with resistances (arousing them through reacting to the patient), and his emphasis on the function of transference as resistance (giving up responsibility by lingering in a phantasistic relationship). Analysis would result in an experience of truth as the outcome of negating illusions, providing a model for what a better lived life feels like.

The same principles resulted in Fromm's *political* goals: achieving a better society, oriented to joy and solidarity. This was expressed in his conflict with Marcuse and the New Left. The Fromm/Marcuse debate in *Dissent* was on the surface a quarrel over Freud's legacy. It occurred in a period of relative stability in the United States, but was followed by a series of political upheavals surrounding the Cuban missile crisis, the civil rights movement, Vietnam war, the Black power movement, the women's liberation movement, the failure of Eugene McCarthy's bid for the Presidency, the Nixon presidency etc. These historical events brought the real basis of their disagreements into the open. They had different ethical sensibilities, and correspondingly divergent appraisals of the political forms required to bring about radical change. As the 1960s unfolded, both adopted different attitudes toward the New Left, the burgeoning student movement and counter-culture – Fromm's being acutely ambivalent, Marcuse's being predominantly positive. Fromm favored a religious model for political organization, orienting them to the fulfillment of a common vision, whereas Marcuse worked with aesthetic relations, based on shared pleasure and phantasy.

3 Mobilization

Fromm's *social psychology* resulted from a large chain of transpositions, in which different experiential elements were joined in common formulations, and single experiential determinations were diffracted into multiple conceptual nuclei. From the 1950s on, this amounted especially to a theoretical convergence of clinical and political experiences, formulated in terms of the consubstantiality of liberation processes. A crossed-structure was formed: clinical determinacies reappeared within political vocabulary, and political determinacies recurred in Fromm's therapeutic approach.

Fromm expressed the identity of clinical and political emancipation as the coincidence of negation and affirmation. An analysis of his models for subjective and social change led us to a discrepant result. Both clinical and political work started with the negation of illusions, but their subsequent development was not the same. The paroxistic transformation of character, as a result of long-harbored perlaboration, brought the negative and affirmative moments into effective coincidence. They were joined in the conscious grasp of the repressed and its emotional repercussions. The result was a deep current of vitality in concentrated self-experience, which emerged as an experiential value, preparing further change. In political mobilization, the reversion of indifference or suffering into hopeful action did not present the same characteristics. Political practice required the collective elaboration of a common vision orienting action. Affirmation came, not as the immediate consequence of praxis, but as the promise of a better society, subsequent to the political struggle.

This theoretical structure and its problems had a real correspondence in the political movements supported by Fromm. Practical humanism emerged from the transposition of ethical social relations onto the political realm. Originating within religious and political communities, these relations had to be abstracted from their previous practical and conceptual expressions, and given a new form. This amounted to the passage from a multiplicity of particular communities, each organized by a common ethical commitment, into a broader coalition – a political formation mobilized by shared moral concern, negative of its opponents and circumstances. This form of *mobilization* first capacitated its subjects for action by relating them in the interest of self-preservation. However, it sublated their previous particular organizations into a general association. A common, positive vocabulary and practice were not anymore possible, except in reaction to its others. There was a basic clash between the social conditions allowing an emergence of humanistic ethics in Fromm's terms, which are characteristic for small, oppressed communities, and the mass range he found necessary to effect social change. A secondary, narcissistic relatedness developed as a practical response to this contradiction, cementing political relations through idealization and identification. Leadership and representation were selected in terms of personal, ethical exemplarity. Fromm's corresponding theoretical response was an unresolved dialectic between activity and contemplation – an oscillation between a praxiological understanding of the realization of values, and their idealization, in abstraction from practice.

4 Means

According to Fromm's *sociology*, human groupings originated different modes of production and reproduction of life through history – relations of production associated to the employment of certain productive forces. From these derived particular economic and political structures. Each social class faced specific conditions of life, amidst which a characteristic practice of life developed, being finally objectified in a collective mode of life. For most of human history, practice of life was under the yoke of subjective alienation – more than ever under capitalism. The scope of freedom was restrained by the exteriorization of human vital forces and the reification of social relations.

Fromm's choice of political *means* was based both on these premises and on his ethics. We discovered him as a socialist of deep trust in democratic institutions. Fromm favored establishing majority coalitions and steering institutions non-violently. He sought common ground between radicals and conservatives, treating the formation of a humanist center as a condition for future radicalism. This induced a series of specifications of his political goals, sometimes to the point of contradiction. A tension developed between his treatment of civil society as the end of progressive politics, and as the means for controlling government decisions. His attempt at securing large majorities led him to privilege the avoidance of war and the establishment of peace above most domestic goals, including socialist developments, while still trying to steer international relations toward a constellation allowing socialist revolutions.

Differences in political strategy were another aspect in Fromm's conflict with the New Left. Both Fromm and Marcuse tried to bridge the gap between present political forms and a future society – but in radically different ways. Marcuse's position was marked by historical discontinuity. He thought minority organizations could act as a vanguard first, prompting the activation of political interest in larger groups afterwards – and without necessarily dispensing with the use of violence. Present-day society could be overcome through a series of diffuse, spontaneous movements, whose decentralized character would provide the anatomy for a new society. Fromm was in favor of optimal decentralization in production, defending worker self-management as a basic economic form. However, he thought a political transition into socialism was unthinkable without previous majority formation and disciplined, concerted action. He envisioned a democratic renaissance, a reactivation of local political activity, which would also set the grounds for a future socialism – but only if oriented to the construction of a larger movement, instead of being pulverized in isolated currents. Each implied a different form of political organization.

5 Organization

Fromm's psychoanalysis is specified by its concern with *reflexivity* – the reaction of the psychic process to itself, in the process of relating to others. This property is explicit in the concept of modes of existence. They conceive one's capacity or incapacity for change in terms of the global transit between consciousness and unconsciousness, as a function of one's dominating modes of relatedness. Being a general subjective category, reflexivity is specified in a series of particular relations. These fall in the sphere of self-awareness. Practice of life resumes the opposition between psychic activity and reactivity. In its abstract sense, it implies the priority of action over character, and leads us to a voluntaristic, negative understanding of subjective and social change. In its concrete sense, practice of life is the expression of an already formed character structure, deriving the necessity of preparing a modification in praxis through previous, affirmative insight. This formal duality is unified in that both movements require normative orientation – a goal. Fromm's concept of self expresses this relation. For him, a sense of self develops in correspondence with the effective values we experience in the process of acting. These values appear as partial self-apperceptions, concomitant to our object relations. They are reunited in the category of conscience, which expresses one's relatedness to oneself as conditioned by values. Humanistic conscience engenders other reflexive affections, such as joy, sadness, and guilt. These emerge as total apprehensions of the vital process by itself.

For Fromm, self-experience would be the basis for identifying the values a political vision should strive to realize. However, we found out Fromm often faced difficulties in effecting enduring political alliances on the basis of moral mobilization. Their survival was hampered, both by competition with other forms of socialization, and by the instability implied in their psychological structure. Humanistic political mobilization presupposed agreement on core values, on the basis of which shared concerns could be elaborated. Previously formed religious and political communities were seen as a privileged infrastructure for *organization* and diffusion of political ideas. Where these were absent, political action was impaired.

Fromm's tendency to introvert reciprocal relations into unilateral conceptual determinations reflected these practical difficulties. His understanding of critique was an attempt at resolving them. His endeavor as a public intellectual was centered on the problem of influencing public opinion, with the purpose of having an indirect repercussion over decisions made in the state – and through them, over foreign affairs. He thought theory should help precipitate the experience of humanistic values, inducing organization where it was not socially given. The operations Fromm believed effective in fostering these experiences were sublimated in the *logical structure* of his critical theory. Fromm took instances of progressive determination – both subjective and social – as the paradigmatic moments of fulfillment of freedom. Neither sheer indeterminacy, nor accomplished determination, but the movement toward it was for him the essential basis for critique. For this reason, his became a theory of the passage from negation into affirmation.

In political action, a common positive ethics appeared therefore as both presupposed to, and deriving from participation in humanistic political relations. This was reflected in the various conflicting strains within Fromm's ethics. Norms could be either interpreted as natural, spontaneous givens of human constitution, or as products of lived social experience. Each of these interpretations resulted in a different way of grounding normative judgments. A naturalistic treatment of norms derived a biological teleology, in which optimal human development is prefigured as an inner drive. Norms were represented as ideals or ends in themselves, and political action as basically negative. This interpretation safeguarded criteria for a universal ethics, but proved incoherent with Fromm's ontology. The opposite problem happened within a pedagogical interpretation: psychic development might happen as predicted by Fromm's characterology, but no immanent criterion was given for favoring some outcomes over others. The only strain in which all requisites of a normative humanism were reconciled fell with a sociological treatment of norms. In this case, the indeterminacy of character formation as a process was emphasized, and norms were embodied as the experiential values concomitant with growth. These values could now serve the purpose of grounding an immanent, universal ethics – not due to the particular goals they represent, but due to their functional properties within the personality. In this conception, experiential values are norms to the extent that they preserve and enhance the capacity of the psychic structure to keep changing.

6 Structure

In most of our previous considerations, relations between political agents appeared as relations between equals. A given division of political labor was presumed, but we tackled neither its conditions of existence, nor the interests and institutions sustaining it. This is an effect of the sources we used: they concerned mainly exchanges between intellectuals and leaderships, reaching other segments of humanistic movements only indirectly. To the extent that these exchanges help constitute the remaining extremes in a political power, the consequences we deduce here remain true. They determine the *structure* of humanistic praxis as intended by Fromm. Changes within any of its categories send the corresponding social relations into other possibilities and constraints – Fromm's radical humanism is only one among other historical variants.

Fromm's political goals induce the option for non-violent political means; but this choice determines their retroactive specification: avoidance of war takes precedence over fostering socialist revolutions. Within democratic societies, pacific action implies working through institutionally given mechanisms. This requires a specification of organization as well. Humanistic formations have to strive to consolidate majorities, gathering a large number of agents – now particularly as voters. The subordination of political organization to the task of majority formation gives Fromm's strategy its centrist character, postponing the realization of its most radical purposes – a contradiction between form of organization and political goals. The subordination of national to international concerns, of socialism to pacifism, results in the vacillation of civil communities between subjects and objects, ends and means of the political process.

This later opposition unfolds into further difficulties. The promise of a better life feeds into the previous organization of political and religious communities, being realized in a series of positive practices – the ethical methods purported to realize this good. They are the presupposition to political alliances relying on moral concern: without a previous inculcation of values, no shared sensibility is possible. At the same time, this form of mobilization is the immediate negation of organization as it was given. Common ethical goals are first presupposed to it, later sublated in it. Mobilization suspends common practice and thought for the sake of cooperation with more and different groups. Subsuming given communities to broader political goals pulls social relations out of their spontaneity: reproducing them is now a necessity for sustaining the political movement as a social power. Common values must be induced and regenerated by necessity, lest the political formation should dissolve. There develops a previously absent stratification. In a common ethics, practice of life and its goals coincide immediately; social relations are the means and ends of each subject's purpose. In a shared morals, the immediate satisfaction of ethical goals is suspended. Political relations are themselves political means – an instrument set between desire and its future realization. This determines their primary instability. Political alliance is sustained only negatively: the more it approximates fulfilling its immediate purpose, the more it dissolves into its original differences, preparing a subsequent conflict – a contradiction between form of mobilization and political goals. Humanistic alliances face a contradiction between their existence and their efficacy.

Fromm's works are an expression of this struggle and an attempt at pacifying it. They represent one among other attempted solutions at reconciling the unity of political goals with the diversity of ethical means and creeds sustaining them. Radical humanism as he proposes it derives from its position in the global structure of humanistic movements. Around the 1960s and 1970s, when Fromm's activism was at its peak, their social bases were spread among varied countries and social classes, addressing different political issues in each case. A non-exhaustive summary should include at least the following: in Latin America, humanism was part of the religious movements inspired by liberation theology and other progressive fractions within the Catholic church. In Eastern Europe, it was especially related to the anti-

Stalinist opposition in the satellite countries, and to the justification of alternative models of socialism to the one enforced by the USSR. In Africa, it was one of the currents feeding into anticolonial struggles. In Western Europe and the US, it fed also into some of the fractions of the student organizations and of the Black movement.

Until the early 1970s, Fromm was living in Mexico, and his political interventions addressed mainly the US. He was in contact with a global network of activists, leaderships, and intellectuals involved in the above movements; but few of them were in the immediacies of his life. Being more than an observer, Fromm was not also a direct participant in many of the political processes he endorsed. He wanted to precipitate forms of political organization whose most consequent development was carried outside the societies in which he lived. His works should be understood as anticipations – as mediating forms, which try to operate the necessary abstraction of given ethical relations from their immediate forms of expression, such that they can be regrouped under new political formations. In Fromm's theory, the conceptual movement corresponds to the passage from a religious model of relatedness into a secular, political formulation. In other cases, mediation goes the other way: political relatedness is brought into the life of religious institutions. Both strategies have to deal with the fundamental tension they engender – between a movement's morphology and its template for action.

This tension is expressed in Fromm's resistance to formalization, and addressed by his theory of liberation. Analysis showed that private and public forms of "affirmation of life" are incomplete when taken in isolation. The anticipation of a better life in clinical experience had to be completed with a change in practice, and political action had to be complemented with knowledge of what a better life feels like. From this insight derived a correction to Fromm's logic. He came to see the immediate affirmativeness of experiential values and the mediate affirmativeness of political visions as mutually presupposed, negative of each other. Thus conceived, the anticipation of the good life and the anticipation of the good society are stratified as complementary, non-equivalent experiences. Each corresponds to a distinct realm of emancipatory praxis, criticizing and fostering the other from without. Liberation as it is experienced in analysis works as a corrective and preparation for political liberation: one's experience of values is the criterion from which political visions can be judged, and strengthen one's responsiveness to others. Conversely, political action struggles to guarantee conditions of life in which values can be fulfilled. This articulation corresponds to a developed concept of liberation, in which "positive" and "negative" freedom both include positive and negative moments.

Index

Note: Locators in *italic* refer to figures; Locators followed by "n" indicate endnotes.

Abraham, Karl 12, 30, 32, 161
act 11, 18, 19, 52, 53, 55, 60, 61, 63, 72, 78, 91, 113, 125, 128, 133, 134, 137, 141, 145, 149, 157, 159, 159, 176, 187, 189, 191, 195, 199–201, 205, 207, 208, 210, 211, 213, 214, 215, 229, 231, 234, 235, 245, 271, 273, 275; characterological consequences of 189; cricuits of 200
active: prescription 164; technique 163, 174, 273
activity 19, 29, 32, 36, 52, 53, 57, 60, 63, 64, 70–77, 109, 113, 125, 131, 133, 134, 142–149, 164, 170, 174, 176, 185, 189, 191, 199, 202, 206, 208, 212, 213, 217, 218, 223, 224, 230, 238, 244, 248, 254, 272, 273, 275, 276
Adams, James Luther 166, 247
adaptation 28, 72, 54, 128, 156; dynamic 22, 189; static 22, 146, 189; in therapy, *see* Clinic
Adler, Alfred 12, 85
Adorno, Theodor 2, 33–37, 245
aesthetics 13, 34–35, 104–106, 114n3; ethos 104; relationships 113, 227, 273; style 247
affect 2, 18, 23, 28–31, 73, 125, 127, 128, 132, 133, 143, 146, 148, 149, 154, 159, 176, 187, 188, 193, 196, 197, 202, 206–209, 211, 216, 230, 233, 273; knowledge 196; sphere, *see* Spheres of Activity
affinity, *see* Ontological Categories
affirmation 2, 34–36, 50–52, 61, 108, 149, 191, 195, 204–219, 226, 234, 272–279; of difference 202, 236; of essence 176;

of life 20, 64, 69, 76, 279; of objects 78, 129
African identity 110
After November Committee 240
aggression 21, 23, 55, 70, 89, 140; aggressiveness 60, 140, 141; animal 54; benign 60, 62, 139; conformist 61; defensive 54; as instinct instinct 60–62; instrumental 61; life-serving 62; malignant 60, 139, 186; narcissistic 62, 141; predatory 54; pseudoaggression: 60; reactive 54; readiness for 60; resisting 62; revolutionary 61, 94
Alexander, Franz 13, 22, 30
alienation 33, 67, 71, 75, 85, 96, 108, 149, 169, 193, 195; estrangement 65, 67–68, 75; externalization 163; idolatry 24, 76, 226, 235; intellectual 96; mode of 74–76; objective 67–68, 207, 272; self-estrangement 71; subjective 67, 75–76, 125, 160, 252, 275; of work 107
alloplastic behavior 54
alternativism 201, 214; real possibilities 69, 78
Althusser, Louis 89
ambivalence 31–32, 58, 95, 96, 99, 110, 273
American capitalism, *see* Capitalism
American Humanist Association 227
American politics, *see* Politics
analytic social psychology, *see* Psychoanalysis
anamnesis, *see* Clinic
anatomical structure 55
animal sexual instinct, *see* Sexuality
Anshen, Ruth Nanda 90, 238–239, 256

anthropology 23, 55, 62, 69, 71, 108, 137, 272; cultural 9
anticipation 130, 191, 211, 229, 240; anguished 229; catastrophic apocalyptic 229
anti-intellectualism 95, 98, 251
anxiety 29, 30, 60, 73, 196, 229, 230; castration 59; neurotic 29; realist 61; separation 139
apathy 94, 243
Aquinas, Thomas 34
archaic orientation, *see* Orientation
Arendt, Hannah 224
Aronson, Ronald 95
arousal 29, 57
art 100–107, 110–112; of listening 153; of living 106–107, 114n5, 190
assimilation 75, 136; concrete 202; genetic interpretation 137; modes of 133, 137, 186
attention: free-floating 163; concentrated 163
attitudes 125, 210, 255, 271; character-conditioned 127; character-rooted 145; conjunctive 126, 144, 200; conscious 185; defined 126; emotional 30, 128, 129; exploitative 133, 197; feminine 57; hoarding 165; masculine 57; moral 227; objective 225; narcissistic 132; necrophilous 164; neurosis 11; non-productive 197, 201; objective 225; primary 126, 136, 271; productive 201; religious 242; revolutionary 133, 250; sadistic 132; secondary 136, 271; syndrome of 129, 139, 185
authoritarian 113; anti-authoritarian radicals 94; character, *see* Character; conscience, *see* Conscience; discipline 105; post-authoritarian 101
automaton conformity 87
autonomous restrictions 50
autonomy 24, 109, 111, 208, 234, 260
awareness 19, 34, 172, 173

Bachofen, Johann Jakob 13, 33
Baeck, Leo 224
Balabanoff, Angelica 251
Balint, Michael 12, 250
Bally, Gustav 114n6
Bateson, Gregory 27
behaviorism 23, 87, 107
being, mode of 68, 185–187

Bell, Daniel 225
Benedict, Ruth 23
Benenson, Peter 256
Benjamin, Walter 245
Biblical language 247
biological: constitution 51; dichotomy 65, 68; factors 55; orientation 85; revulsion 91; teleology 206
biophilia 91, 103, 141, 144, 185, 201, 202, 228; ethics 204, 252; as orientation, *see* Orientation
bisexuality, *see* Sexuality
Black movement 110, 273, 279
blends, *see* Ontological Categories
Bloch, Ernst 247
bottom-up approach 144
bourgeois materialism, *see* Materialism
Brandt, Heinz 256–257
Breuer, Joseph 29, 174, 211
Brown, Norman 90, 104
Buddhism 3, 10, 101; Zen 87, 100
bureaucracy 108, 109, 157, 240
Bureau for Factfinding 237
Burma 262

Câmara, Dom Hélder 256, 257
capacity, psychic 61, 63–64, 70, 76, 126–128, 132–133, 163, 198, 209, 272
capital 71, 259, 261
capitalism 24, 71, 75, 261; American 260
care 129
Casals, Pablo 105
castration 57; anxiety, *see* Anxiety
catalysts 109, 112
categories 186; adult memory 86; of consciousness 23; substantive 18
cathartic method 174
Catholicism 3, 239, 246, 253, 278
cerebration 133–134
change 19, 51, 62; cultural 199; historical 72; political 199, 225; qualitative 102; radical 88; routinized behavior 189; social 20, 98, 112, 199, 274, 276; subjective 199, 274–276
character 12, 189; anal 13, 186; analysis 156; authoritarian 93–94, 133, 158; bicentric model 136, 137; biological function 188; biophilic 185; change 199, 206; concept of 13; figure of 14; flexibility 198; formation 206; functional appreciation of 188; genital 12; hoarding 137, 186; masochistic 136;

necrophilous 164, 185–186; neurosis 11; normal 31, 159; orientation 139; orientations 126; psychological function 188; primary social determinants in 23; receptive 135; reflexive 32; revolutionary 133, 250; sadistic 60, 132, 133, 140, 186; schizoid 159; social, 15, 87, 143, 144, 165, 188, 196; social function 159, 188; structure 25, 28, 32, 75, 88, 126, 127, 144, 172, 188, 272, 276; syndromes 271; system 78, 134, 188–189; traits, *see* Trait; transformation, 213; types 135
characterology 10, 12–13, 30, 136, 143, 160, 277; social 1, 154
character-rooted attitudes, *see* Attitude
character-rooted passions, *see* Passion
childhood: amnesia 86; development, *see* Development; relationship to parents 174, 204; sexual experience 59
Chomsky, Noam 250
Christianity 10, 20, 110, 114n, 230, 246
Citizens for Reason 225, 230, 238, 241, 243
civilization 70, 87, 110, 231
civil society 35, 109, 240, 254, 255, 257, 275
classless society, *see* Society
clinic 2; adaptationist 156; analytic technique 5, 163–164; anamnesis 165; clinical interview 14; cure 11, 19, 156, 157, 166, 214, 216; diagnosis 164, 252; elaboration 20, 202, 213, 274; perlaboration 211, 216, 274; practice 214; prognosis 164, 171; prophylaxy 163, 167, 170, 229; psychotherapy 156, 174; treatment 5, 12–13, 18, 30, 154–156, 161, 163–164, 167, 169–170, 174, 210, 213; termination 171; therapeutic approach 274; therapeutic desire 168; therapeutic effect 162; therapeutic relationship 174; transtherapeutic goal 156, 170
clubs 109, 227, 238, 240, 241
Coffin, Tristram 102, 242, 249
Cohn-Bendit, Daniel 97
cold war 24, 99, 228, 237, 258, 261–262
collaboration 226–227
colonialism 260–261
colonial revolutions, *see* Revolution; anticolonial struggles 112, 279
Committee of Correspondence 253

communication 27, 63, 134, 158, 161, 193, 209, 212; paradigm of 27; public 155
communism: centralized, bureaucratic 108; Chinese 261–262; Soviet, *see* Soviet Union
community 19, 113, 140, 227, 236, 239–240, 246–247, 253–254, 274, 278; ethically-oriented 236, 242,
compensatory drives, *see* Drive
compensatory reaction, *see* Reaction
comprehension, modes of 129, 149
compromise formation 18, 31, 132, 139, 210
compulsion 28, 50, 70, 139, 147, 166, 175; repetition 49, 70
concentration 60, 190
conception of psychic determination, *see* Psychic Determination
condition of existence, *see* Existence
conditions of life, *see* Life
conflict 18, 19, 30, 66, 76, 97, 99, 103, 162, 167, 170, 172, 203, 213, 214, 226, 232, 239, 242, 251, 254, 257, 258, 260, 262, 278; political 35; primary 32, 135; psychic 210, 272; real 135
conflicting tendencies 128
conformist aggression, *see* Aggression
conjunctiveness, *see* Attitude
conscience 187–197, 232; authoritarian 195; humanistic 91, 195, 196, 197; motherly 196
conscious (cs) 17, 66, 109, 161, 186, 195, 208, 212, 213; awareness 187–197; categories of 23; deliberation 188; false 210; simple 53
constitutional: factor 214; genetic basis 71; traits 127
consubstantiality 214, 274
contemplation 144–149, 199, 275
contemporary psychoanalysis, *see* Psychoanalysis
controlled imagination, *see* Imagination
conventionalization 87
convergence, *see* Ontological Categories
conviction 192; lack of 195
cooperation 72–74
coprophilia 59
Coser, Lewis 84
counterrevolution, *see* Revolution
countertransference 169–170
counter-violence 112

creation, *see* Work
credibility 249
critical political sociology 3
critical theory 2, 4, 5, 9, 11, 19, 26, 33, 36, 37, 91, 94, 95, 102, 196, 206, 209, 216
critical thinking 106, 210
criticism 94, 95, 158, 162, 219, 261
critique 2, 28, 37, 205–218, 276–277
Cuban missile crisis 273
cultural anthropology, *see* Anthropology
culture 9, 22, 65, 73, 110, 144, 155, 158; change 199; differences 111; education 95; needs 91; orientation 85; pattern 22; repression 70; revolution 112; transformation 199
culture and personality 22
cultural relativism 23
culturalism 22–23
cure, *see* Clinic; paroxistic 211, 216–217, 274
cybernation 24
cybernetic religion, *see* Religion
Czechoslovakia 232

Davis, Mike 95
death 61, 66, 67, 89, 105, 147, 185, 201; drive 29, 49, 59, 89, 114n; instinct 88–89; organic 52–53; psychic 52–53, 67, 163
decentralization 108–109
Declaration of Conscience 225
defensive aggression, *see* Aggression
de Forest, Izette 250
degree: of abstraction 15, 270; of psychic development 77; differences in 143, 200; of repression 57, 200; of self-awareness 73
democratic socialism, *see* Socialism
depression 159, 161, 196, 229, 234
de Sade, Marquis 90, 103–104
despair 103, 216, 223, 228, 229, 231, 232–234
destructiveness 60, 77, 88–89, 96, 98, 102, 104, 140, 205; attitude, *see* Attitude; destructive hate 94; orientation, *see* Orientation
determination: absolute 50; conception of, *see* Psychic Determination; endogenous 138; instinctive 55, 65, 73; organic 21, 127; organization of 49; physiological 58; progressive 205; psychic 58, 165; reciprocal 127, 133, 144; social 21, 88; unilateral 49
development 55, 63, 262, 274; character 15; childhood 197; economic 255; historical 65; mode of 11, 63; intellect 66; ontogenetic 70; psychic 64, 129, 147, 197; psychosexual 12, 58–59; self-limiting 50; sexual 58; subjective 208; unilateral 53
diagnosis, *see* Clinic
dialectics 26, 34, 36; of activity and contemplation 146–147, 275; of experience 194; of mysticism and messianism 146; of necessity and freedom 49, 147, 272; of polarities 33
dialectical logic, *see* Logic
dialectical materialism, *see* Materialism
dictatorship 111
difference 16, 16, 21–23, 25, 28–31, 35–37, 49, 50, 54, 57–59, 63, 73, 93, 94, 100, 102, 103, 106, 108, 110, 111, 126, 127, 130, 132, 134, 139–143, 148, 154, 159, 194, 195, 200, 202, 205, 212, 213, 216–218, 226, 228, 236, 239, 242, 245, 274; human diversification 70
differentiation 63, 66, 197–206; primary 272
directness 161
disequilibrium, *see* Equilibrium
disillusionment 210, 223
disintegration, *see* Society
Dissent 84–91, 97, 102, 106–108
dissociation 160
division of labor 67, 71, 75, 77, 87; gendered 59; political, *see* Politics
diversification 50, 70, 139
diversity 68, 137, 143, 209, 236
Dobrenkov, Vladimir 20
Dolci, Danilo 249
Donaldson, Ivanhoe 240
dream 17, 22, 86, 113, 148, 153, 170, 171, 193, 194, 215; interpretation, *see* Interpretation
drive 23, 28–32, 55, 59–60, 64–65, 71, 77–78, 88, 126, 134, 139, 145, 197, 272, 277; compensatory 87; death, *see* Death; emancipatory 87; for freedom, *see* Freedom; life, *see* Life; of vital forces 64
drug culture 99–101
Dunayevskaya, Raya 33, 97, 114n6, 248
dynamics, *see* Psychodynamics

dynamic adaptation, *see* Adaptation

Eckhart, Meister 177, 248
ecology 88; of attitudes or traits 126, 140, 200, 206; disaster 21; of mind 27;
economy 17, 29, 31, 63, 125–128, 200, 216; of consciousness 134; development 15, 74, 255; factors 74, 157; psychic 31, 125–128, 143, 209; structure 75, 275; unconsciousness 134
education 91, 109, 205
effective freedom, *see* Freedom
effectiveness, *see* Existential Needs
ego 12, 13, 16, 28, 37, 55, 59, 73, 87, 88, 101, 106, 126, 146, 174, 189; mastery 106; pleasure-ego 66; psychology 13, 16; reality-ego 66
Einstein, Albert 27, 224
emancipation 19, 102, 110, 147, 214–215, 236, 274, 279; drives, *see* Drive
emergency energies 215, 229
emotion 56, 73, 176
emotional: attitudes, *see* Attitude; forces, *see* Force; intensity 103; matrix 14
empathy 168–169
encouragement 233
Encyclopedia of the philosophical sciences 35
energy 55, 134–135; concept of 145; discharge 55; general human 135; neutral 88; psychic 55, 143; quantum of 88; specific 135; surprlus 54
Engels, Friedrich 13, 53, 68, 72, 73, 76
enthusiasm 228, 233
environmental factors 55
envy 61
epigenesis, *see* Ontological Categories
epistemology 18
equality 193; of sexual practices 58
equilibrium: disequilibrium 67; physical 62; psychic 62, 68
Eros 51, 87–91, 97, 102, 103, 107, 112; eroticism 54, 56–60, 57
Eros and civilization 87, 90, 97, 102, 107, 112
essence 62, 64, 65–69, 104; concept of 65; contradiction 68; existential contradiction 68; of human existence 62; progression 69; regression 69; subjective alienation 67
essential faculties 63
essential qualities 62–64; of life 198

estrangement, *see* Alienation
ethically-oriented communities, *see* Community
ethics 2, 5, 32, 49, 90, 91, 96–107, 128, 176, 185–219, 206, 273; biophilic 204, 252; common commitment, 227, 232, 244, 253, 274; efficient factor 236; evaluation 10; exemplarity 245; humanistic 203; naturalistic strain 203–206, 277; pedagogical strain 205, 277; sociological strain 204, 206, 277; transformation 106
ethnographic methods 11
eudaimonism 146; teleology 114n5
evolution 53–54; hominization 54; phylogenetic inheritance, *see* Phylogenesis; process 24, 72; thinking 71
excitation, *see* Existential Needs
exercise: of human capacities 53, 61, 63, 65, 129–130, 145, 163, 185, 190, 204, 272 physical 55; social 63; in true activity 148
existence 62, 63, 78; conditions of 11, 54–62, 69, 73, 75, 96, 129, 140, 271; defined 185; factual expression 63; future 77; modes of 127, 155, 185–187, 189–190, 211, 277; pacification of 112
existential: contradiction 68–69, 273; dichotomy or dichotomies 52, 65, 67, 68, 78, 147; split 66, 146, 149, 273
existential needs 74, 128, 199, 207; effectiveness 128; frame of reference or orientation; 10, 128, 157, 243; object of devotion 128, 199; relatedness 73, 128, 186, 234, 276; rootedness 128, 236; sense of identity 99, 110, 128; sense of unity 128; stimulation and excitation 128; transcendence 128
experience 16–20, 28, 32, 34, 36; common 15; model 5; mode of 9–10, 67, 76; nucleus 19; quality 204; saturation of 204
experiential values, *see* Value
experiential spheres, *see* Spheres of Experience
exploitativeness 186, 197; attitude, *see* Attitude; orientation, *see* Orientation
expression 27, 53, 55, 63, 78, 145, 188, 200, 207–208, 218, 272; self-expression 52, 54, 61
externation, *see* Life

externalization, *see* Alienation

faculty, psychic 139, 191
faith 10, 157, 224, 226, 228, 231, 246, 247
false consciousness 210
fanatical 235
fear 60, 61, 229, 255; of ostracism 73
Fellowship of Reconciliation (FOR) 237
feminine character 57, 59
Feminism 57–59
Fenichel, Otto 88, 114n1
Ferenczi, Sándor 12, 13, 30, 145, 163, 174, 211
fetishism 59, 133
For a Cooperation Between Jews and Arabs 224
force 18, 63; emotional 145; opposing 34; polar 31, 34, 138, 140–141, 200, 270–272; political 148; productive 75, 143; psychic 17, 166; vital 145, 163, 187, 202, 205–208, 211, 234
foreign policy 11, 258–261
formal: analogies 18; deduction 32; resistance 24
frame of reference or orientation, *see* Existential Needs
free association 158, 160, 163, 170, 171, 174, 215
freedom 37, 61, 68, 69, 70, 147, 197–206, 272, 273; drive for 91, 197; effective 78, 199; escape from 200; negative 199, 218, 279; positive 199, 218, 279; subjective 138, 148
Freire, Paulo 248
Freud, Sigmund 1, 5, 10, 12–15, 17, 19, 26, 29–31, 49, 51, 54–59, 60, 62, 64, 66, 70, 71, 73, 76, 85, 88, 89, 93, 101, 103, 125, 130, 134, 143, 160, 170–172, 174, 175, 210, 211; characterology, *see* Characterology; metapsychology, *see* Metapsychology; materialism, *see* Materialism; paradigm 9, 18, 71; technique 154
Freudianism 4, 9, 18, 20, 23; orthodox, *see* Psychoanalysis
Fromm, Erich 1, 9–37, 49–51, 54, 55, 57–60, 61–64, 66–69, 72, 75, 76, 129, 132, 134, 136, 137, 140, 146, 149; and Marcuse debate 84–114, 273; political activities 21, 223–263; political interest 13, 18, 244, 255, 257, 275; politics

2, 10, 14, 20, 35, 36, 90, 93, 94, 107–113, 167, 223–263; research in neurophysiology and systems biology 21; strategy, tactics, and principles 244–254; style 9–11
Fromm-Reichmann, Frieda 161
frustration 29, 61, 99, 105, 238
Fulbright, J. W. 254, 260–261
function 128, 143, 166, 188, 198, 277; approach to character 188

Garaudy, Roger 239
gender 57, 58, 144; equality 58; liberation 58
generalization 12, 14, 18, 19, 64, 144; of attitude into orientation 126, 139; social 252
General systems theory 21
generative perception, *see* Perception
generativity, *see* Ontological Categories
generic being 66, 72, 75
genital: character 12; organization 90; primacy 106
German expansionism 259
Gershman, Herbert 104
goal, political, *see* Politics
Goldwater, Barry 242
good life, *see* Life
Gorz, André 89
gradation: of attitudes or traits 141–3, 271; of positive freedom 200
Graham, Billy 251
Graham, Dom Aelred 114n4
Granfil, Toma 232
Greatness and limitations of Freud's thought 17
Great Refusal 85, 106, 114n2
Greeman, Richard 97
Groddeck, Georg 174–175
Groups 1, 19, 70, 72, 100, 101, 105. 111, 126, 144, 198, 201, 227, 237, 238, 240, 241, 245, 252, 275, 278
growth 55, 138; absolute 53; defined 50–51; psychic 62, 212; pure 50; structured 60, 62, 68, 198, 209, 272; syndrome of 185
guilt 29, 30, 70, 136, 195, 196, 226, 232, 276; unconscious, *see* Unconscious Guilt Feelings

Hagan, Roger 253
hallucination 148

happiness, *see* Joy
having, mode of: 185–187, 197
Hegel, Georg 10, 33–37, 50, 62, 67, 95
Heisenberg, Werner 27
helplessness 66, 67, 73, 196, 273
heterodox psychoanalysis 157–158
heterosexuality, *see* Sexuality
historical: changes 72; development 65; method 11; process 65; thinking 71
Hitler, Adolf 259
hoarding 136, 137, 165, 185, 186; character, *see* Character
hominization 71
homo economicus 88
homosexuality, *see* also Sexuality; etiology of paranoia 30; libido 70
hope 25, 63, 90, 94, 96, 97, 100, 106, 108, 109, 128, 167, 189, 193, 216, 217, 224–226, 228–233, 237, 242, 246, 251, 259, 260, 263
hopelessness 94, 108
Horkheimer, Max 2
Horney, Karen 22, 26, 84, 85, 162
Howe, Irving 84, 86
Hughes, H. Stuart 92
human development 11, 52, 70, 277
human experience: realms of 63
humanism 21; as political formation 224–232; alliances 253, 278; center 253; contemporary 249; ethics 203, 274; Marxist 1, 21, 37, 238, 250, 272; normative 3, 20, 276–277; planning 109; politics 210; psychoanalysis 248; radical: 1, 35, 224, 277, 278; renaissance of 250; socialist 89, 248, 250, 262; values 276
humanistic conscience, *see* Conscience
humanistic experience 202
humanistic political mobilization 276
humanity 65, 96, 202; mission of 53
humanization 70
human nature 62–69, 197; essence 62, 65–69; essential qualities 62–64; laws 62, 64–65
human situation 55, 65
Hungary 232
hydraulic metaphor 88
hysteriform symptoms, *see* Symptom

id 12, 64, 88, 126, 174, 175, 187
idea 9–11, 16, 18, 19, 23, 27, 29, 31–32, 36, 54, 59, 86–88, 95, 96, 102–103, 106–112, 125, 130, 133, 135, 136, 142, 149, 153, 157, 168, 174–177, 189–190, 192–193, 195, 213, 215, 229, 238, 240, 244
ideal 13, 17, 95, 130, 134, 135, 143, 144, 191, 194, 195, 206, 213, 218, 226, 243, 250, 262, 270
idealization 105, 113, 233–235, 243, 274, 275
ideal type 17, 130, 135, 143, 144, 195, 270
ideology 13, 133, 157, 193, 196, 210, 218, 235
identification 59, 110, 168, 169, 219, 227, 229, 235, 274
identity 99, 110, 185, 192, 217, 274; African 110
idolatry, *see* Alienation
Illich, Ivan 256–257
imagination 65, 72, 103, 105, 107, 111, 125; controlled: 169
implicit political theory 237
incestuous symbiosis, *see* Symbiosis
India 262
indifference: affective 73, 132, 139, 141, 159, 274; to life 21, 229
individuation 37, 63–67, 77, 107, 127, 139, 202–203; pre-individuation 69
infantile sexuality 56
inferiority feelings 12
insanity 61, 65, 69, 74
insight 4, 19, 26, 37, 86, 104, 154, 158, 162, 165, 168, 171, 173, 177, 191, 195, 211, 213, 214, 216, 217, 229, 238, 242, 276, 279
instinct: aggressive, *see* Aggression; death, *see* Death; determination 55, 65, 73; foundation for solidarity 91; life, *see* Life; reflex mechanism 54; sexual, *see* Sexuality
instrumental aggression, *see* Aggression
integrity 78, 195, 200, 235
intellect 64, 66, 68, 110, 131, 132, 145, 194, 207; activity 131; differences 236; experience 192; maturation 69; sphere, *see* Spheres of Activity
intelligence 54, 127; pragmatic 54
interest 13, 14, 18, 21, 27, 29, 31, 32, 61, 62, 70, 76, 84, 90, 95, 100, 104, 105, 109, 113, 128, 129, 132, 166, 194, 217, 226, 227, 230, 238, 240,

241, 243, 244, 246–248, 251, 254, 255, 259, 260, 262, 272, 274, 275
interpellation 215
interpersonal psychoanalysis, *see* Psychoanalysis
interpersonal relation 73, 85
interpretation 15, 17, 165, 168; of dreams 171; orthodox 166
introjection 15, 196, 234, 272
introversion 27, 49, 51, 67, 75, 113, 137–138, 190, 276
irrationalism 10
irrational passions, *see* Passion
isolation 63, 67, 72, 73, 127
Israel 241; foreign policy 242

Jay, Martin 28
jealousy 61
Judaism: 1, 3, 10, 19; law 10; mysticism 100; nationalism 235; prophets 1, 93, 95, 113, 194, 215, 229, 246; sabbath 20; tradition 10, 84, 224–225
Johnson, Lyndon 252
Johnson, William 240
Jones, Ernest 250
joy 103, 176, 191, 212, 217, 226, 234, 273, 276; happiness 51, 102, 163, 196, 216; sexual joy 57
Jung, Carl 10, 245
justice 13, 95, 128, 129, 254

Kaiser Wilhelm II 259
Kant, Immanuel 95
Kardiner, Abraham 22
Khoury, Gérard 231, 241
Khrushchev, Nikita 260
Kissinger, Henry 242
Klein, Melanie 12, 30
knowledge 129, 131, 165, 172; therapeutically-oriented 129; unconscious 173

Lacan, Jacques 27
Laing, Ronald 10
Lamarckian 91
language 20–28, 110, 132, 149, 193, 209, 211; in clinic 153–177; speech 23; thought 10, 22, 23, 27, 66, 76, 87, 102, 110, 125, 132, 155, 161, 167, 193, 209, 247
Latin America 231, 278

law 62, 71; of human nature, *see* Human Nature; Jewish, *see* Judaism
leadership 243, 244, 274, 277, 279; political 215, 241
Lenin 112
Lens, Sidney 247
Lévi-Strauss, Claude 27
liberation 101, 103, 106, 156, 170, 172, 190, 198, 199, 211, 214, 256, 278, 279; gender 58
libido 9, 28, 29, 85, 88, 270; narcissistic 29
life 207; affirm 51; characterization 64; concept of 21, 49–53, 61; conditions of 19, 21, 52, 70, 71, 77, 155, 188, 189, 236; drive 89, 145; expression of 56; externation 55; good life 102, 203, 279; growth 50; infinitude 53; instincts 88; mode of 74, 77; objectivation 55; organic 49–52; organization of 63; phenomena 103; preservation 51; process 62, 78, 139, 175, 189, 196, 202, 204; progressive form of 69; psychic 49–52, 67; practice of 13, 14, 21, 28, 75, 77, 106, 188–190, 206, 213, 219, 236, 252, 276; regressive forms of 69; social 56, 72; spheres of 63; as structured growth 60, 62, 68, 198, 209, 272; substance 51, 76; tendency 50, 51; thwarting of 89, 140; unlived 140
Linton, Ralph 22
living process, *see* Life
living substance, *see* Life
Loewenthal, Leo 89
logic 2, 32–37, 185–219; dialectical 33; non-identity 34; paradoxical 33; of polarities 34
logical structure 2, 5, 37, 206, 276
loneliness 234
love 20, 29, 56–60, 76, 102–103, 129–133, 141, 149, 191, 196–197, 201, 235–236
Luban-Plozza, Boris 229, 231

Maccoby, Michael 237, 240, 255
madness 67, 148, 207
majority formation, *see* Politics
malignant aggression, *see* Aggression
malignant narcissism, *see* Narcissism
Mallet, Serge 89
man 58; survival of 72
Maoism 95
Marinetti, Filippo 104

Marcuse, Herbert 2, 5, 84–114, 248, 273, 275; criticism 94–95; ethics 95–107; hedonism 113; phantasy 107; politics 107–113; superimposed needs 87; theory 85–95; theory of revolution 108; traditional values 95
marketing orientation, *see* Orientation
Marković, Mihailo 248
Marx, Karl 1, 5, 13, 18, 26, 33, 35, 37, 49, 50, 53, 54, 56, 63, 66, 67, 68, 71–73, 75, 76, 86, 92, 93, 95, 98, 107, 112, 130, 250
Marxism 13, 20, 22, 32, 37, 95, 100, 248; humanism, *see* Humanism
Marxism-Leninism 95
masculine character, *see* Character
masochism 59, 60, 126, 139–141; character, *see* Character; passions, *see* Passion; orientation, *see* Orientation; masochistic sex, *see* Sexuality
mass psychology, *see* Psychology
materialism: bourgeois 90; dialectical 91; Freudian 28; historical 1, 33, 234, 272; immanent 32, 270; mechanistic 248
material, historical 234
matriarchy 196
maturation 68
May man prevail? 89, 237
McCarthy, Eugene 93, 98, 223, 227, 229, 231, 237, 240–242, 244, 245, 253, 254, 256, 273
McIntyre, Alasdair 97
McLuhan, Marshall 114n3
Mead, Margaret 22–24, 26
means, political, *see* Politics
mechanistic materialism, *see* Materialism
mental health 61, 62, 91, 135; self-annihilation 68
mental survival, *see* Self-Preservation
Merton, Thomas 177, 226, 227, 238, 239, 243, 247
messianism 106, 146–147; apocalyptic 106; secular 36
metaphysics 33; gendered 57, 58; speculation 65
metapsychology 9, 28, 85–88, 134, 198
method 3, 255; psychoanalytic, *see* Psychoanalysis
minority politics, *see* Politics
mobilization; of drives: 88, 94, 113; of energy: 161, 164, 170, 175; of leaders: 247; political, *see* Politics

mode of assimilation, *see* Orientation
mode of comprehension 129, 149
mode of existence, *see* Existence
mode of experience, *see* Experience
mode of production 12, 71, 74–76, 275; objective factors 74
mode of socialization, *see* Orientation
mode of life, *see* Life
morality 71, 224; attitude, *see* Attitude; radicalism 91; sensibility 96, 241, 251, 278; shared concern 11, 232–234, 252, 276
Morgenstern, Oskar 24
motherly conscience, *see* Conscience
motivation 13, 56, 172, 242, 255, 271; unconscious 17
Mullahy, Patrick 84
Mumford, Lewis 94, 96, 225, 230, 238
Muste, Abraham 225, 255
mutual affirmation 202
mutual presupposition 129, 132, 138, 141, 208, 218, 271, 279
mysticism 10, 28, 100; non-theistic 146–148, 172, 177, 218, 226

narcissism 31, 105, 106, 126, 132, 141–142, 161, 163, 233, 234, 235; aggressiveness, *see* Aggression; attitude, 132; malignant 139
narcissistic attitude, *see* Attitude
narcissistic libido, *see* Libido
Nasser, Gamal 262
national politics, *see* Politics
naturalism 196–197, 203–206, 277; eudaimonism 203
necessity 3, 16, 33, 49, 51, 53, 61, 63, 67, 69, 72, 74, 77, 104, 107, 145, 147, 155, 157, 166, 170, 201, 207, 227, 242, 254, 258, 272, 276, 278
necrophagia 59
necrophilia 87, 138–139, 141, 144, 164, 186, 201–202; character, *see* Character; pseudonecrophilia 164; orientation, *see* Orientation
necrophilous character, *see* Character
needs: artificial 87; existential, *see* Existential; physiological 53; psychic, *see* Existential Needs; redefinition of 102; superimposed 87; true and false 87; vital 109

negation 2, 32–37, 49–53, 61–62, 64–65, 86, 91, 106, 113, 172, 206–219, 271–279
Negations 92
negative freedom, *see* Freedom
negative psychology 35
negative theology 173
Nehru, Jawaharlal 262
neocathartic method 30, 211
neo-Freudian 17, 84, 157, 158
Neumann, John von 24
neurophysiology 55, 60; regression, *see* Regression
neurosis 11–19, 159; character, *see* Character; chronic 12; quasi-neurotic behavior 19
neurotic anxiety, *see* Anxiety
New Left 5, 93, 94, 100, 102, 109, 111, 273, 275
nihilism 85–86, 97
non-productive attitudes, *see* Attitude
non-productive orientations, *see* Orientation
non-theism 1, 10, 12, 238; language 177; mysticism 146
norms 3, 13, 19, 36, 129–132, 142, 148, 189–197, 203, 213, 217, 273, 276–277; social 12, 31; system 190
normal character, *see* Character
normative humanism, *see* Humanism
normative theory, *see* Normativity
normative psychology, *see* Normativity
normativity 1–3, 5, 12, 32–33, 36, 130, 191, 194–197, 199, 201, 203–205, 213, 272, 276–277
nuclear war, *see* War

objectivation, *see* Life
objective alienation, *see* Alienation
objective attitude, *see* Attitude
objective dichotomy, *see* Biological Dicothomy
object 67, 133; choice 56–57, 59; libido 29; of devotion, *see* Existential Needs; relations, *see* Relation
Oedipus complex 12, 196
Old Testament 251
One-dimensional man 89, 95, 102, 114n5, 248
ontogenesis 49, 70, 204, 273
ontological categories 5, 128, 208, 272; affinity 134–137; blend 138–144; convergence 138–144; epigenesis 142, 209; generativity 134–137, 208; mutual presupposition 128–135, 208; reflection 32, 128–135; structuration 128–135
ontological forms, *see* Ontological Categories
ontology 2, 5, 28, 34, 198, 203, 205–206, 270, 277
openness 148, 172, 185–186, 200–203, 213, 224, 236
optimism 86, 229
organic: constitution 67; death 52–53; determinations 127; needs 199; repression 71; self-productiveness 67; substance 52
organism 50–57, 72, 78; integrity 54
organization: of direct democracy 109; of life, *see* Life; political, *see* Politics
oriental religion, *see* Religion
orientation 128, 135, 136, 139, 141–142, 144, 155, 165, 271; archaic 200; biophilic 185; character 126; exploitative 186, 197; masochistic 30, 60, 133, 136; marketing 195; mode of assimilation 75, 133, 136–137, 186–187; mode of relatedness 136; mode of socialization 15, 75, 133, 137, 141; necrophilic 141, 186; non-productive 142; productive 142; quality of 141; receptive 133, 135, 138, 192; syndromes of 138, 144; unconscious 185
Orpheus and Narcissus 103

pacification of existence, *see* Existence
pacifism 1, 237, 239, 250, 258, 263, 278; Peace Movement 109, 223, 255, 257
Palestine 27, 224, 257, 261
paradoxical logic, *see* Logic
passion 56, 64, 61, 64, 66, 69, 99, 108, 125, 128, 134, 138, 142, 144–145, 191, 194, 200; character-rooted 87; destructive 61, 139; irrational 59, 77, 87, 127, 135, 189, 200–201, 207–208, 218, 273; masochistic 133; rational 77, 87, 127, 135, 200–201, 208; sadistic 61, 133
pathology 11, 33, 59, 163–164, 197; of cultural communities 19; of normalcy: 11, 13; pathogenic conditions 77; pathogenic factor 159; social 19, 159

patriarchy 58, 70–71, 84, 91, 158, 196, 261; traditional authoritarian 94
paroxism, see Cure
Pauling, Linus 27
Payne, Robert 92, 250
Peace Movement, see Pacifism
pedagogy: analytic 12–13; methods 196
perception 23, 34, 101, 128, 133, 187; generative 125, 133, 148; reproductive 125, 148
periodization 2–3
perlaboration, see Clinic; elaboration, see clinic
personality 11, 85, 87, 128, 155; organization 62, 198; structure 127, 271; systemic character of 187, 192, 209
perversion 59–60, 103, 105, 205, 140–141
pessimism 229
Petrović, Gajo 248
phantasy 20, 35, 107, 112–113, 126, 146, 148, 169, 173, 194–195, 213, 273
phenomenology 15, 16, 125–128, 142, 143, 168
Phenomenology of spirit 35
philosophy 11, 36–37, 105, 114n5, 252
Philosophy and revolution 249
Philosophy of religion 33
Philosophy of right 35
phylogenesis 49, 70–72; phylogenetic inheritance 70; psychic inheritance 71
physical exercise 55
physiological needs, see Needs
physiological sexuality, see Sexuality
Plastrik, Stanley 86
Plato 95
pleasure 31, 33, 55, 103, 113, 134, 146, 153, 273; sensuous 55; sexual gratification 59, 70; sexual joy, see Joy
pleasure-ego, see Ego
Poland 232
Polanyi, Karl 224, 228
polarity 33–34, 52, 57–59, 272; of forces, see Force; polarization 57, 198
politics 2, 63, 94, 173; alliance 3–4, 10, 113, 226, 232–234, 246, 253–254, 258, 276–278; American 94, 97, 262; change 199, 225; circumstances 102, 233–234, 236; coalition 242, 274–275; community 227, 236, 253, 274, 276; conflict 35; division of labor 277; forces 105, 148, 260; form 3, 113, 214, 254, 273, 275; formation 3–4, 37, 113, 217, 224–232, 243, 253–254, 274, 278–279; goals 217–218, 232, 246, 253–254, 273–278; interest 18; issues 19, 27; leadership 4, 215, 240–244, 274, 277, 279; life 214; majority 110–112, 246–247, 252–253, 275; Marcuse 107–113, 273–275; means 112, 241, 254, 275, 277, 278; minority 110–112, 254, 275; mobilization 2, 214–216, 225–226, 229, 234, 241, 243–244, 247, 253, 274–275, 278; national 256; organization 2, 98, 102, 103, 109, 111, 113, 240–241, 244–246, 253, 273–279; practice 217; praxis 99, 216; principles 224, 226–227, 237, 244–246; strategy 230, 237, 246–254. 275; radicalism 91, 105; relations 278; sociology 4, 270–279; structure 75, 255, 275; superstructure 5, 75; tactics 237, 244–254; theory 49; transformation 199; transition 106, 109, 247, 263, 275; unity 148, 226–227; value 94; violence 25; vision 217, 219, 244, 276, 279; work 217, 234, 274
polymorphous sexuality, see Sexuality
Pope Paul VI 238, 244
positive freedom 138,199, 202, 218, 279
position (positive) 34–37, 86, 91, 113, 138, 142, 188, 205, 208–209, 237, 271–273, 277–279
potency, see Potentiality
potentiality 36, 51–53, 63, 67, 76–78, 87, 101, 114n1, 127, 129, 149, 175, 185, 187, 195, 198, 202–208, 273; inherent 78; primary 77, 127, 205, 272; secondary 77, 87, 127, 205, 207, 272
power 23, 25, 63–64, 67, 74, 78, 93, 101, 105, 113, 135–136, 157, 176, 185, 198, 201, 206–207, 212, 227, 241, 242, 244, 255, 259, 273, 277–278; social, see Social
practical spheres, see Spheres of Experience
practice of life, see Life
praxis 13, 99, 146–147, 187, 189, 195, 217, 238, 274, 276
Praxis school 232
preconscious (*pcs*) 16, 30, 53, 64, 126
predatory aggression, see Aggression
pride 231–235
primary: attitude 57, 126, 135–136, 271–273; process, see Process

principles, political, *see* Politics
process 15, 16, 20–28, 50, 62, 186; primary and secondary 23, 31; self-limiting 129, 138
productive attitude, *see* Attitude
productive force 74–75, 143, 275
productiveness 24, 37, 51, 60, 67, 142, 148, 171, 201, 204; attitude, *see* Attitude; orientation, *see* Orientation; traits, *see* Trait
productivity 108
prognosis, *see* Clinic
progression 54, 106; determination 205, 277; orientation 69–70, 200; politics 10, 21, 108–109, 251, 258, 275, 278
projection 15, 76, 133, 194, 234
property 61, 65; private 61
property-structured existence, *see* Having
prophylaxy, *see* Clinic
Protestantism 3, 239, 253
pseudoaggression, *see* Aggression
pseudo-necrophilia, *see* Necrophilia
pseudo-religious, *see* Religion
pseudo-revolutionary, *see* Revolution
psychic: conflict, *see* Conflict; death, *see* Death; development 13, 64, 129, 147, 197–198, 204, 206, 277; dichotomies, *see* Existential Dicothomies; psychic economy, *see* Economy; inheritance, *see* Phylogenesis; psychic energy, *see* Energy; psychic forces, *see* Force; psychic life, *see* Life; needs, *see* Existential Needs; organization, *see* Personality Structure; paralysis, *see* Psychic Death; process 18, 126, 175, 209, 270; self-preservation, *see* Self-Preservation; structure, *see* Personality Structure; survival, *see* Self-Preservation; system, *see* Personality; vulnerability 167
psychic determination, conception of 20, 27, 165, 199, 270; systemic 142, 270–271
psychoanalysis 3, 4, 5, 19, 23, 27, 28, 49, 90, 153, 156, 210, 248; analytic social psychology 2, 4, 5, 14, 21, 32, 88, 274; ego psychology 12–13, 55; heterodox 58, 157–158; interpersonal 84, 272; legitimate method 11–16, 22, 27, 29, 143, 156, 163, 171, 174, 211; orthodox 17, 28, 157–158, 163, 166; pedagogical application of 12; post-Freudian 14,

16; sociopsychoanalysis 11, 14; termination of, *see* Clinic; treatment and technique, *see* Clinic
psycho-biological relation 58
psychodynamics 1, 15–18, 22–23, 29–32, 86, 139, 169, 191, 271
psychogenesis 59
psychology 35, 61, 108, 165, 168, 176, 206; mass 14; ego, *see* Psychoanalysis
psychopathology 11, 163–164
psychosexual development, *see* Development
psychosis 61, 68, 74, 128, 161, 188
psychotherapy, *see* Clinic
public opinion 173, 248, 254, 256–257, 276; communication 155

qualitative: aspect 270; change 102; difference 102; factors 30, 54; synthesis 130
quality 28–32, 140, 191; of energy 88; experiential 204; homogeneous 143; of orientations 141; of sexual experience 60
quantitative: aspect 143–144, 270; determination 29; factors 30, 54
quantity 28–32, 88
quasi-religious attitude, *see* Religion

Rabinkow, Shlomo 245
radicalism 90–91, 95, 97, 105, 113, 275; character 95; character change, *see* character; character structure 88; social change 98, 112; social transformation 102
Radical Education Project (REP) 93
radical humanism, *see* Humanism
Rahner, Karl 228
Rank, Otto 10, 14, 30
rationalization 133, 171, 193, 242
rational passions, *see* Passion
rational vision, *see* Vision
reaction: affective 28–30, 32, 64, 77, 125, 127–128, 139, 145–146, 187–190, 196, 205, 208, 211, 213, 216–217, 228, 233, 276; compensatory 32; formation 31, 70, 164, 235; modes of 30; moral 254
reactive aggression, *see* Aggression
realist anxiety, *see* Anxiety
reality 28, 34, 65, 78, 104, 107, 113, 146, 148, 159, 162, 166–177; concept of 148, 172; realism 57, 130, 229, 243;

real objects 191; sense of 113; to touch reality 173
reality-ego, *see* Ego
real possibilities, *see* Alternativism
reason 10, 20, 54, 65–66, 69, 72, 77, 101, 125, 127–134, 142, 201, 227, 230, 258, 272
Reason and revolution 87
receptiveness; character, *see* Character; orientation, *see* Orientation; traits, *see* Traits
reciprocal implication 138, 209, 271
reconciliation 35
reflexivity 32, 49, 66, 176, 185–187, 191, 194–197, 201, 208, 273, 276; primary 273
reflection, *see* Ontological Categories
regression 16, 69–70, 95–96, 146, 148, 158; collective 70; degrees of 142; infantile 95; neurophysiological 71; progressive function of 106
Reich, Wilhelm 13, 30
Reik, Theodor 14, 15, 210
relatedness, *see* Existential Needs; modes of, *see* Orientation
relation 36, 64, 137, 208; class 75; to desire 186; economic 75; interpersonal 59, 73; intersubjective 73, 133; object 27–28, 30, 126, 189, 191, 213, 272, 276; political, *see* Politics; of production 75, 108, 188, 275; social, *see* Social
relief 113, 163, 170, 210, 212, 228, 233
religion 2, 3, 10, 11, 63, 70, 157; attitude 215, 242; authority 238; community 253, 273, 276, 278; cybernetic 24; ethos 104; form 113; institution 254; movement 3, 14; oriental 100; pseudo-religion 100; quasi-religious attitude 241; of technology 24, 88, 96
'Religious Revival' movement 251
repetition compulsion, *see* Compulsion
repression 28–31, 105, 113, 126, 132–133, 135, 146, 155–161, 167, 170, 188, 195–196, 200, 202, 206, 209–215, 273; cultural 13, 70; needs 103; organic 71; primary 126; of truth 173–174; ways of 31
reproduction: of character 12, 13, 56, 127, 142, 271; social 15, 75, 87, 126, 143, 166, 188, 198, 254
reproductive perception, *see* Perception

repulsion 31, 138
resistance 62, 157, 163, 167, 169, 170, 173, 206, 210, 215, 273
resistance to formalization 10–11, 279
revision: scientific 1, 17, 21, 24, 30, 84–86
revolution 36, 91, 94, 98, 100–101, 108–113, 216–217, 231–232, 246, 250–251, 257–258, 262, 275, 277; character, *see* Character; colonial, 261; counter-revolution 98; non-revolutionary circumstance 93; revolutionary aggression, *see* Aggression; revolutionary character, *see* Character; pseudo-revolutionary 102; theory of 108
Riesman, David 237, 241, 249, 253
robotism 107
rootedness, *see* Existential Needs
Russell, Bertrand 225, 256

sadism 59–61, 104, 125–126, 139–141; attitude, *see* Attitude; character, *see* Character; passion, *see* Passion; sex, *see* Sexuality; character, *see* Character
sadomasochism 31, 104, 105, 139
Sane Nuclear Policy (SANE) 237, 241
sanity 61, 67, 69, 73, 92–93, 128, 272
Sartre, Jean-Paul 107, 245
Schachtel, Ernst 23, 86, 159
Schaff, Adam 228, 232, 238, 247, 248
Schatz, Oskar 98
Schecter, David 153
science 11, 18, 22, 24, 26, 104, 173, 190, 238; natural 27; social 1, 272
Science of Logic 33, 35
schizophrenia 159, 161
schizoid character, *see* Character
SDS (Students for a Democratic Society) 93–95
secondary: attitudes 136, 271; potentialities, *see* Potentiality; process, *see* Process; tendency 136; traits 138
secular messianism, *see* Messianism
self 73, 78, 87, 100–101, 127, 139, 141, 174–175, 189, 191–192, 195, 203–205, 276; loss of 195; sense of 191, 195, 198, 199, 276
self-apperception 196, 201, 206, 213, 276
self-apprehension 187, 191, 194, 202, 208, 212–213, 276

self-awareness 54, 65, 66, 72, 73, 125, 176, 187–197, 201, 208, 233, 276; effective 191; self-consciousness 79
self-consciousness, *see* Self-Awareness
self-determination 111; 261–262
self-estrangement, *see* Alienation
self-experience 62, 65, 128, 148, 177, 191–195, 204, 213, 216, 219, 274, 276
self-expression, *see* Expression
self-management 275
self-orientation 191
self-preservation 21, 23, 53, 55, 60, 61, 66, 70, 72, 78, 135, 232, 233, 234, 272; mental survival 61, 69, 73; physical equilibrium, *see* Equilibrium; physical survival 61, 69, 73; psychic 62–63, 68, 272; survival 52, 53, 62, 70, 72, 171, 257, 276
sensation 31, 64, 100, 103, 125, 138, 145–146, 187–188, 194, 271; sensory or sensuous sphere, *see* Spheres of Activity
sense of identity, *see* Existential Needs
sense of self, *see* Self
sense of urgency 215, 229
sensibility 66, 68, 96, 99–101, 128, 191, 194, 205, 215, 218, 241, 278; moral, *see* Morality
sensitivity 101, 169
separation 66–68; anxiety, *see* Anxiety; between subject and object 147, 149
sexual: behavior 56, 57; difference 57; experience 56; quality 60; sphere, *see* Spheres of Activity
sexuality 11, 31, 56–58, 103, 160; animal instinct 53–54; bisexuality 57–58; desire 56–57; development: *see* Psychosexual Development; heterosexuality 58, 59; homosexuality 57, 59; infantile 56; instinct 56–60; masochistic 60; needs 55; physiological 57; polymorphous 91, 105; psychic bisexuality 56; roles 58; sadistic 60; sensuality 57
Shakespeare, William 104
Sheen, Bishop 251
sick society 90–92
Simmel, Georg 3
Siqueiros, David 240
Siteman, Stephen 225
Skinner, B. F. 227
slip, Freudian 170

social: change 1, 18, 20, 91, 99, 106, 113, 199, 251–252, 272, 274, 276; class 144, 155, 157, 275; conditions 154; development 15, 70; differentiation 63; function 188; life, *see* Life; movement 11; pathology, *see* Pathology; power 76; process 71, 188, 203; product 75; psychology, *see* Psychology; concepts 270; of humanistic movements 232–236; relations 3, 63, 68, 73, 75, 103, 129, 188, 189, 196, 197, 209, 278; structure 75, 155, 206, 255; theory 26
social character, *see* Character
social characterology, *see* Characaterology
social filters 23, 155, 210; socially-conditioned 86
social content: 232–236
social form 19, 69, 232–236, 244: political, *see* Politics; religious, *see* Religion
social formation 15, 35, 32, 123 189, 232–236: political, *see* Politics
social unconscious, *see* Unconscious
socialism 2, 13, 19, 36–37, 84, 86, 102, 105–109, 223–224, 231–232, 237, 244, 248, 250, 254–255, 258–259, 261–263, 275, 279; democratic 1, 254, 259, 262
socialist humanism, *see* Humanism
Socialist humanism 89, 239, 245, 248, 250
Socialist Party 223, 224, 237
socialization, form of: 247, 276; modes of, *see* Orientation
society 18, 69–78, 155; classless 250; concept of 75; disintegration of 25; survival of 72
sociology 3, 10–11, 137, 275
sociopsychoanalysis, *see* Psychoanalysis
solidarity 111, 138, 233, 236; humanistic concept of 111; violent 111
Solzhenitsyn, Alexander 250
Sontag, Susan 105
Soviet Union 260; Russian managerialism 261; satellite countries 232, 248, 262, 279
spheres of activity 63, 74, 127, 136; affective 63, 126, 129, 133, 142, 273; intellectual 63, 126, 133, 142, 187, 273; sensory or sensuous 63, 126, 142, 187–188; sexual 57, 63
spheres of life 63, 75, 165

spheres of experience 14, 19, 28, 34, 37, 218
Spinoza, Baruch 10, 37, 176
state 35, 63, 69, 100, 237, 240, 244, 255, 259, 261, 276
static adaptation, *see* Adaptation
statistics 13–14, 143–144, 255
stimulation, *see* Existential Needs
Story of O. 105
strategy, political, *see* Politics
structuralism 9
structure 20, 55, 128, 277–279; character, *see* Character; logical, *see* Logic; personality, *see* Personality; psychic, *see* Personality; political, *see* Politics; social, *see* Social
structured growth, *see* Life
structuration, *see* Ontological Categories
style, *see* Aesthetics
Styles of radical will 104
subjective alienation, *see* Alienation
subjective change, *see* Character Change
subjective freedom, *see* Freedom
subjective transformation, *see* Character Transformation
sublimation 2, 36, 89, 276
suffering 19, 35, 54, 64, 66–68, 154–164, 166 167, 169, 172, 204, 211 219, 233 234, 236, 251–252, 261, 274
Sullivan, Harry Stack 84, 85, 161
superego 13, 196
superstructure 5, 75
suppression 77, 191, 212
surplus energy, *see* Energy
surrealism 104–105
survival, *see* Self-Preservation; of man, *see* Man; of society, *see* Society
Suzuki, Daitero 245
symbiosis 77, 137–140; incestuous 139, 141
symptom 12, 15, 17, 30, 59, 156, 159, 165–166, 171; analysis 13, 156, 174; hysteriform 29, 174; obsessional 31–2; paranoid 31–2; transitory 210
syndrome 126; of attitudes, *see* Attitude; of character, *see* Character; of decay 138; of growth 185; of orientations, *see* Orientation; of values, *see* Value
system 20–29, 32, 34, 165–166; analysis 20; character, *see* Character; of factors 55; flexibility 198; of norms, *see* Norm; psychic, *see* Personality; regenerative power 198; religious and philosophical 147, 193; social and political 72, 109, 111, 143; of strivings 126
systems theory 4, 9, 25–26, 272; organism-oriented 25

tactics, political, *see* Politics
Tausk, Viktor 15
technique 105, 107, 111; analytic, *see* Clinic
technology, religion of: *see* Religion
teleology, *see* Eudaimonism

The anatomy of human destructiveness 21, 249
The art of being 99
The ego and the id 89
The heart of man 138, 185

theism 1, 10, 12–13, 20, 146, 177, 226, 238
therapeutically-oriented knowledge, *see* Knowledge
therapy or therapeutic, *see* Clinic

The revolution of hope 90, 94, 96, 97, 100, 108, 237

The surrealist revolution in France 104

The working class in Weimar Germany 14

Thompson, Clara 22, 84
thought, *see* Language
thwarting of life, *see* Life
Tito, Josip Broz 262
To have or to be? 22, 99, 185
topology 12–13, 16–18, 30, 77, 134, 186, 270; typical constellation 134
touch reality, *see* Reality
tradition 10, 84, 90, 93, 95, 96, 106, 108, 103, 194, 199, 225, 247, 251; values, *see* Value
trait 12, 13, 30, 105, 126, 142, 143, 185; constitutional 127; productive 57, 143, 185; necrophilic 141, 186; non-productive 142; receptive 135 142; secondary 138

transcendence, *see* Existential Needs; of nature 66
transference 76, 133, 154, 161, 169, 170, 210, 213, 235, 273
transformation: of character, *see* Character; social, *see* Social
transition, political, *see* Politics
transposition: ideal 20, 27, 144, 214, 217; real 3, 113, 254, 274
transtherapeutic, *see* Clinic
trauma 30, 174
Trotskism 95
truth 54, 172–177, 243; negative concept 172; repression of 174; truthfulness 176, 245

uncertainty 212
unconscious (*ucs*) 14, 16, 36, 67; mode of 134, 155, 212; guilt feelings 30; knowledge 173; mode of 134; orientation 185; social 160–161; as subjective objectivity 173
unilateral determination, *see* Determination
unity 2, 34, 68–70, 78, 101, 111, 128, 139, 144, 146–149, 195, 199, 202, 209, 216, 218; political, *see* Politics; sense of, *see* Existential Needs

psychic bisexuality, *see* Sexuality

unlived life, *see* Life
Urquhart, Clara 168, 223, 224, 228, 231, 238, 256
USSR, *see* Soviet Union
utopian 91, 102–103

value 62, 71, 99, 109, 125, 191, 192, 194, 195, 212, 213, 217, 226; of disillusionment 223; effective 204, 213, 276; experiential 2, 130, 191, 195, 196, 219, 243, 277, 279; moral 129; political 94; psychic 147; syndrome 129; system 190; traditional 95; transformation 99

Vietnam war, *see* War
violence 61, 87, 94, 199, 250, 252, 254, 261, 262, 275; benign 141; counter-violence 112; political 25
vision 111, 113, 194–195, 213, 217, 219, 226–227, 229, 244, 250, 252, 273–274, 276, 279; rational 194; political, *see* Politics
vital: forces, *see* Force; drive, *see* Drive; interest 61, 62; needs, *see* Need; process, *see* Life Process; self-expression, *see* Expression
vitality 164–171
Voice of American Conscience 238
von Bertalanffy, Ludwig 21, 24, 25
von Foerster, Heinz 21

war 21, 24, 27; nuclear 21, 27, 223, 231, 237, 258; Vietnam 21, 226, 273; World War I 21, 160; World War II 259
Warburg, Siegmund 238
Watts, Alan 114n4
Weber, Alfred 3, 17, 130
well-being 52, 61, 107, 112, 157, 191, 210, 213
Whitehead, Alfred 114n5
Whorf, Benjamin 23
Wiener, Norbert 24, 25
Wittes, Sarah Sue 104, 110, 177n1
woman 58, 70
Women's Liberation Movement 58, 273
work 11, 12, 20–27, 67, 71, 75, 84, 105, 209, 210, 274; creative 77, 107, 128, 142, 148; political, *see* Politics

xenophobia 251

You shall be as gods 251
Yugoslavia 232, 262

Zen Buddhism, *see* Buddhism
Zionism 3, 13

1844 Manuscripts 108

For Product Safety Concerns and Information please contact our EU
representative GPSR@taylorandfrancis.com
Taylor & Francis Verlag GmbH, Kaufingerstraße 24, 80331 München, Germany

www.ingramcontent.com/pod-product-compliance
Lightning Source LLC
Chambersburg PA
CBHW070746020526
44116CB00032B/1995